Nietzsche:
A Critical Reader

BLACKWELL CRITICAL READERS

Blackwell's *Critical Readers* series presents a collection of linked perspectives on continental philosophers, social and cultural theorists. Edited and introduced by acknowledged experts and written by representatives of different schools and positions, the series embodies debate, dissent and a committed heterodoxy. From Foucault to Derrida, from Heidegger to Nietzsche, *Blackwell Critical Readers* address figures whose work requires elucidation by a variety of perspectives. Volumes in the series include both primary and secondary bibliographies.

David Wood: *Derrida: A Critical Reader*

Hubert Dreyfus and Harrison Hall: *Heidegger: A Critical Reader*

Gregory Elliot: *Althusser: A Critical Reader*

Douglas Kellner: *Baudrillard: A Critical Reader*

Peter Sedgwick: *Nietzsche: A Critical Reader*

Nietzsche:
A Critical Reader

Edited by
Peter R. Sedgwick

BLACKWELL
Oxford UK & Cambridge USA

Copyright © Blackwell Publishers, 1995

First published 1995

Blackwell Publishers Ltd
108 Cowley Road
Oxford OX4 1JE
UK

Blackwell Publishers Inc.
238 Main Street
Cambridge, Massachusetts 02142
USA

British Library Cataloguing in Publication Data
A CIP catalogue record for this book is available from the British Library.

Library of Congress Cataloging-in-Publication Data
Nietzsche: a critical reader/edited by Peter R. Sedgwick.
    p. cm. – (Blackwell critical readers)
  Includes bibliographical references and index.
  ISBN 0-631-19044-9 (hard). – ISBN 0-631-19045-7 (pbk)
  1. Nietzsche, Friedrich Wilhelm, 1844–1900. I. Sedgwick, Peter R.
II. Series.
B3317.N44836 1995
193 – dc20
                                    94-40792
                                           CIP

Typeset in Plantin on 10/12 pt by Best-set Typesetter Ltd, Hong Kong
Printed in Great Britain by TJ Press Ltd, Padstow, Cornwall

This book is printed on acid-free paper.

Contents

Contributors

Keith Ansell-Pearson teaches philosophy at the University of Warwick.

Daniel W. Conway teaches philosophy at the Pennsylvania State University.

Jacques Derrida is Professor at the Ecole des Hautes Études en Sciences Sociales, Paris. His books include *Margins of Philosophy, Spurs: Nietzsche's Styles, The Ear of the Other* and, most recently, *Politiques de l'amitié*.

Rosalyn Diprose teaches philosophy at the Flinders University of South Australia.

Andrew Edgar teaches philosophy at the University of Wales, College of Cardiff.

Martin Heidegger is widely acknowledged to have been one of the most influential philosophers of the twentieth century. He taught at the University of Marburg (1923–8) and the University of Freiburg-im-Breisgau (1928–58).

R. J. Hollingdale has written extensively on Nietzsche, and translated many of his works into English, including *Thus Spoke Zarathustra, Beyond Good and Evil, Daybreak*, and *Human, All-Too-Human*.

Walter Kaufmann was one of the most influential figures in post-war Nietzsche criticism. As well as publishing *Nietzsche: Philosopher, Psychologist, Antichrist* in 1950, he wrote numerous essays on Nietzsche's thought and influence, and also produced many of the first reliable translations of Nietzsche's works in English.

Sarah Kofman was, until her death in October 1994, professor of philosophy at the Sorbonne. She wrote numerous articles and books on Nietzsche, including *Nietzsche and Metaphor* and *Explosion I* and *II*. 'Accessories', from *Explosion II*, appears here for the first time in English. Professor Kofman's presence on the scene of Nietzsche scholarship will be sorely missed.

Nick Land teaches philosophy at the University of Warwick.

Will McNeill teaches philosophy at De Paul University, Chicago.

William Outhwaite teaches sociology at the University of Sussex.

Richard Schacht teaches philosophy at the University of Illinois at Urbana Champaign.

Alan D. Schrift teaches philosophy at Grinnell College, Iowa.

Alessandra Tanesini teaches philosophy at the University of Wales, College of Cardiff.

Acknowledgements

'The Significance of Michel Foucault's Reading of Nietzsche: Power, the Subject and Political Theory' by Keith Ansell-Pearson, reprinted from *Nietzsche Studien*, Vol. 20, 1991, pp. 267–84, by permission of the author.

'Interpreting Signatures (Nietzsche/Heidegger)' by Jacques Derrida, translated by Diane Michelfelder and Richard E. Palmer, reprinted from *Philosophy and Literature*, Vol. 10, No. 2, October 1986, pp. 246–62, by permission of the publisher.

'Nietzsche, Ethics and Sexual Difference' by Rosalyn Diprose, reprinted from *Radical Philosophy*, No. 52, summer 1989, pp. 27–33, by permission of the publisher.

'Kant's Doctrine of the Beautiful. Its Misinterpretation by Schopenhauer and Nietzsche' by Martin Heidegger, reprinted from *Nietzsche*, Vol. I, trans. David Farrell-Krell (London: Routledge & Kegan Paul, 1981), by permission of the publisher.

'Theories and Innovations: Logic, Theory of Knowledge and Metaphysics' by R. J. Hollingdale, reprinted from *Nietzsche* (London: Routledge & Kegan Paul, 1973), pp. 127–39, by permission of the author.

'Nietzsche's Attitude toward Socrates' by Walter Kaufmann, reprinted from *Nietzsche: Philosopher, Psychologist, Antichrist* (Princeton: Princeton University Press, 1974), pp. 391–411, by permission of the publisher.

'Accessories (*Ecce Homo* "Why I Write Such Good Books", "The Untimelies", 3)' by Sarah Kofman, translated by Duncan Large from *Explosion II: Les enfants de Nietzsche* (Paris: Galilée, 1993), appears here for the first time in English by permission of Athlone Press. Duncan Large's complete translation of *Explosion II: The Children of Nietzsche* will be published by Athlone in 1998.

My sincere thanks to the following for their assistance in the preparation of this volume: Keith Ansell-Pearson (for his negotiating skills), Duncan Large (for the Sarah Kofman translation and also many helpful comments), Christopher Norris (for his invaluable advice and encouragement); also to Richard Cochrane and Simon Malpas for proof-reading.

Peter R. Sedgwick

Introduction:
Nietzsche's Institutions

Peter R. Sedgwick

Nietzsche's texts and their criticism have a long and varied history. His name is a term which embraces both the books and notes he left behind and the multitude of readings which have been offered of those texts and fragments. Indeed, reading Nietzsche is a process which is rendered problematic by the twists and turns of his own prose and by his notorious, restless scepticism with regard to the manner in which philosophical issues and problems have been dealt with by thinkers from Plato to Kant and Schopenhauer. Who Nietzsche actually is, and what his thought can be construed to mean and imply, are questions which have been addressed in such a variety of ways by authors ranging from Lukács and Adorno to Kaufmann and Derrida, that no single reading seems able to dominate or determine the entire scene of Nietzsche's textuality.

Nietzsche criticism itself is perhaps best understood as a field of contention, a site of debate in which readings are offered up for critical consumption and judged according to specified (but often wildly disparate) criteria of correctness. This site of debate is not a neutral or unified space which has been determined in advance of critical understanding and particular acts of interpretation. Each reading which is presented modifies that space according to other, additional criteria. For example, an approach which emphasizes the rhetorical strategies used by a text will bring to bear different standards of judgement from an epistemologically accented account of the same piece. Each reading recasts the value and significance of Nietzsche's work by resorting to different rules of interpretation. Reading Nietzsche is thus not a practice which is validated merely by way of reference to the 'content' of his works as if that were a value-free term. The 'additional criteria' which I mentioned above are more than merely additional; they are in fact constitutive of the traditions of Nietzsche scholarship; they form its history, and are therefore essential to a critical appreciation of his work and influence.

If one examines the history of Nietzsche interpretation, it seems that three principal traditions or methodologies of reading have exerted decisive and important influences upon our understanding of his writings. These can be designated as:

1 *The 'German tradition'*: readings which tend to situate Nietzsche within the context of issues in modern philosophy, aesthetics and social theory as delineated by the writings of Kant, Goethe and Marx respectively. These include the work of Marxists such as Lukács and the Frankfurt School, and the hermeneutic tradition epitomized by Heidegger and Gadamer.
2 *The 'French tradition'*: this includes the readings of Bataille, the existentialists, and the postmodern, poststructuralist and deconstructive approaches of the early Jean-François Lyotard, of Gilles Deleuze, Paul de Man, Michel Foucault, Jacques Derrida, and Sarah Kofman. Here questions of language, style, rhetoric, and force are often highlighted in relation to Nietzsche's texts, as well as the constitution of human subjectivity in the context of psychoanalysis or social relations of power.
3 *The 'Anglo-American tradition'*: epitomized by Arthur Danto, Walter Kaufmann, and R. J. Hollingdale, this tends to relate Nietzsche's work to more classically determined conceptions of truth, politics and subjectivity as they have been addressed within the domain of Anglo-American analytic philosophy. A more recent variant on this model can be found in Richard Rorty's view of Nietzsche as a Jamesean pragmatist and iconoclastic 'strong textualist', whose thought can be opposed to the practice of analytic philosophy.[1]

Each of these traditions, of course, can be related to more general tendencies within western philosophy. These tendencies have functioned to mark out boundary lines between the ways in which philosophy has been practised over the last hundred years – the most marked of these divisions perhaps being that between 'analytic' and 'continental' philosophy. Nietzsche's work has exerted its influence upon these traditions in different ways and, reciprocally, has been read differently within them. None of these traditions has rigid, fixed boundaries. Derrida's work, for example, owes a significant debt to the writings of Heidegger. Hence, I am not suggesting that these 'traditions' be taken as absolutely defined limits to the process of enquiry into Nietzsche's thought. Rather, they form a basic historical framework for enquiry which comprises a set of presuppositions and concerns that have both allowed for and justified the presentation of particular interpretations of key terms and ideas as they have occurred or have been read in relation to Nietzsche's work.

What I have loosely defined as 'traditions' of Nietzsche interpretation may also more accurately be considered as 'institutions' of Nietzsche scholarship, that is, structures within which a shared, public referent (in this case signified by a proper name) is presented for discussion and analysis according to shared criteria of understanding. These shared criteria are composed of sets of reading practices which frame particular readings by providing standards of justification which validate them.

At first glance, any talk of institutions related to Nietzsche's name may seem antithetical to much of the force of his own thinking. With regard to the institution of academia, for example, Nietzsche could honestly say, in the words of Zarathustra, 'I have moved from the house of the scholars and I even banged the door behind me.'[2] He spent most of his philosophically active life outside this institution, and came to consider his younger self, the author of *The Birth of Tragedy*, as 'one who concealed himself for the time being under the scholar's hood'.[3] Yet Nietzsche's institutions themselves have been given shape within academia – his most significant interpreters have themselves often been academics, and the audience that their readings have in turn exerted an influence upon (students, professional philosophers and critical theorists, for example) are also inextricably linked to this institution.

Nietzsche also famously decried that most significant of all nineteenth-century institutions, the state, in the first part of *Thus Spoke Zarathustra*:

> State? What is that? [. . .] State is the name of the coldest of all cold monsters [. . .] Everything about it is false; it bites with stolen teeth, and bites easily. Even its entrails are false [. . .] All-too-many are born: for the superfluous the state was invented [. . .] Only where the state ends, there begins the human being who is not superfluous: there begins the song of necessity, the unique and inimitable tune.
> (*Thus Spoke Zarathustra*, First Part, 'On the New Idol')

It would be easy to deduce from this comment, as it would from 'A Glance at the State' in *Human, All Too Human*,[4] that Nietzsche's hatred of the state implies an outright rejection not only of it, but of all institutions. But I do not think this is the case. The state is the object of Nietzsche's suspicion because it embodies for him a tendency to foster cultural decline. The image of monstrosity in the above quotation is deliberately provocative: lacking creative passion, the state is a cold, impersonal, machine-like structure. It feeds off and destroys the creative self-expression which nurtures a healthy, authentic culture. The monster is none other than the power of the masses, the 'All-too-many'. For Nietzsche, the modern state encourages a morality which has as its consequence a debilitating politics of superfluity, one which springs from its primary objective of self-preservation. The state 'civilizes' human beings (always a derogatory term in Nietzsche) in order to maintain itself, and in doing so it neither welcomes nor helps to create the conditions whereby great culture is possible. Thus, in *Twilight of the Idols*:

> Culture and state – one should not deceive oneself about this – are antagonists: '*Kultur-Staat*' is merely a modern idea. One lives off the other, one thrives at the expense of the other. All great ages of culture are ages of political decline, what is great culturally has always been unpolitical, even *anti-political*.[5]

The modern world, the world in which the state is worshipped above all else (for the state is, after all, the '*New* Idol'), is hence seen by Nietzsche as being the context least conducive to the production of great culture – by which he means that form of culture exemplified by classical Greece, which itself 'evolved *in spite of* the *polis*'.[6] With the advent of the epitome of the modern institution, that is, the state, 'the will to assume responsibility for oneself', which is the hallmark of what Nietzsche terms 'natural morality', is rendered impossible (*Twilight*, 'Skirmishes of an Untimely Man', 38). The state is thus the anti-cultural institution *par excellence* for Nietzsche, since it obstructs the development of natural morality and hence the possibility of attaining the conditions which make culture possible.

Turning to the section of *Twilight of the Idols* entitled 'Morality as Anti-Nature' in this context, it is interesting to note Nietzsche's plotting of the relationship between dominant morality (that is, the hitherto accepted mores of the Christian tradition and contemporary state), and its rejection of 'natural morality'. Here it is a question for Nietzsche of dividing moralities from one another in relation to their response to the natural, the world of passions and drives:

> Every naturalism in morality – that is, every healthy morality, is dominated by an instinct of life [. . .] *Anti-natural morality* [. . .] turns, conversely *against* the instincts of life [. . .] it says No to both

the lowest and the highest desires of life, and posits God as the *enemy of life*. (*Twilight*, 'Morality as Anti-Nature', 4)

Moral estimations thus become quantifiable in relation to their stance toward 'life'. Nietzsche's evaluation of good and bad ethical systems and hierarchies therefore implies that their natures can be distinguished by way of reference to the poles of affirmation and negation in respect to the question of life.

How, then, does Nietzsche define life? Certainly not, it seems, with any deference to a Darwinian model of the instincts, with its emphasis on a 'struggle for life' (*Twilight*, 'Skirmishes of an Untimely Man', 14). Rather, a particular *form* of life is affirmed. If Nietzsche, like Rousseau,[7] speaks of a 'return to nature', it is nevertheless not strictly a return but an '*ascent*' which marks out the parameters of Nietzsche's naturalistic discourse. This ascent is in fact conceived in opposition to Rousseau, in opposition to the 'tyranny of the majority' which marks both the latter's and the Darwinian figuration of the natural (*Twilight*, 'Skirmishes', 48). Nietzsche's affirmation of nature in this context is none other than the negation of a negation, the enacted refutation of an anti-natural morality; but it must also carefully plot its way through the maze of other naturalisms unfitted to Nietzsche's conception of the necessity of hierarchy, one example of which is the thought of Herbert Spencer.[8] The notion of *amor fati* (love of fate) has a role to play here as a means of controlling the negational mode as it feeds into Nietzsche's conception of the human, so that this mode does not itself recoil into an unhealthy naturalism:

No one *gives* man his qualities [. . .] One is necessary, one is a piece of fatefulness, one belongs to the whole, one is in the whole [. . .] But there is nothing besides the whole. (*Twilight*, 'Morality as Anti-Nature', 8)

Nietzsche's project may be to re-integrate humanity into nature, but this is nevertheless not an arbitrary or indiscriminate re-integration.[9] Hierarchy is consistently reinstated into the natural in the form of a division between the poles of affirmation and negation, the one privileged over the other in the form of an 'ascent'. Moral judgements, in turn, become signs, marks to be read semiotically within the conflicting frames of ascent and decline (*Twilight*, 'The "Improvers" of Mankind', 1). These signs mark out the boundaries between culture and civilization, the one affirmative and 'natural', the other negative and 'anti-natural'. In consequence, it is not uncoincidental that Nietzsche reads what he considers to be the decline and negation of the function of the instincts (the 'natural') – which is the hallmark of modernity – in terms of the institution:

> The whole of the West no longer possesses the instincts out of which institutions grow, out of which a *future* grows: perhaps nothing antagonizes its 'modern spirit' so much. (*Twilight*, 'Skirmishes', 39)

A particular kind of institution (exemplified by Christianity) destroys the instincts out of which affirmative institutions develop, and the future of humanity is thereby placed in jeopardy. Much of Nietzsche's critique of modern civilization is predicated on the diagnosis of this decline, exemplified in the form of the modern state, as resulting from the dominance of anti-natural ethical codes, which contain the potential of their own inevitable self-destruction.

It is in turn possible to consider Nietzsche's famous Dionysian principle (which in his later work becomes synonymous with life affirmation) in this context as having a relationship to institutional structures in two ways: (1) a positive mode in relation to natural moralities – expressed in the Greek affirmation which occurred during the Dionysian festivals; and (2) a negational mode, which results in a polarized conflict with anti-natural mores – expressed in the form of Nietzsche's own critical negation of Christianity. Examining Nietzsche's last ruminations on the Dionysian in *Twilight of the Idols*, which are couched in the form of considerations on aesthetics, it is possible to delineate this model of the drives at work in relation to the institution:

> What is the meaning of the conceptual opposites which I have introduced into aesthetics, *Apollinian* and *Dionysian*, both conceived as kinds of frenzy? The Apollinian frenzy excites the eye above all, so that it gains the power of vision [. . .] In the Dionysian state, on the other hand, the whole affective system is excited and enhanced so that it discharges all of its means of expression at once and drives forth simultaneously the power of representation, imitation, transfiguration, transformation [. . .] The essential feature here is the ease of metamorphosis [. . . the Dionysian type] enters into any skin, into any affect: he constantly transforms himself. (*Twilight*, 'Skirmishes',10)

The Dionysian state is not a stable one, and requires the frenzied ordering instinct of the Apollinian as its means of expression. In escaping this order the Dionysian nevertheless displays its nature and force in terms of a *mimetic* quality: it can enter into, and imitate, any form; its transformation relies upon the prerequisite of the formal and form-based, Apollinian type. In entering 'into any skin', the Dionysian thus reveals its ability to mimic as the precondition of the 'discharge' or expulsion of contained energy which defines its affect. It is the destabilizing element, but it only destabilizes *through* mimesis as a parodic and excessive contrary which bears an intimate relation to the structuring principle.[10] As such, it does not follow that Nietzsche accedes to an unconditional affirmation of the Dionysian, since its function springs from the inherent tension engendered by the play of 'conceptual opposites'.

In its relation to nature the Dionysian defies conventional morality by partaking of what Walter Kaufmann termed the 'vital force'.[11] This, as Kaufmann notes, embodies an expression of the will to power, one which, Nietzsche writes, 'is explicable only in terms of an excess of force' (*Twilight*, 'What I Owe to the Ancients', 4). The Dionysian, then, becomes enmeshed in a reading of affirmative natural morality, which it grounds; it is the ' "will to life" ' of the Hellenic instinct: 'Here [in the Dionysian festivals] the most profound instinct of life, that directed toward the future of life, the eternity of life, is experienced religiously' (*Twilight*, 'Ancients', 4). Here is the 'return to nature' which Nietzsche argues for: an affirmation of life in all its aspects, one which subsumes the most negative forces within itself and transfigures them into joy, 'the eternal joy of becoming' (*Twilight*, 'Ancients', 5). Significantly, this is linked to the idea of 'the future of life' – a future which western culture is no longer in a position to think about (*Twilight*, 'Skirmishes' 39 – cited above).

Nietzsche's critique of the institution thus becomes the critique of institutional structures which foster decline and alienate or negate the Dionysian element. It is, though, as I have already noted, not a critique of institutions as such. It is perhaps worth recalling here that the figure of 'the architect' (*Twilight*, 'Skirmishes', 11), a giver of order and structure 'under the spell of power', the practitioner of a *'grand style'* which is 'neither a Dionysian nor an Apollinian state', is equated by Nietzsche with an 'institutional' structure that affirms 'a kind of eloquence of power in forms'. Architectural structures are an expression of the will to power. They bear witness to a power which is self-sufficient and transcends any need to justify itself. Here the contending contraries of force and form achieve an equilibrium in which the need for the Dionysian/Apollonian dichotomy vanishes due to the perfect balance achieved within the structure itself. This equally demands that one consider Nietzsche's affirmation of the Dionysian in the context of a critical position which does not simply deny the necessity of form or formalized principles. What Nietzsche affirms are the drives hitherto negated by anti-natural morality, of which Christian morality is a paradigm case.

This leads to a series of contrary movements in Nietzsche's work which does not simply oppose structure to nature, or form to force, but which surveys various structures (institutions, such as that of Christianity) in terms of their related oppositions: '*Dionysus versus the Crucified*'.[12] If the Dionysian, with its mimetic capability, overcomes these oppositions through a transfigurative process, there is nevertheless a residue of structure discernible in its dynamic. It cannot wholly break with the necessity for institutions. In consequence, Nietzsche redefines negation in terms of the resistance which erupts from the inherent conflict between the natural and healthy (i.e. life-affirming) drives and anti-natural morality. What Nietzsche conceptualizes as 'anti-nature' in fact provides the conditions for his affirmation of 'nature' (*Twilight*, 'Morality as Anti-Nature', 3). Within this context, the Nietzschean definition of the world itself as will to power provides the means of invoking nature and individuality in terms of '*physis*'.[13] The relationship between humanity and nature is thus envisaged in terms of physiology, and natural morality meets the demands of the body and the passions by placing them first. As a result there can be no fixed moral order for Nietzsche; moralities and institutions must change to suit the requirements of life, subordinated as they are to the will to power:

> And do you know what 'the world' is to me? Shall I show you in my mirror? This world: a monster of energy, without beginning, without end; a firm, iron magnitude of force that does not grow bigger or smaller [. . .] enclosed by 'nothingness' as by a boundary; not something blurry or wasted, not something endlessly extended, but set in a definite space as a definite force [. . .] as force throughout, as a play of forces [. . .] this, my *Dionysian* world of the eternally self-creating, eternally self-destroying, this mystery world of the twofold voluptuous delight, my 'beyond good and evil', without goal, unless the joy of a circle is itself a goal; without will, unless a thing feels good will towards itself [. . .] *This world is the will to power and nothing else besides!* And you yourselves are the will to power – and nothing else besides![14]

This conception of the will to power, taken from Nietzsche's notebooks, invokes a notion of natural order, one in which the idea of natural morality and life-promoting institutions has its place. Hence Nietzsche's view of classical Greek institutions as erupting from their will to power as a result of 'preventative measures taken to protect each other against their inner explosives' (*Twilight*, 'What I Owe to the Ancients', 3). Seen in this light, institutions are for Nietzsche not merely acceptable but *necessary* expressions of the Dionysian element.

Returning to the question of 'Nietzsche's institutions', then, it would seem that the coinage I have proposed is not as antithetical to Nietzsche's project as it might at first seem. Whether or not these institutions of Nietzsche scholarship themselves are is, perhaps, a matter for further consideration and debate. However, it is important to note that a critical understanding of Nietzsche's work and thought is not only based upon the existence of such sets of interpretative conventions. Criticizing these conventions (or aspects of them), or even rejecting outright some or all of the central concerns which define them, actually itself presupposes their importance. Nietzsche's institutions, in other words, are implicitly invoked as soon as one enters into a critical discussion of the significance of his thought. Reading Nietzsche, in this context, becomes an immanent practice wherein it is possible to play the concerns and presuppositions of one set of interpretative priorities and procedures off against another. Our understanding of Nietzsche's achievement is, I believe, thereby enhanced – for the variety and power of his views can only be done justice through a critical appreciation of the significant contributions offered within these institutions of Nietzsche scholarship, and of their limitations.

The present volume is intended to be read in this spirit; and this is, in a crucial sense, a Nietzschean spirit – the spirit invoked by the term 'perspectivism':

> There is *only* a perspective seeing, only a perspective knowing; and the *more* affects we allow to speak about one thing, the *more* eyes, different eyes, we can use to observe one thing, the more complete will our 'concept' of this thing, our 'objectivity', be.[15]

What this volume offers is a selection of perspectives generated from within, or written in relation to, each of the contending traditions or institutions of Nietzsche scholarship which I have outlined above. Obviously, it has not been possible to provide an exhaustive selection of viewpoints, but the essays and selections contained in this volume serve in each case to exemplify some aspect of one of these institutions of Nietzsche interpretation. Each contribution can be read as offering a stimulating engagement with a significant strand of Nietzsche's thought from within the boundaries of one of these traditions, or in relation to the work of other significant thinkers who have themselves been part of them (be it Heidegger or Deleuze, Rorty or Adorno).

NOTES

My sincere thanks to Siân Davies, Duncan Large, Christopher Norris, and Alessandra Tanesini for their helpful comments on various drafts of this introduction.

1 See Richard Rorty, *Consequences of Pragmatism* (Brighton: Harvester Press, 1982), pp. 155, 152, 226. A 'strong textualist', according to Rorty, is someone who has their own vocabulary 'and doesn't worry about whether anybody shares it' (p. 152).

2 Nietzsche, *Thus Spoke Zarathustra*, trans. Walter Kaufmann, in *The Viking Portable Nietzsche* (London: Chatto & Windus, 1971), Second Part, 'On Scholars'. All further references are given in the text with part number and section title.

3 Nietzsche, *The Birth of Tragedy*, trans. Walter Kaufmann in *Basic Writings of Nietzsche* (New York: Modern Library, 1968), 'Attempt at a Self-Criticism', 3.

4 See Nietzsche, *Human, All Too Human*, Book 1, trans. R. J. Hollingdale (Cambridge: Cambridge University Press, 1986), sections 438–82.

5 Nietzsche, *Twilight of the Idols*, trans. Walter Kaufmann in *The Viking Portable Nietzsche*, 'The "Improvers" of Mankind', 4. All further references are given in the text with section title and number.

6 Nietzsche, *Human, All Too Human*, Book 1, section 474.

7 For a brief discussion of Nietzsche's attitude to Rousseau's 'return to nature *in impuris naturibilis*' (*Twilight*, 'Skirmishes', 1), see Walter Kaufmann, *Nietzsche: Philosopher, Psychologist, Antichrist* (Princeton: Princeton University Press, 1974), pp. 167–70. For a more extensive account of Rousseau and Nietzsche see Keith Ansell-Pearson, *Nietzsche contra Rousseau: A Study of Nietzsche's Moral and Political Thought* (Cambridge: Cambridge University Press, 1991).

8 Spencer, of course, was most noted for his so-called 'adaptation' of Darwinian theories to social theory. For Nietzsche's views on Spencer see, for example, *The Gay Science*, trans. Walter Kaufmann (New York: Vintage Books, 1974), section 373.

9 With regard to this, see Nietzsche, *Beyond Good and Evil*, trans. Walter Kaufmann in *Basic Writings of Nietzsche*, section 230, where Nietzsche considers the project of knowledge as being part of this reintegration.

10 See the chapters devoted to Nietzsche in Paul de Man, *Allegories of Reading: Figural Language in Rousseau, Nietzsche. Rilke, and Proust* (New Haven & London: Yale University Press, 1979) for a discussion of this.

11 Kaufmann, *Nietzsche: Philosopher, Psychologist, Antichrist*, p. 267.

12 Nietzsche, *Ecce Homo*, trans. Kaufmann in *Basic Writings*, 'Why I Am a Destiny', 9.

13 Nietzsche, *The Gay Science*, section 39.

14 Nietzsche, *The Will to Power*, trans. Walter Kaufmann and R. J. Hollingdale (New York: Vintage Books, 1968), section 1067.
15 Nietzsche, *On the Genealogy of Morals*, trans. Kaufmann in *Basic Writings*, III, section 12.

1
The Significance of Michel Foucault's Reading of Nietzsche: Power, the Subject, and Political Theory

Keith Ansell-Pearson

Introduction

There are a number of reasons why Nietzsche's writings do not play a prominent part, if a part at all, in most standard treatments of the history of political theory, and which have ensured that he has remained on the margins of debate amongst political theorists.[1] Most important of all, of course, is the historical identification of Nietzsche's Machiavellian-inspired philosophy of 'beyond good and evil' with the ideology of European Fascism, which led a host of post-war commentators to engage in a project of dehistoricization, depoliticizing Nietzsche's philosophy of power in order to rehabilitate his writings from the abuse they had suffered in the hands of his sister, Elisabeth, and the Nazi ideologists whose work she encouraged and inspired.[2] However laudable the intentions behind this work were, it had the deleterious effect of foreclosing a debate about one of the central facets of Nietzsche's work and his legacy, that is, the nature of his politics and his status as a political thinker. Another reason for Nietzsche's neglect by political theorists lies in the fact that Nietzsche described his own status as a political thinker in terms of being 'the last anti-political German'.[3] This pronouncement has been taken at face value, rather than understood in the specific context in which Nietzsche articulates his opposition to the development of German *Reichspolitik*, under Bismarckian nationalism and statism. In *Ecce Homo* Nietzsche makes clear his fundamental opposition to the theory of *Machtpolitik* put forward by the historian Heinrich von Treitschke to justify the nationalist and militarist aspirations of the nascent German Reich: ' "German" has become an argument,' Nietzsche writes, *'Deutschland, Deutschland über Alles* a principle; the Teutons represent the "moral world order" in history – the carriers of freedom versus the *Imperium Romanum* [. . .] There is now a historiography that is *reichsdeutsch*; there is even, I fear, an anti-Semitic one – there is a *court* historiography, and Herr von Treitschke is not ashamed.'[4]

The question of Nietzsche's politics, and of his relation to political theory, has been further compounded by a generation of commentators who have sought solace and enlightenment in his ethical and political speculations, but who have found in them only empty rhetoric and the misguided yearnings of a maladjusted personality, the speculations of, as one commentator on this very topic has put it, 'a lonely hero fit to be used and destroyed'.[5] The devaluation of Nietzsche's political thought has continued up to the present day with one commentator referring to 'the embarrassingly political Nietzsche'.[6] It is fair to say that an impasse on the question of Nietzsche's politics, and of Nietzsche's status as a political theorist, has been reached by commentators adopting the practice of reading Nietzsche's overt or alleged politics back into the premises of his philosophy of power, and in this way discrediting the entire philosophical site on which Nietzsche had erected his political edifice. Yet for anyone aware of the pivotal role that Nietzsche's writings have come to play in contemporary intellectual debates in critical theory, poststructuralism, and deconstruction, the question of Nietzsche's status as a political theorist poses an enigma in need of some enlightenment.

The great significance of Michel Foucault's reading of Nietzsche is that it is the first to take Nietzsche's work seriously for the concerns of political theory. The implications of this reading are not only far-reaching for our understanding of the tradition of modern political thought but equally for *Nietzsche-Studien* and research. Foucault's reading of Nietzsche sheds a great deal of light on two crucial notions in Nietzsche's corpus: the notion of power and the notion of the subject. Moreover, unlike most interpreters and readers of Nietzsche, Foucault is able to show in what way Nietzsche's use of these notions is crucial for political theory. Thus, the aim of this chapter is to indicate how Foucault's reading of Nietzsche shows a way forward out of the impasse which has been reached on the question of Nietzsche's politics and on the relation between Nietzsche and modern political theory. We are experiencing a burgeoning interest in Nietzsche's writings amongst political theorists and it is Foucault's interpretation of Nietzsche which stands at the forefront of this interest. This chapter concurs with the position adopted by Henning Ottmann in his excellent and comprehensive study of the relation between 'philosophy' and 'politics' in Nietzsche. Ottmann argues that Nietzsche's philosophy is neither an apologia for capitalism nor a celebration of liberalism, neither fascist nor anarchist; rather the importance of Nietzsche's thinking for politics resides in its confrontation with the 'modern' itself and its dialectical possibilities.[7]

Indeed, Foucault's work has attempted to reconstruct the question, what is modernity? He has attempted to displace both the liberal and Marxist paradigms for understanding the nature of the modern world, detecting in both a Whiggish prejudice and a humanist delusion which adheres to the belief that modernity represents a simple struggle for rational and enlightened political institutions and transparent social relations. In order to disrupt the certainties and comforts offered by these models of understanding modern reality, Foucault employs Nietzsche's method of genealogy and locates dissonance at the heart of modernity and its discontents;[8] where liberalism and Marxism posit teleology and emphasize continuity, Foucault locates rupture and discontinuity; where Marxism posits a realm of freedom untainted by relations of domination, Foucault detects a hidden will to power, a will which wants to gain control of reality and master it for the purposes of satisfying our anthropomorphic desires.[9] Like Nietzsche, Foucault uses the method of genealogy to unsettle and undermine the philosophical premises on which humanity erects its political hopes and aspirations. As Nietzsche wrote, reflecting on the causes of European nihilism:

All the values by means of which we have tried so far to render the world estimable for ourselves and which then proved inapplicable and therefore devaluated the world – all these values are, psychologically considered, the results of certain perspectives of utility, designed to maintain and increase human constructs of domination – and they have been falsely *projected* into the essence of things. What we find here is still the *hyperbolic naiveté* of man: positing himself as the meaning and measure of the value of things.[10]

On a number of occasions Foucault has openly acknowledged his debt to Nietzsche.[11] Nietzsche influenced Foucault in a number of ways, but they can basically be reduced to two. Firstly, Nietzsche's understanding of power in terms of relations of forces had a tremendous influence on Foucault's attempt to think about power in a way which went beyond the juridical understanding of power prevalent in political theory. Secondly,

Nietzsche's critique of modern metaphysics and its privileging of the subject (a subject that was construed as rational and free but at the same time dehistoricized and disembodied) had an enormous impact on Foucault and the way in which he came to construe the problem of human freedom and creativity.

The chapter will proceed as follows: firstly, I shall show in what way Foucault understands Nietzsche's philosophy of power and its significance for modern political thought; secondly, I shall examine Foucault's reading of Nietzsche's deconstruction of the human subject and show in what way this project is crucial for politics and political thinking in the late-modern or post-modern age. Foucault's reading of Nietzsche is not without its limitations, however, and the shortcomings of his reading will be touched upon, as well. The chapter will conclude by suggesting that the significance of Foucault's reading of Nietzsche is that it provides a positive way forward for posing anew the question of the relationship between Nietzsche and political theory. If we take cognizance of the full impact of Foucault's reading, it should no longer be possible, or even desirable, for commentators to keep referring to 'the embarrassingly political Nietzsche'.

1 Power

For Foucault Nietzsche is *the* philosopher of power: 'If I wanted to be pretentious,' he wrote, 'I would use the "genealogy of morals" as the general title of what I am doing. It was Nietzsche who specified the power relation as the general focus, shall we say, of philosophical discourse – whereas for Marx it was the production relation. Nietzsche is the philosopher of power, a philosopher who managed to think of power without having to confine himself within a political theory in order to do so.'[12] What we need to explain is the apparent paradox in Foucault's appropriation of Nietzsche which lies in the argument that Nietzsche's philosophy of power is important for political theory because it is the first to construe the problem of power *without* the constraints of a political theory. What is meant by arguing that Nietzsche thinks about power outside of the confines of a political theory? Reflecting on this question will govern our discussion of Foucault in this section of the essay.

Foucault's understanding of power is entirely nominalistic: power (*le pouvoir*) in the substantive sense does not exist.[13] Instead, Foucault focuses our attention on the exercise of power where 'power' denotes not a property or a possession belonging to a dominant class, sovereign, or state, but rather points to a strategy referring to a multiplicity of force relations. Power is neither an institution nor a structure but rather, Foucault argues, following Nietzsche, 'it is the name one attributes to a complex strategical situation in a particular society.'[14] Above all, Foucault's Nietzschean understanding of power aims to combat the prevalent view in political thought which conceives of power exclusively in negative terms: power as prohibition, power as exclusion, as rejection, as obstruction, as denial. In opposition to this dominant juridical model of understanding power – juridical in the sense that it is the 'law' which prohibits, excludes, obstructs, denies, etc. – Foucault argues that power is essentially *productive*. Foucault's argument here follows closely the one Nietzsche evinces in *On the Genealogy of Morals*. The great innovation of Nietzsche's thinking about power in that text is that it sees power not in terms of the strenuous effects of a founding human subject, but rather that it sees power as *productive* of the human subject. In other words, the priority of the subject over power (the object) within the tradition of Western metaphysics is reversed and overturned. We will return to these key points on the human subject shortly, but for the moment it is necessary to focus attention on the notion of power and the specific way in which it is understood by both Nietzsche and Foucault.

Traditionally, Foucault argues, modern political thought has posed the fundamental questions of political philosophy in terms of a philosophy of righ/law (*Recht*). It asks: what are the limits of power? How can power be given 'rights' to restrict its use and abuse? In contrast to this question concerning the legitimacy of (political) power, Foucault poses a different type of question: what rules of right are implemented by the relations of power in the production of discourses of truth, that is, what is the will to power behind the will to truth in political philosophy? Since the Middle Ages, he argues, it has been the major preoccupation of political theorists to determine the legitimacy of power with a theory of sovereignty. However, behind this discourse of right within modern political thought Foucault detects a hidden discourse of power. He writes:

When we say that sovereignty is the central problem of right in Western societies, what we mean basically is that the essential function of the discourse and techniques of right has been to efface the domination intrinsic to power in order to present the latter at the level of appearance under two different aspects: on the one hand, as the legitimate rights of sovereignty, and on the other, as the legal obligation to obey it. The system of right [. . .] is designed to eliminate the fact of domination and its consequences.[15]

Here Foucault traverses a recognizably and distinctly Nietzschean path, locating a discourse of power where none was expected – in the very discourse of modern political thought itself.

Why is Foucault so opposed to the hegemony of the juridical model of power in political theory? And what are the implications of his reliance on Nietzsche's philosophy of power for understanding many of the traditional problems of political philosophy? Concerning the first question, Foucault argues that the juridical model is incapable of comprehending how power operates in modern disciplinary societies. As in the *Genealogy of Morals*, Foucault understands the exercise of power not in terms of 'right' but in terms of technique, not in terms of law but in terms of normalization, not in terms of abuse but in terms of punishment and control. Our modern political rationality, according to Foucault, has developed alongside a new political technology of power which has produced the 'individual' as a subject of the state with rights and obligations: a subject not in the sense of sovereignty but in the sense of discipline.[16] As Nietzsche astutely notes in section 117 of the *Gay Science*, our conception of the individual subject as being the locus and origin of moral actions and ethical responsibility, a conception which constitutes the starting-point for present-day teachers of law and jurists, is a peculiarly modern one. In former times – namely, the prehistoric period Nietzsche calls the 'morality of custom' (*die Sittlichkeit der Sitte*) – one was sentenced to individuality as a form of punishment. Today, however, history has reached the dangerous and uncanny point 'where the "individual" appears, obliged to give himself laws and to develop his own arts and wiles for self-preservation, self-enhancement, and self-redemption'.[17]

According to Foucault we moderns are unable to accept the naked cynicism of power – what Nietzsche refers to as 'the Machiavellianism of power'[18] – and instead we prefer to veil it with a cloak of freedom by erecting discourses of right which impose limits on so-called 'abuses' of power. Foucault invites us to abandon the juridical model of power which has held its grip on our political thinking since the Middle Ages and, instead of conceiving power in terms of a fundamental lawfulness, we learn to think of the mechanisms and strategies of power in a way that is not reducible to the representation of law.

Concerning the second question raised above, Foucault's understanding of power – which draws its main inspiration from Nietzsche's conception of power in terms of relations of domination (*Herrschafts-Verhältnissen*) which are immanent in a multiplicity of force relations[19] – has enormous implications for how we are to construe the problem of modernity and how political theory has conceptualised that problem. By rejecting the juridical model of power common to both liberalism and Marxism, Foucault conceives of power neither in terms of a group of institutions which ensure the obedience of citizens to the State nor in terms of a mode of subjugation which, in contrast to pure naked violence and coercion, has the appearance of law. For Foucault, the analysis of power must not 'assume that the sovereignty of the state, the form of the law, or the overall unity of a domination are given at the outset; rather, these are only the terminal forms power takes [. . .] power must be understood in the first instance as the multiplicity of force relations immanent in the sphere in which they operate and which constitute their own organization'.[20] Like Nietzsche, Foucault posits the omnipresence of power not in terms of any noumenal or metaphysical substance and not 'because it has the privilege of consolidating everything under its invincible unity, but because it is produced from one moment to the next, at every point, or rather in every relation from one point to another. Power is everywhere; not because it embraces everything, but because it comes from everywhere'.[21] The implications of Foucault's reliance on a Nietzschean model of power for political theory should be fairly self-evident. Contra the Marxian model, for example, Foucault is arguing that the function and operation of power cannot be reduced to the mere maintenance of relations of production and of class domination. Foucault's Nietzscheanization of the problem of power in political philosophy means, contra Marxian theory, that relations of power can neither be construed in terms of a position of exteriority with respect to other types of relationships (for example, economic relationships), but rather must be seen to be immanent in them, nor in terms of a base/superstructure metaphor in which power plays a merely secondary role of prohibition; rather relations of power have a directly productive role to play.

Foucault's philosophy of power, derived, as we have seen, from a reading of Nietzsche, eschews the modern paradigm of understanding power in terms of a discourse on the nature of law and sovereignty and in its place puts forward a conception of power in terms of a multiplicity of force relations. Perhaps the most notable feature of this philosophy of power is the radical and disconcerting claim that power is productive of the human subject and that, far from constituting a neutral point of reference, the so-called emancipated and autonomous subject of modernity is in fact fully constituted by power and discipline. It is to this aspect of Foucault's appropriation of Nietzsche that I now wish to turn in the next section of the chapter.

2 The Subject

Nietzsche's *Genealogy of Morals* shows that even the most cherished notions of modern political culture are the product of a specific historical labour of discipline and culture, what Nietzsche prefiguring Freud calls 'civilization' (*Kultur*). For Nietzsche all our 'moral' capacities and attributes such as conscience, responsibility, and free will must be seen to have a history and a genealogy. Indeed, Nietzsche begins the second essay of the *Genealogy* by posing the fundamental question of political philosophy, that is, the problem of breeding a political animal (Aristotle) which can be bound to obligations and held accountable to the *social contract* because it has 'the *right* to make promises': 'To breed an animal *with the right to make promises* – is not this the paradoxical task that nature has set itself in the case of man? Is it not the real problem regarding man?'[22] For Nietzsche political obligation takes place through the historical cultivation of a sense of responsibility by which man is made regular, calculable, and necessary:

> The tremendous labour of that which I have called the 'morality of mores' (*die Sittlichkeit der Sitte*) – the labour performed by man upon himself during the greater part of the existence of the human race, finds in this its meaning, its great justification, notwithstanding the severity, tyranny, stupidity, and idiocy involved in it: with the aid of the morality of mores and the social straitjacket, man was actually *made* calculable.[23]

At the centre of Nietzsche's critique of metaphysics – a critique which emerges directly out of his construal of the problem of breeding a political animal – is a critique of traditional conceptions of the human subject. According to Nietzsche metaphysics has throughout its history posited a conception of a timeless epistemological subject as the foundation of all knowledge and experience of man and the world. But for Nietzsche this constitutes a fundamental error. He writes in the *Genealogy*:

> A quantum of force is equivalent to to a quantum of drive, will, effect – more, it is nothing other than precisely this very driving,

willing, effecting and only owing to the seduction of language (and of the fundamental errors of reason which are petrified in it) that conceives and misconceives all effects as conditioned by something that causes effects, by a 'subject', can it appear otherwise. For just as the popular mind separates the lightning from its flash and takes the latter for an *action*, for the operation of a subject called lightning, so popular morality also separates strength from expressions of strength, as if there were a neutral substratum behind the strong man, which was *free* to express strength or not to do so. But there is no such substratum; there is no 'being' behind doing, effecting, becoming; the 'doer' is merely a fiction added to the deed – the deed is everything.[24]

It is precisely this non-metaphysical and non-teleological understanding of the subject which informs Foucault's philosophy of power. Indeed, in an interview conducted as late as 1983 in which he reflects on his relation to the pantheon of modern European thought (Marx, Nietzsche, Freud), Foucault admits that the determining experience reading Nietzsche had for him as a student of phenomenology was that of liberating him from the notion of the founding act of the subject.[25] By developing further Nietzsche's reversing of the priority of the subject over power within the metaphysical tradition, Foucault is able to show in what way this Nietzschean deconstruction of the subject is crucial for conceiving a post-modern conception of the self.

Following Nietzsche, Foucault argues that the individual which lies at the foundation of our modern view of the world – what Heidegger calls the modern metaphysics of subjectivity, which commences with Descartes's *cogito* – is not to be construed in terms of a preconstituted entity of autonomous action which is simply seized upon and repressed by the exercise of power. Instead, we need to construe this individual subject as the product of a certain form of power peculiar to modern societies which Foucault identifies as disciplinary power, and which determines a whole range of modern discourses (on madness, on punishment, on sexuality, etc.) that constitute certain bodies as individuals and provide them with gestures and desires. Individuals, Foucault argues, are to be understood as the vehicles of power, not its point of application. It is with this argument on the constitution of the individual as an effect of power that Foucault challenges the model of the *Leviathan*:

Let us not ask, therefore, why certain people want to dominate, what they seek, what is their overall strategy. Let us ask, instead, how things work at the level of on-going subjugation, at the level of

those continuous and uninterrupted processes which subject our
bodies, govern our gestures, dictate our behaviours, etc. In other
words, rather than ask ourselves how the sovereign appears to us
in his lofty isolation, we should try to discover how it is that subjects are gradually, progressively, really and materially constituted
through a multiplicity of organisms, forces, energies, materials,
desires, etc. We should try to grasp subjection in its material instance as a constitution of subjects. This would be the exact opposite of Hobbes' project in the *Leviathan*, and of that, I believe, of all
jurists for whom the problem is the distillation of a single will [. . .]
from the particular wills of a multiplicity of individuals.[26]

For Foucault the domain, the territory, of political theory has definitely
shifted. Inspired by Nietzsche's genealogy of the subject, it is no longer
for him a question of uniting the particular and the universal through a
notion of the general will (as in Rousseau and Hegel, for example), but
rather of analysing the different modes in which individuals have been
constituted as human subjects that are equipped with a 'free' will and
on account of which they can be held responsible for their actions.
Nietzsche's deconstruction of the founding act of the subject culminates
in Foucault's rejection of the liberal model of an autonomous subjectivity – a subject supposedly freed from constraining social hierarchies
and political domination – since this model is itself implicated in modern
disciplinary forms of power. According to Foucault we need an entirely
different, nonjuridical notion of subjectivity in order to think about the
nature of human freedom and subjectivity in a new way. Thus, on two
fronts – on the question of power and on the question of the human
subject – Foucault employs Nietzsche's writings as a way of moving
beyond the parameters set by political theory in thinking about the
nature of modernity and its dialectical possibilities.

One notable attempt to take up Foucault's challenge and to advance
his argument on the need for a post-modern notion of subjectivity is to
be found in a work on the problem of modernity in political theory, in
which Nietzsche assumes a pivotal role.[27] William Connolly has argued
that there are two ways of construing Nietzsche's philosophy of power.
Either we take the most obvious and widely accepted reading which
interprets the will to power in terms of a notion which advocates a kind
of Hobbesian universal mastery and domination (over nature, persons,
and things), or we can follow a Foucaultian path and construe the will to
power in terms of a recognition and affirmation of forms of otherness.[28]
For Connolly political modernity is characterized by a quest for trans-
parency and the overcoming of all natural and man-made obstacles

which stand in the way of the realization of this goal. However, the price to be paid for the attainment of this end-state is the assimilation and domination of 'otherness', including, most destructively of all, nature itself. Things which escape human control and mastery are defined as 'forms of otherness' and held to be in need of rationalization and normalization (madness, perversity, chaos and disorder, etc.). The importance of Nietzsche in thinking through the relation between political theory and modernity lies in Nietzsche's affirmation of these forms of otherness and of a space in which they can be recognized without incorporating them into some grand dialectical system of absolute thought and knowledge. Modern political theory from Rousseau to Hegel and Marx, however, has supported the ideal of an ethico-political community in which suppression and subjugation is accepted for the sake of realizing the goal of social harmony and collective unity.[29] But the desire for unity and harmony expressed in the search for the common good can only result in a totalitarian denial of otherness, an otherness which arises by necessity from this quest for completion.

Connolly invites us to interpret the modern project of freedom and emancipation in terms of an imperialistic discourse of mastery and domination that is blind to its own unexamined assumptions about the self and the world. He argues that any set of norms or standards which becomes endowed with legitimacy and authority must represent an ambiguous achievement in so far as it succumbs to the temptation of establishing its own hegemony by excluding and denying that which does not fit into its confines. With Foucault, Connolly shares a deep suspicion towards notions of an integrated and harmonious self because this integration and harmony can only be achieved at the cost of subjugating a form of otherness which is resistant to harmony and unity.

The importance of Nietzsche in this context is that the absence of a political theory in his writings allows him the advantage over other modern thinkers – Hegel, Marx, etc. – of being able to examine the presumptions of modernity without advocating in advance of this interrogation a single theory of politics.[30] Thus, unlike many commentators, Connolly does not view the lack of a coherent or systematic political theory in Nietzsche in terms of a lacuna in need of reconstruction, but rather as a source of strength in thinking about the problem of modernity without the certainties and the comforts provided by a totalizing and foundational philosophical system.

With the thought of will to power, Connolly suggests, Nietzsche provides a counter-ontology of resistance which puts into doubt the anthropomorphic desire behind modernity that the world should be made susceptible to human mastery and the desire of utopian politics for a community united in its understanding of the common good. Modernity has created a political animal, but one which is full of rancour and *ressentiment*, resentment both towards that within itself which resists subjectification and towards that in others which deviates from its own moral standards and norms. In both instances the self as subject refuses to accept difference in itself and others and converts this irreducible difference into an otherness which must be excluded and denied. As Connolly points out:

> The subject is not simply or unambiguously the self which establishes its unity, freedom, independence and self-transparency; it is also the self required to interiorize a complex set of socially imposed standards and to regulate that in itself which deviates from those norms. The subject is ambiguously an instrumentality of modern order and a claimant of rights within it, an independent centre of knowledge and a bearer of socially established criteria of knowledge, a seeker of self-transparency and an interiorizer of social norms. This ambiguity is its essence; but its denial is crucial to its identity. Is there, then, no trace of resentment in the self which bears the impress of subjectivity? Is there no drive to revenge in the accusations, corrections, improvements, verdicts, and punishments individuals mete out to each other or in the treatment they accord to those falling below the threshold of subjectivity?[31]

Nietzsche offers a form of selfhood in which discipline and self-control are affirmed while the tarantula of revenge and resentment, as Zarathustra calls it, is refused: 'For that man may be delivered from revenge: that is for me the bridge to the highest hope, and a rainbow after long storms.'[32] The human subject learns to affirm the contingency and finitude of its existence and to accept the fragility of the world and its place in it. For Connolly this 'brave ethic' of Nietzsche's constitutes, in contrast to the ethic of mastery and domination characteristic of modernity, an ethic of 'letting be'.[33]

The interiorization of the subject which Nietzsche analyses in the *Genealogy* in terms of the development of a bad conscience has all too often been understood in terms of an advocation on Nietzsche's part of some grandiose and ahistorical return to pagan aristocracy (the 'blond beasts' of Nietzsche legend).[34] But this is a mistaken reading of Nietzsche's intentions. Nietzsche accepts the historicization and the socialization of the human subject and the necessity of the slave revolt in morality which has deepened the human animal in that it has cultivated a 'soul' – and with it the knowledge of 'evil.' In contrast to the reading of Nietzsche as a neo-conservative, Connolly, inspired by Foucault's critique of modernity in which Nietzsche plays a decisive part, succeeds in showing us the outlines of a Nietzschean ethic which may take us beyond the antinomies of political modernity.

Concluding Reflections

Foucault's reading of Nietzsche is bold, challenging, and imaginative. It has inspired some original construals of Nietzsche's relation to political theory. However, it is not without exegetic problems. In spite of the fact that Foucault was a self-declared intellectual anarchist who had little respect or regard for the fidelity of his textual interpretations – Foucault argues strongly that there is no single Nietzscheanism[35] – it is necessary to question the accuracy of his reading of Nietzsche in the two aspects we have concentrated our attention on.

Foucault's use of Nietzsche's philosophy of power in order to shift the boundaries of political thought rests on the argument that Nietzsche thinks of power outside of the confines of a political theory. This is true to a certain extent, but it should be noted that Nietzsche does not reject the juridical model of power as completely and unequivocally as Foucault does. Thus, for example, we find that in *Thus Spoke Zarathustra* Nietzsche relates the teaching of will to power in terms of a teaching on the nature of law and sovereignty. This is evident in two notable parables in the book. First, in the parable on 'Of the Way of the Creator' (*Vom Wege des Schaffenden*), Nietzsche has Zarathustra present a notion of sovereignty in which self-mastery is understood to involve not only the self-legislation of the will but also self-execution of power. In other words, the notion of will to power can be read in terms of Nietzsche's attempt to show the inseparability of 'will' (legislation) and 'power' (execution), to show that we cannot think of one without the other. In this way Nietzsche shows the unity of the doer and the deed, that the human self only discloses itself through human action. In this way Nietzsche departs radically from the Kantian conception of autonomy, in which the emphasis is placed not on the consequences of human action (on what Nietzsche calls 'doing') but on the intentions behind it, and which posits a morally good and pure rational agent, but one which is conceived in purely ahistorical and noumenal terms. Thus, Zarathustra asks: 'Can you furnish yourself with your own good and evil and hang up your own will above yourself as a law? Can you be judge of yourself and avenger of your law?'[36] Secondly, in the parable on 'Of Self-

Overcoming' (*Von der Selbst-Ueberwindung*) Nietzsche has Zarathustra inform us that wherever he found a living creature he found the will to power, 'even in the will of the servant I found the will to be master.' 'All living creatures,' Zarathustra relates, 'are obeying creatures [. . .] he who cannot obey himself will be commanded [. . .] Only where life is, there is also will: not will to life, but – so I teach you – will to power!'[37]

This point on the will to power as a teaching of sovereignty has implications for understanding Nietzsche's notion of subjectivity. As we have seen, Foucault abandons the notion of autonomous subjectivity found in liberal theory on the grounds that it is little more than an insidious model of self-determination by which the disciplinary institutions of modern society (the prison, the asylum, the clinic, etc.) gain normalized control of the human subject and create spurious hierarchical distinctions between the normal and the insane, the healthy and the sick, the free and the oppressed in order to train the 'normal' (and normative) self to accept responsibility for its conduct. In contrast to Foucault, however, Nietzsche does not embark on a complete abandonment of a notion of subjectivity but instead puts forward an alternative aesthetic model of human freedom and creativity. In *The Gay Science*, for example, Nietzsche speaks of creating the self in terms of a notion of artistic wholeness:

> To 'give style' to one's character – a great and rare art! It is practiced by all those who survey all the strengths and weaknesses of their nature and then fit them into an artistic plan until every one of them appears as art and reason and even weaknesses delight the eye [. . .] For one thing is needful: that a human being should *attain* satisfaction with himself, whether it be by means of this or that poetry and art; only then is a human being at all tolerable to behold. Whoever is dissatisfied with himself is continually ready for revenge, and we others will be his victims, if only by having to endure his ugly sight.[38]

In this aesthetic model of subjectivity we see the outlines of the kind of model of the self which Connolly conceives as being a positive and creative form of selfhood which does not resent its own mode of organization and rage against the temporality of the human condition. While not embracing the view that the subject is to be construed in terms of a mere effect of power, this does not mean that Nietzsche posits a metaphysics of the subject or that he views the creation of the self as something prior to the constitution of power. On the contrary, Nietzsche views subjectivity in terms of a labour of self-overcoming which is inseparable from relations of power. Indeed, in his last work on ethics Foucault was to recognize that his notion of the subject as a mere effect of power constituted one of the major deficiencies of his thinking, and it was precisely to a Nietzschean aesthetic conception of ethics that he turned in thinking about an alternative nonjuridical model of selfhood.[39]

The significance of Nietzsche's notion of character is that it envisages a form of self-creation and self-legislation which does not rely on notions of *moral* judgement. In section 290 of the *Gay Science* we have quoted from, for example, Nietzsche says that the human being that is able to subject itself to the constraint of style does not conceal what is ugly about their nature but knows how to make it sublime. 'In the end,' Nietzsche says, 'when the work is finished, it becomes evident how the constraint of a single taste governed and formed everything large and small.' Nietzsche's key point is that the important thing is not whether this taste is 'good' or 'bad,' but that it reflects a single taste, that is, a taste which reveals that the self which imposes the discipline of style upon itself is able to give a coherence and unity to its character. This unity of the self, however, is not a *moral* unity but an *aesthetic* one – more, it is one which is truly beyond the oppositions of moral judgement, that is, *beyond good and evil*.

Notwithstanding the criticisms I have made, Foucault's reading of Nietzsche maintains its originality. His reading shows that Nietzsche's philosophy of power can be fruitfully deployed in order to re-think some of the central problems of political philosophy in a fresh and invigorating way. Indeed, one commentator has recently argued, in the wake of Foucault's reading, that Nietzsche's overt 'neo-conservative' politics can be disengaged from his philosophy of power without jeopardising the coherence and originality of his thought. Mark Warren has argued that there exists no necessary logical connection between Nietzsche's philosophy of power and his aristocratic politics, but rather that Nietzsche's politics only follow from his philosophy of power if we accept, as he did, several uncritical assumptions about the nature and limits of politics in modern societies, such as, for example, the belief that all societies, both ancient and modern, require a rigid and institutionalised division of labour and order of rank in which society is divided into masters and slaves.[40] Thus, following in the footsteps of Foucault's pioneering work, Warren suggests that attention is not focused on Nietzsche's regressive and debilitating politics, which constitutes the least interesting aspect of his work, but rather on his philosophy of power, which is the aspect of his work least explored by political theorists. For Warren, the great significance of Nietzsche's philosophy of will to power is that it is the first which can be seen to explicitly break with the metaphysical assumptions

of modern political thought about the nature of human agency by
conceiving the subject as entirely contingent, dependent upon historical
and cultural practices for its realization in the social world.[41]

Behind the imaginative readings of Nietzsche's importance for post-
modern politics put forward by Connolly and Warren there lies the
inspirational work of Michel Foucault, which, if deployed in the way
it is intended to be, makes it impossible for critics of Nietzsche to
keep on discussing the political import of his work solely in terms of
'the embarrassingly political Nietzsche.' Foucault's work points the
way forward beyond the impasse which has been reached on the question
of Nietzsche's politics and his status as a political thinker. His reading
of Nietzsche should serve to inspire a whole programme of Nietzsche
research in an effort to open up the neglected question of Nietzsche's
relation to the major thinkers of the tradition of modern political thought
(Machiavelli, Hobbes, Rousseau, Kant, and Hegel) and to pose the
crucial question of Nietzsche's importance for post-modernity. A
number of the major philosophers of this century – Jaspers, Heidegger,
Deleuze, Derrida – have thrown up a 'new Nietzsche' for discussion and inspiration. It is unlikely that we will find one that is as
challenging and inspiring as the one to be found in the work of Michel
Foucault.

NOTES

1 Werner Dannhauser, 'Friedrich Nietzsche', in L. Strauss and U. Cropsey,
  History of Political Philosophy (Chicago, Chicago University Press, 1987 –
  third edition), pp. 829–51, suggests that the relation of Fascism to Nietzsche
  recalls the relation of the French Revolution to Rousseau. Previous attempts
  to examine the question of Nietzsche's politics in the wider context of his
  principal theoretical concerns include, Tracy B. Strong, *Friedrich Nietzsche
  and the Politics of Transfiguration* (Berkeley, University of California Press,
  1975), and Ofelia Schutte, *Beyond Nihilihm. Nietzsche Without Masks*
  (Chicago, University of Chicago Press, 1984).
2 On the mythologization of Nietzsche by his sister see the Prologue to
  Walter Kaufmann's classic study, *Nietzsche, Philosopher, Psychologist, and
  Antichrist* (Princeton, Princeton University Press, 1974 – fourth edition).
  Kaufmann's study is a classic instance of the process of depoliticization
  Nietzsche's writings underwent in the aftermath of the Second World War.
  For Kaufmann 'the leitmotif of Nietzsche's life and thought' is 'the theme of
  the antipolitical individual who seeks self-perfection far from the modern
  world' (p. 418).
3 See EH, 'Warum ich so weise bin', section 3, in KSA 6. For an excellent
  biographical study see, Peter Bergmann, *Nietzsche. The Last Anti-Political
  German* (Bloomington, Indiana University Press, 1987).
4 EH, 'Der Fall Wagner', 2.

5 John S. Colman, 'Nietzsche as *Politique et Moraliste*', in *Journal of the History of Ideas* 27 (1966), p. 568.

6 See Walter H. Sokel, 'The Political Uses and Abuses of Nietzsche in Walter Kaufmann's Image of Nietzsche', *Nietzsche-Studien* 12 (1983), p. 441.

7 Henning Ottmann, *Philosophie und Politik, bei Nietzsche* (Berlin and New York, Walter de Gruyter, 1987), preface.

8 For Nietzsche's description of genealogy as a 'historical method' see GM H, 12 in KSA 5.

9 See Foucault's essay, 'Nietzsche, Genealogy, and History' in M. Foucault, *Language, Counter-Memory, Practice*, ed. D. E Bouchard (Oxford, Basil Blackwell, 1977).

10 Nietzsche, *The Will to Power*, tr. Walter Kaufmann and R. J. Hollingdale (New York, Random House, 1968), section 12 B.

11 See especially, Michel Foucault, *Philosophy, Politics, and Culture. Interviews and Other Writings 1977–84*, ed. L. D. Kritzman (London, Routledge, 1988), pp. 250–1, p. 312.

12 Michel Foucault. *Power/Knowledge. Selected Interviews and Other Writings 1972–1977*, ed. C. Gordon (Brighton, Harvester Press, 1980), p. 53.

13 Ibid., p. 198.

14 Michel Foucault, *The History of Sexuality*. Volume 1, tr. R. Hurley (Harmondsworth, Penguin, 1979), p. 93.

15 Foucault, *Power/Knowledge*, p. 95.

16 Michel Foucault. 'The Political Technology of Individuals', in Luther H. Martin et al., *Technologies of the Self. A Seminar with Michel Foucault* (London, Tavistock Publications, 1988), pp. 150–4.

17 JGB 262, KSA 5.

18 Nietzsche *The Will to Power*, sections 304 and 776.

19 JGB 19.

20 Foucault, *History of Sexuality*, p. 92.

21 Ibid., p. 93.

22 GM II, 1.

23 Ibid., II, 2.

24 Ibid., I, 13.

25 Foucault, *Philosophy, Politics, and Culture*, p. 24.

26 Foucault. *Power/Knowledge*, p. 97.

27 I am using the term 'post-modern' very loosely to refer to a way of thinking about notions of autonomy and subjectivity which differs in significant respects from how these notions are conceived in the modern tradition. However, I very much agree with Agnes Heller and Ferenc Fehér, who argue that postmodernity (including the postmodern *political* condition) does not denote a new historical era, but rather that it is parasitic on modernity in as much as it lives and feeds on modernity's achievements and dilemmas. 'What is new in the situation,' they write, 'is the novel historical consciousness developed in *post-histoire*; the spreading feeling that we are permanently going to be in the present and, at the same time, after it'. See Heller and Fehér, *The Postmodern Political Condition* (Oxford, Basil Blackwell, 1989), pp. 10–11. I have argued along very similar lines – chiefly that postmodernity is one more way of refashioning the discontents of modernity and that the relation between the two has to be construed in terms of a fundamental entwinement – in my unpublished paper, 'Foucault and the Post-modern Turn in Political

Theory' (first delivered at a conference entitled *Postmodernism and the Social Sciences* held at the University of St Andrews, Scotland, August 1989). For insight into how we might construe Nietzsche's philosophy in the debate on modernity and postmodernity see, Robert B. Pippin, 'Nietzsche and the Origin of the Idea of Modernism', *Inquiry* 26 (1983), pp. 151–80, plus his essay, 'Nietzsche's Farewell: Modernity, Pre-Modernity, and Post-Modernity', in B. Magnus (ed.), *Nietzsche* (Cambridge, Cambridge University Press, forthcoming) and Ian Forbes, 'Nietzsche, Modernity, and Politics', in J. R. Gibbin, *Contemporary Political Culture. Politics in a Postmodern Age* (London, Sage, 1989), pp. 218–36.

28 W. Connolly, *Political Theory and Modernity* (Oxford, Blackwell, 1988), p. 161. For a reading of the will to power in terms of a principle of domination see, J. P. Stern, *Nietzsche* (Glasgow, Collins, 1978); for a reading of the notion in terms of a principle of self-overcoming and self-mastery see, Kaufmann, *Nietzsche*; for an attempt to mediate between these two readings see, O. Schutte, *Beyond Nihilism*. For a comprehensive and informative reading of Nietzsche's teaching see, Wolfgang Müller Lauter, 'Nietzsches Lehre vom Willen zur Macht', *Nietzsche Studien* 3, 1974, pp. 1–60.

29 Connolly, *Political Theory and Modernity*, p. 132.

30 Ibid., p. 168.

31 Ibid., pp. 156–7.

32 Za II, 'Von den Taranteln', KSA 4.

33 Connolly, *Political Theory and Modernity*, p. 161.

34 See Detlef Brennecke, 'Die Blonde Bestie. Vom Mißverständnis eines Schlagworts', *Nietzsche-Studien* 5 (1976), pp. 113–45.

35 Foucault, *Philosophy, Politics, and Culture*, p. 32.

36 Za I, 'Vom Wege des Schaffenden'.

37 Ibid., 'Von der Selbst-Ueberwindung'.

38 FW 290, KSA 3.

39 See Michel Foucault, 'On the Genealogy of Ethics: An Overview of Work in Progress', in P. Rabinow (ed.). *The Foucault Reader* (Harmondsworth, Penguin, 1984), pp. 340–72.

40 Mark Warren, *Nietzsche and Political Thought* (Cambridge, Mass, MIT Press, 1988), preface and pp. 226–7, pp. 237–46.

41 Ibid., pp. 152–9. I have critically examined in some detail the claims Warren makes on behalf of Nietzsche's alleged break with the metaphysical assumptions of modern political thought in my essay, 'Nietzsche: A Radical Challenge to Political Theory?', in *Radical Philosophy* 54 (spring 1990), pp. 10–19.

2
Returning to Nature: Nietzsche's *Götterdämmerung*

Daniel W. Conway

> Nature is a bad economist: its expenditure is much larger than the income it procures; all its wealth notwithstanding, it is bound sooner or later to ruin itself.
> Friedrich Nietzsche, *Schopenhauer as Educator* (1874)

> I too speak of a "return to Nature," although it is really not a going back but an *ascent* – up into the high, free, even terrible Nature and naturalness where great tasks are something one plays with, one may play with.
> Friedrich Nietzsche, *Twilight of the Idols* (1888)

Introduction

Upon finishing his eleventh book, provisionally entitled *The Idleness of a Psychologist*, Nietzsche sent the manuscript to his friend Peter Gast (Heinrich Köselitz) for a final, pre-publication review. Upon reading the manuscript, Gast hurriedly scribbled his impressions, including the "editorial" suggestion that Herr Nietzsche adorn the book with "a more sumptuous, resplendent title."[1] Heeding, as always, his friend's sycophantic advice, Nietzsche promptly renamed his little book:

Götzen-Dämmerung.

Oder:

wie man mit dem Hammer philosophirt

[*Twilight of the Idols. Or: How One Philosophizes With a Hammer*].[2]

Playing on (and perverting) the title of the concluding opera of Wagner's *Ring* tetralogy, *Götterdämmerung* (*Twilight of the Gods*),[3] Nietzsche unveiled the hammer with which he would expose and demolish the hollow idols of late modernity.

While Nietzsche's mischievous wordplay yields a provocative title for the product of his "idleness," Wagner's original title may actually afford a more compelling insight into the development of Nietzsche's own thought. Indeed, his eleventh-hour decision to dignify his idleness tends to obscure the *Götterdämmerung* that transpires within the complex economy of his own philosophical development. His most influential contribution to philosophy, the explication of the aesthetic principles that he associates with Dionysus and Apollo, respectively, virtually disappears from his later writings. While a transfigured incarnation of Dionysus occasionally presides over his later writings, Nietzsche rarely rehearses the aesthetic principles that he originally associated with the two gods,[4] and he never again appeals to their dual aegis. In his "review" of *The Birth of Tragedy*, he mocks the idea that tragedy represents the dialectical synthesis of Apollo and Dionysus, and he wrinkles his nose at the "offensively Hegelian" odor that clings to the book as a whole (EH: bt 1).[5] Following *The Birth of Tragedy*, he apparently exiles Dionysus and Apollo, and his subsequent writings negotiate the theoretical space that is cleared by the gods' mysterious retreat. Having broken with Wagner for good in 1876, Nietzsche orchestrates a *Götterdämmerung* of his own.

While Nietzsche's *Götterdämmerung* may be consistent with the atheism and iconoclasm with which he is popularly identified, it is also only apparent. As it turns out, he does not retire the patron deities of his philosophy so much as the "artists' metaphysics" that they inelegantly served. While the *Götterdämmerung* I have described marks a fundamental turning in Nietzsche's thought, this turning involves the transformation, rather than the exile, of Dionysus and Apollo. In his post-Zarathustran writings, Nietzsche investigates the (apparent) tension between Life and Nature, which reproduces in naturalistic terms the original opposition between Apollo and Dionysus.[6] Having abandoned the "artists' metaphysics" of *The Birth of Tragedy*, he transforms the aesthetic categories eponymously associated with Dionysus and Apollo into the economic principles of Nature and Life, respectively. Nietzsche's *Götterdämmerung*, his apparent apostasy from the patronage of Dionysus and Apollo, thus sheds light on the naturalistic development of his philosophy. Although absent in name, Apollo and Dionysus continue to preside over his thought – albeit now transfigured into the economic principles that govern his "return to Nature."

1 Returning to *The Birth of Tragedy*

In his "Attempt at a Self-Criticism," which he appends in 1886 as a Preface to *The Birth of Tragedy*, Nietzsche sets out to reclaim his much maligned book and to recover its political dimension. Not coincidentally, he makes no attempt in this retrospective Preface to defend or embellish his original account of the aesthetic principles he named for Apollo and Dionysus. The 1886 Preface in fact diverts the reader's focus to the latter term of this famous dyad, claiming that the book it reclaims answers the question, "What is Dionysian?" (BT: AS 4).[7] He ridicules the "artists' metaphysics" of *The Birth of Tragedy* (BT: AS 2), which distracted everyone – including the book's author – from the political importance of this question. His perceived need to re-raise this question not only attests to the failure of *The Birth of Tragedy* to execute its original design, but also reinforces the new, self-consciously political orientation of his project. *The Birth of Tragedy* succeeded in considering "science in the perspective of the artist," but only confusingly and incompletely managed to frame art itself "in the perspective of Life" (BT: AS 2).

The signal political insight of *The Birth of Tragedy*, which even Nietzsche initially failed to glean, lay in the supposition that tragedy played a justificatory role in Greek culture. In the original *Birth of Tragedy*, he introduced this idea only parenthetically, announcing that:

It is only as an aesthetic phenomenon that existence (*Dasein*) and the world are eternally *justified* (*gerechtfertig*). (BT 5; cf. BT 24)

Along with Apollo and Dionysus, the term "aesthetic justification" disappears from Nietzsche's subsequent books.[8] Yet the idea of an "aesthetic justification," of which the collaboration of Apollo and Dionysus was supposedly representative, continues to fascinate Nietzsche, and it stands at the center of his post-Zarathustran political thinking.

A primary aim of the 1886 Preface is to discredit the "artists' metaphysics" that unduly burdened *The Birth of Tragedy*. In the original *Birth of Tragedy*, Nietzsche locates the justificatory power of tragedy in the "metaphysical comfort" it provides:

We are to recognize that all that comes into being must be ready for a sorrowful end; we are forced to look into the terrors of the individual existence – yet we are not to become rigid with fear: a metaphysical comfort tears us momentarily from the bustle of the changing figures. (BT 17)

The "metaphysical comfort" furnished by tragedy forcibly wrenches the spectator's gaze from the terrifying Dionysian *Ur-eine*. Only the sublime, saving illusions of Apollo stand between the painful, individuated lives of the tragic Greeks and their remersion into the inexhaustible stream of life. The union of Apollo and Dionysus thus produced for the ancient Greeks an aesthetic justification of their existence.

In his early writings, then, Nietzsche conceives of the "metaphysical comfort" dispensed by tragedy as a positive, constructive, unifying force. In a passage representative of the *bathos* that pervades the original *Birth of Tragedy*, he gushes,

Let us imagine a coming generation with such intrepidity of vision, with such a heroic penchant for the tremendous. . . . Would it not be necessary for the tragic man of such a culture, in view of his self-education for seriousness and terror, to desire a new art, *the art of metaphysical comfort*. (BT 18)

In the 1886 Preface, however, he repudiates this "art of metaphysical comfort," claiming that it would only reinforce the anti-naturalism of Christianity (BT: AS 7). In its place, he now recommends "the art of *this-worldly* [*diesseitigen*] comfort," which may prepare his readers "some day [to] dispatch all metaphysical comforts to the devil" (BT: AS 7). While he associates "the art of this-worldly comfort" with the lusty, irreverent laughter of Zarathustra, he says nothing more about it, leaving his readers to reconstruct the underlying philosophical position from which this "holy" laughter erupts.[9]

In light of the anti-metaphysical tenor of Nietzsche's post-Zarathustran writings, it seems likely that the recommended "art of this-worldly comfort" comprises some strain of naturalism. Indeed, we might characterize the interpretative project of the 1886 Preface as the recovery of *The Birth of Tragedy* as a naturalist manifesto. As he strips away the super-natural accretions that burden his "firstborn," his guiding commitment to naturalism finally emerges. Greek tragedy represents for him the apotheosis of naturalism, as evidenced by its sustained resistance to metaphysical principles of explanation. What originally attracted him to the Dionysian impulse of tragedy was not the "metaphysical comfort" celebrated by the original *Birth of Tragedy*, but the *justification of life* embodied by Dionysus.

Nietzsche's original, "offensively Hegelian" reconstruction of the "aesthetic" justification furnished by tragedy was virtually indistinguishable from the "metaphysical" justification furnished by the theoretical worldview. Both eventually relied on saving appearances to shield fragile individuals from the Dionysian truth about the world. He subsequently revises his appraisal of tragedy, relocating its justificatory power in its capacity to refuse all "metaphysical comforts":

> Saying Yes to Life even in its strangest and hardest problems, the will to Life rejoicing over its own inexhaustibility even in the very sacrifice of its highest types – that is what I called Dionysian, *that* is what I guessed to be the bridge to the psychology of the *tragic* poet. Not in order to be liberated from terror and pity . . . but in order to be *oneself* the eternal joy of becoming. (TI 10: 5)

Dionysus thus represents the indestructability of Life, but Life is indestructible only as a transient subsystem within the boundless economy of Nature.[10] To become a disciple of Dionysus thus requires one to pursue a strict, thoroughgoing naturalism. A genuine justification of human existence, like that delivered by tragedy, must regard Life *as it is*, as fully natural, as bearing no transcendent meaning or beauty whatsoever.

To affirm Life as strictly natural, one must therefore dispense with all those metaphysical comforts and supernatural palliatives that have traditionally made Life bearable for the majority of human beings. The key to a justification of existence lies not in the "metaphysical comfort" engendered by the union of Apollo and Dionysus, but in the negotiation of exchange between the competing economies of Life and Nature. The Zarathustran laughter that Nietzsche associates with the "art of this-worldly comfort" is therefore symptomatic of a strict, thoroughgoing naturalism. As a disciple of Dionysus, Nietzsche laughs at the folly expressed by the need for metaphysical comfort. In a passage that conveys the cosmology that motivates his turn to naturalism, he asks,

> What alone can be our doctrine? That no one *gives* man his qualities – neither God, nor society, nor his parents and ancestors, nor he himself . . . No one is responsible for man's being there at all, for his being such-and-such, or for his being in these circumstances or in this environment. (TI 6: 8)

Adumbrations of Nietzsche's turn to naturalism appear in *The Birth of Tragedy* itself, for his discussion there of Apollo and Dionysus accommodates the transformation of these aesthetic categories into economic principles. Notwithstanding his characterization of tragedy as a collaboration between Apollo and Dionysus, *The Birth of Tragedy* reveals that the two gods are not equal partners in the business of delivering an aesthetic justification. While Greek tragedy owes its provenance to the patronage of both gods, Nietzsche assigns a certain priority to the "tragic wisdom" of Dionysus. While Apollo presides cheerfully over those simulacra of life that sustain the illusory meaning of individual existence, Dionysus affords his epopts a glimpse of life *as it is*, in its paralyzing monistic unity. While the wisdom of Apollo is necessary to preserve the *principium individuationis* that governs the career of the tragic hero, the wisdom of Dionysus is true to Life itself, independent of the psychological and existential needs of individual human beings. Apollo's "metaphysical comfort" enables an aesthetic justification not of life as it is, as the indestructible, all-consuming *Ur-eine* celebrated by Dionysus, but of separate lives operating under the illusory *principium individuationis*.

As a shelter for individuation, the Apollinian impulse of tragedy is therefore subordinate to its Dionysian counterpart, which celebrates the inexhaustible unity of all forms of life:

> The metaphysical joy in the tragic is a translation of the instinctive unconscious Dionysian wisdom into the language of images: the hero, the highest manifestation of the will, is negated for our pleasure, because he is only phenomenon, and because the eternal life of the will is not affected by his annihilation. "We believe in eternal life," exclaims tragedy; while music is the immediate idea of this life. (BT 16)

According to the argument of *The Birth of Tragedy*, then, only Life itself is truly meaningful. Any justification of the individuated lives of separate human beings is merely "aesthetic" in nature.

In his "review" of *The Birth of Tragedy*, Nietzsche calls attention to the "Hegelian" concepts (and stench) of the book, suggesting that the original "antithesis" of the Apollinian and Dionysian is only apparent, only "dialectical" (EH: bt 1). The union of Dionysus and Apollo is attained in tragedy, but only because the Apollinian impulse is in reality a manifestation of the Dionysian impulse. Dionysus thus represents a monistic principle to which Apollo stands in what is merely a dialectical opposition. The priority that Nietzsche assigns to Dionysus over Apollo thus serves as an instructive model for his later attempt to subsume Life within Nature. In the economic terms that he favors in his post-Zarathustran writings, the Apollinian impulse represents an ephemeral moment suspended within the boundless, tragic economy of Dionysus.

2 The Economies of Life and Nature

In various essays and fragments inspired by his obsession with Nietzsche, Georges Bataille distinguishes between two models of economy. A *general* economy is bounded by no external conditions imposed on its internal regulation of intake and expenditure, and it consequently squanders itself in the generation of excess. By way of contrast, a *restricted* economy must govern its internal regulation in accordance with externally imposed conditions or restrictions. The calculated, measured expenditures of a restricted economy are therefore incompatible with the generation of genuine sumptuary excess.[11] While Bataille's reading of Nietzsche has little or nothing to do with the latter's "return to Nature," we may nevertheless borrow his distinction to chart the transformation of the aesthetic impulses associated with Apollo and Dionysus into the economic principles of *Life* and *Nature*.

Like most of the constituent terms of Nietzsche's post-Zarathustran vocabulary, "Life" and "Nature" enter his thought unannounced. He deploys these terms as if their meaning were perfectly clear to his readers, and he offers very little explanation of his reliance on them for his various critical evaluations. He furthermore treats his various appeals to Life and Nature as philosophically decisive. For example, he reserves his greatest enmity for those opponents whom he deems either "anti-natural" or "inimical to Life," and he apparently expects his readers to appreciate, if not share, his enmity. While the rhetoric of his post-Zarathustran writings may suggest that he wields these terms as transcendent standards of evaluation, he deploys them primarily as economic principles, which regulate the naturalism that emerges from those writings.[12]

Just as the Apollinian represents "only" an ephemeral moment *within* the tragic economy of the Dionysian, so Life comprises a subsystem sheltered within the boundless economy of Nature. While Nature partakes of the model of general economy, unrestricted by conditions governing its intake and expenditure, Life partakes of the model of restricted economy, conditioned by the peculiar needs of human existence. Although Apollo and Life may appear to constitute forces independent of Dionysus and Nature, respectively, their independence from these latter, monistic forces is only illusory. No permanent antagonism obtains either between Apollo and Dionysus or between Life and Nature. Each of the

latter terms accommodates the illusory opposition and engulfs its corresponding former term in an all-consuming economy. Indeed, the
apparent antithesis is *itself* Dionysian, or natural. As an expression or
manifestation of Nature, Life only appears to favor certain human beings
and their designs; in the end, all is subsumed within the totalizing
economy of Nature.

As described by Nietzsche in his post-Zarathustran writings, Nature is
unbounded, independent of and indifferent to the peculiar needs and
demands of Life. Nature admits of no other, whether hospitable or
hostile to Life, that imposes conditions upon the internal regulation of its
economy. To those philologically inept "physicists" who claim to deduce
democratic principles from the canon of natural law, Nietzsche rejoins,

> Somebody might come along who, with opposite intentions and
> modes of interpretation, could read out of the same "Nature," and
> with regard to the same phenomena, rather the tyrannically
> inconsiderate and relentless enforcement of claims of power. (BGE
> 22)

Nature consequently need not, and does not, regulate itself in accordance with any super-natural laws that might favor or frustrate specific
forms of Life. In accordance with the model of general economy, Nature
squanders itself in an unprincipled expenditure of vitality, utterly indifferent to the forms of Life that flourish or perish within its boundless
economy. To the Stoics, who propose to live "according to Nature,"
Nietzsche cautions,

> Imagine a being like Nature, wasteful beyond measure, indifferent
> beyond measure, without purposes and consideration, without
> mercy and justice, fertile and desolate and uncertain at the same
> time; imagine indifference itself as a power. (BGE 9)

In light of the indifference of Nature, living "according to Nature" is
either trivially accomplished – "supposing your imperative 'live according to Nature' meant at bottom as much as 'live according to Life'"
(BGE 9) – or utterly impossible to sustain.[13] The mortality that
Nietzsche originally associated with the Dionysian impulse he here at-
taches to Nature: living "according to Nature" would entail a degree of
profligacy, of indifference, which is incompatible with the nomothetic
character of Life. To live "according to Nature" is therefore to abjure
Life in favor of an unprincipled, formless, and eminently mortal existence – the diametric opposite, that is, of Stoic morality.

Whereas Nature is boundless, indifferent and amoral, Life remains bounded by a horizon of anthropocentric preferences and values. The internal regulation of the economy of Life is restricted by the human need for nomothesis. Life itself requires us to legislate, to design, to register preferences – in short, to "deviate" from Nature and regulate the economy of Life. To live, according to Nietzsche, is to legislate a hierarchy of values with the human at its center:

> Living – is that not precisely wanting to be other than this Nature?
> Is not living – estimating, preferring, being unjust, being limited,
> wanting to be different? (BGE 9)[14]

Living beings may "want to be other than" Nature, but Nature eventually co-opts all instances of defiance. As a restricted subsystem suspended within the general economy of Nature, Life constitutes a specific configuration of Nature – one that "wants to be different" – rather than an alternative or external force. Despite the heroic attempts of metaphysicians and priests to endow Life with a supernatural capacity all its own, human beings can neither alter nor postpone the natural regulation of the economy of Life. The antagonism between Life and Nature, which all forms of Life necessarily presuppose, is therefore only dialectical; indeed, the appearance of antagonism is itself fully natural. Life thus comprises all those subsystems resident within the economy of Nature that strive (albeit in vain) to defy the indifference of Nature.

Nietzsche thus suggests that it is perfectly natural for human beings to attempt to defy Nature in the perceived interests of Life. As Strauss remarks, "*Physis* calls for *nomoi* while preserving the distinction, nay, the opposition, of *physis* and *nomos*."[15] The nomothetic tasks of preferring, estimating, and evaluating, which alone sustain the transient subsystem of Life, eventually fall to philosophers:

> *Genuine philosophers, however, are commanders and legislators*: they
> say, "*thus* it *shall* be!" . . . With a creative hand they reach for the
> future, and all that is and has been becomes a means for them, an
> instrument, a hammer. Their "knowing" is *creating*, their creating is
> a legislation, their will to truth is – will to power. (BGE 211)

Humankind can ill afford to emulate the indifference of Nature, and it is the task of philosophers to regulate the restricted economy of Life. As commanders and legislators, they must introduce order and discipline into the formless economy of Nature, thus "correcting" for Nature's

profligacy. Toward this end, philosophers legislate a hierarchy of values
that both promotes the flourishing of certain forms of Life and excludes
other forms. Nature does not exclude, but the philosopher *must* do so, if
the prescribed forms of Life are to defy even temporarily the indifference
of Nature.

As legislators, philosophers must defy Nature in order to regulate the
economy of Life. Whatever success they achieve is ephemeral, however,
for the indifference of Nature ensures the eventual negation of their
legislations. Indeed, the legislation of principles, norms and laws is no
more natural than their obliteration or decay. As a lawgiver, the philosopher thus occupies a dialectical, interstitial space that lies at the intersection of Life and Nature, in that irruptive subsystem of Nature that
"wants to be different." Nietzsche consequently cautions his readers
to observe the "law of Life," which decrees that all human triumphs
must eventually precipitate their own demise: "All great things bring
about their own destruction through an act of self-overcoming
[*Selbstaufhebung*]" (GM III: 27). This "law of Life," which regulates the
subsystem of Life in accordance with the economy of Nature, ultimately
countermands the philosopher's legislations, thereby serving as a rude
reminder that Life is fully natural.

While Life cannot afford to emulate the indifference of Nature, it may
appear amoral – or even immoral – to anyone inured to the "metaphysical comforts" dispensed by Western morality:

> Life itself is *essentially* appropriation, injury, overpowering of what
> is alien and weaker; suppression, hardness, imposition of one's
> own forms, incorporation and at least, at its mildest, exploita-
> tion. . . . Life simply *is* will to power. (BGE 259)[16]

Especially in his later writings, Nietzsche figures Life as *will to power*, as
an agency that transumes, but is not reducible to, the lives of individual
human agents. He insists, for example, that "Life itself forces us to posit
values; Life itself values through us when we posit values" (TI 5: 5). Life
is will to power, which originates beyond the periphery of individual
human "agents," flowing through them and suffusing them with vitality.
What we commonly call "individuals" are not so much agents as patients
of the will to power; they are the embodied media through which Life
expresses itself.

Nature too is an expression of will to power, which infuses inanimate
and animate entities alike (BGE 22). In fact, Nietzsche customarily
figures the will to power, like Nature, on the model of general economy.
The nomothetic restrictions "imposed" on the will to power by the

conditions of Life are therefore only apparent. He more regularly identifies Life with will to power because the artificial defiance of Nature's indifference, which transpires within the restricted economy of Life, affords us a unique – albeit dialectically constructed – immanent perspective on the nature of will to power. Partaking of the model of general economy, Nature admits of no other in comparison with which its principles of internal regulation might appear in sharper relief. Nothing stands to Nature as Nature stands (dialectically) to Life. In fact, we know of the will to power in its general, unrestricted manifestation (that is, Nature) only indirectly, from the analogy Nietzsche draws between it and the will to power in its restricted manifestations (that is, Life).

3 Nietzsche's Naturalism

The indifference of Nature not only compels the philosopher's intervention, but also complicates the task of legislation. Those philosophers who dare to legislate cannot appeal to Nature for help, for "Nature is a bad economist" (SE 7).[17] If Life is to sustain a hierarchy of values, then philosophers must proceed solely on their own authority; Nature cannot serve in any objective capacity to ground or justify their legislations.

This point bears further elaboration, especially in light of Nietzsche's own experiment with naturalism.[18] In a representative passage, he declares that he and his "friends" now view humankind as strictly natural, rather than as a homeless hybrid of the natural and super-natural:

> We no longer derive man from "the spirit" or "the deity"; we have placed him back among the animals. We consider him the strongest animal because he is the most cunning: his spirituality is a consequence of this. (AC 14)

In a succinct statement of the naturalism that informs his own legislations, he describes his "task" as an attempt

> To translate man back into nature; to become master over the many vain and overly enthusiastic interpretations and connotations that have so far been scrawled and painted over that eternal basic text of *homo natura*; to see to it that man henceforth stands before man as

even today, hardened in the discipline of science, he stands before the rest of nature. (BGE 230)

While eager to recommend his version of naturalism, Nietzsche is also quick to dissociate his "task" from the "return to Nature" he associates with Rousseau:

> This miscarriage, couched on the threshold of modern times, also wanted a "return to Nature"; to ask this once more, to what did Rousseau want to return? I still hate Rousseau in the French Revolution: it is the world-historical expression of this duality of idealist and rabble. . . . The doctrine of equality! There is no more poisonous poison anywhere: for it seems to be preached by justice itself, whereas it really is the termination of justice. (TI 9: 48)[19]

While his resistance to the super-natural principles of metaphysics is clear, the positive content of his own naturalism is not. Indeed, the further we pursue his naturalism, the more apparent his dilemma becomes: Nature may serve either as a standard for nomothetic legislations or as an indifferent, amoral agency, but it cannot serve in both capacities simultaneously.[20]

One source of confusion here is that Nietzsche offers only a minimal positive characterization of the Nature to which he "returns."[21] While he clearly feels that a "return to Nature" after the manner of the Stoics, or of Rousseau, would be impossible, his own alternative remains mysterious:

> I too speak of a "return to Nature," although it is really not a going back but an ascent – up into the high, free, even terrible Nature and naturalness where great tasks are something one plays with, one may play with. To put it metaphorically: Napoleon was a piece of "return to Nature," as I understand the phrase. (TI 9: 48)[22]

Nietzsche thus endows the Nature to which he "returns" with no positive content or character, offering instead a strictly privative account of it. Nature is simply whatever remains when all super-natural principles of interpretation have been subtracted from our understanding of the world. He similarly refuses to advance positive or synthetic characterizations of the will to power; it is simply that which resides at the most basic level of intelligibility.[23] The "return to Nature" that he envisions thus involves a return to *human* nature as the sole authority or justification for the nomothetic preferences required by the restricted economy of Life. Nature functions as a standard for the philosopher's legislations, but only negatively, as the lack of all supernatural constraints on what the legislator may "play with." Here we encounter the "existentialist" Nietzsche, who apparently understands Nature as the field or space within which human nature expresses itself in its brute immanence.

Nietzsche's "return to Nature" thus takes the form of a principled resistance to all metaphysical or super-natural interpretations of the human condition. This resistance frees Nature from the constraints imposed on it by pre-determined accounts of its powers and possibilities, thereby allowing Nature to define itself in its own spontaneous expression and unfolding, in the unbridled play of will to power. He thus describes *homo natura* as an *Urtext*, from which he vows to scour the "many vain and overly enthusiastic interpretations and connotations that have so far been scrawled and painted over [it]" (BGE 230). In order to "translate man back into Nature," Nietzsche must somehow erase the graffiti of previous philosophers without adding an equally distorting scrawl of his own.[24]

Nietzsche's problem, however, is that he cannot indefinitely resist the natural temptation to impress his own signature onto the *Urtext* of *homo natura*. After rescuing Nature from all previous interpretations, he involuntarily inscribes the privative space that he has cleared, interpreting *homo natura* in terms of the expression of affective engagement. When he brands a foe as "anti-natural," he refers not to some deviation from the economy of Nature, but to the anti-affective animus that motivates his foe's position. In his post-Zarathustran writings, he often employs "Nature" synechdochally, to refer to the affects; metaphysical speculations are "anti-natural" insofar as they deny the embodied, affective reality of human existence (BGE 258). For example, he denounces Christian morality as "anti-natural" not because it somehow defies or disrupts the economy of Nature, but because its recourse to super-natural principles of regulation threatens to extirpate the affects. He similarly equates all forms of "idealism" with "anti-nature," for he views "idealism" as an indictment of the body and the affects (EH: gb 5).

But even if we accept Nietzsche's criticism of these "enemies of Nature," it still does not follow that Nature furnishes a warrant for his naturalism. While the super-natural (or metaphysical) impulse of morality may be anti-affective, it is nevertheless fully natural. Similarly, the victory of slave morality is no more or less natural than the millennial reign of the "natural aristocracy" that Nietzsche applauds (BGE 257).

4 The Philosopher as Mythwright

If philosophers are to succeed as legislators, then they cannot very well pledge their allegiance publicly to the "law of Life." In fact, in order to gain support for their legislations, philosophers and priests have traditionally lied about Life, denying that Life is natural and promising to preside over a form of Life that is immune to the indifference of Nature. Nietzsche thus contends that:

> The so-called *pia fraus* . . . [is] the heirloom of all philosophers and priests who "improved" humankind. Neither Manu nor Plato nor Confucius nor the Jewish and Christian teachers have ever doubted their *right* to lie. (TI 7: 5)

Rather than criticize this recourse to noble fictions, Nietzsche attributes it to the divided office that necessarily falls to philosophers. The philosopher is not only a legislator, but also a mythwright.[25] The successful lawgiver must provide a mythic context within which his legislations become justified. The purpose of such myths is not so much to deliver the truth of the matter as to establish an aesthetic setting within which the legislated form of Life might take root and flourish. Nietzsche consequently insists that a just legislator both may and must deviate from the truth:

> The higher reason in such a procedure lies in the aim, step by step to push consciousness back from what had been recognized as the right life (that is, *proved* right by a tremendous and rigorously filtered experience), so as to attain the perfect automatism of instinct – that presupposition of all mastery, of every kind of perfection in the art of life. To set up a code of laws after the manner of Manu means to give a people the chance henceforth to become master, to become perfect – to aspire to the highest art of life. *To that end, it must be made unconscious*: this is the aim of every holy lie. (AC 57)

Along these lines, Nietzsche describes *revelation* and *tradition* as the "double wall" that any healthy people must erect in order to insulate its founding legislations from corrosive internal criticism (AC 57).

The prescriptive thrust of Nietzsche's naturalism is therefore attributable to the philosopher's role as mythwright. His "ought," his appeal to Nature as a standard for regulating the economy of Life, both trades on and furthers the founding myth of his naturalism. Certain (aristocratic) forms of Life, he maintains, are favored by Nature itself, and any refusal of the patronage of Nature will exact a prohibitive, and eventually mortal, expenditure of vital resources.[26] While explaining his admiration for Manu, the Hindu lawgiver, Nietzsche avers that

> Nature, not Manu, distinguishes the pre-eminently spiritual ones, those who are pre-eminently strong in muscle and temperament, and those, the third type, who excel neither in one respect nor in the other, the mediocre ones – the last as the great majority, the first as the elite. . . . To be a public utility, a wheel, a function, for that one must be destined by Nature. . . . For the mediocre, to be mediocre is their happiness; mastery of one thing, specialization – a natural instinct. (AC 57)

Nietzsche consequently links the decadence of a people or epoch to its deviation from the general prescriptions of Nature.

By mythically aligning Nature with Life, Nietzsche actually reproduces the "offensively Hegelian" formula he proposed in *The Birth of Tragedy*. Much as Dionysus and Apollo collaborate to deliver an aesthetic justification of human existence, so Nature co-operates with Life to secure the conditions of human flourishing, thus conferring a divine sanction upon certain forms of Life. In both cases Nietzsche attributes a distinct moral sensibility to forces (Dionysus and Nature) that he elsewhere describes as amoral and indifferent; in both cases he appeals to a general economy that miraculously satisfies the conditions of a restricted economy. We might think of the "aesthetic justification" provided by Dionysus and Apollo as an example of the founding myth that sacralizes the philosopher's legislations. *The Birth of Tragedy* purveys such a myth, claiming that Dionysus and Apollo can be persuaded, under the right cultural conditions, to collaborate for the benefit of mortals. Their collaboration, functional if not friendly, yields an aesthetic justification of human existence. Nietzsche's post-Zarathustran writings circulate a similar myth, claiming that an otherwise indifferent Nature smiles upon aristocratic forms of Life. In neither case does he offer any direct indication that he is aware of his own mythmaking.

Nietzsche's account of Nature as "indifferent beyond measure" ultimately militates against any appeal to Nature – including his own – as the ground or warrant of the philosopher's legislations. Although Nietzsche's own lawgiving tends to favor naturalistic reforms, Nature itself neither endorses nor encourages this nomothetic tendency. Nature would show his preferred principles of legislation the same indifference that it shows to all other principles. As a consequence, he cannot legitimately claim an epistemic privilege for his naturalism, as if it were somehow "true" to Nature itself. If his account of Nature is correct, then the ridicule he heaps upon the Stoics ultimately rebounds to discredit his own "return to Nature" as well.

Life too is ultimately indifferent to Nietzsche's naturalism, for Life requires *simply* that we legislate, and it evinces no preference for naturalistic principles of legislation. When philosophers intervene to nurture a specific form of Life, they act solely on their own authority, in accordance only with their own legislative preferences. Although Life comprises a subsystem of Nature, a naturalistic account of Life commands no epistemic advantage over an anti-natural or supernatural account of Life. Even the ascetic ideal, which apparently countenances an assault on Life itself, is natural, and Nietzsche acknowledges that it functions to preserve certain forms of (degenerating) Life (GM III: 13). *What* we choose is of no concern either to Life or to Nature, and *that* we choose is no more natural than that we do not. Indeed, all of those agencies that Nietzsche denounces as "anti-natural" or "hostile to Life" fit seamlessly within the boundless economy of Nature, which stands utterly indifferent to his nomothetic preferences.

It would appear, then, that Nietzsche's "return to Nature" trades on an equivocation of the term "Nature." On the one hand, he figures Nature on the model of a general economy, as a boundless force that is utterly indifferent to human concerns. On the other hand, he occasionally appeals to Nature as the affective ground of human agency, as the human "nature" that ascetic disciplines are designed to extirpate. It is in this latter sense that he occasionally invokes Nature as a normative standard for his own legislations, thereby implying that Nature provides some sort of warrant or justification for certain forms of Life as opposed to others. With this sense of "Nature" in mind, he registers a preference for those cultures and political regimes that encourage the expression of affective engagement.[27]

My aim here is not to debunk or to challenge Nietzsche's naturalism. My point is simply this: the Nature that favors aristocratic forms of Life cannot be the Nature that he describes as "indifference beyond measure" (BGE 9). Even if we are willing to grant that sustained empirical observation supports his claim that human societies "naturally" tend toward pyramidal organization, it does not follow that such organizations are *therefore* preferable – especially if Nature is indifferent to human flourishing. In order to summon the prescriptive thrust that informs his naturalism, Nietzsche must commit what is popularly known as the "naturalistic fallacy": he moves effortlessly from Nature as fact to Nature as norm.

5 The Natural Philosopher

Rather than defend Nietzsche's naturalism or explain away the equivocation upon which it trades, we might view his "return to Nature" as indicative of the plight of the philosopher. If we apply to Nietzsche his own account of the activity of philosophizing, if we interpret his naturalism as "the personal confession of its author and a kind of involuntary and unconscious memoir" (BGE 6), then we see that he cannot help but add his own distinctive scrawl to the palimpsest that obscures the *Urtext* of *homo natura*.

After chiding the Stoics for forcing themselves "to see Nature the wrong way, namely Stoically," Nietzsche explains that

> What formerly happened to the Stoics still happens today, too, as soon as any philosophy begins to believe in itself. It always creates the world in its own image; it cannot do otherwise. Philosophy is this tyrannical drive itself, the most spiritual will to power, to the "creation of the world," to the *causa prima*. (BGE 9)

Here he suggests that it is perfectly natural for philosophers to arrogate to themselves a super-natural authority. Indelibly inscribed into the *Urtext* of *homo natura*, it would seem, is the inclination to oppose *nomos* to *physis*. As a consequence of their nature, philosophers cannot help but believe the foundational lies they tell about Life, even if they knew them to be lies at one time. Nietzsche's problem with the Stoics thus lies not in their unwitting creation of the world in their own image, which they cannot help but undertake, but in the world they create and the image that informs it. While all philosophers create the world in their own image, and "cannot do otherwise," some of these "worlds" are preferable to others.

It would seem, then, that the philosopher's mythcraft is not an entirely conscious and deliberate enterprise. The philosopher too is a piece of Nature, thereby representing an expression, rather than a transcendence, of the will to power. Hence the philosopher too needs myths. To intervene into the economy of Nature, in the full knowledge that Nature equally subsumes all forms of Life, apparently requires more strength and fortitude than mere mortals – especially decadent mortals – can muster. We might think of the philosopher, then, as the unwitting instrument of the cunning of Life. In order for Life to exist at all, the philosopher must exempt himself from his most basic psychological insights. The philosopher will see (and expose) his rivals as mythwrights, but he cannot afford to cast a similarly critical eye on himself. He consequently "creates the world in his own image," for he "cannot do otherwise." In attending to its own interests, Life endows all philosophers with a prodigious will to power, which effectively blinds them to the mythic content of their own legislations. The curse of philosophy, the incapacity to forge the self-referential link in the concatenation of one's own psychological and philosophical insights, thus stands as the precondition of Life itself.[28] In order for Life to flourish, philosophers must inherit the sins of Oedipus.

Nietzsche is no exception to this general principle; he too is a piece of Nature. While perfectly adroit at exposing and debunking the foundational myths of other philosophers, he is quite blind to his own mythmaking. Like Oedipus, who solved the riddle of the Sphinx only to exempt himself tragically from his solution, Nietzsche has great difficulty extending his general account of philosophizing to include himself. He not only articulates the hypothesis of will to power, but also corroborates this hypothesis in his own lawgiving; he too creates the world in his own image. We might therefore conclude from the case of Nietzsche that philosophers are naturally as blind to their own mythmaking as they are destined to engage in it. If this is the case, then it would make little sense to take Nietzsche to task as a mythwright; he has already shown us that he engages in a process of mythmaking to which he is not privy.[29]

If I am right in identifying the mythic component of Nietzsche's naturalism, then the standard epistemic objections to his "return to Nature" are both accurate *and* irrelevant. *All* philosophers, he insists, not only resort to mythcraft, but also eventually come to believe the myths they create to supplement their legislations. Unless we have good reason to exempt Nietzsche from this general account of the nature of philosophizing, we should expect him to succumb eventually to the spell of his own mythcraft. Even if he *does* suppose his naturalism to be justified on epistemic grounds – based, for example, on some correspondence with Nature – his own authorial intentions are ultimately irrelevant. Following his own lead, we might reject his founding myth on epistemic grounds, while endorsing it nonetheless on pragmatic grounds – for example, as the philosophical armor that affords us our best chance of surviving the twilight of the idols.

Conclusion

If we refuse to issue Nietzsche an exemption from his own account of the nature of philosophizing, then we come to see why his "return to Nature" necessarily falls short of its mark. Like all philosophers, he creates the world in his own image and "forgets" that he has done so; he cannot do otherwise. Having labored assiduously to discredit all previous philosophical attempts to project onto Nature the constitutive virtues of specific peoples, he eventually yields to the natural temptation to add his own interpretation to the palimpsest of Nature.

Viewed as a moment within the career of an individual philosopher, Nietzsche's "return to Nature" appears to be a failure. Despite his enormous success in dispensing with metaphysical principles of explanation, he fails in the end to subject *himself* to the naturalistic categories that he unflinchingly applies to other philosophers. Viewed as a project that transcends the peculiar quirks of any single philosopher, however, his "return to Nature" appears somewhat more successful. If his account of the nature of philosophizing is correct, then we cannot expect *him* to complete the task of "naturalizing Nietzsche." This task falls instead to the next generation of naturalistic philosophers, the generation trained by Nietzsche himself, who stand to Nietzsche as Nietzsche stands to his own philosophical predecessors. Indeed, if he is to complete posthumously his "return to Nature," then *we* must forcibly revoke the supernatural privilege he involuntarily claims for himself.

NOTES

This essay is dedicated to my colleague Stanley Rosen, in friendship and gratitude, on the occasion of his retirement from The Pennsylvania State University.

1 An excerpt from Gast's letter to Nietzsche on 20 September 1888 is cited by Walter Kaufmann in *The Portable Nietzsche* (New York: Viking Penguin, 1982), p. 464.

2 *Friedrich Nietzsche: Sämtliche Briefe, Kritische Studienausgabe in 8 Bänden*, herausg. G. Colli and M. Montinari (Berlin: Walter deGruyter/Deutscher Taschenbuch Verlag, 1986), Band 8, #1122, s. 443.

3 In his letter to Gast on September 27, 1888, Nietzsche describes his new title as venting "even more malice [*Bosheit*] against Wagner." *Sämtliche Briefe*, Band 8, #1122, s. 443.

4 A notable exception occurs in TI 9: 10–11, where Nietzsche presents the Apollinian and Dionysian as "kinds of frenzy."

5 When recounting the "decisive innovations" of *The Birth of Tragedy*,

Nietzsche points to "its understanding of the Dionysian phenomenon among the Greeks," but he mentions neither the Apollinian phenomenon nor any collaboration between the two gods (EH: bt 1).

6 For an excellent appraisal of Nietzsche's various appeals to Nature as a standard for the philosopher's lawgiving, see Leo Strauss, "Note on the Plan of Nietzsche's *Beyond Good and Evil*," collected in *Studies in Platonic Political Philosophy* (Chicago: University of Chicago Press, 1983) pp. 174–91.

7 With the exception of occasional emendations, I rely throughout this chapter on Walter Kaufmann's translations/editions of Nietzsche's books for Viking Press/Random House, and on R. J. Hollingdale's translations for Cambridge University Press. Numbers refer to sections rather than to pages, and the following key explains the abbreviations for my citations. AC: *The Antichrist(ian)*; AS: "Attempt at a Self-Criticism"; BGE: *Beyond Good and Evil*; BT: *The Birth of Tragedy*; EH: *Ecce Homo*; GM: *Toward a Genealogy of Morals*; SE: *Schopenhauer as Educator*; TI: *Twilight of the Idols*.

8 Nietzsche again refers to the term in his 1886 Preface to the new edition of *The Birth of Tragedy*: "In the book itself the allusive [*anzügliche*] sentence is repeated several times, that the existence of the world is *justified* only as an aesthetic phenomenon" (BT: AS 5).

9 I pursue this question further in "Nietzsche's Art of This-Worldly Comfort: Self-Reference and Strategic Self-Parody," *History of Philosophy Quarterly*, Vol. 9, No. 3 (1992), pp. 343–57.

10 For an exhaustive account of the polysemous myths surrounding Dionysus, see Karl Kerényi, *Dionysos: Archetypal Image of Indestructible Life*, Ralph Manheim, trans. (Princeton NJ: Princeton University Press, 1976).

11 Georges Bataille, *Inner Experience*, Leslie Anne Boldt, trans. (Albany: SUNY Press, 1988); and "The Notion of Expenditure," in *Visions of Excess*, Allan Stoekl, ed., Allan Stoekl, Carl R. Lovitt, Donald M. Leslie, Jr, trans. (Minneapolis: University of Minnesota Press, 1985), pp. 116–29. My interpretation of Bataille is indebted to Jacques Derrida's essay, "From Restricted to General Economy: A Hegelianism Without Reserve," in *Writing and Difference*, Alan Bass, trans. (Chicago: University of Chicago Press, 1978), pp. 251–77.

12 My attempt to chart the economic currents of Nietzsche's thought is indebted to Henry Staten's study, *Nietzsche's Voice* (Ithaca: Cornell University Press, 1990), especially chapters 1 and 4.

13 "Nature is *chance*" (TI 9: 7).

14 Nietzsche's ridicule of the Stoics militates against any transcendence of the restricted economy of Life. Death alone links human beings to a general economy – namely, that of Nature, in which expenditure transpires unrestricted by conditions of exchange. Within the restricted economy of Life, all expenditure is channeled through the ascetic ideal, which ultimately governs (and restricts) the conditions of all human economies.

15 Strauss, "Note on the Plan," p. 183.

16 Nietzsche similarly contends that "The total appearance of Life is not the extremity, not starvation, but rather riches, profusion, even absurd squandering – and where there is struggle, it is a struggle for *power*" (TI 9: 14).

17 *Untimely Meditations*, R. J. Hollingdale, trans. (Cambridge: Cambridge University Press, 1983), p. 178. "The *first* truth of aesthetics," Nietzsche maintains, is that "nothing is beautiful, except man alone" (TI 9: 20).

18 In *Nietzsche and Modern Times* (New Haven: Yale University Press, 1993), Laurence Lampert persuasively argues that Nietzsche's naturalism (which Lampert helpfully identifies as a form of "immanentism"), requires a bold departure from the practice of esotericism that marks the history of philosophy. According to Lampert, "Nietzsche aims to bring philosophy out from behind its shelters and to construct a new accord between philosophy and the public. Nietzsche's openness, his rashness, his betrayal of Platonic sheltering, forces a confrontation with perhaps the most profound and problematic of all the issues of Nietzsche's thought, his true radicality: Can a human community be built on the deadly truths known to philosophy?" (pp. 277–8).

19 For a thorough discussion of Nietzsche's critique of Rousseau, see Keith Ansell-Pearson, *Nietzsche contra Rousseau* (Cambridge: Cambridge University Press, 1991), especially chapter 3.

20 This dilemma, and Nietzsche's attendant vacillations with respect to Nature, are explored by Strauss, "Note on the Plan," especially pp. 182–7.

21 For a sympathetic reconstruction of Nietzsche's experiment with naturalism, see Richard Schacht, *Nietzsche* (London: Routledge & Kegan Paul, 1983), especially chapters 5 and 6.

22 Nietzsche describes Goethe as "a magnificent attempt to overcome the eighteenth century by a return to nature, by an *ascent* to the naturalness of the Renaissance" (TI 9: 49).

23 Alphonso Lingis further articulates this interpretation in his essay "The Will to Power," collected in *The New Nietzsche*, David B. Allison, ed. (New York: Delta, 1977), pp. 37–63.

24 For a thorough treatment of Nietzsche's naturalism, and of its promise as the foundation for an ethical teaching uniquely suited to "modern times," see Lampert, *Nietzsche*, chapter 14.

25 My discussion of the philosopher's mythcraft is indebted to Stanley Rosen's essay, "Suspicion, Deception, and Concealment," *Arion* (3rd series), Vol. 1, No. 2 (1991), pp. 112–27.

26 For an excellent survey of the political implications of Nietzsche's esotericism, see Stanley Rosen's essay, "Nietzsche's Revolution," in *The Ancients and the Moderns* (New Haven: Yale University Press, 1989), pp. 189–208.

27 In discussing the history of Israel, for example, Nietzsche argues that "at the time of the kings, Israel also stood in the correct, *that is, the natural*, relationship to all things" (AC 25, emphasis added).

28 Nietzsche discusses at length the philosophers' unwitting projection of themselves into the world in TI 3: 5 and 6: 3.

29 Martin Heidegger contends that Nietzsche's emphasis on the legislation of new values betrays an irrecuperable complicity in the metaphysical tradition: "Despite all his overturnings and revaluings of metaphysics, Nietzsche remains in the unbroken line of the metaphysical tradition when he calls that which is established and made fast in the will to power for its own preservation purely and simply Being, or what is in Being, or truth." "The Word of Nietzsche: God is Dead," *The Question Concerning Technology and Other Essays*, William Lovitt, trans. and ed. (New York: Harper & Row, 1977), p. 84. In criticizing the residual "humanism" of Nietzsche's thought, however, Heidegger overlooks the dialectical relationship that Nietzsche proposes between Life and Nature. While any philosopher, Nietzsche and Heidegger

included, may lose sight of his situation within the economy of Nature, Nietzsche nowhere advertises the anthropocentric "will to power" as Being or Truth. On the contrary, the hypothesis of will to power is designed to account for, and to counteract, the peculiarly humanistic myopia that informs the philosopher's lawgiving.

3
Interpreting Signatures (Nietzsche/Heidegger): Two Questions

Jacques Derrida

The first question concerns the *name* Nietzsche, the second has to do with the concept of totality.

I

Let us begin with chapters 2 and 3 of Heidegger's *Nietzsche* – dealing with "The Eternal Recurrence of the Same" and "The Will to Power as Knowledge," respectively. We will be turning especially to the sub-section on chaos ("The Concept of Chaos," I, pp. 562–70) and to "The Alleged Biologism of Nietzsche" ("*Nietzsches angeblicher Biologismus*"). In view of the fact that the same interpretation is regularly at work throughout, the risks involved in choosing this strategy are, I hope, quite limited. In each instance, a single system of reading is powerfully concentrated and gathered together. It is directed at gathering together the unity and the uniqueness of Nietzsche's thinking, which, as a fulfilled unity, is itself in a fair way to being the culmination of occidental metaphysics. Nietzsche would be precisely at the crest, or ridge, atop the peak of this fulfillment. And thus he would be looking at both sides, down both slopes.

What about this unity – this doubled unity? What is its connection to the name – or rather, the signature – of Nietzsche? Does Heidegger take any account of this question – which others might call biographical, autobiographical, or autographical – of the singularity of a signature ostensibly the proper name of Nietzsche? To put the matter another way,

if one can glimpse behind Heidegger's reading of Nietzsche the foundations of a general reading of Western metaphysics, then the question
arises: To what extent does this interpretation of metaphysics in its
totality and as a whole contain an interpretive decision about the unity or
singularity of thinking? And to what extent does this interpretive decision
also presuppose a decision about the "biographical," about the proper
name, the autobiographical, and about signature – about the politics of
signature?[1]

Heidegger's position on this subject I will indicate first of all with a
summarizing and simplifying statement, which one could, I hope, dem-
onstrate is not wrong: there is a unity in Nietzschean thought even if it
is not that of a system in the classical sense. This unity is also its
uniqueness, its singularity. A thesis explicitly advanced by Heidegger is
that every great thinker has only one thought. This uniqueness was
neither constituted nor threatened, neither gathered together nor
brought about, through a name or proper name – nor by the life of
Nietzsche, either normal or insane. This unique unity is something it
draws from the unity of Western metaphysics which is gathered together
there at its crest, which one could also compare to the simple unity of a
line created by a fold. The result of all this is that biography, autobiography, the scene or the powers of the proper name, of proper names,
signatures, and so on, are again accorded minority status, are again given
the inessential place they have always occupied in the history of metaphysics. This points to the necessity and place of a questioning which I
can only sketch here.

Such would be a simplified version of the question. Now let us read
Heidegger a little more closely and seek to confirm the strongest coherence of his interpretation or, beyond its coherence, his deepest thought.
As a provisional concession to the classical norms of reading, let us take
this book at its beginning, or even before its beginning at the beginning
of the preface. Naturally, this preface was, like so many others, written
later. As we know, the book goes back to a series of lectures given
between 1936 and 1940, and to some treatises written between 1940 and
1946. One should take most careful note of these dates if one is to bring
this interpretation, as a whole and in detail, into connection with the
historico-political and institutional field of its presentation. The preface,
however, dates from 1961. The intention of the two pages in this case,
as almost always, is to justify the publication of this collection by reference to the essential unity of its totality: "This publication, rethought
(*nachgedacht*) as a whole (*als Ganzes*) should provide a glimpse of
the path of thought which I followed between 1930 and the *Letter on
Humanism* (1947)." The unity of this publication and of this teaching is,

then, also the unity of the path of thought of Heidegger at a decisive moment and traced through a period of over fifteen years. But at the same time this also means that the unity of his interpretation of Nietzsche, the unity of Western metaphysics to which this interpretation is referred, and the unity of the Heideggerian path of thought are here inseparable. One cannot think the one without the other.

Now what are the first words of this preface? What does one find in that first phrase? To be elliptical, let us say one finds *two things*, and both of them have a literal connection with the *name* of Nietzsche.

First, the name is placed in quotation marks.

Now what happens when a proper name is put between quotation marks? Heidegger never asks himself. Still, his whole undertaking, although entitled "Nietzsche," has perhaps put all its powers together in such a way as to nullify the urgency and necessity of this question.

Second, let me read you the first sentence of the preface in the French translation by Klossowski: "'Nietzsche' – the name of the thinker here names the *cause* of his thinking [*intitulé ici la cause de sa pensée*]."[2] Heidegger's next paragraph explains and, up to a point, justifies Klossowski's translation of a certain German word (*Sache*) by "cause." For in Heidegger's next paragraph we read: "A case, the legal case, is, in itself, *ex-pli-cation* – or in German, *Aus-einander-setzung* – one party taking a position in relation to another. To let our thought be penetrated by this 'cause' – to prepare it for this – that is the content of the present publication."[3]

Now to someone who simply opens up this book without knowing the German text, such an approach could seem both odd and at the same time consonant with the latest modernity, not to say the latest style: the *name* of the thinker would thus be the *cause* of his thought! The thinking, then, would be the *effect* caused by his proper name! And here is a book on the name Nietzsche and on the connections between his name and his thought. Taking into account the fact that in this French edition, through a strange typographical error, the name Nietzsche is cut in two (Niet-zsche), who knows what heights this new reader, in the freshness of his too great or too limited perspective, could attain in his analysis of the schism of the proper name, an analysis which, through a parceling out of the signifier or the semantic elements, could make a connection between the Slavic (Polish) origin of the name, on the one hand, and what Nietzsche himself said about the negativity of his own name and the destructive power of his thought, on the other. And if this analysis were carried to delirious extremes, it would then connect this negative element, *Niet-* (and why not? why stop half-way?) with the only two cities in which he said in 1887 he could think or wanted to think: Venice and Nice (specifically, in a letter to Peter Gast dated September 15, which Heidegger cites near the beginning of the book and chapter on *The Will to Power as Art*).[4] These two cities remain the only cure for Nietzsche, the only possible escape. Ah, says our ingenuous and zealous reader, "I see, I see! *il veut Nice, il Venise, il veut Nietzsche, il veut et il ne veut pas*,[5] there you have the two places, the two said places, the toponyms of his *Will to Power!*" But unfortunately this sequence can only work in French and the delirium must come to a halt the moment one notices that Venice in German is *Venedig* and Nice in German is *Nizza*. As Nietzsche says, cited by Heidegger: "*Somit läuft es auf Venedig und Nizza hinaus . . .*" – "Therefore it has turned out to be a matter of Venice and Nice . . ." (*N*, I, p. 22; Eng. I, p. 14).

But then, pursuing his reading, our French reader still asks: What does it mean, "Nietzsche, the name of the thinker stands as title for his thinking"? Even within the confines of the French translation the content of the next paragraph is enlightening for it clearly says, Do not take the word *cause* in its opposition to *effect* as material, efficient, formal, or final cause of his thought but understand it as the Latin *causa*: legal debate, litigation, opposition of two parties. Still, this perspective too can exercise a kind of modish temptation for the French reader of today: the name Nietzsche as contentiousness of thinking, as stake in a game, war, or legal battle – that scarcely sounds classical any more. Such, taking this new, fresh start, would be an initial reading. But if he consults the original text, the reader discovers something else, quite different from *cause* either in the derivative sense *or* the usual sense of the word: "'Nietzsche,' the name of the thinker stands as title for *die Sache seines Denkens*," the *subject-matter* (*Sache*) of his thought, for *what* he thinks.

The German word that one usually translates into French as *cause* (English: "cause") is *Ursache* (the cause or reason for something). Because the two words are alike, Klossowski felt justified in translating *Sache* as "cause." But normally *Sache* designates the "thing" – not the sense object or even the thing at hand but the thing in question, the affair, which eventually can lead to litigation. In this sense, the Latin *causa*, cause in the sense of litigation or a trial, is a good translation. It poses not only the thing in question but the question of the thing (*Die Frage nach dem Ding*), which is dealt with elsewhere, namely in Heidegger's great meditation by that title and above all in reference to the relation to all semantic determinations of cause. Indeed, the translation of *Sache* by the French word *cause* (instead of *chose*, thing) can find, as we have said, support in the course of the text itself. For

Heidegger continues, *"Die Sache der Streitfall, ist in sich selbst Auseinandersetzung"* – "the matter, the point of dispute, is in itself a placing in opposition, a confrontation."

But when he says that the name of the thinker stands as title "for the *Sache* of his thinking," he certainly does not intend to make the name the cause of an effect that would be the thinking. The genitive "of" here designates the *Sache* (matter) *as* his thinking. Everything will confirm this once one considers the proper name not as that of an individual or of a signatory; it is the name of a thought, of a thought whose unity gives in return sense and reference to the proper name. "Nietzsche" is nothing other than the name of this thinking. The syntax of the genitive misleads us in the other direction, if one may put it that way, for the name is not before the thought, it is the thing that is thought; it is produced and determined by it. Only in thinking this thought will one think the possessive, the genitive, and the proper name. One will learn *who Nietzsche is* and what his name says only from his thinking – not from card files packed with more or less refined biographical facts.

At this point two paths present themselves. One would consist in taking a new approach to the problematic of the name, at the risk of seeing the name dismembered and multiplied in masks and similitudes. We know what Nietzsche risked in this respect. The name would be constituted on the far side of the "life" of the thinker, from the vantage point of the future of the world, from an affirmation of the "eternal recurrence."[6]

The other path would be to determine the essentiality of the name from the "subject matter of thought," of thought itself defined as the content of theses, and to let fall into inessentiality the particular proper name, which has become the index of the "biography" or a "psychology" of an individual. In legitimately scorning biographism, psychologism, or psychoanalysis, one instead embraces reductionist empiricisms which in turn only cover up what is given as thinking. This is what Heidegger does, for the best reasons in the world. But in doing this does he not thereby fall back on a gesture of classical metaphysics, indeed at the very moment in which he is appealing for something other than metaphysics – i.e., at the moment when he situates Nietzsche on the crest of that metaphysics? This classical gesture also reappears in his dissociating the matter of life or of proper name from the matter of thought. Hence the beginning of Heidegger's lecture course: In a very conventional fashion he dissociates his summary and "official" biography of Nietzsche, on the one hand, from the grand questions which stretch the great philosopher to the limit of his powers, on the other. Such is the form of this first lecture, which conforms to the old pedagogical model: very quickly one runs through the "life of the author" in its most conventional features, then turns to the thought, that which Heidegger calls "the authentic philosophy of Nietzsche." This philosophy, Heidegger notes, "does not arrive at a definitive elaboration nor is it ever published as a work."

Then, criticizing the edition of the complete works, Heidegger notes some of its limitations. They adhered to the principle of integrality (*Vollständigkeit*, completeness), that pushed everything and which re-surrected nineteenth-century models, to the point of that biologism and psychologism which are like a monstrous perversion of our age. Heidegger criticizes that editorial enthusiasm that "proceeds in the man-ner of biological and psychological elucidation," which "traces minutely all the data" of the life of the author, including the opinions of con-temporaries. It is an "excrescence" (*Ausgeburt*, monstrosity, product), a "monstrous product of the addiction of our time to the psycho-biological (*der psychologish-biologischen Sucht unserer Zeit*)." Says Heidegger, "Only the proper preparation of an authentic edition of the *Works* (1881–1889), if that task is ever accomplished in the future, will bring access to the 'works of Nietzsche,' properly speaking." Furthermore, Heidegger adds, "This will never be genuinely accomplished if in the questioning we do not grasp Nietzsche as the end of Western metaphysics and press over to the quite different question of the truth of Being" (*N*, I, pp. 18–19; Eng. I, p. 10). To pose the question of the truth of Being, beyond ontology, and to determine the place of Nietzsche as the end of Western metaphysics – these are the prerequisite conditions if one wishes eventu-ally to gain access to the "biography" of Nietzsche, to the name, and above all to the textual corpus of Nietzsche – if one wishes, in other words, to know "who Nietzsche was."

Prior to all other questions, we need to be attentive to the fundamental necessity for such a schema as Heidegger puts forward, and also attentive to everything in a certain historical and political situation which could justify it. The psychological and biological eagerness in the *style* he so often practices circles around and thereby misses the *content* of a thought – its necessity and its internal specificity. A well-known schema. Besides, at the time he was teaching his "Nietzsche," Heidegger had begun to put some distance between himself and Nazism. Without saying anything in his lecture itself that was directed against the government and the use it was making of Nietzsche (on so much prudence and silence one can certainly put an interpretation – but elsewhere), Heidegger is in the process of overtly criticizing the edition that the government is in the process of supporting. Heidegger appears at first to have been associated with it, then he backed out; the issue had to do with instituting, in cooperation with Nietzsche's sister, falsifications in that edition:

"For knowledge of Nietzsche's biography," Heidegger continues, "the presentation by his sister, Elisabeth Förster-Nietzsche, *The Life of Friedrich Nietzsche* (published between 1895 and 1904), remains always important. As with all biographical works, however, use of this publication requires great caution. We will refrain from further suggestions and from discussion of the enormous and varied secondary literature surrounding Nietzsche, since none of it can aid the endeavor of this lecture course. Whoever does not have the courage and perseverance of thought required to get involved in reading Nietzsche's own writings has no need to read anything *about* him either" (*N*, I, p. 19; Eng. I, pp. 10–11).

Here and elsewhere one of the targets of Heidegger is what he calls "philosophy of life." The object of Heidegger's attack here was Nazism, but also a classical university tradition as well, which made of Nietzsche a "philosopher-poet," a life-philosopher without conceptual rigor whom one could denounce "from the height of German chairs of philosophy." But in either case one praises or condemns that "philosophy of life" which Heidegger from *Being and Time* onward had combatted as an absurdity.

This critique of psycho-biologism underlies also his critique of Nietzsche's "alleged biologism" (*"Nietzsches angeblicher Biologismus,"* *N*, I, pp. 517–27). It answers the question of the name of Nietzsche, the question "What is that we call Nietzsche?" There, once again, in response to the question, "Who is Nietzsche?", right at the opening of the third chapter, "The Will to Power as Knowledge," in the first subsection (again the first words), which has the title "Nietzsche as Thinker of the Fulfillment of Metaphysics":

Who Nietzsche *is* and above all who he *will be* we know as soon as we are in a position to think that thought which he stamped into the world-framework of *The Will to Power*. Nietzsche is that thinker who went the way that the train of thought led him – to the will to power. Who Nietzsche is we never find out through a historical account of his life history, and also not through a presentation of the content of his writings. Who Nietzsche is we do not will to know and also are not meant to know if and so long as we have in mind only the personality, the historical figure, the psychological object and its productions. But wait. (*N*, I, p. 473)

At this point, Heidegger brings forward an objection he will soon reject. Before going into this, however, I should like to offer a cautionary remark against oversimplifying the question I am directing to Heidegger's procedure. Doubtless there is an effort by Heidegger to reduce the name of Nietzsche or the "Who is Nietzsche?" question to the unity of Western metaphysics, even to the uniqueness of a limit situation on the crest of that metaphysics. Nevertheless, the question "Who is X?" was a rare question when applied to a thinker; it is so still if one does not understand it in a biographically trivial way – as the man and the work, the man behind the work, the life of Descartes or Hegel associated with a kind of doxography. But to ask in another sense "Who is Nietzsche?" – to make his name the title of a book on his thought – that is something not so conventional.

Here is the objection Heidegger raises in a *pro forma* way just after he has rejected psychobiography: "But just a minute! Has not Nietzsche himself as a last act completed a work for publication entitled *Ecce Homo: How One Becomes What One Is?* Does not *Ecce Homo* speak as Nietzsche's last will and testament, to the effect that one must deal with this man, and let it be said of him what the excerpts of that writing suggest: 'Why I am so wise? Why I am so intelligent? Why I write such good books? Why I am a destiny?' Does this not point to an apex in unrestrained self-presentation and measureless self-mirroring?" Heidegger answers: *Ecce Homo* is not an autobiography, and if anything culminates in it, it would be the final moment of the West, in the history of the era of modernity. Without a doubt things get knotted together right in this place. One can admit, easily enough, that *Ecce Homo* is not Nietzsche's autobiographical history. But when Heidegger simply lets stand the conventional concept of autobiography instead of reshaping it, and only opposes to it the destiny of the West whose "carrier" Nietzsche would be, then one has to ask: Does Heidegger himself escape a fairly traditional opposition between biographical factuality – psycho-biographical, historical – and an essential thinking on the order of a historical decision? One can also ask what interest is served by this Heideggerian discourse being carried out along these lines.

By means of this strategy, Heidegger intends to rescue Nietzsche from his own singular fate. This fate has remained ambiguous. It has provoked odd uses of his thinking, uses which turned against what Heidegger calls Nietzsche's "innermost will." Thus it is a matter of gaining access to this innermost will and to oppose it to the duplicity of the empirical figure of Nietzsche as well as to the ambiguity of its subsequent effects – its immediate after-effects, for Heidegger believed that the future will work to restore that innermost will. After saying this in order to rescue Nietzsche from ambiguity, Heidegger directs this whole interpretation of Nietzsche's essential and singular thinking to the following argument: this thinking has not really gone beyond the end of metaphysics; it is still itself a great metaphysics and even if it points to such an overcoming, it is just barely, just enough to remain on the sharpest crest of the boundary. Or, in other words, to remain in complete ambiguity.

This, then, is essential ambiguity! Not just Nietzsche's, as Heidegger sees it, but also Heidegger's own ambivalence with regard to Nietzsche. It remains constant. In saving Nietzsche, Heidegger loses him too; he wants at the same time to save him and let go of him. At the very moment of affirming the uniqueness of Nietzsche's thinking, he does everything he can to show that it repeats the mightiest (and therefore the most general) schema of metaphysics. When he is pretending to rescue Nietzsche from this or that distortion – that of the Nazis, for example – he does so with categories which can themselves serve to distort – namely, with that opposition between essential and inessential thinkers, authentic thinkers and inauthentic ones, and with the definition of the essential thinker as someone selected, chosen, marked out or, I would even say, "signed" (*gezeichnet*). Signed – by what? By whom? By nobody – by the history of the truth of Being. Nietzsche was sufficiently chosen for that, and yet he was condemned by this same destiny to bring metaphysics to its completion, and without reaching a decision which he alone had prepared, even without recognizing the scope of that decision: "between the hegemony of *beings* and the lordship of *Being*" ("*Zwischen der Vormacht des Seienden und der Herrschaft des Seins*"). For all these points I refer you to the first pages of the chapter, "The Will to Power as Knowledge," whose first section carries the heading, "Nietzsche as Thinker of the Fulfillment of Metaphysics" (*N*, I, p. 473ff).

It was doubtless necessary to set up this interpretation-schema of Nietzsche's *biographein* in order to penetrate to his "alleged biologism." There too it is a matter of rescuing – in a most ambiguous way – the uniqueness of a thinking from the ambiguity of a life and work. The marking out of the boundaries of the biographical and of the proper name opens up the general space in whose interior the interpretation of the biological occurs.

Before the first words I quoted moments ago from the Preface there is an exergue.[7] It is taken from the *Gay Science* and its first word is "life." "Life" stands at the extreme outset of Heidegger's book – even before its beginning, before any decision between biography and biology. Here, strangely enough, Heidegger is not satisfied with breaking off the passage before its end. He also skips over a few words and replaces them with ellipses: "Life . . . more mysterious since the day the great liberator came over me – the thought that life should be an experiment of knowers." Among the words he skips over are the words "true" and "desirable," both of which pertain to life. Here is the fragment from Nietzsche in its – if one may speak this way – integral character.

In media vita! No! [These four words – the title, in short – and above all, these two exclamation points, are omitted by Heidegger – this time without ellipses. JD] Life has not disappointed me! On the contrary, I find it truer, more desirable and mysterious every year – ever since the day when the great liberator came over me: the idea that life might be an experiment of knowers – and not a duty, not a calamity, not trickery! And knowledge itself: let it be something else for others; for example, a bed to rest on, or the way to such a bed, or a diversion, or a form of leisure – for me it is a world of dangers and victories in which heroic feelings, too, find places to dance and play. "*Life as a means to knowledge*" – with this principle in one's heart one can live not only boldly but even gaily, and laugh gaily, too! And who knows how to laugh anyway and live well if he does not first know a good deal about war and victory? (*Gay Science*, § 324)

These are fundamentally secretive assertions, very difficult to interpret, just like the title *In media vita!* That makes life out to be a medium – as much in the sense of a mean between two extremes as in the sense of an elementary milieu in which the experiment of knowledge finds its place. In situating itself within life, this experiment uses life as a means, steers it from the inside, and – with this power to steer the living – comes to be beyond and outside of life, on the side of its end and its death, and so on. One can see why Heidegger took this passage as an exergue. He appears to be making a biological reading of Nietzsche more difficult in advance, whether one understands this reading in the sense of a subordination under the model of biology or as a celebration of life as the ultimate aim – even to the determination of life as the Being of beings, or being as a whole.

This choice of an exergue is sufficient evidence that the question about life and the "alleged biologism" stand at the active center of Heidegger's *Nietzsche*. And yet the paradoxical character of this passage (*In media vita!*) could also thwart Heidegger's hermeneutical strategy. Life does have a beyond, but it does not allow itself to be made into something secondary. As itself and in itself it unfolds the movement of truth or knowledge. It is in itself as its own beyond. Not to mention the stresses and the joys, the laughter and the war, the question marks and exclamation points – those things which Heidegger, considering how he effaces or conceals them, obviously does not want to hear spoken of here.

I would like to point out a second thing about this exergue – or rather, once again, a first thing, something completely first – pre-first. I said "life" was the first word of the citation. Strictly speaking, it is the first word in the quotation from Nietzsche. Before this quotation Heidegger adds a short sentence which – strangely enough – presents the exergue itself: "Nietzsche himself names the experience that determines his thinking: '. . .'". Hence, it is Nietzsche himself who *names* what determines his thinking, the patient experience of his thinking. And, if the name of the thinker designates the matter of his thinking, as Heidegger wants to show immediately afterwards, then the exergue as a whole means: Nietzsche names himself, he names himself from that out of which one must be able to name him. He will give himself a name from out of the experience of his thinking, and from it he receives his name. And so the thinking, so named, must rightly be understood from within this autonomous circle. But is it correct to say, as Heidegger so positively claims, that this thinking is one? – that Nietzsche then has only one name? Does he name himself only once? For Heidegger, his naming takes place only once, even if the place of this event retains the appearance of a borderline, from which one can get a look at both sides at once, at the summit of Western metaphysics, which is gathered together under this name.

But who ever has said that a person bears a single name? Certainly not Nietzsche. And likewise, who has said or decided that there is something like a Western metaphysics, something which would be capable of being gathered up under this name and this name only? What is it – the oneness of a name, the assembled unity of Western metaphysics? Is it anything more or less than the desire (a word effaced in Heidegger's Nietzsche citation) for a proper name, for a single, unique name and a thinkable genealogy? Next to Kierkegaard, was not Nietzsche one of the few great thinkers who multiplied his names and played with signatures, identities, and masks? Who named himself more than once, with several names? And what if that would be the heart of the matter, the *causa*, the *Streitfall* (point of dispute) of his thinking?

As we have just now seen, Heidegger wants to save Nietzsche at any cost, to save him from ambiguity by a gesture which is itself ambivalent. And what if it would be this rescue, which must be called into question in the name or names of Nietzsche?

When reading Heidegger's lectures on Nietzsche it is possibly less a matter of suspecting the content of an interpretation than of an assumption or axiomatic structure. Perhaps the axiomatic structure of metaphysics, inasmuch as *metaphysics itself* desires, or dreams, or imagines its own unity. A strange circle – an axiomatic structure which consequently demands an interpretation, one, gathered up, around a thinking unifying a unique text and, ultimately, the unique name for Being, for the experience of Being. With the value of the *name* this unity and this oneness mutually guard themselves against the dangers of dissemination. Here, perhaps – to take the words from Heidegger's preface – lies the *Streitfall* or the *Auseinandersetzung* between the Nietzsches and Martin Heidegger, between the Nietzsches and so-called (*ladite*) Western metaphysics. Since Aristotle, and at least up until Bergson, "it" (metaphysics) has constantly repeated and assumed that to think and to say must mean to think and say something that would be a *one*, one *matter*. And that not thinking-saying some one matter or principle is not thinking-saying at all, but a loss of the *logos*. Here is perhaps what the Nietzsches have put in question: the *legein* of this *logos*, the *gathering* of this logic.

This plurality starts to look like the family names of wanderers and tightrope walkers. It leads one away to the feast. Nietzsche and Heidegger speak of this feast with added emphasis. I leave it to you to consider this defference:

The error will be recognized only when a confrontation with Nietzsche is at the same time conjoined to a confrontation in the realm of the grounding question of philosophy. At the outset, however, we ought to introduce some words of Nietzsche's that stem from the time of his work on "will to power": "for many, abstract thinking is toil; for me, on good days, it is feast and frenzy" (XIV, § 24).

Abstract thinking a feast? The highest form of human existence? Indeed. But at the same time we must observe how Nietzsche views the essence of the feast, in such a way that he can think of it only on the basis of his fundamental conception of all being, will to power. "The feast implies: pride, exuberance, frivolity; mockery of all earnestness and respectability; a divine affirmation of oneself, out of animal plenitude and perfection – all obvious states to which the Christian may not honestly say Yes. "*The feast is paganism par excellence*" (*Will to Power*, § 916). For that reason, we might add, the feast of thinking never takes place in Christianity. That is to say, there is no Christian philosophy. There is no true philosophy that could be determined anywhere else than from within itself. For the same reason there is no pagan philosophy, inasmuch as anything "pagan" is always still something Christian – the counter-Christian. The Greek poets and thinkers can hardly be designated as "pagan." Feasts require long and painstaking preparation. This semester we want to prepare ourselves for the feast, even if we do not make it as far as the celebration, even if we only catch a glimpse of the preliminary festivities at the feast of thinking – experiencing what meditative thought is and what it means to be at home in genuine questioning. (*N*, I, pp. 14–15; Eng. I, pp. 5–6)

What happens in the course of the feast to the *legein* of this *logos*, which demands of the thinking-saying of the essential thinker that it be a thinking-saying of the one and the unique? The Nietzsches' feast risks tearing it into pieces or of dispersing it in its masks. Certainly it would protect it from any kind of biologism, but because the "logism" in it would lose its hold from the start. And another style of autobiography would come into being, bursting open (in every sense of the expression *faire sauter*) the unity of the name and the signature, disturbing both biologism and its critique, so far as it operates, in Heidegger, in the name of "essential thinking."

These are the preliminary remarks that I wanted to suggest for a future reading of Heidegger's *Nietzsche* – for this ambiguous life-saving act, in the course of which one stretches out the net for the tightrope walker, the one who runs the greatest risk overhead on the narrow rope, only insofar as one has made sure that he – unmasked and protected by the unity of his name, which in turn will be sealed by the unity of metaphysics – will not be taking any risks. In other words: he was dead before he landed in the net.

Certainly none of that will have taken place in *Zarathustra* – nor in Basel, Venice, or Nice – but in Freiburg im Breisgau, between 1936 and 1940, during the preparation for a feast, preparation for a "being at home in genuine questioning" (*N*, I, p. 15; Eng. I, p. 6).

II

Since I have been speaking for far too long (and I hope you will excuse me), I will be even more schematic in linking up a second question to the one we have just discussed. All this will be barely even preliminary, and, as I indicated at the beginning, will have to do with the concept of totality. One knows that the reference to the "totality of beings" in Heidegger's interpretation of Nietzsche, as well as in Western metaphysics itself, plays a structuring role. In order to speed things up, I am first of all going to mention two quotations. Heidegger takes the first one from the notes for *The Will to Power*: "Our whole world is the *ashes* of countless *living* creatures: and even if the animate seems so miniscule in comparison to the whole, it is nonetheless the case that *everything* has already been transposed into life and so departs from it." After this quotation Heidegger continues: "Apparently opposed to this is a thought expressed in *The Gay Science*, number 109: 'Let us guard against saying that death is the opposite of life; the living creature is simply a kind of dead creature, and a very rare kind.'"

The first thought points to a paradox in totality as a value. It shows itself disrespectfully in the face of the assurance of all that one generally thinks under the category of totality. But let us not forget that Heidegger defines metaphysics as the thinking of beings as a whole so that the question of the Being of beings is excluded; and on the basis of this definition he often makes Nietzsche out to be the last metaphysician. Without getting tangled up in the complexity of this whole question, one can already surmise just by reading this one passage that Nietzsche by no means trusts any thought of totality. He who says, "Even if the animate seems so miniscule [*sic*] in comparison to the whole, it is nonetheless the case that *everything* has already been transposed into life and so departs from it," expresses a thought about life and death which by no means subordinates itself to an unequivocal meaning of totality, of the relation between a whole and a non-whole. The idea of the eternal recurrence, obviously pervading this statement, is not a thought about totality. But Heidegger presents it *as* a thought about totality. It is one of the most insistent and most decisive themes of his reading. For instance, he writes at the end of the entire interpretation, which began with the two quotations that I recited:

> For one thing, we have circumscribed the field in which the thought of return belongs and which the thought as such concerns: we have surveyed this field of being as a whole and determined it as the interlacing unity of the animate and the lifeless. For another, we have shown how in its foundations being as a whole – as the unity of animate and inanimate – is structured and articulated: it is constituted by the character of force and the finitude of the whole (at one with infinity) that is implied in the character of force – which is to say, the immeasurability of the "phenomenal effects." (*N*, I, p. 355; Eng. II, pp. 96–7)

We must remember that Heidegger takes the will to power to be the principle of the knowledge of the eternal recurrence of the same. It is the *Verfassung* (composition) of beings (their *quid*, their *quidditas*, their *essentia*); the eternal recurrence is the modality (the *quomodo, die Weise* [the manner of being]) of beings as a whole (*N*, I, p. 425). In order to analyze Nietzsche's metaphysical *Grundstellung* (fundamental position), Heidegger must examine the accepted answer to the question about beings as a whole. The answer, he finds, is a two-fold one: the totality of beings is will to power and it is eternal recurrence. Whether or not these two answers are compatible, complementary, or combinable is basically less determinable from their content than their mutual relation. In point of fact, they are responses to two questions which throughout metaphysics form a pair (Being as *quidditas* or *essentia*; Being as manner of existing). As Heidegger sees it, because we did not know to identify this "metaphysical" pair of questions, we have erred up to now before the enigma of this twofold answer. But you can very well see that in each of these two questions the question of beings as a totality remains implied. This question about beings as a whole is one that Nietzsche, as the metaphysician he is (according to Heidegger), would stubbornly seek to answer.

And now my question: If in the first of the two statements Heidegger cites ("even if the animate seems so miniscule [*sic*] in comparison to the whole, it is nonetheless the case that *everything* has already been transposed into life and so departs from it") the thought of the eternal recurrence does not coincide either with the thought of totality or any opposition of whole and part, is it perhaps hasty to make Nietzsche out to be a metaphysician, albeit the last one? – At least if a metaphysician is, as Heidegger sees it, a thinker who adheres to the thought of beings as a whole. It just may possibly be that Nietzsche is not at all a thinker of beings, if indeed an essential connection exists between beings as such and totality.

Is it not also worth noting that it is life-death which deprives the value of totality of any privileged status? Is it not to be thought – following a very Nietzschean gesture, for we could well have other indications – that the living (the-living-the-dead) is not an existent being, does not fall within an ontological determintion? Nietzsche had one day proposed to think the word "being" starting from life and not the other way around.

A second preliminary remark: Heidegger has put these two quotations together on the ground of their apparent contradiction. He notes that they appear to "stand opposed" (*entgegenstehen*) to one another. Even if what we have here is an hypothesis or a feigned objection, it seems to me that its very principle is thwarted in Nietzsche's sentence. There, opposition or contradiction no longer constitutes a law dictating prohibitions to thought. And that without dialectic. Life and death (life-death), from which we think everything else – are not the whole. Neither are they opposites: "Let us guard against saying that death is the opposite of life; the living creature is simply a kind of dead creature, and a very rare kind." In one blow Nietzsche thwarts all that governs the thought or even the anticipation of totality, namely the relationship of genus and species. Here we are dealing with a unique inclusion – without any possible totalization – of the "whole" in the "part." With a metonymizing free from limits or positive devices. Let us defend ourselves against all our defenses – Nietzsche seems to be saying, at the beginning of a long

aphorism (*Gay Science*, § 109), which, one more time, Heidegger does
not quote in its entirety. – Yet another metonymical violence that engages his interpretation, it seems to me. But I do not want to impose
upon your time; somewhere else, some other time, perhaps I will come
back to these matters. Here I simply wanted to take the risk of sketching
out two questions.

NOTES

Translated by Diane Michelfelder and Richard E. Palmer. This essay was
presented at the Goethe Institute in Paris on April 25, 1981, at a colloquium
organized by Philippe Forget which brought together Hans-Georg Gadamer and
Jacques Derrida. Papers from the colloquium, including among others the presentation by Gadamer, Derrida's reply, and Derrida's own contribution have
appeared in German as *Text und Interpretation*, edited by Philippe Forget
(Munich: W. Fink, 1984). The translators wish to thank Philippe Forget for his
generous assistance in this project.

1 Derrida elsewhere develops this theme further, and in relation to Nietzsche.
  See his "Nietzsches Otobiographie oder Politik des Eigennamens: Die Lehre
  Nietzsches," *Fugen: Deutsch-Französisches Jahrbuch für Text-Analytik* (1980).
  J. D. (For the English version of this article, see note 7 below.)
2 Martin Heidegger, *Nietzsche*, trans. Pierre Klossowski (Paris: Gallimard,
  1971).
3 Martin Heidegger, *Nietzsche* (Pfüllingen: Neske, 1961), p. 9; English edition,
  Nietsche, vol. 1: *The Will to Power as Art*, trans. David F. Krell (New York:
  Harper & Row, 1979), p. xv. Where Derrida provides a French translation, we
  have worked from the French rather than using Krell's translation. Where the
  German is presented untranslated, we have sometimes used the Krell translation and sometimes supplied our own.
4 Heidegger, *Nietzsche*, I, 22; Eng. I, 14. Hereafter the abbreviation *N* will refer
  to the original two-volume German edition. The English translation, when
  given, will follow a semicolon.
5 The point Derrida is making relies on the French sounds. A translation would
  be: "He wants Nice, he venices, he wants Nietzsche" – all of which sound close
  enough to each other in French to invite the play on words.
6 This is the interpretation proposed by Derrida in the essay cited in footnote 1
  above. J. D.
7 Fr. "exergue." See the significant reference in Derrida's "Otobiographies: The
  Teaching of Nietzsche and the Politics of the Proper Name," in *The Ear of the
  Other: Otobiography, Transference, Translation*, ed. Christie V. McDonald (New
  York: Schocken Books, 1985), pp. 11–12: "Between the Preface [of *Ecce
  Homo*] signed F. N., which comes after the title, and the first chapter . . . there
  is a single page. It is an outwork, an *hors d'oeuvre*, an exergue or a flysheet
  whose topos . . . strangely dislocates . . . the time of life's *récit*. . . ."

4
Nietzsche, Ethics and Sexual Difference

Rosalyn Diprose

There are many women in Nietzsche's texts. There is the old woman, the sceptic and the enigmatic love object, or woman as masquerade. There is The Woman, the *jouissance* of which is Lacan's God – the Truth behind the veil. There is the other as object of evaluation and there is the reactive, castrating feminist. And there is the woman as mirror who, like the scientist, is an instrument – a reflection of forms not her own. Like the rest of Nietzsche's philosophy, his comments about women are often offensive, always colourful and never black and white.

The subject of this paper is Nietzsche's feminist, although his other women will necessarily enter the scene. For it is Nietzsche's anti-feminism which has attracted the more black and white responses from commentators. The following small sample may indicate why:

> Woman, the more she is a woman, resists rights hand and foot: after all, the state of nature, the eternal war between the sexes, gives her the first rank. . . . Has my answer been heard to the question of how one cures a woman – 'redeems' her? One gives her a child. Woman needs children, a man for her is only a means.[1]

And so on. Offensive? Yes. Descriptive or prescriptive? It's hard to tell.

Kaufmann apologises for Nietzsche's lapse in decency when addressing the subject of feminism,[2] and Christine Allen blames Nietzsche's attitude on his failed seduction of Lou Salomé[3] – a possibility I don't discount. More recently, Kelly Oliver has offered a psychoanalytic reading of Nietzsche's anti-feminism as symptomatic of his desire to possess woman as mother. This is posited against Derrida's claim (or, more correctly, against Krell's reading of Derrida's claim) that Nietzsche

desires to *be woman*.[4] In another recent critique, Ellen Kennedy argues
that Nietzsche opposes women's emancipation because it serves to 'destroy the will to power and to encourage the herd mentality'.[5] According
to this reading, Nietzsche's woman is determined by her biology and,
hence, should remain in her subservient position as wife and mother.
Kennedy's is a particularly curious reading despite its neat fit with the
quote given above. The will to power cannot be destroyed and there is no
essential biology for Nietzsche, rather, a socially constructed arrangement of forces.

While Nietzsche's feminist is my subject, I wish to distance myself
from these readings. Not because I condone Nietzsche's mysogyny but,
rather, because my objection to his anti-feminism can only be raised via
a different path. We could, of course, ignore Nietzsche's wider philosophy and thus reduce his comments on women to unconditional and
personal mysogyny. Yet there may be something of interest to salvage,
even beyond a 'proper' interpretation of a nineteenth-century philosophy. The path I will take to Nietzsche's anti-feminism is one that
attempts to salvage what is, ironically, of use to feminism – his critique
of the liberal subject and the ethics of self-creation that this critique
entails.

Contemporary feminists, for all their differences, seem to share a
discomfort with the assumed authenticity of the rational subject as he is
positioned at the norm of a politics of equality. Michèle Le Doeuff, for
example, claims that in order to avoid the existential equation between
oppression and moral error, feminism 'needs another problematic than
that of the subject, and another perspective than that of morality'.[6]
Marion Tapper, in her paper 'Can a Feminist be a Liberal', argues that
liberalism's abstract conception of the individual obscures the way in
which the evaluation of sexual difference operates to disadvantage
women in the public sphere.[7] And Catharine Mackinnon reaches a
similar conclusion: the concept of equality reproduces the power imbal-
ance between men and women. She argues that, as the social norm of
valued subjectivity is the male body, then the evaluation of sexual difference is an expression of power, in that difference means dominance, and
'equality' as sameness is impossible.[8]

It might seem somewhat paradoxical to claim that Nietzsche, while
lacking this specific detail and hardly a champion of women's rights,
does share these sentiments about equality, difference and dominance.
In *Twilight of the Idols* and elsewhere, he condemns 'equality' as a 'certain
actual rendering similar' which, as an expression of the will to power,
'belongs to decline'.[9] Against this he evokes a morality of 'many coloured
actions', a celebration of a 'multiplicity of types' and the 'will to be

oneself'.[10] To support this distinction between equality and a celebration of differences, Nietzsche provides a notion of the subject as a corporeal entity – socially constructed in relation to the other's difference. This notion, in turn, allows him to undermine the supposed autonomy, rationality and moral responsibility of the liberal individual and to unmask the ethical mode of evaluation which sustains this subject as the norm in the democratic state.

1 Ethics, the Creation of the Self and the Other

In order to fully appreciate Nietzsche's ethics of self-creation and the place of sexual difference within it, it is necessary to look closely at his understanding of morality. Morality, he claims, is 'a system of evaluations that partially coincides with the conditions of a creature's life'.[11] It is also defined by him as a 'theory of relations of dominance under which the phenomenon "life" arises' (BGE 19). Thus Nietzsche foreshadows Foucault's nexus between knowledge, power and the body by positing an intimate relation between 'moral systems of evaluation', 'relations of dominance' and the 'creation of life'.

Evaluation and the creation of life

For Nietzsche, the operation of systems of evaluation involves more than the attachment of the moral values 'good' and 'bad' to individual actions. The production of all knowledge involves interpretation (WP 481) whereby 'our values are interpreted *into* things' (WP 590). Morality, as the evaluation of all sensations and activities is, it seems, at work everywhere:

> As soon as we see a new image, we immediately construct it with the aid of all our previous experiences, *depending on the degree* of our honesty and justice. All experiences are moral experiences, even in the realm of sense perception. (GS 114)

To say that 'our values are interpreted *into* things' suggests, not only that moral evaluation is all-pervasive, but that it produces more than a point of view. It creates life. At a most general level this means that, for Nietzsche, neither the object of interpretation nor its value and meaning exists in essence prior to our evaluation of it. It is through the process of interpretation, drawing upon a shared system of evaluation, that we transform what is 'in flux, incomprehensible and elusive' into apparently organized, enduring 'things':

> The reputation, name and appearance, the usual measure and weight of a thing, what it counts for . . . all this grows . . . until it gradually grows to be part of a thing and turns into its very body. (GS 58)

This applies to any 'thing' and any 'body'.

The body of particular interest to feminism is the sexed body. On this subject Nietzsche would appear to have little to say. However, appearances can be deceiving. The space for the creation of the sexed body can be located in more general references to the creation of a particular part of life – the phenomena we call 'self' and 'other'. Nietzsche's concern with the way in which moral evaluation governs the creation of, and relation between, self and other undermines what is most sacred to a liberal empiricist tradition and what is most frustrating to feminism – the notion of an autonomous, rational, morally responsible individual.

It follows from Nietzsche's more general claims about the relationship between systems of evaluation and the creation of 'life' that it is through the process of interpretation that the phenomenon 'self' arises, as well as the phenomenon 'other'. Let me first consider the constitution of the self as the subject, although, in practice, this cannot be separated from his relation to the other. Nietzsche insists that the unity of Descartes' subject, as the cause of mental and other acts, cannot be presupposed. The will, ego or 'I' is a unity 'only in a word'.[12] Nor is the body a pregiven unity, separate from the mind but, rather, is a multiplicity of activities. The body, as we know it, is a product of a relation between commanding and obeying forces (BGE 19) and consciousness is a reflection of this relation (WP 477 and GS 354).

While the 'mind is an idea of the body' it is an idea mediated by those systems of evaluation which organize life in general. A plurality of material sensations, a multiplicity of forces of constraint, compulsion, resistance, pressure and motion is organized by the introduction of social norms – moral values and concepts like 'cause' and 'effect' – and through this imposition the unity of the 'self' is created. In *On the Genealogy of Morals*, for example, Nietzsche describes how the creation of a selective memory through the mnemotechnics of pain and punishment unifies the subject according to social convention (GM II 1 and 2). Memory brings unity to a selection of activities, effects and disparate events, past, present and future, such that the subject can safely say 'I will have done'.[13] This creation of a subject 'who makes promises' also involves a tradition of disproportionate evaluation of different parts of the body, used as a system of guarantees against failure to fulfil a promise or repay a debt (GM II 5). And 'forgetting' is transformed into an active, socially convenient, faculty of repression against the dangers of social psychosis. Forgetting ensures that 'chance' sensations and unending, unmediated impressions do not disrupt the uniformity of, and link between, discrete events now belonging to the responsible subject (GM II 1). Thus Nietzsche can claim that 'everything of which we become conscious is [always already] arranged, simplified, schematized, interpreted through and through' (WP 477). The 'I' represents only a conscious symptom of part of the body's possibilities – possibilities already organized and interpreted according to social convention.

The more obvious implication of Nietzsche's observations on this unified, responsible subject is that it is a fiction. It is only through convention and the 'interpretation of surface phenomena that accompany acts' that we separate the doer from the deed. We thereby assume a unified will that causes the deed and a substantial ego as causal antecedent to thought (TI p. 49). Both the authenticity and the unity of the rational subject are consequently thrown into doubt. A further implication is that, while the subject is divided, this division is between socially mediated consciousness and the repressed, not between mind and body. The body is the seat of subjectivity, not in the sense of a pre-given causal biology, but as a socially constructed arrangement of forces. Hence, sexual difference cannot be located in either an essential causal biology or in a purely mental state as the object and product of axial conditioning. Rather, Nietzsche's model of subjectivity suggests that, just as the male subject is a product of interpretation which draws upon a shared system of evaluation, so is the mark of sexual difference.

As I have suggested, the mark of sexual difference can be located in the distinction between subject and other. The subject is fundamentally divided – not just between consciousness and the repressed, but between self and other. In that, given the work involved in the 'active forgetting' necessary to maintain the subject's unity, he must at times suffer an identity crisis. It is to prevent the collapse of the assumed autonomy and unity of the subject that a certain construction of the other is required. And allow me to introduce some of Nietzsche's more attractive women in this context:

When a man stands in the midst of his own noise, in the midst of his own surf of plans and projects, then he is apt also to see quiet,

magical beings gliding past him and long for their happiness and
seclusion: *women*. He almost thinks that his better self dwells there
among the women. (GS 60)

A certain image of woman, operating at a distance, seems to hold the key
to the completion of the subject's identity. His better self appears to
dwell there in an image that promises to organise and silence the noise
of the repressed. His desire, then, is to possess this image. Or, as
Nietzsche puts it: 'Our pleasure in ourselves tries to maintain itself by
again and again changing something new *into ourselves*: that is what
possession means' (GS 14). To incorporate the other woman, what he is
not, would secure the presence of the subject's identity. But, Nietzsche
warns: 'The magic and most powerful effect of woman is, in philosophical language, action at a distance . . . but this requires first of all –
distance' (GS 60).

What these passages reveal, in the first instance, is the position of
woman in relation to the male subject – she is his other and, as such, is
crucial to the creation and maintenance of his identity. Thus the autonomy of the subject is also thrown into doubt in that the social systems
of evaluation which give rise to the subject only do so in a field of
relations with others. And, as Nietzsche's definitions of morality suggest,
this field is one of domination as well as one of interpretation. To say
that morality is a 'theory of relations of dominance' brings Nietzsche's
notion of the will to power onto the scene of interpretation and the
creation of the subject.

Evaluation and relations of dominance

If the apparent unity of the subject is a product of interpretation then, as
Nehamas suggests, the notion of an interpreter behind the interpretation
is also a fiction.[14] If this is the case then who or what interprets? Our
needs, manifest as drives, interpret, answers Nietzsche, and 'every drive
is a lust to rule' (WP 481). Or, to put this another way, as he does: 'the
will to power *interprets* . . . it defines, limits, determines degrees' (WP
643). This power is not so much something that the subject 'has' but is
the productive force of interpretation of which the delimited subject is an
effect. It is a relational entity 'designated by the effect it produces and
that which it resists' (WP 634).

By equating interpretation with productive power in this way,
Nietzsche is claiming that 'reality' consists, not of fixed, passive entities,
but of material centres of force which seek to extend their own effects

and activities. Centres, including the phenomenon 'self', which seek to grow stronger and resist domination by others through the interpretation and evaluation of their own effects as separate from, and in relation to, others. Hence:

> every centre of force adopts a perspective toward the entire remainder, i.e. its own particular valuation, mode of action and mode of resistance. . . . Reality consists precisely in this particular action and reaction of every individual part toward the whole. (WP 567)

Translating this general claim into the specific question of the human Being Nietzsche proposes that 'the only "Being" vouchsafed for us is changing, not identical with itself, it is involved in relationships'[15]: relationships of power and dominance which are established and reinforced by the interpretation of the subject's own activities as distinct from others.

We can perhaps begin to see how the corporeal image of the other woman is, at least partially, an effect of the subject's will to power. Woman, like the male subject, is not born of an essence but of an interpretation. What defines the subject as unified and separate from her is the selective interpretation of his activities and of his relations with, and differences from, other collections of effects. Just as 'the thing is the sum of its effects' (WP 551), 'I am an effect' (BGE 19) and so is woman. The division between inner and outer world, the subject and object, the subject and other is an arbitrary (although enduring) product of interpretation wherein we assume some effects belong together. This process of production generates a hierarchy of identity in that, given woman's role in constituting and maintaining the subject's boundaries, her corporeal image is constructed in deference to his and is, therefore, less discrete.

Woman is socially inscribed as the ambiguous point against which the subject identifies himself. At a distance the corporeal image of woman thus created operates to re-affirm the subject's unity and autonomy; as a possible source of increased power for the subject, in the sense of a proliferation of his effects, she is the object to be possessed. A contradictory double image of virtue and shame is essential to the self-certainty of the subject – a self-certainty maintained at woman's expense. This precarious, ambivalent relation between subject and other is the essence of sexual difference and the creation of the subject relies on such an interpretation of difference: 'it is man who creates for himself an image of woman, and woman forms herself according to this image' (GS 68).

The apparent willingness with which women act out the subject's fantasy is a bit of wishful thinking on Nietzsche's part. Women are not merely 'reactive' – they have their own modes of action and valuation beyond the needs of the subject. Nietzsche at least admits to the impossibility of maintaining simultaneously both virtue and shame and suggests that women's scepticism and silence 'casts anchor at that point' (GS 71). But silence and retreat are not the only avenues of resistance women have to the power of interpretation. Any active expression of subjectivity beyond the needs of the subject would have its material effects upon the subject's identity. Nietzsche acknowledges this when claiming that woman would be unable to hold men if 'we did not consider it quite possible under certain circumstances she could wield a dagger (any kind of dagger) *against us*. Or against herself – which in certain cases would be a crueler revenge' (GS 69).

Finally, sexual difference is not just a symptom of interpretation which organises materiality and establishes and maintains relations of dominance. But, as I have suggested, interpretation implies the designation of value. The only fundamental ontological differences that Nietzsche seems to admit, including presumably those between the sexes, are 'variations in power' – differences in quantity arising from the 'desire to be more' (WP 564). While there is no quality or value-in-itself, differences in quantity are felt and interpreted as differences in quality (WP 563). The quantitative reckoning, weighing and measuring of the self as distinct from the other involves the construction of a hierarchy of qualitative differences between self and other. Neither exists *in essence* apart from their relational effects and the interpretation of those relations as differences in quality. Hence it is no accident that women are evaluated differently from men against a male norm – the norm itself is maintained in its dominant position by such evaluation.

Given that Nietzsche's understanding of morality firmly re-inserts politics, epistemology and ontology back into the realm of ethics, it is not surprising that his philosophy continues to provoke some discomfort. The ethical problem for him is that in order to delimit the subject as autonomous, authentic and re-located at the centre of the universe we need to 'invent and fabricate the person with whom we associate – and immediately forget we have done so' (BGE 138). This is not for him a harmful or indifferent process. The system of evaluation which gives rise to the liberal subject is inflected with the will to domination. Yet we cannot simply unmask the essential self or other behind the power of interpretation – for neither exists. Rather, Nietzsche's genealogy of morals unmasks the subject's investments and the violation, appropriation and domination involved in circumscribing and evaluating intersubjective differences. However, it remains to be seen whether his concern can stretch to include the violation of women – the subject's other *par excellence*.

2 Towards an Ethics of Difference

That a particular kind of individual endures indicates, Nietzsche suggests, that a particular species of interpretation also endures (WP 678). The kind of individual that endures is the subject that operates normatively in our democratic institutions. The species of interpretation which maintains this creature is the mode of evaluation which we would call 'dichotomous'. It is within an excursion through dichotomous systems of evaluation that Nietzsche's explicit critique of a politics of equality can be found.

Through his gesture *Beyond Good and Evil* Nietzsche attacks the apparent indifference of dichotomous systems of evaluation. Contrary to appearances, he claims, nothing and no one is good-in-itself: 'It might even be possible,' he suggests,

> that *what* constitutes the value of those good and honoured things
> resides precisely in their being artfully related, knotted and cro-
> cheted to those wicked, apparently antithetical things. (BGE 2)

The designation of value is not indifferent to difference, nor is it without its material effects. We create valuable things through the devaluation of difference. The thing is fetishized – becomes a valuable thing-in-itself – by forgetting this process of production. 'We put value into things and this value has an effect on us long after we have forgotten that we were the donors.'

But what *is* the effect on us? In particular, what is the effect on the subject of assigning value to the other's difference? Nietzsche's most systematic answer can be found in *On the Genealogy of Morals*. In describing how *ressentiment* creates values, he claims that: 'slave morality from the outset says No to what is "outside", what is "not itself", and this No is its creative deed' (GM I 10). The negation of the other's difference is the subject's denial of heterogeneity and this is creative in an ontological sense. The man of the 'herd' reacts against difference: he creates the other as evil, as an opposite and from this he, himself, evolves. The constitution, status and identity of the subject is, therefore, an effect, more precisely an after-effect, of evaluating the other's difference.

As 'translation is a form of conquest' (GS 83), the other does not emerge from this process unscathed. Creating and maintaining the normative subject through a contempt for difference is merely a veiled expression of the will to power: the subject's will to extend his own activities, impose his own values and 'create the world in his own image'. As a result of this reaction to difference, the other may be deemed socially inferior and marginalized accordingly. Or the other's difference, so determined, may be effaced through the process of 'making equal' or making the same. Either way, the creative power of dichotomous evaluation lies in giving rise to a certain kind of subject as an after-thought to creating, then negating the other's difference.

Putting aside the specific question of sexual difference temporarily, I want to trace the general sentiment of Nietzsche's opposition to this mode of self-creation as it operates in an ethico-politics of equality. Rather than being measured and measuring others against a social norm of value, Nietzsche proposes a 'morality of many coloured actions'. 'We *want to become what we are*,' he says, 'human beings who are new, unique, incomparable, who give themselves laws, who create themselves' (GS 335). Rather than negating the other's difference, we seek our honour, our value through affirming ourselves (TI p. 46).

The problem with Nietzsche's alternative ethics of affirmation for a liberal empiricist tradition is locating what is affirmed and from where new values can emerge. The position from which we can create ourselves by affirming what is new, different and incomparable is, it seems, the position of 'other' to reactive evaluation. Nietzsche's wider definition of the 'other' as the profound spirit, the enigmatic, the poet and the artist allows the space for us to insert into this position anyone who is interpreted as profoundly different to the social norm (on the basis of sex, colour, ethnicity, sexuality etc.) by a dichotomous mode of evaluation.

Where the normative subject is created and maintained through a comparative distaste for otherness, the 'other' will always remain enigmatic. The corporeal image of the other is, in part, an image *for* the subject. Such consideration of difference by the subject involves the selection of a few effects and characteristics from a continuum of possibilities. And just as the other's possibilities can never be fully appreciated in this way, the other's difference can never be fully captured, silenced and effaced by an ethico-politics of equality. As Nietzsche claims in *Beyond Good and Evil*:

Every profound spirit needs a mask, more around every profound spirit a mask is continually growing thanks to the constantly false, that is to say *shallow* interpretation of every word he speaks, every step he takes, every sign of life he gives. (BGE 40)

The process of reactive evaluation creates the mask that is the other's socially inscribed difference. But, unlike in Hegel's synthesis of the dialectic, a remainder of difference is always deferred in the creation of this mask. This is particularly the case if the other does not merely 'react' or conform to the subject's interpretation. This remainder, itself constantly shifting, is the space that allows the possibility of affirming oneself against the social norm of interpretation. What Nietzsche affirms here is not unlike what Derrida describes under the motif of *différance* – the infinite deferral and delaying of the presence of meaning and value.[16]

It is clear from Nietzsche's descriptions of the operation of morality that there is no *essential* corporeal value behind the mask to be retrieved and affirmed. Rather, there is a 'tempo of one's style' which is lost in translation (BGE 28); a multiplicity of possible permutations and combinations of effects which resists simplification. Or, as Nietzsche would have it, an excess feeling of power, abundance and plenitude which seeks to create the self differently rather than subtract from the other (TI p. 72). Hence, in Nietzsche's ethics of self-creation there is no end point of self-realization or authentic subjectivity as Stern suggests[17] – no unmasking or construction of an essential self. What Nietzsche describes is an inevitable, yet positive mode of resistance to social domination and normalization; a process of re-interpreting one's own activities and effects; a will to ambiguity and self-affirmation which draws upon what exceeds interpretation and which finds its pleasure in thwarting and subverting a mode of evaluation that seeks to simplify and efface differences.

Feminists, self-defined or not, are, or course, familiar with this will to ambiguity. It is practised every day. Not in a simple reversal of the values that re-inforce women's oppression but in the way women oppose, re-interpret and weave around the simplistic categories that evaluate their differences from men. And, given Nietzsche's recognition of the unique role that sexual difference plays in sustaining the subject's status and identity, one would expect that women would be given a privileged place in his ethics of self-affirmation. However, just as the liberal subject which Nietzsche attacks is male, so is the 'we' located at the creative site of undecidability.

For Nietzsche, the 'other' placed most at risk by an ethics of equality is not woman but the sometimes cruel, sometimes enigmatic, always exceptional Noble spirit. The way Nietzsche appears to single out a sole aristocratic victim is somewhat surprising to a contemporary reader and has drawn criticism from some commentators. However, that Nietzsche appears to seek to save an elite and somewhat frightening figure from the workings of the democratic state is, in part, a product of historic necessity. It was the noble man, embellished by a memory of Greek nobility, who, more than any other, symbolized what was thrown into relief by the rise of the liberal individual in the nineteenth century. But this is no longer the case: a century of 'equality' has created its own hierarchy of value and, hence, its own order of differences to be marginalized and effaced. All the same, on the question of Nietzsche's explicit exclusion of women from this possibility of self-creation, the excuses run out.

So, what about the masks behind woman's mask of virtue and shame? What of the dagger of other possibilities wielded beyond the dance to man's tune? At times Nietzsche comes close to recognizing the power of women's positive resistance to the domination of social sameness. This is certainly implicit in his acknowledgement of the role of woman as the subject's other, as in comments that hint at feminine dissatisfaction as the necessary pre-condition to change (GS 24). On the question of other possibilities for women he, at times, hypothesizes:

> All at once we believe that somewhere in the world there could be women with lofty, heroic and royal souls, capable of and ready for grandiose responses, resolutions and sacrifices, capable of and ready for rule over men because in them the best elements of man apart from his sex have become an incarnate ideal (GS 70).

However, he is quick to discount this possibility: 'such voices always retain some motherly and housewifely coloration'. This is, in part, a denial of an essence behind the mask of woman a belief that motivates man's desire for more – and of the futility of simply reversing existing oppositions. But it is also a sign that Nietzsche remains unsympathetic to feminist attempts, in any form, to improve woman's lot. More than unsympathetic – he seems positively hostile.

Nietzsche's anti-feminism is not so much inconsistent but symptomatic of his own *ressentiment*. His opposition to feminism of equality is in keeping with his opposition to the material effects of reducing all differences to a social norm. However, there is a small but significant difference between feminism and democratic normalization in general. Feminists of equality may implicitly seek to make women the same as the male subject – at least for the purposes of evaluation before the law. But, as Nietzsche himself implies, the norm is male, making such a project partial, at best. More important, for feminism to be a threat to Nietzsche's *male* poet, artist and enigmatic noble spirit, it would have to have the power to make men the same as women. Such a power has not, to my knowledge, ever been a reality.

So why this stubborn obsession? A hint of an answer can be found, I think, in the comments prefacing Nietzsche's more vitriolic attacks on feminism. In *Beyond Good and Evil*, for example, he claims that the comments to follow on 'woman as such' are spoken by an 'unchangeable "this is I" '. They are, therefore, '*my* truths' he claims, emphatically (BGE 231). Similarly, in *Ecce Homo* and in a manner reminiscent of Lacan's 'love letters',[18] Nietzsche introduces an even more notorious attack on female emancipation (which includes the quote given at the beginning of this paper) with the following:

> May I venture to say that I *know* women? That is part of my Dionysian dowry. Who knows? Perhaps I am the first psychologist of the eternally feminine. They all love me – an old story – not counting *abortive* females, the 'emancipated' who lack the stuff for children. (EH p. 266)

Bearing in mind the uncertainty of this 'know', Nietzsche claims to know women – perhaps better than they do themselves. He is venturing his truths – not just in the sense of his opinion, but in the sense of what his 'this is I' requires of woman to ensure its unity. The 'we' who practise this ethics of affirmative self-creation require, it seems, the same image of the eternally feminine to guarantee its value. Nietzsche insists that this 'we' should not be 'deprived of the stimulus of the enigmatic' (WP 470). But the feminists wield the dagger that threatens to take away this enigmatic image of the eternally feminine – the mirror that gives him back his own reflection. Nietzsche, on the question of 'woman as such', lines up with the liberal subject which he seeks to subvert – they are both interpreting an image of themselves at woman's expense. The difference is that Nietzsche admits it.

But he is doing more than ambiguously acknowledging man's debt to woman. He also claims to speak from experience – from the position of the eternally feminine ('that is part of my Dionysian dowry'). The problem that 'woman as such' presents for Nietzsche is that the corporeal image of woman is already ambiguous, divided in-itself. Whilst the 'other' position women thus occupy is a result of a 'shallow interpretation' (to adopt Nietzsche's phrase) and is not to be envied, nor uncritically embraced, it does make women the obvious source of other possibilities – for affirming the otherness of the other. Yet Nietzsche would have us believe that, at the site of affirmative subversion of dichotomous evaluation, he would be a more effective 'woman' than women. As hard as he tries, he cannot occupy that particular position and perhaps that is where his scepticism and silence, on the question of the dagger women wield against the normative subject, casts its anchor.

If we can still speak of origins then I can venture to say that Nietzsche sowed the seeds for an ethics of difference based on a genealogy of the divided self. An anti-philosophy, if you like, which can be mapped to the present through psychoanalysis, structuralism and semiotics. His philosophy is, therefore, useful to feminism for its observations, rare in Western philosophy, on the subject as a material construction – the unity of which is dependent upon the domination and devaluation of an indiscrete and contradictory image of woman. It is useful too for the space it thereby opens to women to explore possibilities for change beyond the impasse of equality. However, just as with the philosophy of Nietzsche's contemporary male disciples, we need to tread carefully through this new terrain. A celebration of differences runs the risk of reproducing modes of subjectivity and power relations which fall within familiar and esteemed boundaries. And it occasionally shows signs, explicit in Nietzsche's philosophy, of what Spivak calls the 'double displacement of woman' – a displacement of woman from the site of otherness[19] – just when this site has been acknowledged as both the condition of possibility of the subject's authenticity as well as the source of his possible demise.

NOTES

1 Friedrich Nietzsche, *Ecce Homo*, p. 267 in *On the Genealogy of Morals and Ecce Homo*, Walter Kaufman (trans.), Vintage, New York, 1967. Hereafter referred to as GM (followed by essay and section number) and EH (followed by page number for this edition).

2 See, for example, Kaufmann's introduction to *The Gay Science*, Walter Kaufmann (trans.), Vintage, New York, 1974, p. 24. Hereafter referred to as GS followed by section numbers.

3 Christine Allen, 'Nietzsche's Ambivalence about Women', in Lorenne Clark and Lynda Lange (eds), *The Sexism of Social and Political Theory*, University of Toronto Press, Toronto, 1979, p. 125.

4 Kelly Oliver, 'Nietzsche's Woman: the Poststructural Attempt to do Away with Women', *Radical Philosophy*, No. 48, 1988. While I share Oliver's concerns I have only touched on the important debate about 'writing as woman' as Derrida presents it in *Spurs/Eperons*, Alan Bass (trans.), University of Chicago Press, Chicago, 1979. A more detailed critique is provided by Gayatri Spivak in 'Displacement and the Discourse of Woman', Mark Krupnick (ed.), *Displacement: Derrida and After*, University of Indiana Press, New York, 1982 and 'Love Me, Love My Ombre, Elle', *Diacritics*, Vol. 14, No. 4, winter 1984.

5 Ellen Kennedy, 'Nietzsche: Woman as Untermensch', in Ellen Kennedy and Susan Mendus (eds), *Women in Western Political Philosophy*, Wheatsheaf, Sussex, 1987, p. 190.
6 Michèle Le Doeuff, 'Operative Philosophy', *Ideology and Consciousness*, No. 6, autumn 1979, p. 57.
7 Marion Tapper, 'Can a Feminist be a Liberal', *Australasian Journal of Philosophy*, Supplement to Vol. 64, June 1986.
8 Catharine A. Mackinnon, *Feminism Unmodified: Discourses on Life and Law*, Harvard University Press, Cambridge, 1987, especially chapter 2.
9 Nietzsche, *Twilight of the Idols*, R. J. Hollingdale (trans.), Penguin, Harmondsworth, 1968, p. 91. Hereafter referred to as TI followed by page numbers for this edition.
10 Ibid. and *Beyond Good and Evil*, R. J. Hollingdale (trans.), Penguin, Harmondsworth, 1972, p. 215. Hereafter referred to as BGE followed by section numbers.
11 Nietzsche, *The Will to Power*, Walter Kaufmann (ed. and trans.) and R. J. Hollingdale (trans.), Vintage, New York, 1967, p. 256. Hereafter referred to as WP followed by section numbers.
12 For example, TI p. 37, BGE 19 and WP 485–561.
13 See also TI p. 46 for the notion that the present individual is also his past and future.
14 Alexander Nehamas, *Nietzsche: Life as Literature*, Harvard University Press, Cambridge, 1985. I am partly indebted in this section to Nehamas' refreshing account of the relation between interpretation and the will to power as described in the chapter 'The Thing is the Sum of its Effects'. While Nehamas' account relates to the 'thing' as product of interpretation, I seek to emphasize the effect of interpretation on the subject of interpretation.
15 Nietzsche, *Werke: Kritische Gesamtausgabe*, G. Colli and M. Montinari (eds), Berlin, 1967, Vol. V, section 2, p. 468, quoted in J. P. Stern, *Nietzsche*, Fontana, London, 1978, p. 146.
16 See, for example, Jacques Derrida, 'Différance', *Margins of Philosophy*, Alan Bass (trans.), University of Chicago Press, Chicago, 1982. Such an understanding of Derrida's descriptions of the operation of 'différance' is, in turn, essential to his reading of Nietzsche as 'writing as woman' in *Spurs*.
17 Stern, *Nietzsche*, pp. 76 and 77.
18 'There is a *jouissance* proper to her, to this "her" which does not exist and signifies nothing . . . and of which she herself may know nothing' (p. 145) and to 'these mystical ejaculations . . . Add the Écrits of *Jacques Lacan* which is of the same order' (p. 147) in Jacques Lacan, 'God and the *Jouissance* of The Woman' and 'A Love Letter', Juliet Mitchell and Jacqueline Rose (eds), *Feminine Sexuality*, Macmillan, London, 1982.
19 Spivak, 'Displacement and the Discourse of Woman'.

5
Weber, Nietzsche and Music

Andrew Edgar

The purpose of this chapter is to explore possible relationships between Max Weber's unfinished study, *The Rational and Social Foundations of Music*[1] and Nietzsche's *Birth of Tragedy*.[2] While exploration of the influence of Nietzsche has been a central issue in Weber scholarship at least since Fleischmann's 'De Weber à Nietzsche', and Raymond Aron's 'Max Weber and Power-Politics', both made public in 1964,[3] attention has tended to be focused either on Weber's overtly political writings, or on the sociology of power and politics. By concentrating on a relatively neglected study of music, the Nietzschean interpretation of Weber may be extended, so as to address fundamental problems in the theorization of culture, society and the individual.

Upon initial contact, Weber's and Nietzsche's studies appear fundamentally different in both tone and content. While focusing on the nature and history of Greek tragedy, Nietzsche finds in this the resources to confront an array of issues in metaphysics, aesthetics and epistemology. The essay thereby defies easy summary. In contrast, Weber demarcates a specific problem. He is concerned, through cross-cultural analysis, to provide a rigorous account of progressive rationalization in the theorization of music as a tone system, and the corresponding accounts of such phenomena as harmony, melody and counterpoint, and the development of systems of notation. Further, rationalization is seen in the response of music theorists to more or less heterogeneous social pressures, such as the impact of technological innovation on instrument manufacture and design, the structure of the orchestra and the significance of changes in the composition of music's audiences. Nietzsche's characterizations of *The Birth of Tragedy* in terms of its lack of desire for logical purity, its arrogance and fanaticism, appear to be antithetical to

Weber, whose language is forbiddingly technical, serving the precise articulation of musical and social facts. It is difficult to conceive of Weber leading his fellow-revellers 'to new secret paths and dancing-places'.[4] Similarly, Weber's study seems to be fundamentally different in its intentions, in so far as it is concerned with the deployment of a value-neutral social science. It is not concerned with the aesthetic evaluation of musical rationalization. To paraphrase Nietzsche, art is overtly seen under the lens of science.[5]

This initial impression is misleading. There is in Weber, as in Nietzsche a 'strange voice . . . disguised beneath the scholar's hood, beneath the heaviness and dialectical joylessness of the German'.[6] Weber's sociology as a whole may be seen to share a problematic with Nietzsche and specifically the young Nietzsche of *The Birth of Tragedy*. A common point of influence may be found in Schopenhauer's grounding of metaphysics in the confrontation with the horror and evil of the world. Nietzsche responds to this, in *The Birth of Tragedy*, with the central claim that 'it is only as *an aesthetic phenomenon* that existence and the world are eternally *justified*'.[7] Weber's sociology responds equally emphatically, by positing a 'metaphysical need for a meaning-ful cosmos' as a fundamental motivation to human action.[8] This need is manifest in response to diverse culturally mediated experiences of suffering, impurity and senselessness, and is felt across diverse so-cial groups, such as the disprivileged, the bourgeois rationalist, and (in reflection upon ethical and religious questions) the intellectual.[9] Underpinning this, however, is a more disquieting suggestion, and one at least superficially more in line with Schopenhauer's pessimism. The 'cultivated' member of modern society will share the need for meaning with all humanity, but will have this need increasingly frustrated because of the differentiation of contemporary culture. The individual, whether a passive recipient of existing cultural values and interpre-tations, or their active creator, can occupy only a segment of the culture. Each segment is characterized by a value-orientation that is, for Weber, ultimately incommensurable with any other. The dominant culture of contemporary society is a scientific culture, and as such it is a culture of facts and instrumental rationality, unable to mediate between, or evaluate the worth of, competing value-claims. In consequence, the more complex the culture is, the more trifling the individual's position becomes, and the less certainty they can have that they have grasped the 'essence' of the culture let alone the whole. In sum, the 'advancement of cultural values . . . seems to become a senseless hustle in the service of worthless, moveover self-contradictory, and mutually antagonistic ends'.[10] It is in this context that the strange voice of Weber's sociology of

music begins to be revealed. As Weber's sociology of power and bureaucracy is concerned with the irrational (repressive and anti-demo-
cratic) implicitations of modern rational organization, so his sociology of
music is concerned with the inevitable failure of music theory to provide
a coherent, and thus meaningful, account of music and the value conflict
that underlies this failure. Music thereby serves to focus reflection upon
the agonistic nature of human culture in general.

If Nietzsche describes *The Birth of Tragedy* as an essay on the problem
of science, and further as articulating something novel precisely in recognizing that science is problematic,[11] then Weber's sociology as a whole
takes up this problem. For Nietzsche the problem of science is focused
on Socrates as 'the turning point, the vortex of world history'. Socrates
initiates the 'profound *illusion* . . . that rational thought, guided by causality, can penetrate to the depths of being', and is even capable of
correcting being.[12] In 'Science as a Vocation', while acknowledging the
significance of Indian systems of logic, Weber notes the unique achievement of Hellenic philosophy in developing the concept, and thus
grounding Western science. Echoing the agonistic tone of Nietzsche's
philosophy, and referring explicitly to Socrates, he notes that the concept
is 'a handy means by which one could put the logical screws upon
somebody so that he could not come out without admitting either that
he knew nothing or that this and nothing else was truth'.[13] Socratic
thought is thereby seen to provide Western science with its grounding
presupposition: that all phenomena in the world may be given a definitive explanation. The inexplicable mysteries of magic are thereby banished, and the world disenchanted. *Rational and Social Foundations of
Music* takes up this problem, but, in contradistinction to Nietzsche's
claim that 'the problem of science cannot be recognized within the
context of science',[14] articulates the problem of science through science.
The overt subject-matter of the essay is music theory, and thus the
science of music rather than music itself. Given Nietzsche's distinction
between the poet and the thinker,[15] Weber may be seen to be concerned
exclusively with thinkers. Music theory thereby becomes illustrative, if
not indeed emblematic, of the crisis in Western rationality. Yet this crisis
is articulated through a social science that is equally profoundly
grounded in rationality. Here again, a strange voice begins to emerge
from beneath the scholar's hood.

Two further issues may be found to link *The Birth of Tragedy* and
Rational and Social Foundations, albeit that they stand in a more oblique
relationship to the overt subject-matter of Weber's study. Firstly, while
Rational and Social Foundations does not seek to articulate the achievements of music theory in terms of national culture, and thus does not
seem to take up Nietzsche's championing of German music, nationalistic

elements underpin Weber's explicitly political writings, and more broadly the sociology as a whole is concerned to justify the economic, technical and scientific superiority of Occidental societies over all others. *Rational and Social Foundations* may therefore be intepreted within this framework, and again in relation to *The Birth of Tragedy*. Secondly, in Weber's social and political writings as a whole, an ambiguity hangs over his conceptualization of personal identity. His accounts are divided between models of a socially situated self, determined in its value-orientation and consequent action by an ambient *Weltanschauung*, and of an autonomous self that can freely choose values. This ambiguity may be traced in both Schopenhauer and Nietzsche, and is thematized in *Rational and Social Foundations* in so far as the intellectual music theorist is its hero. These two points may be elaborated upon briefly, before the details of a Nietzschean reading of *Rational and Social Foundations* are spelt out.

In his 1895 inaugural address at Freiburg, 'The Nation State and Economic Policy', Weber explicitly links his political science to his practical politics. The address as a whole is open to a broadly Nietzschean interpretation. Raymond Aron notes that Weber finds struggle everywhere, from the dreariness of everyday existence and the winning of 'elbowroom', to the power politics that is fought out within and between nations.[16] The account is most distinctively Nietzschean in its analysis of the mutation of forms of struggle, so that struggle is seen to be pursued through the semblance of peace or international co-operation.[17] Developmental economic processes are analysed as power struggles, not primarily in the Marxist sense in which class and nation-alist struggle can be reduced to an economic base, but rather in so far as the overtly civilized and fair processes of economic exchange and devel-opment are themselves essentially manifestions of unavoidable conflict. The moment of struggle is further celebrated by appeal to an histori-cal and ultimately nationalist perspective. While the address begins as a scientific, and thus overtly value-neutral, account within political economy. Weber seeks to present the practitioner of a 'human science', and thus of political economy, as always already situated within a nation's culture. As such, their value-neutrality is seen to be mediated by the value-judgements inherent in their culture, which are expressed in 'the distinct imprint of humanity we find in our own nature', and articulated through consideration of the '*quality of the human beings* who are brought up in these economic and social conditions'.[18] Specifically, Weber is concerned here with the struggle between the Polish and German populations in the East Elbian countryside, and with what is, from his German position, the superiority of the German 'race'. Political science thereby comes to be understood as 'the servant of politics', specifically in its subservience to 'the lasting power-political interests of the nation'.[19] This is articulated through an appeal to history and national destiny. Weber criticizes historians for failing to recount 'the warlike deeds of our ancestors',[20] and expresses his concern for 'the *future*, for *those who will come after us*'.[21] This future will contain only struggle, but Weber hopes at once that the German race of the future will be successful in this struggle, and that this future people will recognize 'in our nature the nature of *its own ancestors*'.[22]

While Weber later distanced himself from the 'Address', it may be suggested that something of its agonistic character continues in the mature sociology, albeit that German achievement is largely displaced by Occidental achievement.[23] Thus Weber's introduction to the *Sociology of Religion* begins by pointing to the universal significance and value of Western civilization.[24] The importance of a Nietzschean reading of Weber may therefore be suggested to lie in its role as problematizing the affirmative tone of that account. In highlighting the struggle that underpins Occidental achievement the agonistic nature of both the achievement of rationalization, and of the account of that achievement is emphasized.

In turning to the problem of Weber's account of the self, a similar ambiguity may be remarked in Schopenhauer. As Christopher Janaway describes this: 'While producing a theory that the self is fundamentally a blindly striving, limited, pain-ridden product of organic functions, Schopenhauer never loses a sense that it ought to be a pure Platonic soul.'[25] The embodied, or for Weber, socially determined self, may be seen to underpin the 'Freiburg Address'. Weber openly takes the stance of an economic nationalist. This position cannot be justified by explicating its truth, for, as a value-orientation, he presents it as being incommensurable and antagonistic to any other value-orientation. The position is justified only by Weber situating himself within the bourgeoisie, and as thus having 'been brought up to share their views and ideals'.[26] More broadly, 'the standard of value adopted by a German economic theorist, can be nothing other than . . . a German standard'.[27] These passages suggest that the self is constituted by an ambient *Weltanschauung*, in this case as bourgeois, nationalist, and academic. As a constellation of values, such a *Weltanschauung* satisfies the agent's metaphysical need for a meaningful cosmos, yet implies that any agent's value-judgements are largely pre-determined as expressions of the *Weltanschauung*.

In other writings, and particularly those marked by his methodological individualism, Weber proposes the image of the human agent as a 'soul – as in Plato – [which] chooses its own fate'.[28] The image is used to suggest a self that is non-identical to its *Weltanschauung*. In part, even as a rational being, the self is unable to justify the *Weltanschauung* that it does occupy. Yet further, in so far as it is capable of reflecting upon its values, it may perceive that they are an inadequate response to the metaphysical need for meaning, and so may reconstitute them in terms of a greater inner consistency. In a series of analyses that echo Nietzsche's 'weak will' and 'strong will',[29] Weber proposes a distinction between an ethic of responsibility and an ethic of conviction. In the former, by deploying instrumental rationality, the agent's action is calculated to be the most efficient means to a given end. As such the agent takes the ambient *Weltanschauung* for granted, as the source of its values and goals, and indeed the socially accepted criteria of instrumental efficiency. In the ethic of conviction, a strong will acts with value-rationality, presupposing that its ideal action is an ultimate end, and thus accepts no responsibility for the consequences and costs of so acting. Bad results are attributed, for example, to the world, to other humans, or to God's will.[30] Precisely in so far as Weber grounds the 'dignity of the "personality"' in the consistency that the agent achieves in the coordination of the constitutive values and actions of their *Weltanschauung*,[31] it is suggested that a peculiarly valuable form of autonomous agency is realized in reflection that increases the coherence of the *Weltanschauung*.

In Weber's sociology as a whole, the figure of the intellectual manifests this paradoxical subjecthood clearly. Intellectualism is the purist manifestation of the metaphysical need for meaning in so far as the intellectual is driven to reflection, 'not by material need but by an inner compulsion to understand the world'.[32] Weber identifies intellectualism as characteristic of a particular type of social group, typically a group that is independent from the economic and political pressures of mundane life. This position frees them for seemingly autonomous reflection. Yet by identifying different types of intellectualism, according to the social groups from which the intellectuals emerge or which they serve, Weber also suggests that the products of intellectual reflection remain delimited by an ambient *Weltanschauung*.[33] As modern science is an example of intellectualism, the determinism that Weber gives to his own position in the 'Freiburg Address' is re-asserted. Thus, in its reflection upon science, and with the intellectual figure of the theorist (struggling to give meaning to the micro-cosmos of music) as its hero, *Rational and Social Foundations* also comments upon the ambiguity of the human subject. In this it again opens itself to interpretation in the light of *The Birth of Tragedy*, now in terms of Nietzsche's analysis of the condition of individuation and Schopenhauer's *principium individuationis*.

To summarize the above account, it has been suggested that four elements may be taken to characterize the relationship between Weber and Nietzsche, and more specifically between *Rational and Social Foundations* and *The Birth of Tragedy*. Both texts are concerned with the need for meaning in the face of suffering (and irrationality); the problem of science; the politics of culture; and the nature of personal identity. These themes may be developed in more detail, and with specific consideration of the treatment and possible resolution that they receive in *Rational and Social Foundations*, by considering the study with reference to three accounts that Weber himself gives of it. These serve to situate the study within Weber's sociology as a whole, and so highlight its capacity to bear a Nietzschean interpretation.

Weber appeals to the rationalization of music in the 'Introduction' written for the *Sociology of Religion* in 1920, as evidence of the universality of Western culture. This account begins by remarking that cultural phenomena of universal significance and value developed within Western civilization.[34] (Overtly this claim to universality is justified in terms of the rationality of Western culture.) These phenomena include the natural and social sciences, economic production and distribution, bureaucracy and the law. The arts are presented as the most surprising addition to this list, but thereby as important evidence of the nature of Western culture. Weber briefly outlines the rationality of Western architecture (for example in terms of the use of the pointed arch in Gothic vaulting), and the development of printing. The rationality of music is characterized though reference to the development of Western harmony as the framework within which both vertical and horizontal note intervals are understood. This framework is complemented by the organization of the orchestra, the Western system of notation and development of such instruments as the organ, piano and violin.

This self-interpretation highlights the themes that dominate the middle and later sections of the *Rational and Social Foundations*. Chapter 5 articulates the rational development of music through consideration of the manner in which music theory and practice strives to integrate the demands of the melodic (or horizontal) aspects of music with the harmonic (or vertical). A series of (ideal typical) stages are mapped, beginning with unison and octave singing, and heterophony (in all of which the horizontal element dominates). This continues through polyvocality (in which chord sequences lack any sense of harmonic progression so that the vertical dimension is dominant) and so to contrapuntal polyphony and, for Weber, its perfection in modern chordal harmony (which involves thinking 'musically in two-dimensional terms: vertically across the staff lines and at the same time horizontally alongside these lines'[35]). At a number of points Weber notes, in a tone anticipating that of the *Sociology of Religion*, the superiority of Western developments over those of other cultures. Thus harmonic-homophonic music (entailing 'the subordination of the entire tone setting under one voice carrying the melody') is 'apparently nowhere so far developed as in the Occident as early as the fourteenth century'.[36] This in turn leads to the type of question which informs Weber's sociology as a whole: 'Why did polyvocality appear in some parts of the world but not others?'[37] In sum, given the superiority of Western music over that of all other cultures, music may be subject to the same methods of analysis that Weber uses to account for the uniqueness of Western capitalism as such. In the case of music Weber is able to appeal both to related developments (such as the use of rational systems of notation and the exploitation of instrument design) and to the overcoming of heterogeneous impediments (such as the confinement of music to ritual and religious uses).[38] These developments give music theorists the autonomy necessary to reflect upon the impetus to rationalization inherent in the musical material itself. Weber refers, for example, both to 'the inner logic of tone relations which immediately pushed on toward the formation of modern scales' and to 'the evolution of music into a professional art' as the pre-condition to 'rationalization proper'.[39]

As a guide to interpreting *Rational and Social Foundations*, this account is marked by its suppression of the problematic nature of Western rationality and Western culture, not simply by failing to raise the relationship between rationality and a grounding power struggle, but more significantly by closing off any reflection on the problem of a rational account of music itself. The development of music is constructed retrospectively from the established achievements of the West. However, in *Rational and Social Foundations*, the presuppositions of the account are thrown into question because music is from the first articulated in terms of Western music theory (that has its roots in Pythagorean traditions), thereby exposing the circularity of the account of the sociology of music given in the 1920 Introduction. The original thesis of *Rational and Social Foundations* is simplified to the point of distortion. Crucially, and yet coherently with the affirmative tone of this particular account of Western culture, it is suggested that the harmonic framework of Western music is wholly adequate in terms of its inner coherence, and its account of musical phenomena. *Rational and Social Foundations*, in contrast, dwells upon the unavoidable irrationality of Western music theory. As such, the Introduction is the scholar's hood, that does not merely disguise, but actively conceals, the strangeness of the Nietzschean moment of Weber's sociology.

The idiosyncratic nature of Weber's self-interpretation is highlighted by the introduction (of 1913) to 'The Economic Ethic of the World Religions'. Weber again appeals to music to illustrate a point in the articulation of his sociology as a whole, but now music becomes emblematic, not of the boundless success of Western rationality, but rather of its inevitable limitation. Weber resists the universalist claims of Western science, and ultimately challenges its Socratic underpinnings. Implicitly appealing to the opening pages of *Rational and Social Foundations*, he notes that 'the calculation of consistent rationalism has not easily come out with nothing left over. In music, the Pythagorean "comma" resisted complete rationalization oriented to tonal physics'.[40] Beginning from an account of music in terms of the division of the octave by intervals of the fifth (and fourth), it is argued that: 'If one ascends or descends from a tonic in circles first in the octave followed by fifths . . . the powers of the these divisions can never meet on one and the same tone no matter how long the procedure be continued'.[41] The Pythagorean comma is the discrepancy in a mathematically perfect scale that exists between the note reached at the twelfth perfect fifth and the seventh octave. In sum, what Weber seemingly champions as the most rational account of musical material is incapable of generating a consistent and comprehensive analysis. *Rational and Social Foundations* thereby begins with an outline of the basic elements of Western music theory, albeit orientated to exposing the unavoidable irrationalities. This account continues in order to explore parallel, and indeed greater, problems in alternative attempts to theorize music (including systems grounded in the fourth rather than the Western fifth, or in whole-tone steps and pentatonicism, and also various forms of tempered scale). The exact nature of these irrationalities is, however, left ambiguous, and this uncertainty is echoed in Weber's remark that it 'is not easy to say precisely what in modern tonality . . . gives it a firm foundation'.[42]

Weber's analysis appears to focus on the development of music systems through the selection and privileging of certain intervals within the octave. As such, scales may be grounded in such natural phenomena as the overtone series. Similarly, it is implied that the distinction between rational and irrational intervals is objective, yet the ground of that rationality, like the 'firm foundation' of Western theory, remains elusive. Thus Weber argues that the 'harmonically most perfect intervals, the octave, fifth, and fourth were distinguished by the recognizability which made them paramount for the development of a primitive tonality. . . . As it is easier correctly to remember real as contrasted to unreal events . . . a corresponding condition is present for distinguishing right and wrong intervals'.[43] From this it should be concluded that the remaining irrationalities in Western theory are due to the inadequacy of the theory itself. Yet Weber explicitly argues against this, in so far as the failure to provide a rational account is repeatedly identified as being inevitable.[44] Further, the sundering of music theory from any simple dependence on natural material is suggested in so far as, with reference to the explanation of chord progression given in Western music theory (by such as Helmholtz), it is noted that 'the scale of upper partials does not form the perfect basis of a scale'.[45] In this Weber implicitly challenges what he elsewhere identifies as the necessary presuppositions of Western science, that its rules of logic and method are valid,[46] or in Nietzsche's terms, that it can penetrate the depths of being. Weber's argument may then be presented, consistently with the 1913 Introduction, as suggesting that nature can fundamentally resist science, and more precisely, that music theory continues as a science, paradoxically, despite the strict conditions of its possibility having been removed.

The working through of this paradox may be seen to lie in the suggestion that music theory is peculiar in explicitly responding to natural material as meaningful. Weber notes that the natural sciences are incapable of describing their world as 'worthwhile', or as having any meaning.[47] Yet music theory is presented, not simply in terms of the explanation of a natural phenomenon, but rather in terms of its interpretation.[48] Music is never merely a matter of 'tonal physics', but is rather sound existing towards some end. In sum, music theory does not appeal to what is simply given in nature, but rather explicates 'music material' that is already social, and thus is mediated by the listening practices of those who are cultivated into specific forms of interpretation and expectation. A pre-social music, that might indeed ground modern tonality, is thereby rendered elusive, precisely because music theory is a self-consciously value-laden (and conflict-ridden) science.

The manner in which music theory rests upon value-conflict may be explicated by turning to the third of Weber's interpretations of *Rational and Social Foundations*. In 'The Meaning of "Ethical Neutrality"' (of 1917), the sociology of music is appealed to in order to illustrate the possibility of a value neutral analysis of social progress. Initially, this account appears to be closer to that offered in the 1920 Introduction than to that offered in 'The Economic Ethic of the World Religions'. A purely empirical history or sociology of art is presented as being possible in so far as it entails the analysis of the progress of an art form, with 'progress' being operationalized in precise technical terms through reference to the effective achievement of an explicitly given end. As such, Weber's concern is with an objective instrumental rationality, albeit that his comments on the differentiation inherent in technological progress also suggest that technologies can be analysed in terms of the possibilities that they open up for the artist.[49] The sociology of music illustrates this approach by reconstructing the development of music (and its grounding theory) up to its culmination in modern Europe in terms of the progress towards rational harmony.[50] This account broadly overlaps with chapter 5 of *Rational and Social Foundations*. The account is superior to the 1920 Introduction by clarifying the explanatory mechanism of the sociology of music. Explanation proceeds by explicating a set of conditions that are themselves theorized as solutions to technical problems, that 'cause' the technical refinement in music theory. These conditions include the development of instruments, notation and polyphony. These in turn may be grounded in economic, religious or political imperatives. Thus, centrally, it is noted that '[i]n the early Middle Ages the monks of the northern Occident missionary area . . . rationalized the popular folk po-lyphony for their own purposes instead of following the Byzantine monks in allowing the music to be arranged for them by the Hellenically trained *melopoios*'.[51]

   The seemingly unproblematic and affirmative nature of this account, like that of the 1920 Introduction, is achieved only by suppressing key strands in the argument of *Rational and Social Foundations*. Crucially, 'Ethical Neutrality' suggests that the superiority of Western music lies in the achievement of a consistent harmonic system. Not only is the prob-lem of the comma thereby ignored, but more significantly the tension between harmonic, melodic and other possible ends is barely noted. Indeed, only the reference to the discrepancy between Western and Byzantine monastic practices suggests anything of this tension. *Rational and Social Foundations*, however, focuses upon this. The end of the music system serves to define a value-orientation, and thus the *Weltanschauung*, within which music is grasped and interpreted. The precise nature of the rationalization of music within a given culture will thereby depend upon the musical ends that it privileges. Weber explores the possibilities of purely or predominantly melodic *Weltanschauungen* in terms of both the intervals that may be given priority in the octave, and the scope for reducing 'tonal material to the smallest uniform distance. . . . Indeed, wherever music is not rationalized according to chords, the principles of melodic distance and harmonic division are not in conflict'.[52] This is taken further to suggest the possibility of expression, and even 'fullness of sound' predominating over harmonic and melodic ends.[53] The supe-riority of Western music is thereby presented, not through its single minded and instrumentally effective achievement of harmonic ends (and indeed it is implied that the tension between harmonic and melodic ends is a pre-condition, albeit not one found uniquely in the West, of rational progress in music[54]) but rather through its unparalleled sensitivity to the conflict between diverse ends. The account of Western chordal harmony as thinking musically in two-dimensional terms is thereby enriched.

Weber's argument culminates with the observation that 'an ear which, unlike ours, does not, by training unconsciously interpret each interval born out of pure melodic and expressive needs in harmonic terms, is not restricted to the enjoyment of intervals which it can classify harmonically'.[55] The point is only weakly articulated in *Rational and Social Foundations*, but it may be suggested that this marks the relationship between the socially embodied and the autonomous self, precisely in so far as there is a discrepancy between music as understood and constituted in the society's ambient *Weltanschauung*, and music as it is constituted in the rational reflection of the theorist. 'Ethical Neutrality', by identifying Western music with the achievement of harmonic ends, considers music as it is understood by the socially embodied self. Weber can therefore note, with apparent irony, that he writes on music from 'the standpoint of the interests of the modern European ("value-relevance!")'.[56] Yet Western music theory, itself the product of an autonomous intelligentsia, is distanced from that end. While the empirical sociology of music may take harmonic ends as a given social fact, musicology questions the coherence of that very end. This displacement of the end does not merely raise Weber's distinction between subject and objective instrumental rationality (and thus between efficacy within the world as it is perceived by lay actors, and the objective efficiency, typically identified, at least potentially, by Western science) but rather undermines the possibility of instrumental rationality at all. Again, paradoxically, the science of music continues, despite its necessary presuppositions having been undermined.

This problem is not entirely alien to 'Ethical Neutrality'. The account of an empirical social science is framed by two highly Nietzschean passages. The observations that, '[c]onflict cannot be excluded from social life', and ' "[p]eace" is nothing more than a change in the form of the conflict', preface and give context to a consideration of the possibility and scope of value-neutrality.[57] If all societies are inevitably antagonistic, no universally acceptable evaluation of a social order can be offered. Evaluation therefore is taken to involve necessary reference to the opportunities that are provided to 'certain types of persons' within that order. Science cannot then deem one social order to be better than another, except in so far as that observation is qualified by noting for whom it is better, and in what manner. While this premises Weber's separation of evaluative from non-evaluative disciplines, music, whether studied within musicology or by a sociology of music. disrupts this dichotomy.

An empirical sociology of music can proceed if it can identify coherent ends. 'Ethical Neutrality' suggests the possibility of such a science by presupposing the unproblematic nature of harmony as the core value of the Western musical *Weltanschuung*. *Rational and Social Foundations* goes well beyond this. Western music theory and practice, in contradistinction to the overt *Weltanschuung*, is unable to focus on a single end (such that concern with harmonic ends can no longer be pursued in complete indifference to melodic ends), nor to generate a coherent system of ends. By implicating music in value-conflict at both an aesthetic level (in the tension between vertical and horizontal ends) and further through social conditioning, it exposes the superiority of Western music as lying not in any ahistorical rationality, but rather in its power to displace and encompass all other musical systems. The music theorist, precisely by focusing on the consistency of the system and thus aspiring to intellectual autonomy, becomes the naive witness of, and participant in, inevitable social conflict. *Rational and Social Foundations*, unlike the overtly value-neutral guises of the 1920 Introduction and 'Ethical Neutrality', pays testimony to that witness.

In conclusion, and in an attempt to provide a possible explication of certain of the tensions that run through Weber's sociology of music, it may be suggested that the three accounts that Weber gives of the material originally generated in *Rational and Social Foundations* bear a peculiar relationship to *The Birth of Tragedy*, such that Weber reproduces in his own sociology the decline that Nietzsche traces in tragedy. *Rational and Social Foundations* embodies the vision of the Dionysian-Apolline art of Aeschylus, while the 1920 Introduction represents the final triumph of Socrates' and Euripides' Apolline thinking. In that Weber is concerned with the development of and tension within music theory, it may be suggested that his inquiry parallels Nietzsche's documentation of the Greek's Apolline response to the threat of the Dionysian. Two strands may be separated from Nietzsche's account. On the one hand, the Apolline is the illusion, or ultimately the game, that gives meaning to suffering by representing the will. On the other hand, the Apolline is grounded in the *principium individuationis*, and thereby focuses the tension between the autonomous individual and the socially embodied self.

Nietzsche places at the core of the most profound Apolline culture Silenus's response to King Midas: the most desirable thing for humanity is never to have existed. This Greek sensitivity to suffering is borne only in so far as it can be given aesthetic representation, and so justified as beautiful.[58] The Apolline is thereby characterized in terms of dream and illusion (in opposition to Dionysian intoxication). As such it is a moment of contemplation and reflection, and at its most superficial merely separates the spectator from the spectacle, concealing its urgency and presence. Music, primarily a Dionysian art and yet in Greek culture given Apolline form (both in performance through the exclusion of harmony and emphasis on a regular rhythm, and in interpretation through the role of the lyric poet), avoids superficiality by becoming the appearance of the will. Such music 'symbolically refers to the primal contradiction and the primal suffering within the Primal Oneness, and thus symbolizes a sphere beyond and prior to all phenomena'.[59] It thereby realizes the necessary co-existence of the Dionysian and Apolline moments, such that the Dionysian remains the foundation of the Apolline, and yet a foundation can only be grasped by humanity in so far as it is presented within an Apolline illusion.[60] In consequence, however, the Apolline is necessarily deceptive. While lifting humanity 'out of [its] orgiastic self-destruction', it deceives with the clarity with which it appears to grasp and articulate the Dionysian. The profundity of great tragedy lies in its exposure of this deception (and equally, the weakness of Euripides' drama, and indeed Socratic science, lies in its capitulation to the deception). The tragic conclusion reveals the Apolline as the veiling of the true Dionysian effect: 'This is the Apolline dream state, in which the daylight world is veiled and a new world, more distinct, comprehensible and affecting than the other and yet more shadowy, is constantly reborn before our eyes.'[61] Nietzsche's argument culminates in the 'bold leap' of suggesting that tragedy 'has to convince us that even ugliness and discord are an artistic game which the will . . . plays with itself'.[62] The exposure of the Apolline deception, and thus the exposure of the game as being merely indicative of a deeper grounding wisdom, finds expression in delightful acceptance of musical dissonance, such that the listener does not merely want to go on listening, but to go beyond listening.[63]

Parallels to this account of the Apolline moment of illusion are readily found in *Rational and Social Foundations*. The comma and the tension between harmonic, melodic and other ends occupy the space of primal suffering in Nietzsche's account. Crucially, in relation to Weber's other sociological and political writings, this refers outward to the inevitability of conflict within society as a whole. Yet a doubt may be cast on the depth of such an interpretation, precisely in so far as Weber himself seems to have capitulated to the Apolline deception. In so far as he is concerned with music theory, and not with music, he appears to remain distant from Nietzsche's concern with the Dionysian. More precisely, Weber appears to fall victim to Nietzsche's criticism of those who speak of music through visual images.[64] Music theory reduces both Dionysian excess and the Apolline symbol, not to visual imagery, but to an even more impoverishing mathematical equation. In reply, it may be suggested that Weber merely offers a more profound understanding of music. Nietzsche sets up an opposition between words and music, most notably in his remark that one could not bear to listen to the third act of *Tristan and Isolde* simply as abstract music, unaided by the drama of word and image.[65] Underpinning *Rational and Social Foundations* is the equally disquieting, but less hyperbolic, suggestion that we could not listen to any music, unless it had been given Apolline form and clarity. through the work of music theorists. From this standpoint. Weber may be seen to suggest that contemporary music theory, being the unique achievement of Western culture, attains the point of exposing its own Apolline deception. The comma and the conflict of ends necessarily propels music theory beyond itself, such that it delights in them (and thus in conflict *per se*) as Nietzsche requires us to delight in dissonance (metaphorical and otherwise). Beyond purely Apolline theory (and beyond science) lies the enchantment and meaning of the Dionysian.[66] Music theory thereby procedes as a science only in so far as it is self-conscious of the Apolline deception, and, at least potentially, newly open to the problem of meaning.

The clarity and speculative calm of the Apolline is grounded by Nietzsche in the *principium individuationis*. This serves to characterize the Apolline realm of illusion not simply in terms of the differentiation, or more precisely fragmentation, of the object of contemplation (thereby violating the Primal Oneness of Schopenhauer's will), but more significantly in terms of the individualization and isolation of the spectator. Nietzsche borrows Schopenhauer's image of the lone boatman, trusting in the fragile craft of the *principium individuationis* against the boundless and raging sea of suffering.[67] The craft is fragile not only in terms of the enormity of the Dionysian violence about it, but also in terms of the instability of the very individualization inherent in personhood. Lyric poetry is seen to expose the deception of the Apolline apotheosis of the *principium* (in which the individual transforms suffering into their own redemptive vision), by aspiring to a fusion with the 'primal artist of the world . . . at once subject and object, at once poet, actor and audience'.[68] Tragedy expresses a similar aspiration in the delight taken in the destruction of the individual.[69] An eternal, Dionysian life is revealed behind the *principium individuationis*, continuing despite the destruction of any phenomenal individual. Indeed, Nietzsche suggests that for a long time Dionysius was the only theatrical hero.[70] Individual characters, and their sufferings, are thereby grasped only in terms of their Dionysian ground. The later dramas of Sophocles and Euripides reverse this by focusing on the individuality of the characters portrayed, divorcing them from the universal. The metaphysical consolation of Dionysius is thereby replaced by 'earthly resolution for tragic dissonance. . . . [T]he hero, having been adequately tormented by fate, [wins] his well-earned reward'.[71] These dramas merely confirm the existing phenomenal and fragmented order of the world. The decline of tragedy is thereby associated with the decline of myth, not just in so far as the mythic embodies the metaphysical vision, *sub specie aeterni*,[72] but also in that the communal grounding of the individual is concealed, precisely through the sundering of the Apolline from the Dionysian, and the individual from the community. The Dionysian (and thus communal) moment of the folk-song is lost.[73]

The Apolline individual, protected by the frail craft of the *principium*, finds a strong echo in Weber's figure of the intellectual, and the autonomous self it exemplifies. The Nietzschean reading of *Rational and Social Foundations* again throws new light on this. The intellectual, through a grounding in rational science, aspires to occupy the place of metaphysical vision, and as such, suffers from the same hubris as Nietzsche's Euripides and Socrates. Music theory, precisely by remaining true to the Dionysian moments of the comma and the conflict of ends, denies this aspiration, and thereby throws into question the intellectual's phenomenal autonomy, and the universality of its science.

It is precisely these most Nietzschean aspects that Weber's own subsequent glosses of the sociology of music gradually erode. In effect, the exposure of the Apolline deception of music theory, which *Rational and Social Foundations* embraces with the delight of a participant in the drama, is increasingly suppressed, as the Apolline illusion of an increasingly hermetic sociology serves to distance the sociologist from the spectacle witnessed. If the 1920 Introduction is, as Benjamin Nelson has claimed,[74] the master clue to Weber's sociology as a whole, then it is a clue that must be treated with the utmost caution. This self-interpretation does not merely move away from certain Nietzschean foundations (manifest, for example, in the 1895 Address) to an alternative and more consistent position. Rather, as has been suggested above, comparison of *Rational and Social Foundations* with the 1920 Introduction and the two other glosses, demonstrates that Weber increasingly suppresses or ignores the 'strange voice' of the sociology of music. Weber's response to, and acknowledgement of, the problems to which it gives rise, become increasingly oblique or dogmatic. In contrast, the Weber of *Rational and Social Foundations* does not merely open up new approaches within his own sociology, but poses fundamental questions as to the manner in which he has been appropriated into academic sociology.

NOTES

1 Max Weber, *The Rational and Social Foundations of Music*, trans. Don Martindale, Johannes Riedel, Gertrude Neuwirth, Carbondale: Southern Illinois University Press, 1958. The essay was worked on by Weber in 1911. It was published posthumously as an appendix to the 1921 edition of *Wirtschaft und Gesellschaft*. It was not included in the 'first complete English translation' of *Economy and Society*, edited by Guenther Roth and Claus Wittich, New York: Bedminster Press, 1968.

2 Translations are from Shaun Whiteside and Michael Tanner's edition, *The Birth of Tragedy: Out of the Spirit of Music*, Harmondsworth: Penguin, 1993.

3 E. Fleischmann, 'De Weber à Neitzsche', *Archives Européennes Sociologiques*, 5, 1964, pp. 190–238, and R. Aron, 'Max Weber and Power-Politics', in O. Stammer (ed.), *Max Weber and Sociology Today*, Oxford: Blackwell, 1971. Aron's paper was originally presented to the German Sociological Association in 1964, and was broadly supported by other presentations from Wolfgang Mommsen, Jürgen Habermas and Herbert Marcuse. These accounts served to shift the emphasis of Weberian interpretation away from a basic presupposition that Weber was concerned primarily with democracy, in order to highlight the centrality of power and domination in his thinking. While Fleischmann's account is important for highlighting this and other aspects of Weber's work that do indeed bear a genuinely Nietzschean interpretation, his emphasis on Weber's antipathy to Marx, along with the exploitation of an over-simplified opposition between Marx and Nietzsche, served to exaggerate Weber's alignment with Nietzsche. (For an account of the debates concerning the relationship between Weber and Nietzsche from 1964 onwards, see Martin Albrow, *Max Weber's Construction of Social Theory*, London: Macmillan, 1990, pp. 55–61.)

4 Nietzsche, *The Birth of Tragedy*, 'Attempt at a Self-Criticism', section 3.

5 Nietzsche seeks 'to see science under the lens of the artist, but art under the lens of life', *Birth of Tragedy*, 'Attempt at a Self-Criticism', section 2.

6 Nietzsche, *Birth of Tragedy*, 'Attempt at a Self-Criticism', section 3.

7 Nietzsche, *Birth of Tragedy*, section 5. See Arthur Schopenhauer, *The World as Will and Representation*, trans. E. F. J. Payne, New York: Dover, 1958, volume 2, p. 161.

8 Max Weber, 'The Social Psychology of the World Religions', in *From Max Weber: Essays in Sociology*, London: Routledge & Kegan Paul, 1948, p. 281.

9 See Weber, 'Social Psychology', pp. 280–1 for a list of potential evils from which the individual may wish to be 'redeemed'. *Economy and Society*, p. 499, documents the relationship between the 'metaphysical need' and different social groups. Schopenhauer's account of the role of priests and philosophers in the fulfilling of the need for metaphysics (*World as Will and Representation*, volume 2, pp. 162–4) yields significant comparisons to Weber's account of priests and intellectuals.

10 Max Weber, 'Religious Rejections of the World and their Direction', in *From Max Weber*, p. 357. See also 'Science as a Vocation', in *From Max Weber*, pp. 139–43.

11 Nietzsche, *Birth of Tragedy*, 'Self-Criticism', sect. 2 (p. 4).

12 Nietzsche, *Birth of Tragedy*, sect. 15 (p. 73).

13 Weber, *From Max Weber*, p. 141.

14 Nietzsche, *Birth of Tragedy*, 'Self-Criticism', sect. 2 (p. 4).

15 See Nietzsche, *Birth of Tragedy*, sect. 12 (p. 58) on the distinction between Euripides as poet and as thinker.

16 Aron, 'Max Weber and Power-Politics', p. 85. See Max Weber, 'The National State and Economic Policy (Freiburg Address)', *Economy and Society*, 9 (4), 1980, pp. 428–9, pp. 436 and 438. It may be noted that Aron does not present this as an unequivocally Nietzschean text. For example, the concept of political struggle is initially articulated through Darwinian metaphors of adaptation and selection, and associated images of superior and inferior races.

17 Weber, 'Freiburg Address', pp. 436 and 438.

18 Weber, 'Freiburg Address', p. 437 (Weber's italics).

19 Weber, 'Freiburg Address', p. 438.

20 Weber, 'Freiburg Address', p. 439.

21 Weber, 'Freiburg Address', p. 437.

22 Weber, 'Freiburg Address', p. 437.

23 In a marginal note at the end of the unfinished essay 'Structures of Power' (*From Max Weber*, pp. 159–79), Weber notes that: 'There is a close connection between the prestige of culture and the prestige of power' (*From Max Weber*, p. 448).

24 Max Weber, 'Author's Introduction' to his *The Protestant Ethic and the Spirit of Capitalism*, London: Allen & Unwin, 1930, p. 13. Strictly this is not the introduction to the *Protestant Ethic* but to the series of essays that constitute the *Sociology of Religion*.

25 Christopher Janaway, 'Nietzsche, the Self, and Schopenhauer', in Keith Ansell-Pearson (ed.), *Nietzsche and Modern German Thought*, London and New York: Routledge, 1991.

26 Weber, 'Freiburg Address', p. 444.

27 Weber, 'Freiburg Address', p. 437.

28 Max Weber, 'The Meaning of "Ethical Neutrality" in Sociology and Economics', in his *The Methodology of the Social Sciences*, eds Edward A. Shils and Henry A. Finch, New York: Free Press, 1949, p. 18.

29 F. Nietzsche, *The Will to Power*, trans. Walter Kaufmann and R. J. Hollingdale, New York: Random House, 1967, section 46. 'The multitude and disgregation of impulses and the lack of any systematic order among them result in a "weak will": their coordination under a single predominant impulse results in a "strong will".'

30 See Max Weber, 'Politics as a Vocation', in his *From Max Weber*, pp. 120–1. On instrumental and value rationality, see *Economy and Society*, pp. 24–5.

31 Max Weber, '"Objectivity" in Social Science and Social Policy', in *Methodology*, p. 55.

32 Weber, *Economy and Society*, p. 499. Similarly in 'Structures of Power' Weber remarks that: 'By "intellectuals" we understand a group of men who by virtue of their peculiarity have special access to certain achievements considered to be "culture values", and who therefore usurp the leadership of a "culture community"' (Weber, *From Max Weber*, p. 176).

33 Weber, *Economy and Society*, pp. 500 ff.

34 Weber, 'Author's Introduction', p. 13.

35 Weber, *Rational and Social Foundations of Music*, p. 68. Weber gives the initial outline of these stages between pp. 66 and 69. Polyphony is discussed on pp. 68–76. The development of harmony is discussed on pp. 76–82. See pp. 79–

80 for Weber's discussion of heterophony, and thus the initial transition from predominantly melodic music to a concern with harmony. (It may be noted that the chapters and sub-divisions in the English text have been introduced, generally with great sensitivity, by the translators.)

36 Weber, *Rational and Social Foundations of Music*, p. 76. Similarly, of the type of polyphony developed by Bach, Weber notes that '[n]o other epoch and culture was familiar with it, not even . . . the Hellenes' (p. 69).

37 Weber, *Rational and Social Foundations of Music*, p. 82.

38 See Weber, *Rational and Social Foundations of Music*, pp. 82–8 on notation; pp. 107–17 on instrument design and development; p. 91 on the breakdown of the Church's control over music in the West.

39 Weber, *Rational and Social Foundations of Music*, pp. 61 and 41.

40 Max Weber, 'The Social Psychology of World Religions', in *From Max Weber*, pp. 267–301, p. 281.

41 Weber, *Rational and Social Foundations of Music*, p. 3. Similarly, Weber points to the irrationalities marked by the syntonic comma in the C major scale (p. 11).

42 Weber, *Rational and Social Foundations of Music*, p. 33.

43 Weber, *Rational and Social Foundations of Music*, p. 39.

44 See, for example, Weber, *Rational and Social Foundations of Music*, p. 12.

45 Weber, *Rational and Social Foundations of Music*, p. 9.

46 Weber, 'Science as a Vocation', p. 143.

47 Weber, 'Science as a Vocation', p. 144.

48 See, for example, Weber, *Rational and Social Foundations of Music*, p. 33.

49 Max Weber, 'Ethical Neutrality', pp. 28, 32, and 34.

50 Weber, 'Ethical Neutrality', p. 30. The distinctiveness of Western music is briefly outlined in terms of a music theory grounded in the primacy of fifth.

51 Weber, 'Ethical Neutrality', p. 31.

52 Weber, *Rational and Social Foundations of Music*, pp. 14 and 29–30.

53 See Weber, *Rational and Social Foundations of Music*, pp. 63 and especially 65, which suggests that it is precisely a concern for expression in Hellenic music that prevents it from shifting from melodic to harmonic thinking. See p. 68 on the goal of fullness of sound as providing the best explanation of Bantu music.

54 Weber, *Rational and Social Foundations of Music*, p. 82. This may be further grounded in the drive to develop techniques and explanations of modularization. The technical problem of modularization rests in and focuses the tension between harmonic and melodic ends.

55 Weber, *Rational and Social Foundations of Music*, p. 93.

56 Weber, 'Ethical Neutrality', p. 30.

57 Weber, 'Ethical Neutrality', pp. 26–7. See also p. 36, which suggests the subordination of at least elements of science (and by implication music theory) as 'fiction', 'useful for theoretical purposes'.

58 Nietzsche, *Birth of Tragedy*, pp. 22–3 and 32.

59 Nietzsche, *Birth of Tragedy*, p. 35.

60 See Nietzsche, *Birth of Tragedy*, p. 101–2.

61 Nietzsche, *Birth of Tragedy*, p. 45. I assume that Nietzsche's arguments in section 21 (pp. 99–104) relate back, and give context, to the analysis of tradegy in section 8.

62 Nietzsche, *Birth of Tragedy*, p. 115.

63 Nietzsche, *Birth of Tragedy*, p. 115.

64 Nietzsche, *Birth of Tragedy*, p. 34.
65 Nietzsche, *Birth of Tragedy*, p. 101.
66 See Nietzsche, *Birth of Tragedy*, p. 43.
67 Nietzsche, *Birth of Tragedy*, p. 16.
68 Nietzsche, *Birth of Tragedy*, p. 32.
69 Nietzsche, *Birth of Tragedy*, p. 80.
70 Nietzsche, *Birth of Tragedy*, p. 51.
71 Nietzsche, *Birth of Tragedy*, p. 84.
72 Nietzsche, *Birth of Tragedy*, p. 111.
73 Nietzsche, *Birth of Tragedy*, p. 32.
74 Benjamin Nelson, 'Max Weber's "Author's Introduction" (1920); a master clue to his main aims', *Sociological Inquiry*, 44 (4) 1974, pp. 269–78.

6
Kant's Doctrine of the Beautiful: Its Misinterpretation by Schopenhauer and Nietzsche

Martin Heidegger

At the outset, we know in a rough sort of way that just as "the true" determines our behavior in thinking and knowing, and just as "the good" determines the ethical attitude, so does "the beautiful" determine the aesthetic state.

What does Nietzsche say about the beautiful and about beauty? For the answer to this question also Nietzsche provides us with only isolated statements – proclamations, as it were – and references. Nowhere do we find a structured and grounded presentation. A comprehensive, solid understanding of Nietzsche's statements about beauty might result from study of Schopenhauer's aesthetic views; for in his definition of the beautiful Nietzsche thinks and judges by way of opposition and therefore of reversal. But such a procedure is always fatal if the chosen opponent does not stand on solid ground but stumbles about aimlessly. Such is the case with Schopenhauer's views on aesthetics, delineated in the third book of his major work, *The World as Will and Representation*. It cannot be called an aesthetics that would be even remotely comparable to that of Hegel. In terms of content, Schopenhauer thrives on the authors he excoriates, namely, Schelling and Hegel. The one he does not excoriate is Kant. Instead, he thoroughly misunderstands him. Schopenhauer plays the leading role in the preparation and genesis of that misunderstanding of Kantian aesthetics to which Nietzsche too fell prey and which is still quite common today. One may say that Kant's *Critique of Judgment*, the work in which he presents his aesthetics, has been influential up to now only on the basis of misunderstandings, a happenstance of no little significance for the history of philosophy. Schiller alone grasped some essentials in relation to Kant's doctrine of the beautiful; but his insight too was buried in the debris of nineteenth-century aesthetic doctrines.

The misunderstanding of Kant's aesthetics involves an assertion by Kant concerning the beautiful. Kant's definition is developed in sections 2–5 of *The Critique of Judgment*. What is "beautiful" is what purely and simply pleases. The beautiful is the object of "sheer" delight. Such delight, in which the beautiful opens itself up to us as beautiful, is in Kant's words "devoid of all interest." He says, "*Taste* is the capacity to judge an object or mode of representation by means of delight or revulsion, *devoid of all interest*. The object of such delight is called *beautiful*."[1]

Aesthetic behavior, i.e., our comportment toward the beautiful, is "delight devoid of all interest." According to the common notion, disinterestedness is indifference toward a thing or person: we invest nothing of our will in relation to that thing or person. If the relation to the beautiful, delight, is defined as "disinterested," then, according to Schopenhauer, the aesthetic state is one in which the will is put out of commission and all striving brought to a standstill; it is pure repose, simply wanting nothing more, sheer apathetic drift.

And Nietzsche? He says that the aesthetic state is rapture. That is manifestly the opposite of all "disinterested delight" and is therefore at the same time the keenest opposition to Kant's definition of our comportment toward the beautiful. With that in mind we understand the following observation by Nietzsche (XIV, 132): "Since Kant, all talk of art, beauty, knowledge, and wisdom has been smudged and besmirched by the concept 'devoid of interest.' " Since Kant? If this is thought to mean "through" Kant, then we have to say "No!" But if it is thought to mean since the Schopenhauerian misinterpretation of Kant, then by all means "Yes!" And for that reason Nietzsche's own effort too is misconceived.

But then what does Kant mean by the definition of the beautiful as the object of "disinterested" delight? What does "devoid of all interest" mean? "Interest" comes from the Latin *mihi interest*, something is of importance to me. To take an interest in something suggests wanting to have it for oneself as a possession, to have disposition and control over it. When we take an interest in something we put it in the context of what we intend to do with it and what we want of it. Whatever we take an interest in is always already taken, i.e., represented, with a view to something else.

Kant poses the question of the essence of the beautiful in the following way. He asks by what means our behavior, in the situation where we find something we encounter to be beautiful, must let itself be determined in such a way that we encounter the beautiful *as* beautiful. What is the determining ground for our finding something beautiful?

Before Kant says constructively what the determining ground is, and therefore what the beautiful itself is, he first says by way of refutation what never can and never may propose itself as such a ground, namely, an interest. Whatever exacts of us the judgment "This is beautiful" can never be an interest. That is to say, in order to find something beautiful, we must let what encounters us, purely as it is in itself, come before us in its own stature and worth. We may not take it into account in advance with a view to something else, our goals and intentions, our possible enjoyment and advantage. Comportment toward the beautiful as such, says Kant, is *unconstrained favoring*. We must freely grant to what encounters us as such its way to be; we must allow and bestow upon it what belongs to it and what it brings to us.

But now we ask, is this free bestowal, this letting the beautiful be what it is, a kind of indifference; does it put the will out of commission? Or is not such unconstrained favoring rather the supreme effort of our essential nature, the liberation of our selves for the release of what has proper worth in itself, only in order that we may have it purely? Is the Kantian "devoid of interest" a "smudging" and even a "besmirching" of aesthetic behavior? Or is it not the magnificent discovery and approbation of it?

The misinterpretation of the Kantian doctrine of "disinterested delight" consists in a double error. First, the definition "devoid of all interest," which Kant offers only in a preparatory and path-breaking way, and which in its very linguistic structure displays its negative character plainly enough, is given out as the single assertion (also held to be a positive assertion) by Kant on the beautiful. To the present day it is proffered as *the* Kantian interpretation of the beautiful. Second, the definition, misinterpreted in what it methodologically tries to achieve, at the same time is not thought in terms of the content that *remains* in aesthetic behavior when interest in the object falls away. The misinterpretation of "interest" leads to the erroneous opinion that with the exclusion of interest every essential relation to the object is suppressed. The opposite is the case. Precisely by means of the "devoid of interest" the essential relation to the object itself comes into play. The misinterpretation fails to see that now for the first time the object comes to the fore as pure object and that such coming forward into appearance is the beautiful. The word "beautiful" means appearing in the radiance of such coming to the fore.[2]

What emerges as decisive about the double error is the neglect of actual inquiry into what Kant erected upon a firm foundation with respect to the essence of the beautiful and of art. We will bring one example forward which shows how stubbornly the ostensibly self-evident misinterpretation of Kant during the nineteenth century still obtains today. Wilhelm Dilthey, who labored at the history of aesthetics with a passion unequaled by any of his contemporaries, remarked in 1887 (*Gesammelte Schriften* VI, 119) that Kant's statement concerning disinterested delight "is presented by Schopenhauer with special brilliance." The passage should read, "was fatally misinterpreted by Schopenhauer."

Had Nietzsche inquired of Kant himself, instead of trusting in Schopenhauer's guidance, then he would have had to recognize that Kant alone grasped the essence of what Nietzsche in his own way wanted to comprehend concerning the decisive aspects of the beautiful. Nietzsche could never have continued, in the place cited (XIV, 132), after the impossible remark about Kant, "In *my* view what is beautiful (observed historically) is what is visible in the most honored men of an era, as an expression of what is *most worthy* of honor." For just this – purely to honor what is of worth in its appearance – is for Kant the essence of the beautiful, although unlike Nietzsche he does not expand the meaning directly to all historical significance and greatness.

And when Nietzsche says (WM, 804), "*The* beautiful exists just as little as *the* good, *the* true," that too corresponds to the opinion of Kant.

But the purpose of our reference to Kant, in the context of an account of Nietzsche's conception of beauty, is not to eradicate the firmly rooted misinterpretation of the Kantian doctrine. It is to provide a possibility of grasping what Nietzsche himself says about beauty on the basis of its own original, historical context. That Nietzsche himself did not see the context draws a boundary line that he shares with his era and its relation to Kant and to German Idealism. It would be inexcusable for us to allow the prevailing misinterpretation of Kantian aesthetics to continue; but it would also be wrongheaded to try to trace Nietzsche's conception of beauty and the beautiful back to the Kantian. Rather, what we must now do is to allow Nietzsche's definition of the beautiful to sprout and flourish in its own soil – and in that way to see to what discordance it is transplanted.

Nietzsche too defines the beautiful as what pleases. But everything depends on the operative concept of pleasure and of what pleases as such. What pleases we take to be what corresponds to us, what speaks to us. What pleases someone, what speaks to him, depends on who that someone is to whom it speaks and corresponds. Who such a person is, is defined by what he demands of himself. Hence we call "beautiful" whatever corresponds to what we demand of ourselves. Furthermore, such demanding is measured by what we take ourselves to be, what we trust we are capable of, and what we dare as perhaps the extreme challenge, one we may just barely withstand.

In that way we are to understand Nietzsche's assertion about the beautiful and about the judgment by which we find something to be beautiful (WM, 852): "To pick up the scent of what would nearly finish us off if it were to confront us in the flesh, as danger, problem, temptation – this determines even our aesthetic 'yes.' ('That is beautiful' is an *affirmation*.)" So also with *The Will to Power*, number 819: "The firm, mighty, solid, the life that rests squarely and sovereignly and conceals its strength – that is what '*pleases*,' i.e., that corresponds to what one takes oneself to be."

The beautiful is what we find honorable and worthy, as the image of our essential nature. It is that upon which we bestow "unconstrained favor," as Kant says, and we do so from the very foundations of our essential nature and for its sake. In another place Nietzsche says (XIV, 134), "Such 'getting rid of interest and the ego' is nonsense and imprecise observation: on the contrary, it is the thrill that comes of being in *our* world now, of getting rid of our anxiety in the face of things foreign!" Certainly such "getting rid of interest" in the sense of Schopenhauer's interpretation is nonsense. But what Nietzsche describes as the thrill that comes of being in our world is what Kant means by the "pleasure of reflection." Here also, as with the concept of "interest," the basic Kantian concepts of "pleasure" and "reflection" are to be discussed in terms of the Kantian philosophical effort and its transcendental procedure, not flattened out with the help of everyday notions. Kant analyzes the essence of the "pleasure of reflection," as the basic comportment toward the beautiful, in *The Critique of Judgment*, sections 37 and 39.[3]

According to the quite "imprecise observation" on the basis of which Nietzsche conceives of the essence of interest, he would have to designate what Kant calls "unconstrained favoring" as an interest of the highest sort. Thus what Nietzsche demands of comportment toward the beautiful would be fulfilled from Kant's side. However, to the extent that Kant grasps more keenly the essence of interest and therefore excludes it from aesthetic behavior, he does not make such behavior indifferent; rather, he makes it possible for such comportment toward the beautiful object to be all the purer and more intimate. Kant's interpretation of aesthetic behavior as "pleasure of reflection" propels us toward a basic state of human being in which man for the first time arrives at the well-grounded fullness of his essence. It is the state that Schiller conceives of as the condition of the possibility of man's existence as historical, as grounding history.

According to the explanations by Nietzsche which we have cited, the beautiful is what determines us, our behavior and our capability, to the extent that we are claimed supremely in our essence, which is to say, to the extent that we ascend beyond ourselves. Such ascent beyond ourselves, to the full of our essential capability, occurs according to Nietzsche in rapture. Thus the beautiful is disclosed in rapture. The beautiful itself is what transports us into the feeling of rapture. From this elucidation of the essence of the beautiful the characterization of rapture, of the basic aesthetic state, acquires enhanced clarity. If the beautiful is what sets the standard for what we trust we are essentially capable of, then the feeling of rapture, as our relation to the beautiful, can be no mere turbulence and ebullition. The mood of rapture is rather an attunement in the sense of the supreme and most measured determinateness. However much Nietzsche's manner of speech and presentation sounds like Wagner's turmoil of feelings and sheer submergence in mere "experiences," it is certain that in this regard he wants to achieve the exact opposite. What is strange and almost incomprehensible is the fact that he tries to make his conception of the aesthetic state accessible to his contemporaries, and tries to convince them of it, by speaking the language of physiology and biology.

In terms of its concept, the beautiful is what is estimable and worthy as such. In connection with that, number 852 of *The Will to Power* says, "It is a question of *strength* (of an individual or a nation), *whether* and *where* the judgment 'beautiful' is made." But such strength is not sheer muscle power, a reservoir of "brachial brutality." What Nietzsche here calls "strength" is the capacity of historical existence to come to grips with and perfect its highest essential determination. Of course, the essence of "strength" does not come to light purely and decisively. Beauty is taken to be a "biological value":

> For consideration: the extent to which our value "beautiful" is completely anthropocentric: based on biological presuppositions concerning growth and progress –. ("Toward the Physiology of Art," no. 4)

> The fundament of all aesthetics [is given in] the general principle that aesthetic values rest on biological values, that aesthetic delights are biological delights. (XIV, 165)

That Nietzsche conceives of the beautiful "biologically" is indisputable. Yet the question remains what "biological," *bios*, "life," mean here. In spite of appearances created by the words, they do *not* mean what *biology* understands them to be.

NOTES

1 Immanuel Kant, *Kritik der Urteilskraft*. Akademieausgabe, B 16.
2 *Das Wort "schön" meint das Erscheinen im Schein solchen Vorscheins.* Although the words *schön* and *Schein* vary even in their oldest forms (see Hermann Paul, *Deutsches Wörterbuch*, 6th ed. [Tübingen, M. Niemeyer, 1966], pp. 537b f and 569b f), their meanings converge early on in the sense of the English words "shine" and "shining," related to the words "show," "showy." Perhaps the similar relationship between the words "radiate" and "radiant" comes closest to the German *Schein* and *Schön*. But it is not simply a matter of alliterative wordplay: the nexus of *schön* and *Schein* is, according to Heidegger, what Plato means by *ekphanestaton*; and if Nietzsche's task is to overturn Platonism, this issue must be near the very heart of the Heidegger–Nietzsche confrontation. On the relation of *Schein* and *schön* see also Martin Heidegger, "Hegel und die Griechen," in *Wegmarken*, pp. 262, 267, and elsewhere.
3 Neske prints §§ 57 and 59, but this is obviously an error: *die Lust am Schönen*, as *Lust der blossen Reflexion*, is not mentioned in § 57 or § 59, but *is* discussed indirectly in § 37 and explicitly in §39. See especially B 155.

7
Theories and Innovations in Nietzsche: Logic, Theory of Knowledge and Metaphysics

R. J. Hollingdale

Logic

Nietzsche was not a logician, but he did undertake a critique of logic in the sense of raising one specific objection to the claims normally made on its behalf. This objection is worth considering in a little detail, since, whatever value it may have for the science of logic, it adds a dimension to our picture of Nietzsche himself and his attitude towards thought and truth.

Let us recall his assertion that 'nothing is "given" as real except our world of desires and passions' and that 'we can rise or sink to no other "reality" than the reality of our drives – for thinking is only the relationship of these drives to one another' (*BGE*, 36). This assessment of the relation between thought and the 'drives' is repeated elsewhere, and is in general Nietzsche's view of the matter: it is stated, for example, in a note of the winter of 1887–8 which refers to the 'misunderstanding of passion and *reason*, as if the latter were an independent entity and not rather a relationship between different passions and desires; and as if every passion did not have in it its quantum of reason' (*WP*, 387). A similar conclusion had already been drawn in *The Gay Science*, where the 'course of logical thought and inference in our present brain' is said to correspond 'to an operation and struggle of drives which are all in themselves individually very illogical and unjust' (*GS*, 111). Such a view of the nature of thought conflicts with any idea involving its objective validity: it abolishes the 'faculty' of thought altogether, and thus calls in question the objective validity of the 'science of reasoning', logic.

A long and very interesting note published as section 516 of *The Will to Power*, starting from a criticism of the Aristotelian 'law of contradiction', concludes by denying that logic has anything at all to do with truth. 'We are incapable of affirming and denying one and the same thing: this is a subjective law drawn from experience, it does not express any "necessity" *but only an incapacity*': this is the basic objection. If, as Aristotle says, the law of contradiction 'is the most certain of all principles . . . then one should consider all the more strictly what assertions it already *presupposes*'. Either 'it is supposed to assert something in regard to reality, to being, as if one already knew this from another source: namely that antithetical predicates *cannot* be ascribed to it', or 'that antithetical predicates *ought not* to be ascribed to it': in the latter case 'logic would be an imperative, *not* to knowledge of what is true, but to the positing and arrangement [*Zurechtmachung*] of a world *which we shall call true*'. The question at issue is: 'are logical axioms adequate to reality, or are they standards and means for us to *create* the real, the concept "reality"?' In order to affirm the first alternative, one would have 'to know being already, which is certainly not the case'; consequently, the law of contradiction 'contains no *criterion of truth*, but is an *imperative* in regard to that which *ought* to count as true'. Logical axioms, in fact, in so far as they are assumed to possess objective validity, repose upon a metaphysical view of the world: every law of logic and mathematics presupposes a 'self-identical A', the substratum of which is inevitably a 'thing': '*our belief in things* is the presupposition of the belief in logic'. But a 'thing' is, as Nietzsche never wearies of insisting, a construct, and if we do not grasp that fact but 'make of logic a criterion of *true being*, we are already on the road to positing as realities all those hypostases substance, predicate, object, subject, action, etc.: that is to say, to conceiving a metaphysical world'. The 'most primitive acts of thought' affirmation and denial, 'holding for true and holding for not true', are already dominated by the belief that our judgments correspond with what is true in itself; but, since thoughts are a product of sensations, this belief amounts to a belief that 'sensations teach us *truths* about things'. This belief is at least questionable; quite apart from the fact that the foundation of the law of contradiction – 'I cannot have two antithetical sensations simultaneously' – is '*quite crude and false*'. The fact of the matter is that logic, like geometry and arithmetic, 'applies only to *fictitious entities which we have created*. Logic is the attempt to comprehend the real world by means of a scheme of being we ourselves have posited: more correctly, to render it formulatable and calculable to us'.

Logic thus 'rests on presuppositions with which nothing in the actual world corresponds' (*HA*, 11); 'reality does not appear' in logic or in 'that applied logic, mathematics' at all, 'not even as a problem' (*T*, II. 3). 'Logic is fastened to the condition: assuming there are identical cases. In fact, for logical thought and inference to be possible, this condition must first be imagined as fulfilled; that is to say: the will to *logical truth* can successfully assert itself only after a fundamental *falsification* of all events has been assumed' (*WP*, 512). We have at present a 'subjective compulsion to believe in logic', but this compulsion only reveals that 'long before logic itself entered our consciousness, we did nothing but introduce its postulates into events': it is we 'who have created the "thing", subject, predicate, act, object, substance, form, after we had long been engaged on '*making* identical, *making* crude and simple' (*WP*, 521). Logic is thus the 'science' of a fictitious world created by man and believed to be true. Why was it created? Because a 'logical' world, a 'calculable' world, is useful (*WP*, 507), or answers 'physiological demands' (*BGE*, 3). It may even be that the ability for '*making* identical, *making* crude and simple' was once a decisive factor in natural selection:

> He who . . . did not know how to discover the 'identical' sufficiently often in regard to food or to animals hostile to him, he who was thus too slow to subsume, too cautious in subsuming, had a smaller probability of survival than he who in the case of every similarity at once conjectured identity. But it was the prevailing tendency to treat the similar at once as identical, an illogical tendency – for nothing is identical – which first created all the foundations of logic. (*GS*, 111)

The 'logical' view may even be a 'condition of human life' (*BGE*, 4). Moreover, through the fictions of logic one *dominates* reality: '*the will to make equivalent is the will to power*' (*WP*, 511).

The theory that the categories of reason are fictions, and are recognized as such, does not, however, for Nietzsche carry with it the corollary that they should be set aside (even if that were possible): for logical fictions are *necessary*. That, indeed, is why they were brought into existence; and while you may recognize that an error is an error, you ought not to condemn it simply on that account, for it may be a necessary error – necessary, that is, for the preservation and enhancement of mankind:

> The falseness of a judgment is to us not necessarily an objection to a judgment. . . . The question is to what extent it is life-advancing, life-preserving, species-preserving, perhaps even species-breeding; and our fundamental tendency is to assert that the falsest judgments . . . are the most indispensable to us, that without granting

as true the fictions of logic, without measuring reality against the purely invented world of the unconditional and self-identical, without a continual falsification of the world by means of numbers, mankind could not live – that to renounce false judgments would be to renounce life, would be to deny life. (*BGE*, 4)

Theory of Knowledge

In some remote corner . . . of the universe there was once a star on which clever animals invented knowledge. It was the most arrogant and mendacious moment of 'universal history': but only a moment. Nature took but a few breaths and the star grew cold; and the clever animals had to die. – Someone might invent such a fable as this and yet still not have illustrated well enough how pitiful, how shadowy and fleeting, how aimless and capricious the human intellect appears within nature. There were eternities in which it did not exist; when it has gone again nothing will have happened. For there exists for that intellect no mission extending beyond the life of man.

Here, at the beginning of an unfinished and unpublished essay of 1873, 'On Truth and Falsehood in an Extra-Moral Sense', is the essence of what was also Nietzsche's final attitude towards the nature of human knowledge: it is before all else an *instrument*, designed in accordance with, and limited to the satisfaction of human needs. In the sense in which philosophers are accustomed to use the word, therefore, there is *no* 'knowledge'.

The consequences of this fact permeate the published works, especially the later ones; the grounds by which it is established are confined largely to the posthumously published notebooks, and *The Will to Power* contains very many epistemological speculations which have no parallel in the published books. In so far as failure to publish a line of speculation indicates in general that Nietzsche was not yet satisfied with it, we must say that he never arrived at a formal 'theory of knowledge'; but his thinking on this subject is unmistakable, and can be detected at every stage of his development; so that, in this case, it seems that the unpublished notes served to clarify to his own mind and bring clearly into the open that which was presupposed in much of what he had already published. If we too avail ourselves of this explicit clarification we can present Nietzsche's 'theory of knowledge' briefly and in an orderly fashion.

The world is in a constant state of change: in philosophical jargon, it is 'becoming' and not 'being'. But a 'becoming' world cannot be 'known'. This is the conceptual basis of Nietzsche's denial of the possibility of knowledge: we can 'know' only the simulacra of being which we ourselves have constructed.

> Continual transitions forbid us to speak of an 'individual' etc.; the 'number' of beings is itself in flux. We would know nothing of time or of motion if we did not, in a crude fashion, believe we observed 'that which is at rest' beside 'that which is in motion'. The same applies to cause and effect, and without the erroneous conception of 'empty space' we would never have arrived at the conception of space. The law of identity has as its background the 'appearance' that there are identical things. A world in a state of becoming could not in a strict sense be 'comprehended' or 'known'; only in so far as the 'comprehending' and 'knowing' intellect discovers a crude ready-made world put together out of nothing but appearances, but appearances which, to the extent that they are of the kind that have preserved life, have become firm – only to this extent is there anything like 'knowledge': i.e. a measuring of earlier and later errors by one another. (*WP*, 520)

Thinking itself is possible only on the basis of an 'assumption of beings . . . logic deals only with formulas for that which remains the same': but this assumption 'belongs to our perspectives'. Because 'the world in a state of becoming' is 'unformulatable', and 'knowledge and becoming exclude one another', 'knowledge' must be something other than knowledge: 'there must first be a will to make knowable, a kind of becoming must itself create the *illusion of beings*' (*WP*, 517).

Knowledge is 'not "to know" but to schematize – to impose upon chaos as much regularity and form as suffices for our practical requirements'; in the evolution of reason what was decisive was 'the requirement, not to "know", but to subsume, to schematize, for the purpose of intelligibility and calculation'; the evolution of reason is 'adaptation [*Zurechtmachung*], invention, in order to produce similarity, identity – the same process every sense impression goes through' (*WP*, 515). Knowledge, again, is 'a *determining, designating, making-conscious of conditions* (*not* a *fathoming* of entities, things, "things in themselves")' (*WP*, 555); and this is true of all knowledge, deductive as well as empirical: 'An illusion that something is *known* when we possess a mathematical formula for an event: it has only been *designated, described*; nothing more!' (*WP*, 628). In brief: 'The whole apparatus of knowledge is an apparatus for abstraction and simplification – directed, not at knowledge, but at obtaining possession of things: "end" and "means" are as remote from its essence as are "concepts". With "end" and "means" one obtains possession of the process (– one *invents* a process which is graspable), with "concepts", however, of the "things" which constitute the process' (*WP*, 503).

This conception of the nature of knowledge is repeated and reformulated scores of times, and we need not labour it further. Out of it emerge all his other suggestions as to why the 'knowledge' we have is of the kind it is and not of some other kind – suggestions which would be redundant if our 'knowledge' of reality and the nature of reality coincided. Since 'there are no facts', all knowledge of facts is interpretation, 'introduction of meaning – *not* "explanation"' (*WP*, 604): and the attempt to discover what we know thus resolves itself into an attempt to discover why we interpret as we do.

One line of investigation begins from the necessity we are under to think in words, and the illusion this gives us that a word is an explanation: 'man has for long ages believed in the concepts and names of things as in *aeternae veritates* . . . he really thought that in language he possessed knowledge of the world. The sculptor of language was not so modest as to believe that he was only giving things designations, he conceived rather that with words he was expressing supreme knowledge of things' (*HA*, 11). Words are also the chief agents in our construction of 'facts', that is to say the imposition of 'being' on the flux of 'becoming': through words and the concepts formed from them we are 'continually tempted to think of things as being simpler than they are, as separated from one another, as indivisible, each existing in and for itself' (*WS*, 11). And the structure into which all our words are fitted, that is to say grammar, fixes in advance according to what scheme our thinking as a whole will be directed – which explains the 'singular family resemblance between all Indian, Greek and German philosophizing . . . Where, thanks to a common . . . grammar . . . there exists a language affinity it is quite impossible to avoid everything being prepared in advance for a similar evolution and succession of philosophical systems: just as the road seems to be barred to certain other possibilities of world interpretation' (*BGE*, 20).

The basis of *our* grammar, Nietzsche insists, is the subject–predicate relationship. The consequence of introducing this relationship into all our thinking is that we impose the idea of subject and object, deed and doer, on to the world itself: 'In every judgment there lies the entire, full, profound belief in subject and predicate or in cause and effect (namely, as the assertion that every effect is an activity and that every activity presupposes an agent)' (*WP*, 550). The cause of the relationship itself is our belief in the existence of the ego, of an 'I' which we are, and which is the primal 'subject' and causal agent: ' "Subject", "object", "predicate" – these distinctions are *created* and are now imposed as a schematism upon all apparent facts. The fundamental false observation is that I believe it is *I* who do something, suffer something, "have" something, who "have" a quality' (*WP*, 549). But the ego is, as here indicated, an error; it is indeed the simplest and most primitive 'assumption of being': but, through becoming the basis of language construction, it leads ineluctably to the most comprehensive of all such assumptions: 'I fear we are not getting rid of God because we still believe in grammar', the reason being that language 'sees everywhere deed and doer . . . believes in the "ego", in the ego as being, in the ego as substance, and . . . *projects* its belief in the ego-substance on to all things – only thus does it *create* the concept "thing" . . . Being is everywhere thought in, *foisted on*, as cause; it is only from the conception "ego" that there follows, derivatively, the concept "being" (*T*, III. 5). 'Things' are projections of the ego as causal agent, and God is only the biggest 'thing'.

When he seeks to penetrate further and discover why this initial assumption of an ego is made, Nietzsche discovers it in physiology, in the life-forms of the races of man: 'the spell of definite grammatical functions is in the last resort the spell of *physiological* value judgments and racial conditions' (*BGE*, 20). The kind of knowledge we possess is determined by what we are physically, and 'it is improbable that our "knowledge" should extend further than what exactly suffices for the preservation of life' (*WP*, 494). We 'know' precisely what we need to 'know' for our survival: 'we have . . . no organ whatever for *knowledge*, for "truth": we "know" . . . precisely as much as may be *useful* in the interest of the human herd, the species.' Naturally, we do not necessarily 'know' correctly even that which is really 'useful' to us: 'what is here called "utility" is . . . perhaps precisely that fatal piece of stupidity through which we shall one day perish' (*GS*, 354).

With which observation we are back with the thought that the 'clever animal' which invented knowledge 'had to die', and that when the human intellect has gone again 'nothing will have happened'.

Metaphysics

Nietzsche wanted to be a phenomenalist, and you fail to appreciate a whole dimension of his greatness unless you see that his philosophy is at heart a phenomenalism. But his antecedents again and again undermined his capacity to fulfil this desire, and he remained until the end and against his will a writer of metaphysics. Or perhaps it was his artistic nature, which wanted to produce powerful effects, which continually pushed him back into metaphysics. An account of Nietzsche as a phenomenalist – or, better, an edition which excised everything that was not strict phenomenalism – would contain the hard core of his philosophy, including his ethical philosophy, which is an attempt at a phenomenalism of morals, but almost all the 'poetry', almost everything pertaining to him as 'the lyrist of cognition', would be gone, and with it a great part of his 'influence'.

Philosophy is not exactly a majority interest, and there is no reason it should be; but even the minority who do read the subject are for the most part attracted to it by the same force which attracts them to *art*: philosophy which possesses no affective content is really philosophy for professionals, for men and women who specialize in it as a livelihood or are committed amateurs, and there is no more reason it should have any popular following than that the study of the properties of elastic gases and fluids ('pneumatics') should have such a following.

Recall how Nietzsche, according to his own account, was attracted to philosophy: he bought *The World as Will and Idea* and allowed the 'energetic and gloomy genius' of Schopenhauer to 'operate upon me . . . Here I saw a mirror in which I beheld the world, life and my own nature in a terrifying grandeur . . . here I saw sickness and health, exile and refuge, Hell and Heaven' (*Retrospect of My Two Years at Leipzig*). If this has in it the ring of truth, as it surely does have, is that not because it is, in all essentials, an account of how most of us were first attracted to philosophy? But if the name of, say, Beethoven, were substituted for that of Schopenhauer, would it not still ring true? It is an affective response to a work of art which is being described – the work of art in this instance being a metaphysical philosophy. This seems to me no accident: I would even go so far as to say that it is metaphysics which has hitherto recruited philosophers, and has made of philosophy a subject of 'general interest' which has been studied by non-professionals in the same way as music is studied by people who have no intention of becoming professional musicians.

Now, it was part of Nietzsche's complex attitude towards art to suggest that artists are falsifiers, in the sense that art is a means of disguising the real nature of existence; and in so far as metaphysics is art it is open to the same objection: that is why Nietzsche wanted to get past metaphysics. But, at the same time, metaphysics supplied him with an outlet for the side of his nature which could be satisfied only with artistic expression: and so, until the end of his active life, and perhaps sometimes without being fully aware of it, he continued to express ideas which have to be called metaphysical.

I will give two examples of Nietzsche writing metaphysics after 1876, when he had in intention turned away from it. The first is the passage written in 1885 and printed by the editors of *The Will to Power* as the last section of the book (1067): a rhapsody on universal 'will to power':

And do you know what 'the world' is to me? Shall I show it to you in my mirror? This world: a monster of energy, without beginning, without end; an immovable, brazen enormity of energy, which does not grow bigger or smaller, which does not expend itself but only transforms itself; as a whole of unalterable size, a household without expenses or losses, but likewise without increase or income; enclosed by 'nothingness' as by a boundary; not something flowing away or squandering itself, not something endlessly extended, but as a definite quantity of energy set in a definite space, and not a space that might be 'empty' here or there, but rather as energy throughout, as a play of energies and waves of energy at the same time one and many, increasing here and at the same time decreasing there; a sea of energies flowing and rushing together, eternally moving, eternally flooding back, with tremendous years of recurrence, with an ebb and a flood of its forms; out of the simplest form striving towards the most complex, out of the stillest, most rigid, coldest form towards the hottest, most turbulent, most self-contradictory, and then out of this abundance returning home to the simple, out of the play of contradiction back to the joy of unison, still affirming itself in this uniformity of its courses and its years, blessing itself as that which must return eternally, as a becoming that knows no repletion, no satiety, no weariness –: this my *Dionysian* world of the eternally self-creative, the eternally self-destructive, this mystery-world of the twofold delight, this my 'beyond good and evil', without aim, unless the joy of the circle is itself an aim; without will, unless a ring feels goodwill towards itself – do you want a *name* for this world? A *solution* for all your riddles? A *light* for you too, you best concealed, strongest, least dismayed, most midnight men? – *This world is the will to power – and nothing beside!* And you yourself are also this will to power – and nothing beside!

This is only an unpublished note; yet it was not something hastily thrown off and forgotten, for it replaces an earlier, erased excursus on the same theme. What does it mean? What, even if we ignore and discount the 'poetic' form of delivery as a piece of self-indulgence, does it mean to say that the 'world' is 'will to power'? *Whose* power? Power over *what*? Or, if these questions are misdirected, what is 'power' intended to mean? Energy, in the sense in which we speak of 'electrical power'? If so, what does 'will' mean? Not, certainly, a 'drive' or a 'complex of drives and emotions', since the detection of these phenomena would indicate that the 'world' is an organism, which is patently not what is meant by a 'sea of energies flowing and rushing together'. Or, if these questions too are misguided, what is there in this passage which could be verified or disproved? Is it not the kind of utterance which is neither true nor false, but rather a release of an internal tension, like 'Yippee!'? Finally, if the phrase 'the world' in this passage were, wherever it occurs, replaced by 'the last movement of the *Hammerklavier* sonata', or by 'the process of combustion', or by any phrase designating something characterized by the appearance of energetic action, would the sense of the passage as a piece of description suffer in any way? In other words, is it not a description of *the appearance of energetic action* itself, and of no other specific thing? In short, the passage seems to possess no specific meaning of the kind obviously intended. What it *sounds* like is a description of Schopenhauer's undifferentiated 'will' as the ground of being with mental images evoked by the word 'power' added to it: in other words, an extension, impermissible to Nietzsche, of the will to power beyond the realm of phenomena into the word-intoxicated realm of metaphysics.

The second example is his persistent worrying of the ancient problem of appearance and reality. For the sake of his theory of knowledge and critique of logic, he needs the postulate that 'being is an empty fiction' (*T*, III. 2), and he rightly sees as a corollory to this that 'the "apparent" world is the only real one' (ibid.); what he does not see, apparently, is that the distinction between 'being' and 'becoming', and between 'appearance' and 'reality', is altogether irrelevant to the phenomenalism to which he had, in intention, committed himself when he repudiated metaphysics. Moreover, for all his continuing concern with this metaphysical problem, he never seriously considers whether the solution to it he discovered at the age of twenty was in any way inadequate: so far as I can see, he never subjected it to the slightest critical inspection. The solution in question comes from F. A. Lange's *History of Materialism*, which Nietzsche first read in 1866 and subsequently recommended as a work offering great enlightenment. Lange argues that all knowledge is knowledge of the phenomenal (apparent) world – the fact of our knowing a thing being the proof that that thing is a phenomenon – and that consequently all the ideas we have, including the ideas of a dichotomy between an apparent and a real world and the content of that real world, can only be phenomena. Nietzsche accepted this argument and repeated it, in differing formulations, again and again throughout the remainder of his life: 'The "real world", however it has been conceived of hitherto – it has always been the apparent world *once more*' (*WP*, 566), he wrote in a note of the winter of 1887–8, and this formulation may stand as a paradigm of all the others. Now this 'proof' is no more than the assertion that we cannot *imagine* a 'real' world that does not turn out to be the world we know once more: it does not touch upon the question whether a 'real' world might not be a necessary postulate even if we cannot imagine what it might be like. Fundamentally, Nietzsche realizes this, but he has no interest in emphasizing it because all his interest is directed towards asserting the limitation of our knowledge to knowledge of phenomena and then to decrying as instances of 'world-denial' and 'decadence' all attempts to establish the existence of anything beyond or behind phenomena: 'To talk about "another" world than this is quite pointless, provided that an instinct for slandering, disparaging and accusing life is not strong within us: in the latter case we *revenge* ourselves on life by means of the phantasmagoria of "another", a "better" life . . . To divide the world into a "real" and an "apparent" world . . . is only a suggestion of *décadence* – a symptom of *declining* life' (*T*, III. 6). This is all very well as far as it goes, but it does not go nearly far enough. To reduce the problem of appearance and reality to a psychological (or physiological) problem is to do no more than trifle with it: the question whether, aside from the *motive* one may have for believing in the existence of a 'real' world, reason does or does not *compel* us to posit some such thing, is not even touched upon: and the reason Nietzsche halts at this problem with a solution he discovered ready-made when he was hardly out of his teens is, I think, that he had ceased to be interested in metaphysics and could not be bothered to give much serious thought to what had come to seem to him irrelevant issues. What Lange's argument really establishes (if you go along with it) is a basis for an exclusive occupation with phenomenalism – not because everything is proved to be phenomenon, but because within this discipline the dichotomy of 'appearance' and 'reality' no longer plays any role. If Nietzsche grasped this, determined to devote himself to phenomenalism, but was against his will diverted from this path back on to that of metaphysics, the unsatisfactory character of his speculations about reality and appearance would be explained.

There is a parallel between Nietzsche's development in this regard and the historical scheme of Comte. According to Comte, mankind began by explaining phenomena theologically (in terms of the operations of gods and spirits), moved on to metaphysical explanations (in terms of impersonal essences and faculties), and finally arrived at phenomenalism (explanation as the description of the relations between phenomena). This course, whether or not it represents a valid account of human intellectual evolution, certainly describes Nietzsche's: one might call him a 'classic case' of the progression from theology to metaphysics to phenomenalism. It is because this is so – because this progression is so marked that even his backslidings into metaphysics cannot obscure it – that a determination to see him as a front-line Protestant theologian, or as the 'last metaphysician of the the West' who demonstrated the impossibility of metaphysics, while it may bring out and highlight some very interesting aspects of him, is a falsification of him as a whole.

NOTES

All references are given by section numbers, which are the same in all editions of Nietzsche's works (including translations).

Key to abbreviations

Human, All Too Human (HA).
The Wanderer and His Shadow (WS).
The Gay Science (GS).
Beyond Good and Evil (BGE).
Twilight of the Idols (T).
The Will to Power (WP).

The relevant pasage from 'On Truth and Lie in an Extra-Moral Sense' can be found in *The Viking Portable Nietzsche*, trans. Walter Kaufmann (London: Chatto & Windus, 1971/New York: Penguin, 1976); also translated as 'On Truth and Lies in a Non-Moral Sense', in *Philosophy and Truth: Selections from Nietzsche's Notebooks of the Early 1870's*, trans. D. Breazeale (New Jersey: Humanities Press, 1979).

8
Nietzsche's Attitude toward Socrates

Walter Kaufmann

... received the decisive thought as to how a philosopher ought to behave toward men from the apology of Socrates: as their physician, as a gadfly on the neck of man.

IV, 404

Nietzsche's attitude toward Socrates is a focal point of his thought and reflects his views of reason and morality as well as the image of man he envisaged. His critics and interpreters have been persistently preoccupied with his critique of Socrates, and it has become a dogma, unquestioned and unexamined, that Nietzsche repudiated Socrates. At best, it is admitted that his attitude was "ambiguous.' What is needed is an examination of all passages in which Nietzsche discusses Socrates as well as some in which Socrates is not named outright. Such a study leads to a new understanding of *The Birth of Tragedy* and of *Ecce Homo,* and it throws new light on Nietzsche's entire philosophy, from his first book to his last. It gives a concrete illustration, sadly lacking in the voluminous Nietzsche literature, of his dialectic; it brings to light the unequaled impact on his mind of the irony and ceaseless questioning of Socrates; and it shows how Nietzsche, for whom Socrates was allegedly "a villain,"[1] modeled his conception of his own task largely after Socrates' apology.

I

The prevalent impression of Nietzsche's attitude toward Socrates depends partly on a misconstruction of his first book, which was written,

124 *Walter Kaufmann*

for the most part, during the Franco-Prussian War and published in 1872. Its origin is thus reminiscent of that of Hegel's first book, the *Phenomenology*, which was completed in Jena in 1806 while the French took the city. *The Birth of Tragedy* also resembles Hegel's work in its fundamentally dialectical conception. Though Nietzsche's uneven style brings out the negative and critical note most strongly, he was not primarily "for" or "against": he tried to comprehend. In a general way, his dialectic appears in his attitude toward his heroes. Like Oscar Wilde, he thought that "all men kill the thing they love" – even that they should kill it. Thus he explained his love of *Carmen* by calling attention to "Don José's last cry on which the work ends: 'Yes! *I* have killed her. *I* – my adored Carmen!' Such a conception of love (the only one worthy of a philosopher) is rare: it raises a work of art above thousands" (W 2). We find no similar commentary on *Othello* – but it is against this background that we must understand Nietzsche's great admiration for Shakespeare's portrait of Brutus.

> Independence of the soul – that is at stake here! No sacrifice can then be too great: even one's dearest friend one must be willing to sacrifice for it, though he be the most glorious human being, embellishment of the world, genius without peer. (FW 98)

Friedrich Gundolf has pointed out, in two books on Caesar and on Shakespeare, that Nietzsche read his own "sacrifice" of Wagner into this drama. Nietzsche's relationship to Wagner, however, is merely the most striking instance of his dialectic. He pictured the second, negative, stage of his own development and of any quest for independence and freedom – as a deliberate renunciation of all one has previously worshiped: old friends and values are given up in a "twilight of the idols" (XVI, 37). If one considers Nietzsche's attitude toward Schopenhauer, one finds the same break: the Brutus crisis. The category "What Nietzsche Hated"[2] is thus inadequate; and we shall now see how the inclusion of Socrates in it is quite untenable.

In *The Birth of Tragedy*, Socrates is introduced as a demigod, the equal of Dionysus and Apollo, man and myth at once. Nietzsche has propounded his thesis of the origin of Greek tragedy out of the "Dionysian" and the "Apollinian"; he has described the great dramas of Aeschylus and Sophocles, and finally the Euripidean attack on these giants. "Euripides, too, was . . . a mask only: the deity who spoke out of him was not Dionysus, nor Apollo, but . . . Socrates" (GT 12). While Socrates is pictured, in the following pages, as the embodiment of that rationalism which superseded tragedy, his superhuman dignity is emphasized throughout. Reverently, Nietzsche speaks of the "logical urge" of Socrates: ". . . in its unbridled flood it displays a natural power such as we encounter to our awed amazement only in the very greatest instinctive forces" (13). He speaks of sensing "even a breath of that divine naïveté and assurance of the Socratic direction of life" and of the "dignified seriousness with which he everywhere emphasized his divine calling, even before his judges" (13). Nor have there been many since Plato who have described Socrates' death with more loving poetry:

> That he was sentenced to death, not exile, Socrates himself seems to have brought about with perfect awareness and without any natural awe of death. He went to his death with the calm with which, according to Plato's description, he leaves the Symposium at dawn, the last of the revelers, to begin a new day, while on the benches and on the earth his drowsy table companions remain behind to dream of Socrates, the true eroticist. (13)

Nietzsche's conception of Socrates was decisively shaped by Plato's *Symposium*[3] and *Apology*, and Socrates became little less than an idol for him. To reconcile this patent fact with the established notion that Nietzsche's attitude was hateful, some of the more careful students of Nietzsche's work have postulated a distinction between "Socratism," which he is then said to have detested, and the personality of Socrates himself.[4] Some such distinction is indeed required – but its validity depends on the definition of Socratism; and the view that Nietzsche merely admired the man Socrates while hating the outlook he embodied is untenable. Even a cursory inspection of § 15 of *The Birth of Tragedy* shows this quite conclusively – and this section marks the climax and conclusion of Nietzsche's long analysis of the problem of Socrates. The original manuscript ended with § 15; the remainder of the work, which consists of the "timely" application of the previous analysis to Wagner's work, was – as Nietzsche later regretted (GT-V) – added as an afterthought.[5] Nevertheless, interpreters have almost invariably ignored § 15 – and on this depends not only Brinton's construction but also Morgan's: "*The Birth of Tragedy* not only formulates the antinomy between knowledge and life: it presages Nietzsche's solution . . . suggesting that the antagonism between Socratism and art may not be necessary."[6] Actually, Nietzsche starts out with the antithesis of the Dionysian and the Apollinian; and their synthesis is found in tragic art. Then Socrates is introduced as the antithesis of tragic art. The antagonism is not one which "may not be necessary." Rather, Nietzsche persistently concerned himself with what he accepted as necessary; and because Socratism seemed necessary to him – he affirmed it. Like Hegel, Nietzsche sought to comprehend phenomena in their necessary sequence; that is part of the significance of his *amor fati*.

In fact, Nietzsche asks explicitly: "Perhaps art is even a necessary corollary and supplement of science?" (GT 14). In the next sentence, he replies: "it must now be said how the influence of Socrates . . . again and again prompts a regeneration of *art*" (15). Far from merely presaging a solution, Nietzsche then tries systematically to show how the "sublime metaphysical delusion" of Socrates is that very instinct which leads science ever again to its own limits – at which it must necessarily give way to art. Socratism – i.e., the rationalistic tendency – was not arbitrarily injected into the Greek mind by Socrates; it was "already effective before Socrates" and "only gained in him an indescribably magnificent expression" (14). What – Nietzsche asks in the end – would have happened to mankind *without* Socratism? He finds

> in Socrates the one turning point . . . of world history. For if one were to think of this whole incalculable sum of energy . . . as *not* employed in the service of knowledge, . . . then the instinctive lust for life would probably have been so weakened in general wars of annihilation . . . that suicide would have become a general custom, and individuals might have experienced the final remnant of a sense of duty when . . . strangling their parents and friends. (15)

This is the final vision of *The Birth of Tragedy* – except for the appended application to Wagnerian opera. Unrestrained pessimism would not only fail to produce great art, but it would lead to race suicide. The Socratic heritage, the elemental passion for knowledge, must "by virtue of its own infinity guarantee the infinity" and continuation of art (15).

In the picture of the "theoretical man" who dedicates his life to the pursuit of truth, Nietzsche pays homage to the "dignity" of Socrates. At the same time his own features mingle with those of his ideal (15). Socratism is the antithesis of tragedy, but Nietzsche asks "whether the birth of an 'artistic Socrates' is altogether a contradiction in terms" (14), and nobody has ever found a better characterization of Nietzsche himself. At the end of section 15 we find another self-portrait: "the *Socrates who practices music*." In Nietzsche's first book as in his last, Socrates is criticized but still *aufgehoben* in – still part of – the type Nietzsche most admires.

Here is Nietzsche's own estimate of *The Birth of Tragedy*:

> It smells offensively Hegelian, and the cadaverous perfume of Schopenhauer sticks only to a few formulas. An "idea" – the antith-

esis of the Dionysian and the Apollinian – translated into the realm of metaphysics; history itself as the development of this "idea"; in tragedy this antithesis is *aufgehoben* into a unity; and in this perspective things that had never before faced each other are suddenly juxtaposed, used to illuminate each other, and *comprehended* [*begriffen*]. (EH-GT 1)[7]

In the summer of 1872, in 1873, and in 1876, Nietzsche, then a professor at the University of Basel, lectured on "The Pre-Platonic Philosophers." His lectures (IV, 245–364) substantiate what has here been said about his attitude toward Socrates. First of all, the significant conception of the "pre-*Platonic*" philosophers (which so pointedly includes Socrates) has been unjustifiably ignored in Oehler's book on *Nietzsche and the Pre-Socratics*; and practically all later interpreters have relied on Oehler's account of Nietzsche's relation to the ancient Greeks. The only English book that gives a detailed account of Nietzsche's "connection with Greek literature and thought" even goes to the extent of rechristening the lectures altogether, refering to them as *The Pre-Socratics*.[8]

Actually, Nietzsche quite specifically includes Socrates: "Socrates is the last one in this line" (1). In his lecture on Heraclitus, Nietzsche says further that three of the pre-Platonics embody the "purest types: Pythagoras, Heraclitus, Socrates – the sage as religious reformer, the sage as proud and lonely truth-finder, and the sage as the eternally and everywhere seeking one" (1). One may suspect that Nietzsche must have felt a special kinship to the ever seeking Socrates. In any case, the lecture on Socrates leaves little doubt about this self-identification. Socrates is celebrated as "the first philosopher of *life* [*Lebensphilosoph*]": "Thought serves life, while in all previous philosophers life served thought and knowledge" (17). Even then, Nietzsche was writing his "untimely" essay on the 'Use and Disadvantage of History for Life." Written in 1873, it appeared in 1874.

His admiration for Socrates, however, prevented him no more than the Platonic Alcibiades from stressing the physical ugliness of Socrates no less than his plebeian descent. His flat nose and thick lips, and his alleged admission that nature had endowed him with the fiercest passions, are all emphasized on the page preceding the praise of the *Lebensphilosoph*.[9]

The lecture draws heavily on the *Apology*: wisdom consists in seeing the limitations of one's own knowledge; Socrates, living in poverty, considered it his mission to be a gadfly on the neck of man; "life without such inquiries is no life." The irony of Socrates receives special emphasis. We may quote parts of the final tribute:

Thus one must consider his magnificent apology: he speaks before posterity . . . he wanted death. He had the most splendid opportunity to show his triumph over human fear and weakness and also the dignity of his divine mission. Grote says: death took him hence in full magnificence and glory, as the sun of the tropics sets . . . with him the line of original and typical "*sophoi*" [sages] is exhausted: one may think of Heraclitus, Parmenides, Empedocles, Democritus, and Socrates. Now comes a new era. (10)

The prevalent view of Nietzsche's repudiation of Socrates ignores these lectures completely; yet the fragments of that period reiterate the same profound admiration. Beyond question the most important of these is *Philosophy in the Tragic Era of the Greeks*, which Knight identifies with "pre-Socratic philosophy," concluding that Socrates must have been conceived as the great villain.[10] Yet the essay, like the lectures, is based on the conception of "the pre-Platonic philosophers as a group that belongs together and to which alone I intend to devote this study" (2); and Nietzsche speaks of "the republic of geniuses from Thales to Socrates" (2).

Of the many quotations that might be added, we shall adduce only two from the lectures on "The Study of the Platonic Dialogues" (IV, 365–443). Here the *Apology* is celebrated as "a masterpiece of the highest rank" (12), and later Nietzsche adds:

Plato seems to have received the decisive thought as to how a philosopher ought to behave toward men from the apology of Socrates: as their physician, as a gadfly on the neck of man. [II, 11]

Even then, in the spring of 1873, Nietzsche began, but did not complete, an "untimely" essay on "The Philosopher as the Physician of Culture" (*Der Philosoph als Arzt der Kultur*, VI, 65–74). Apparently, Nietzsche himself derived his picture of the ideal philosopher from the *Apology*, and Socrates became his model.

II

After what has been said so far, one may suspect that the point must be at hand where Nietzsche's passionate admiration should have been shaken by a "Brutus crisis" – a deliberate attempt to maintain "independence of the soul" by turning against the idolized Socrates. In a fragment, sketched late in 1875, we actually find an enumeration of three brief points regarding "Socratism" which is abruptly terminated by the sentence:

> Socrates, to confess it frankly, is so close to me that almost always I fight a fight against him. (vi, 101)

Now we have previously admitted that some distinction must indeed be made between Nietzsche's attitudes toward Socrates and Socratism, although it is false to say that Nietzsche abominated Socratism, if the latter is taken to mean the outlook Socrates embodied.

Quite generally, Nietzsche distinguishes between (1) men whom he admires, (2) the ideas for which they stand, and (3) their followers. Only in terms of some such categories can one understand Nietzsche's complex attitude toward Jesus, Christianity, and Christendom. Similarly, Nietzsche admired Schopenhauer; respected but criticized Schopenhauer's philosophy; and despised the followers who made his "debauches and vices . . . a matter of faith" (FW 99). Nietzsche admired Wagner and felt drawn to much of his music; but he abominated the ostentatiously Christian nationalists and anti-Semites who congregated in Bayreuth – and his critique of Wagner might be epitomized by saying that he accused Wagner of having become a Wagnerian (EH-MA 2).

Nietzsche's fight against Socrates thus takes two forms: denunciations of his epigoni and respectful criticisms of his own doctrines. The critical period begins, characteristically, with a brief note in which the pre-Socratics and the post-Socratics are contrasted and the increasing concern with happiness after Socrates is deplored (vi, 104). The attack on the epigoni is also foreshadowed by the conception of Alexandrian culture which we find in the closing pages of *The Birth of Tragedy* – but Nietzsche distinguished between the *Lebensphilosoph* Socrates and the mediocrity who knows only the palest pleasures and lacks any conception of life or passion.

Socrates, while definitely a decisive "turning point" in history, is the very embodiment of Nietzsche's highest ideal: the passionate man who can control his passions. Here, as in Goethe, he found a man who had "given style to his character" (FW 290) and "disciplined himself to wholeness" (G ix 49). Such men, however, live, more often than not, on the threshold of what Nietzsche called decadence; and they perform their great deed of self-creation and integration on the verge of destruction and disintegration (cf. x, 412).

Even Schopenhauer does not come up to this ultimate standard. Against both him and Kant, Nietzsche levels the charge that they failed to achieve any true integration of life and learning: "Is that the life of sages? It remains science . . . Socrates would demand that one should bring philosophy down to man again" (VII, 21). The notion that Nietzsche repudiated his earlier view of Socrates as the "theoretical man," when he now described his philosophy as "practical," rests on a basic misunderstanding. There is no new positivistic and pro-Socratic period in which Nietzsche gives up his previous conceptions. Throughout, Socrates is admired for his integration of the theoretical and practical: in the earliest writings he is both the "theoretical man" and the *Lebensphilosoph*; now he is "the theoretical man" who "would rather die than become old and feeble in spirit" (VII, 198).[11]

Socrates is thus the very incarnation of the ideal Nietzsche opposes to his contemporary "Alexandrianism"; and in the essay on Schopenhauer, in the *Untimely Meditations*, Socrates is enlisted on Nietzsche's side: "the conditions for the origin of genius have *not improved* in modern times, and the aversion to original men has increased to such a degree that Socrates could not have lived among us and would not, in any case, have reached the age of seventy" (U III 6).

From Nietzsche's next work, *Human, All-Too-Human*, where Socrates is often referred to with unqualified approval and the notions of the gadfly and the divine calling are still prominent, was shall cite only a single passage:

> *Socrates*: If all goes well, the time will come when, to develop oneself morally-rationally, one will take up the *memorabilia* of Socrates rather than the Bible, and when Montaigne and Horace will be employed as precursors and guides to the understanding of the simplest and most imperishable mediator-sage, Socrates. . . . Above the founder of Christianity, Socrates is distinguished by the gay kind of seriousness and that *wisdom full of pranks* which constitutes the best state of the soul of man. Moreover, he had the greater intelligence. (S 86)

Such passages would seem to render absurd any claim that Nietzsche hated Socrates. Oehler, however, has suggested – and most of the literature has followed him – that Nietzsche's writings are to be divided into three stages of which the second, with its enlightened views, represents a temporary departure from true Nietzscheanism. This untenable dogma was intended to explain away Nietzsche's break with Wagner, his repudiation of nationalism and racism, and his vision of the "Good European." All the ideals of Nietzsche's so-called "middle period," however, can also be found in his later writings and actually receive their most extreme formulation in the last works of 1888. State worship, for example, is denounced in the essay on Schopenhauer in the "early" period; in the aphorisms of the "middle" period; then, even more vehemently, in the chapter "On the New Idol" in *Zarathustra*; and finally in *Götzen-Dämmerung* and *Ecce Homo*.[12] Just as persistent are his antiracism, his appreciation of the Enlightenment – and his admiration for Socrates.

The *Dawn* is the first of Nietzsche's books in which a respectful critique of Socratic doctrines can be found. Socrates and Plato, though they were "great doubters and admirable innovators," shared that "deepest error that 'right knowledge *must be followed* by right action'" (M 116; cf. M 22).

In *The Gay Science* Nietzsche's admiration for Socrates reaches its apotheosis. The genuine simplicity of the dying Socrates is celebrated once more (FW 36), his war on ignorance and unthinking acceptance of the opinions of others is lauded (FW 328), and Nietzsche declares: "I admire the courage and wisdom of Socrates in all he did, said – and did not say" (FW 340). This affirmation, though unqualified, is not blind – and the very same aphorism ends with the words: "we must overcome even the Greeks." As a dialectical thinker, Nietzsche affirms as necessary and admires even what must be overcome. His admiration does not arrest his thinking, and his critique does not detract from his admiration. In his own historical situation, Socrates acted as wisely and courageously as was then possible; but in the same passage Nietzsche claims that Socrates was a pessimist who "suffered life" as a disease. This is what must be overcome – and the following aphorism contains one of the first statements of the conception of eternal recurrence. With this ultimate affirmation of life, Nietzsche would overcome pessimism; but this doctrine obviously bars any idiosyncratic repudiation.

Zarathustra, Nietzsche's next work, contains no explicit mention of Socrates; yet two of its chapters cannot be properly understood apart from Nietzsche's admiration for Socrates: "On the Friend" and "On Free Death." Nietzsche's scornful words about love of one's neighbor are known well enough, but the key sentence of the chapter "On Neighbor-Love" should not be ignored:[13] "Not the neighbor do I teach you but the friend."

Nietzsche's high esteem for the Greeks is a commonplace; but it has been assumed that he wanted to return to the pre-Socratics, while his great debt to Socrates, Plato, Aristotle, and the Stoics has been overlooked.[14] In his attempt to surpass the Sermon on the Mount, Nietzsche goes back to the Socratics. Thus we find an epigram at the end of the first part of *Zarathustra* (quoted again in the preface to *Ecce Homo*): "The man who seeks knowledge must be able not only to love his enemies but also to hate his friends." One is immediately reminded of Aristotle's excuse for his disagreement with Plato (*Nicomachean Ethics*, 1096a): it is a "duty, for the sake of maintaining the truth, even to destroy what touches us closely" since "piety requires us to honor truth above our friends." Nietzsche goes beyond Aristotle by urging his own readers: "One repays a teacher badly if one always remains a pupil only" (Z I 22). Like Socrates, Nietzsche would rather arouse a zest for knowledge than commit anyone to his own views. And when he writes, in the chapter "On the Friend," "one who is unable to loosen his own chains may yet be a redeemer for his friend," he seems to recall Socrates' claim that he was but a barren midwife.

Nietzsche's emphatic scorn for those who would abandon their own path to follow another master, and his vision of a disciple who might follow his master's conceptions beyond the master's boldest dreams are thus no longer enigmatic. We can also understand the episode in Nietzsche's biography when he was looking for such a disciple – just one, not twelve. A "Nietzschean," however, whether "gentle" or "tough," is in a sense a contradiction in terms: to be a Nietzschean, one must not be a Nietzschean.

Nietzsche's hymn on "dying at the right time," in the chapter "On Free Death," has stumped his interpreters: for he obviously does not have in mind suicide. Jesus, moreover, is named explicitly as one who died a "free death," but "too early" and "too young," and not "at the right time." A close reading of the chapter, however, and a comparison with the many passages in which Nietzsche speaks of Socrates' death leave no doubt that we are confronted with another juxtaposition of Socrates and Christ. Nietzsche's general failure to equal his hero could hardly be illustrated more frightfully than by his own creeping death.

In the preface to *Beyond Good and Evil*, Nietzsche's next work, we are told that the influence of Socrates, though it may well have been a corruption, was a *necessary* and fruitful ingredient in the development of Western man: "let us not be ungrateful." We must keep this programmatic preface in mind when we read Nietzsche's violent objection to the Socratic identification of the good with the useful and agreeable, "which smells of the plebes" (190). Although Socrates, "that great ironist, so rich in secrets," recognized the irrational component of moral judgments, his influence led to the misconception that reason and instinct aim naturally for the good (191).

A later passage shows conclusively that Nietzsche has not really changed his mind about Socrates: he is still the ideal philosopher. Short of the value-creating philosopher of the future who has never yet existed – and does not live today (211)[15] – there is none greater than Socrates.

> The philosopher, as a *necessary* man of tomorrow . . . always had to find himself, in opposition to his today. . . . Hitherto all these extraordinary promoters of man, who are called philosophers, and who rarely have felt themselves to be friends of wisdom, but rather disagreeable fools and dangerous question marks, have found their . . . hard, unwanted, inescapable task . . . in being the bad conscience of their time. By applying the knife vivisectionally to the very *virtues of the time* they betrayed their own secret: to know of a *new* greatness of man . . . Each time they have uncovered how much hypocrisy, comfortableness, letting oneself go and letting oneself drop . . . were concealed under the most honored type of their contemporary morality. . . . At the time of Socrates, among men of fatigued instincts, among the conservatives of ancient Athens who let themselves go . . . *irony* was perhaps necessary for greatness of soul – that Socratic sarcastic [*boshaft*] assurance of the old physician and plebeian who cut ruthlessly into his own flesh, as well as into the flesh and heart of the "nobility," with a glance that said unmistakably: "Don't try to deceive me by dissimulation. Here we are equal." Today, conversely, when only the herd animal is honored and dispenses honors in Europe, and when "equality of rights" could all too easily be converted into an equality in violating rights – by that I mean, into a common war on all that is rare, strange, or privileged, on the higher man, the higher soul, the higher duty, the higher responsibility, and on the wealth of creative power and mastery – today the concept of "greatness" entails being noble, wanting to be by oneself, being capable of being different, standing alone, and having to live independently. . . . Today – is greatness *possible*? (212)

Nietzsche realizes that the greatness of Socrates is indubitable, while his own greatness is problematic. The model philosopher is still a physician, but the gadfly has turned into a vivisectionist. The passage also throws light on Nietzsche's aristocratic tendencies. In an age in which there was a "nobility" that deemed itself superior without living up to its exalted conception of itself, greatness could manifest itself in the bold insistence on a fundamental equality. In our time, however, equality is confused with conformity – as Nietzsche sees it – and it is taken to involve the renunciation of personal initiative and the demand for a general level-ling. Men are losing the ambition to be equally excellent, which involves as the surest means the desire to excel one another in continued competition, and they are becoming resigned to being equally mediocre. Instead of vying for distinction, men nurture a *ressentiment* against all that is distinguished, superior, or strange. The philosopher, however, must always stand opposed to his time and may never conform; it is his calling to be a fearless critic and diagnostician – as Socrates was. And Nietzsche feels that he is only keeping the faith with this Socratic heritage when he calls attention to the dangers of the modern idealization of equality, and he challenges us to have the courage to be different and independent. In the modern world, however, is that still possible?

In the *Genealogy of Morals*, Socrates is mentioned only once:

> What great philosopher hitherto has been married? Heraclitus, Plato, Descartes, Spinoza, Leibniz, Kant, Schopenhauer – these were not. . . . A married philosopher belongs *in comedy* . . . and that exception . . . the *sarcastic* [*boshaft*] Socrates, it seems, married *ironically* just to demonstrate *this* proposition. (III, 7)

Eight *great* philosophers are named; only one is a pre-Socratic, though others could have been added easily – and Socrates and Plato are both included.

The posthumously published notes of Nietzsche's last years have sometimes been invoked to prove assertions about Nietzsche that are at odds with the published works. As a matter of principle, it should not be forgotten that the notes, including those which the editors chose to publish as *The Will to Power*, are mostly the scribblings Nietzsche jotted into his notebooks during his long walks – and at night. They cannot balance the lectures and the books; and most of them, including again the material published in *The Will to Power*, appear in Nietzsche's later books, often in a form and a context that yield an unexpected meaning.

In any case, the notes contain no departure from Nietzsche's previous position. Side by side with occasional tributes to the philosophers "before Socrates" (WM 437; XVI, 3, 4), we find, for example, these sentences:

> Some ancient writings one reads to understand antiquity: others, however, are such that one studies antiquity *in order* to be able to

read *them*. To these belongs the *Apology*; its theme is supra-Greek. (XVI, 6)

Nietzsche's references to the ugliness and plebeian descent of Socrates are as continuous with the earlier works as the tributes to his irony and integrity.

The passages about Socrates in *The Will to Power* deal primarily with his alleged decadence (429–32, 437, 441–43, 578). But, as we have seen, Nietzsche explains in the Preface of *The Case of Wagner*: "I am no less than Wagner a child of this age, that is, a *decadent*; but I comprehended this, I resisted it. The philosopher in me resisted." Wagner, it seems, resembled the Athenians who let themselves go, while Nietzsche emulates Socrates, the model philosopher: "What does a philosopher demand of himself, first and last? To overcome his time in himself, to become "timeless.'" This conception of the decadent philosopher who cannot cure his own decadence but yet struggles against it is developed in the *Götzen-Dämmerung*. Like his first book, it contains an extended treatment of what Nietzsche now calls "The Problem of Socrates";[16] and one may generalize that the works of 1888, for all their hyperboles and for all their glaring faults, represent more sustained analyses than any of Nietzsche's works since *The Birth of Tragedy*. However strained and unrestrained they are, they contain some of Nietzsche's most fruitful and ingenious conceptions.

In his chapter on "The Problem of Socrates," Nietzsche recalls the ugliness, plebeian descent, and decadence of Socrates and adds – in a sentence which we shall have to recall later: "Socrates was the buffoon [*Hanswurst*] who *made others take him seriously*" (5). He is also said to have "fascinated" the contest-craving Greeks by offering them a new kind of spiritualized dialectical contest, and – as in *The Birth of Tragedy* – he is considered a great "erotic" (8). Far more significant is the fact that, just as in Nietzsche's first book, Socratism is considered dialectically as something necessary – in fact, as the very force that saved Western civilization from an otherwise inescapable destruction. Socrates "understood that all the world *needed* him – his means, his cure, his personal artifice of self-preservation" (9): "one had only *one* choice: either to perish or – to be *absurdly rational*" (10). In this way alone could the excesses of the instincts be curbed in an age of disintegration and degeneration; Socratism alone could prevent the premature end of Western man. Yet "to *have to* fight the instincts – that is the formula for decadence" (11). Socratism itself is decadent and cannot produce a real cure; by thwarting death it can only make possible an eventual regeneration which may not come about for centuries. Socrates himself realized this: "In the *wisdom* of his courage to die," he recognized that for himself no ultimate cure was possible – except death (12).[17]

III

Ecce Homo was Nietzsche's last work and in many ways the culmination of his philosophy. Much of it can be understood only in terms of a juxtaposition which we have previously encountered: Christ versus Socrates. As Nietzsche assures us in the *Antichrist*, he reveres the life and death of Jesus – but instead of interpreting it as a promise of another world and another life, and instead of conceding the divinity of Jesus, Nietzsche insists: *Ecce Homo!* Man can live and die in a grand style, working out his own salvation instead of relying on the sacrifice of another. Where Kierkegaard, at the outset of his *Fragments*, poses an alternative of Christ, the Savior, and Socrates, the Teacher, and then chooses Christ and revelation, Nietzsche, as ever, prefers Socrates: man's salvation is in himself, if anywhere. Like Kierkegaard – and unlike some "humanists" today – Nietzsche felt that this position entailed a decisive break with Christianity. In any case, it does not involve any departure from Nietzsche's "middle" period. He still considers himself the heir of the Enlightenment: at the end of *Ecce Homo* he cites Voltaire's "*Écrasez l'infâme!*"

This vehement polemic is not incompatible with the *amor fati* stressed in *Ecce Homo*. Thus we are told in the first part: "Nothing that is may be subtracted, nothing is dispensable" (2); and in the second part Nietzsche elaborates: "My formula for the greatness of a human being is *amor fati*: that one wants nothing to be different – not forward, not backward, not in all eternity" (10). If this attitude is not markedly different from Hegel's, Nietzsche's attitude toward Christianity certainly is. Yet both men define their own historical significance in terms of their relation to Christianity. Owing to this, each considers himself, in Nietzsche's words, a destiny. Hegel thought his system reconciled in an essentially secular philosophy the dogmata of Christianity and the heritage of ancient and modern philosophy. He saw himself standing at the end of an era as a fulfillment. Nietzsche answered his own question, "why I am a destiny," by claiming that he was the first to have "uncovered" Christian morality. He believed that after him no secular Christian system would be possible any more; and he considered himself the first philosopher of an irrevocable anti-Christian era. "To be the first one here may be a curse; in any case, it is a destiny" (6). His anti-Christianity, therefore, does not seem to him essentially negative. He is no critic who would have things be different: he lives at the beginning of a new era, and things *will* be different. "I contradict as has never been contradicted before and am yet the opposite of a no-saying spirit" (1).

All this shows the essential continuity of Nietzsche's thought, no less than does his reiteration in the first chapter that he, as well as Socrates, is decadent. In his discussion of *Zarathustra*, Nietzsche ascribes to the overman that "omni-presence of sarcasm [*Bosheit*] and frolics" which he evidently associated with Socrates; and in speaking of *The Case of Wagner* Nietzsche emphasizes his own love of irony. Yet not one of these points is as important as the fact that *Ecce Homo* is Nietzsche's *Apology*.

Brinton remarks incidentally – though, in conformity with almost the entire literature, he fails to discuss *Ecce Homo* – that it "is not apologetic."[18] This, of course, is the basis of our comparison with the *Apology* – that masterpiece for whose sake one studies antiquity. The heading of the first chapter, "why I am so wise," recalls the leitmotif of the *Apology*. Socrates, after claiming that he was the wisest of men, had interpreted his wisdom in terms of the foolishness of his contemporaries, who thought they knew what they really did not know, and in terms of his own calling. Nietzsche answers his own provocative question in terms of "the disparity between the greatness of my task and the smallness of my contemporaries" (EH-V 1). His wisdom, he claims, consists in his opposition to his time – and we have seen that he felt close to Socrates in this respect.

The second question, "why I am so clever," is similarly answered: "I have never pondered questions that are none" (1). Again one recalls the *Apology*, where Socrates scorns far-flung speculations; he confined his inquiries to a few basic questions of morality.

The third question, "why I write such good books," receives a more startling reply: "There is altogether no prouder nor, at the same time, more subtle kind of book: here and there they attain the ultimate that can be attained on earth – cynicism" (3). We are reminded of that Socratic "wisdom full of pranks which constitutes the best state of the soul of man," and of the "sarcastic assurance" of the "great ironist" who vivisected the virtues of his age. Nietzsche concedes that a cynic may be no more than an "indiscreet billy goat and ape," but even so he considers "cynicism the only form in which mean souls touch honesty" (J 26). His position here depends, as it often does, on the conviction that superficially similar forms of behavior may be expressions of profoundly different states of mind: "In sarcasm [*Bosheit*] the frolicker and the weakling meet" (Z I 10); it may be an expression of *ressentiment* or of greatness of soul. Thus Nietzsche expressly associates cynicism with the "new barbarians" who combine "spiritual superiority with well-being and excess of strength" (WM 899). And in a letter to Brandes, on November 20, 1888, he says: "I have now written an account of myself with a cynicism that will become world-historical. The book is called *Ecce Homo*."[19]

In the *Götzen-Dämmerung*, Socrates had been called a buffoon: now "buffoon" and "satyr" (a term the Platonic Alcibiades had used to picture Socrates) become idealized conceptions. Nietzsche, too, would be a satyr (EH-V); he praises Heine's "divine sarcasm without which I cannot imagine perfection" and calls him a satyr; and on the same page he says of Shakespeare: "what must a man have suffered to find it so very necessary to be a buffoon" (EH II 4). In the end, Nietzsche says of himself: "I do not want to be a saint, rather a buffoon. Perhaps I am a buffoon" (EH IV 1).

We may conclude by considering a passage from *Beyond Good and Evil* (295) which is quoted in *Ecce Homo* (III 6). Originally Nietzsche had claimed that he was here describing Dionysus – and indeed this is a picture of him whom Nietzsche has in mind when he writes, in the last line of his last book: "Has one understood me? – *Dionysus versus the Crucified* –"

Who is "Dionysus"? Nietzsche encountered the death and resurrection of a god in both Orphism and Christianity; but the rebirth of Dionysus seemed to him a reaffirmation of life as "indestructible, powerful, and joyous," in spite of suffering and death, while he construed the crucifixion as a "curse on life," and recalled that Goethe already had spurned the cross.[20] When "Dionysus" absorbed the Apollinian, and the reaffirmation of life assumed the meaning of passion sublimated as opposed to passion extirpated, Goethe became Nietzsche's model, and he "baptized" Goethe's faith "with the name of *Dionysus*" (G IX 49). Beyond doubt, the title *Ecce Homo* refers not only to Pilate's famous words about Jesus, but also to the exclamation with which Napoleon greeted Goethe: *Voilà un homme!* When Nietzsche had first cited this phrase (J 209), he had been unable to suppress the comment: "that meant, 'But this is a *man!* I had expected a mere German.'" *Ecce Homo* suggests a larger contrast: Goethe versus Christ, "*Dionysus versus the Crucified*."

Nietzsche, however, is not thinking of Goethe alone. In *Beyond Good and Evil* already, "Dionysus is a philosopher" (295); and while Nietzsche prefaces the quotation in *Ecce Homo*, "I forbid, by the way, any conjecture as to whom I am describing in this passage," we need not conjecture if we remember that Nietzsche called Socrates the "Pied Piper of Athens" – in *The Gay Science*, right after saying: "I admire the courage and wisdom of Socrates in all he did, said – and did not say" (340).

> The genius of the heart, as that great hidden one has it . . . the Pied Piper . . . whose voice knows how to descend into the depths of every soul. . . . The genius of the heart . . . who teaches one to listen, who smooths rough souls and lets them taste a new yearning. . . . The genius of the heart . . . who divines the hidden and forgotten treasure, the drop of goodness . . . under the . . . thick ice. . . . The genius of the heart from whose touch everyone goes away richer, not having found grace nor amazed, not as blessed and oppressed by the goods of another, but richer in himself . . . opened up . . . less sure perhaps . . . but full of hopes that as yet have no name. (J 295)

The last lines may be true of Nietzsche, too – and he goes on to call himself a disciple of this "Dionysus" and, in a later passage, also a Pied Piper (G-V). Yet he fell so pitifully short of Socrates' serenely mature humanity that his very admiration invites comparison with the mad, drunken Alcibiades in the *Symposium*, who also could not resist the fascination and charm of Socrates. And if we seek an epitaph for Nietzsche, we might do well to couple his hymn on the genius of the heart with the words of the Platonic Alcibiades:

> I have been bitten by a more than viper's tooth; I have known in my soul . . . that worst of pangs . . . the pang of philosophy which will make a man say or do anything. And you . . . all of you, and I need not say Socrates himself, have had experience of the same madness and passion in your longing after wisdom. Therefore, listen and excuse my doings . . . and my sayings. . . . But let profane and unmannered persons close up the doors of their ears.

NOTES

1 Crane Brinton, *Nietzsche* (Cambridge, Mass.: Harvard University Press, 1941), 83.
2 Friedrich Gundolf, *Caesar im Neunzehuten Jahrhundert* (Berlin: Bondi, 1926), chapter 4.
3 When Nietzsche graduated from school, he designated the *Symposium* his "*Lieblingsdichtung.*" (Cf. his *curriculum vitae* in E. Förster-Nietzsche, *Das*

Leben Friedrich Nietzsches 1, 109.)

4 Cf. Hidebrandt, *Nietzsches Wettkampf mit Sokrates und Plato* (Dresden: Sybillen, 1922). Here a chronological analysis of Nietzsche's writings is offered, but GT 15 is ignored. A similar view had been suggested earlier (1918) by Ernst Bertram, *Nietzsche: Versuch einer Mythologie* (Berlin: Bondi, 1918), who had, however, avoided any final clarity.

5 The original manuscript, entitled *Socrates und die Griechische Tragödie*, was published in 1933.

One of Rilke's comments on *The Birth of Tragedy*, written in 1900 but not published until 1966, is very perceptive: "It seems to me that the accident of Wagner is to be blamed for the fact that N immediately applied his insights and hopes, which suit the German character so little, to this occasion, which was nearest at hand (too near!); this detracts greatly from the final third of the book. This damage is far greater than his use of Kantian and Schopenhauerian terminology. If Schopenhauer's conception of music in particular did much to advance N's purpose, the immediate application of everything to Wagner's creations spells disappointment: one does not *wish* that all these lofty promises are supposed to have been *already* fulfilled: above all, one believes that the author of the book is himself well qualified (*as a poet*) to make the attempt at a 'resurrection of Dionysus'" Rainer Maria Rilke, marginal comments on GT, written circa March 1900, in *Sämtliche Werke*, VI, (Frankfurt am Main: Insel-Verlag, 1966), (1174ff).

6 George A. Morgan, *What Nietzsche Means* (Cambridge, Mass.: Harvard University Press, 1941, 264; New York: Torch Books (paperback), 1965).

7 Richard Oehler in his very influential book on *Friedrich Nietzsche und die Vorsokratiker* (Leipzig: Dürr, 1904), 28, claims that the early Nietzsche "was completely under the influence of Schopenhauer" and hence a pessimist, and therefore had to repudiate optimistic Socratism. While the literature has, for the most part, followed Oehler, Ernst Troeltsch, *Der Historismus und seine Probleme* (1922), 499ff, recognized Nietzsche's elaborate dialectic and hence found in *The Birth of Tragedy* "more Hegel than Schopenhauer," though he did not consider Nietzsche's attitude toward Socrates.

8 A. J. H. Knight, *Some Aspects of the Life and Work of Nietzsche and particularly of his Connection with Greek Literature and Thought* (Cambridge: Cambridge University Press, 1933), 18. To the inaccuracies that Knight accepts uncritically from Oehler, Bertram, and Frau Förster-Nietzsche he adds many errors of his own: e.g., we are told that "only once does Nietzsche praise" Plato (57) and that "Nietzsche was undoubtedly influenced, in his Superman theories, by . . . Kierkegaard" (138ff and 58). Yet Nietzsche's writings abound in tributes to Plato (who exerted a decisive influence on Nietzsche's thought); while the "Superman theories" were developed long before 1888, when Nietzsche first heard of Kierkegaard (from Brandes), too late to become acquainted with his ideas. Knight, however, follows Bertram in admitting – amid many inconsistencies – that Socrates influenced Nietzsche's conception of the ideal philosopher.

9 Ignoring this, Oehler, *Friedrich Nietzsche und die Vorsokratiker*, 28ff, 31ff, assumes that Nietzsche's later insistence on Socrates' features and descent is proof of his hatred. The literature has generally followed Oehler.

10 Knight, *Some Aspects*, 23, 58. Knight depends on Oehler, who, while granting that Nietzsche himself attached supreme importance to this fragment, as-

sumed that Nietzsche was concerned with the pre-Socratic only (123). The same assumption is at least implicit in Karl Löwith, *Nietzsches Philosophie der Ewigen Wiederkunft des Gleichen* (Berlin: Die Runde, 1935; rev. ed. Stuttgart: Kohlhammer, 1956), 110, and Josef Hofmiller, *Friedrich Nietzsche* (Hamburg-Bergedorf: Stromverlag, no date), 15. The latter even claims that, in the realm of classical philology, Nietzsche was not at all interested "in Plato and Aristotle, but exclusively in the pre-Socratics" (12).

11 Hildebrandt, *Nietzsches Wettkampf*, who would distinguish the anti-Socratic "theoretical" construction and the pro-Socratic "practical" interpretation, overlooks these and many similar passages.

12 Those who would consider Nietzsche's condemnation of the State as somehow anti-Socratic may well be reminded of Socrates' dictum in the *Apology*: "if I had engaged in politics, I should have perished long ago, and done no good to either you or to myself. . . . No man who goes to war with you or any other multitude, honestly striving against the many lawless and unrighteous deeds which are done in a state, will save his life; he who will fight for the right, if he would live even for a brief space, must have a private station and not a public one" (31ff, Jowett). Even in the *Republic*, where the Platonic Socrates describes the ideal City, he concludes: "perhaps there is a pattern set up in the heavens for one who desires to see it and, seeing it, to found one in himself. But whether it exists anywhere or ever will exist is no matter; for this is the only commonwealth in whose politics he can ever take part" (592, Cornford). Nietzsche, to be sure, did not believe in Plato's heaven or his Theory of Forms – but he assumed that Socrates had not believed in them either; and in their opposition to any existing form of government, and perhaps also in their deprecation of business and democracy, both Plato and Nietzsche seem to have considered themselves heirs of Socrates. The scattered notes of Nietzsche's last years in which he toys with notions of breeding philosophers and with a caste system in which nature herself distinguishes between the predominantly spiritual ones (*Geistige*), the warriors, and the mediocre mass, are obviously inspired by the *Republic*, no less than are the notes in which Nietzsche suggests that military discipline must be part of the philosopher's education. Yet who among all the great philosophers was a soldier's soldier – except Socrates?

13 In this respect, Friedrich Jodl's *Geschichte der Ethik* is at one with Morgan, *What Nietzsche Means*; while George Santayana, in his *Egotism in German Philosophy* (New York: Scribner, no date), actually writes: "it is remarkable how little he learned from the Greeks . . . no sense for friendship" (121ff).

14 Thus Oehler ignores Nietzsche's dialectic, his ceaseless questioning, his irony, his discourse on love of one's educator, his conception of sublimation with its incessant allusions to the *Symposium*, his development of Plato's notion of *sophrosyne*, his eulogy of friendship and free death, his *amor fati*, etc. A just recognition of Nietzsche's debt to the pre-Socratics need not entail the claim that Nietzsche despised the later Greeks. Like Richard Oehler's later book on *Friedrich Nietzsche und die Deutsche Zukunft* (Leipzig: Armanen, 1935), his *Friedrich Nietzsche und die Vorsokratiker* depends on a tendentious selection of fragmentary quotations, torn from their context. Oehler's earlier book, however, ends with a quotation which, while supposed to justify the attempt to trace Nietzsche's spiritual ancestry, is actually amusingly at odds

not only with Oehler's *furor Teutonicus,* but also with his central thesis that Nietzsche's preference for the pre-Socratics entailed a repudiation of Socrates and Plato: " . . . In that which moved Zarathustra, Moses, Mohammed, Jesus, Plato, Brutus, Spinoza, Mirabeau – I live, too."

15 In J 44, Nietzsche expressly calls himself a mere "herald and precursor" of the "philosophers of the future".

16 Knight, *Some Aspects,* 128, erroneously declares this chapter to be part of the *Genealogy.*

17 Not only Hildebrandt, *Nietzsches Wettkampf,* 57–59, assumes that this chapter contains another "hateful" repudiation of Socratism, but even Ludwig Klages, *Der Psychologischen Errungenschaften Nietzsches* (Leipzig: Barth, 1926), 181, takes for granted Nietzsche's "passionate repudiation of Socrates . . . in GT and G" – and that in a chapter in which Klages accuses (!) Nietzsche of "Socratism," i.e. of not having been sufficiently irrational. Neither author offers any analysis of the text of G.

18 Brinton, *Nietzsche,* 65. Hildebrandt, in his discussion of Nietzsche's attitude toward Socrates, does not even mention *Ecce Homo.*

19 Morgan, *What Nietzsche Means,* 133ff, writes: "I am unable to account for Nietzsche's extraordinary valuation of *cynicism.*" The present analysis would indicate that it is to be accounted for in terms of Nietzsche's admiration for Socrates. In *Ecce Homo* he tried to outdo Socrates' request for maintenance in the Prytaneum (*Apology,* 36).

20 GT 7; WM 1052; WH 175. Cf. p. 379.

REFERENCES AND KEY TO ABBREVIATIONS

Key to the abbreviations used in the present text.

Die Geburt der Tragödie (The Birth of Tragedy)	GT	1872
Unzeitgemässe Betrachtungen (Untimely Meditations)	U	
I *David Strauss, der Bekenner und Schriftsteller* (David Strauss, the Confessor and Writer)		1873
II *Vom Nutzen und Nachteil der Historie für das Leben* (Of the Use and Disadvantage of History for Life)		1874
III *Schopenhauer als Erzieher* (S. as Educator)		1874
IV *Richard Wagner in Bayreuth*		1876
Menschliches, Allzumenschliches (Human, All-Too-Human)	MA	
I		1878
II *Vermischte Meinungen und Sprüche* (Mixed Opinions and Maxims)		1879
Die Morgenröte (The Dawn)	M	1881
Die Fröhliche Wissenschaft (The Gay Science)	FW	1882
Book v ($343–383) added in 1887.		
Also Sprach Zarathustra (Thus Spoke Zarathustra)	Z	
Parts I and II, 1883; III, 1884; IV, 1885 – first public edition of Z IV, 1892.		
Jenseits von Gut und Böse (Beyond Good and Evil)	J	1886
Der Fall Wagner (The Case of Wagner)	W	1888
Die Götzen-Dämmerung (The Twilight of the Idols) Ten chapters.	G	1889

Der Antichrist (The Antichrist)   A   1895*

Ecce Homo Four chapters; also ten sections on the above   EH   1908*
    titles: EH-GT; EH-U; etc.

    Der Wille zur Macht (The Will to Power) 1067 sections.   WM   **
    Prefaces (*Vorreden*) are abbreviated "V"; e.g., GT-V.

These works are cited by the abbreviations given above and by the numbers of the aphorisms or sections – which are the same in all editions, regardless of language. All other references are to the Musarion edition of the *Gesammelte Werke* (23 vols, 1920–9).

9
Accessories (*Ecce Homo*, 'Why I Write Such Good Books', 'The Untimelies', 3)

Sarah Kofman

Having re-read the first *Untimely Meditation*, and passing over the second in silence, Nietzsche expands on the third and fourth, reprising the themes introduced in the overture, section 1:[1] in these texts, under the names of Schopenhauer and Wagner, it was 'himself' he was speaking about. It would be a pointless effort to read them with the intention of understanding the two 'cases' these names represent and the psychological problems they pose. At the time, Nietzsche did not claim to be performing a diagnosis of either, precisely because he did not yet see them as 'cases', or consider the philosophy of the one, the music of the other, as symptoms. Although he presented himself as a physician of civilization, which he judged to be sick, he did not yet sense sickness in Schopenhauer and Wagner, and instead set them up as saviour figures. Only much later will he write *The Case of Wagner*, and will we be able to find the equivalent of a *Case of Schopenhauer* (which will never be written) in the sections Nietzsche devotes to the philosopher in the Third Essay of the *Genealogy*. Although in the two *Untimely Meditations* he wanted to do something other than psychology[2] (in the new sense he subsequently gives this term), since he 'himself' was nevertheless already – unwittingly – a profound 'psychologist', he could not help having already sensed a few of the fundamental traits of their 'nature', a few details which were essential, like all details. Thus he had already detected and highlighted Wagner's histrionic talent,[3] to which he will continually return afterwards – proof of the sureness of his instinct, or of his flair,[4] which makes him wise and clever enough to go straight to what is essential. Yet the following still needs to be emphasized: the *après-coup*[5] erases the fact that in the 'youthful works' Wagner's comic talent did not have the pejorative connotations it will have in the later texts, where it will be classed as vulgar ham acting and become a form of hysteria, a symptom not of the greatness but of the decadence of the musician who puts his music at the service of his histrionic art and not the other way around. The histrionic art, along with each of the artistic 'corruptions' and infirmities inaugurated by Wagner, will be reduced to an art of lying, a manifestation of physiological degenerescence.[6] The histrionic genius, his characteristic, which leads him, like every man of the theatre, to search only for 'effect', gives him henceforth a place outside the history of music: his dominant instinct makes him anything but a musician.[7]

Nietzsche's dominant instinct, then, immediately sensed Wagner's dominant instinct, the theatrical instinct, discredited in the later texts by a gesture linking back up with the metaphysical tradition which denounces, among other things, the inauthenticity of the actor playing on effects. And in fact grasping this essential 'detail' made him immediately understand Wagner's whole 'psychology', which, like his music, is merely a consequence of this 'genius' dominant in him, and ultimately leads back to specific physiological premises.

So at the same time as he emphasizes the permanence of his psychological flair, which attests to the *unity of his will*, Nietzsche declares that the project of the last two *Untimely Meditations* was not psychological in nature but in fact, much more ambitiously, educational. Here again he was innovating radically, to the extent that in order to express what was unheard-of he was forced to adopt other voices, the masks of Schopenhauer and Wagner. By an educational project, he did not in fact mean a reform of the 'educational establishments'. What was at stake was an educational project without parallel (*ohnegleichen*), no more and no less than the introduction of a completely different concept of culture, conceived as a discipline and defence of the self and rebelling against the prevailing herd culture which results in a generalized levelling out. What was at stake was the introduction of a higher idea of culture: that of a self-discipline carried to the point of hardness, which anticipated Zarathustra's watchword, 'become hard', taken up again in the last section of 'The Free Spirit' in *Beyond Good and Evil*, where Nietzsche the new Stoic will address the philosophers to come. What was being expressed at that stage was a great historic task, the advent indeed of what he was calling at that stage the 'great' man, an 'old word' which designated – though without yet designating him as such – the overman. The incomparable originality and novelty of the task forced Nietzsche, then, before he could dispense with old words and accede in full clarity to 'himself', to the unity of his will and of his 'mission', to take a multiplicity of by-roads. Since his way (*voie*) was not marked out in advance,[8] his voice (*voix*) was at first only able to make itself heard if it smuggled itself in, if it made the most of an opportunity (taking it by the *forelock, Schopf*) which presented itself: the existence of two precursory models, two famous types which were not yet fixed (*noch unfestgestellte Typen* writes Nietzsche, taking up again almost verbatim the expression he had used in *Beyond Good and Evil*, 62 to designate the kind of animal humanity is), and which he could therefore freely fiction by imposing on them – without really knowing it – his own type. Playing on the ho- mophony of *Schopf* and *Schopenhauer*, Nietzsche reduces the latter (and Wagner as well) to an 'opportunity' which he took by the forelock, because it was to hand, handy (*in der Hand*), so as to have in hand some extra means of expression, formulas, and signs – and to try as a result to master what he had not yet mastered: his own language. Nothing but semiotic means, Wagner and Schopenhauer were mere 'manœuvres' in Nietzsche's becoming 'Nietzsche'.

Looking back from a distance, he finds it strange that as early as the third *Untimely Meditation*, and not just in the time of the autobiography, he should have been able to guess with uncanny (*unheimlich*) sagacity that under the names of these two great men it was a question of him alone. Uncanny to be so young and already so perspicacious, because this precociousness leads one to suspect that sagacity results not from deliberate reflexion but from an instinctive flair, always already there, for which one can give no 'reasons', and which over time will simply make its voice heard more and more clearly.

If we refer to the text from that period (section 7), we can note that the rhetorical relationship established in *Ecce Homo* between Nietzsche himself, Wagner and Schopenhauer, is pointed up with reference to Schopenhauer and the relationship he maintains with Kant and Buddha, who were two means among a hundred thousand others and countless hieroglyphics, helping him to accomplish a single task and to express a single meaning, his own. 'Everything he subsequently appro- priated to himself from life and books, from the whole wealth of the sciences, was to him hardly more than colouring and means of expres- sion [*Mittel des Ausdrucks*: in *Ecce Homo* the term is *Sprachmittel*]; he employed even the Kantian philosophy above all as an extraordinary rhetorical instrument [*rhetorisches Instrument*]'.[9] Schopenhauer, who also, like Wagner, had a visionary gaze, which had allowed him to perceive 'a dreadful scene in a supraterrestrial court [. . .], the saint as judge of existence', tried subsequently to reproduce in all his writings this image of life, this tremendous vision which he had already had as a child. Kant and, on occasion, among others, Buddhist and Christian mythology, were just means for trying to express and fix this vision. What Bergson would call a fundamental intuition which to express itself can only use a thousand inadequate conceptual means, *The Birth of Tragedy* called metaphorical language, in other words a carrying over from a language of images to a 'conceptual' language at one further remove – and hence incapable of expressing it – of the essence of life perceived intuitively. It is by referring to the rhetorical model, which he uses in *The Birth of Tragedy* and in the *Philosophenbuch*,[10] that Nietzsche in the third *Untimely Meditation* establishes the link between Schopenhauer's very first vision and his means of expression, which he declares to be 'an extraordinary rhetorical instrument'. Nietzsche is still implicitly referring to these very first texts when, in *Ecce Homo*, he maintains that he himself was at that stage putting to his own use 'formulas, signs, means of expression', or a semiotic. Still more '*unheimlich*' than Nietzsche's youthful sagacity is this description of Schopenhauer, a veritable double of himself, who, before him and in relation to Kant, used the same metaphorical instruments he himself will use later on, so he says, in relation, among others, to this same Schopenhauer. Because he could only draw back in terror from his own double, Nietzsche – looking back from a distance, indeed – prefers to displace the effect of *Unheimlichkeit* onto his 'youthful sagacity' and to reduce the double to the identical: it was not 'Schopenhauer' he was speaking about but really and truly 'himself', which would explain the similarity between 'their' instruments and take away all its strangeness. This is indeed why, in order to have us understand the relationship which Nietzsche establishes between himself and the figures of Schopenhauer and Wagner, *Ecce Homo* will not mention the relationship established in the third *Untimely Meditation* between Schopenhauer and Kant, but instead the one which Nietzsche highlights in other texts as characteristic of the relationship Plato/Socrates,[11] a relationship of instrumentality: the noble disciple used his plebeian master like a means of expressing himself. Under the name of Socrates – nothing but a *chimerical* being, impregnated by him from all directions – it is 'Plato' alone who is speaking. In the interest of its argument, this page of *Ecce Homo* does not admit that Nietzsche does not establish such a simple, one-sided relationship between the master and the disciple. If the latter seizes hold of the figure of his master, it is not only in order to get him pregnant and make him beautiful in his image, but also in order to be impregnated – in other words, in this case, contaminated and poisoned – by 'him', in return, to such an extent that only Nietzsche's genealogical flair can succeed in distinguishing what is 'proper' to the one and to the other. If Nietzsche does not emphasize, as in *Beyond Good and Evil*, the reciprocity of the relationship, it is because he is keen precisely to pass in silence over the fact that he himself, in turn, not only impregnated Wagner and Schopenhauer and made them beautiful in his

image, but was also well and truly contaminated and poisoned by them
and had great difficulty breaking with them, having first united with
them symbiotically and revered them like fathers and masters. *Ecce
Homo*, in its desire to emphasize the continuity of the *œuvre* and to unify
it, forgets the reciprocal erotic 'relationship' and stresses only the rhetorical relationship: Schopenhauer and Wagner were simply *metaphors*
for himself which he seized hold of for his own use. Mere opportunities,
instruments, accessories, means – lackeys – of one who, apparently
merely a disciple, as Plato was of Socrates, was in fact acting as a
subterranean master – and was alone in positing aims, in imposing his
aim. And just as Nietzsche, going beyond the contamination of the most
beautiful plant in antiquity, strives to restore to it all its purity by
separating it typologically from its poisoner, whom he reduces from the
status of master to that of slave, mere instrument, similarly in his own
case he reverses the roles and gets his own back: having been called by
the press at the time one of Wagner's 'literary lackeys'[12] (in the correspondence of the period he himself calls him his 'father' and his 'revered
master', and considers himself merely a disciple of Schopenhauer),
henceforth he grants mastery and nobility to himself alone, and reduces
Wagner and Schopenhauer to the role of mere accessories at his service,
at the service of Nietzsche's becoming Nietzsche. In ultimately reducing
both of them, like Socrates, to typical decadence figures, Nietzsche uses
his genealogical method as a roundabout way of putting an end to the
mastery and the hold which these two pseudo-'masters' had had over
him in his youth: the typological reading proves that they could only ever
have been means – means for *his* use. In the *Untimely Meditations* they
acted as his ventriloquists and were merely figureheads who spoke only
of him (*bloss von mir reden*).

But who 'he'? The Nietzsche he was to 'become', the Nietzsche to
come, who had already been attested to by both *Richard Wagner in
Bayreuth*, which is declared 'a vision of [his] future', and *Schopenhauer as
Educator*, whose watchword, 'become who you are', is like a statement in
miniature (*en abîme*) that this text bears inscribed in itself, in advance,
the innermost history of his becoming. 'He' is thus not so much the
Nietzsche of the period of the *Untimely Meditations* as the promise
(*Versprechen, Verheissung*) which he represented in his own eyes, as if at
that stage he had made a commitment to 'himself' for the future (and he
was fully confident in the knowledge that it would not remain a mere
promise).

The third *Untimely Meditation* 'promises' the Nietzsche to come: a so-
called 'youthful' work, it allows one to maintain that its author 'shows
promise', that his work is 'promising'; it presages his future, authorizes

one to anticipate what he will become – one can *see* it already. But to say of someone that he shows promise is also to assert that he has not yet quite achieved what 'he' is already heralding, that he has not yet become really 'himself'. If indeed, as the *après-coup* seeks to emphasize, there is one and the same will inspiring the Nietzsche of the *Untimely Meditations* and the one he will subsequently 'become', the transition from the youthful Nietzsche to the Nietzsche of *Ecce Homo* required a long road to be travelled, many byways to be taken and many masks adopted. To describe his 'becoming himself' he takes up again the metaphors he used in *Schopenhauer as Educator*: those of the road, of the ladder to be climbed in order to reach a 'self' which is not buried away in the depths but situated above one.[13] They all emphasize the distance and the difference in perspective which still separated 'Nietzsche' from 'Nietzsche', despite their proximity, since he could not already have reached 'his' height – the height for which he was destined and which he had *promised* himself: although his vision had been self-assured, never-theless, like the Hebrews of the Old Testament, at that stage he could only *glimpse* the Promised Land. Before entering it – like that people doomed to wandering and misfortune, which, despite everything, kept its trust in the word of God assuring it of its having been chosen, and an unerring faith – Nietzsche, never doubting his success for a moment, or that he would keep the word which, for his part, committed only himself to himself, Nietzsche, too, had to go more or less miraculously through many perils and aporias, many 'Red Seas', to take roundabout routes, apparent dead ends, to depart and stray[14] from the way which was to lead him to *terra firma* – to the land which he himself (since God is well and truly dead and can no longer make such promises) had promised to himself. A land which he, unlike the Hebrews, will not share with other chosen ones, which he has reserved for himself alone, like a native soil or a secret garden which no one other than he will be invited to enter in order to taste its fruits.[15]

This 'promised' land was situated at such a height that at that stage only a visionary gaze (which he attributed at that stage to Wagner and Schopenhauer but which was his own) could see it with full self-confi-dence and in perfect happiness. The distance between this final height and the less elevated altitude of the 'young' Nietzsche is marked by a difference in expression, the symptom of quite a specific transformation: speaking at that stage the language of Schopenhauer, he was expressing himself in common currency, with words which were still steeped in 'moraline';[16] the language of the one who has acceded to his height, the height of the immoralist, is no longer that of a man but of the flash of lightning which, as we have seen, symbolizes for Nietzsche from very early on 'a free power without ethics'.[17] In the section which it devotes to *On the Genealogy of Morals*, *Ecce Homo* makes this 'overman's' language – the very language of Dionysus, the god of darkness – characteristic of the style of the three Essays: 'Each time a beginning which is *intended* to mislead [. . .]. Gradually an increasing disquiet; isolated flashes of lightning; very unpleasant truths becoming audible as a dull rumbling in the distance [. . .]. At the conclusion each time among perfectly awful detonations, a *new* truth visible between thick clouds.'

It is his use of this language of lightning flashes and detonations, this Dionysian language which no contemporary can hear, that keeps Nietzsche apart: no road can lead from other men to the one who stays in the ice of the Nordic heights, inaccessible to all those who are not, like him, 'Hyperboreans'.[18]

If the 'promise' which the *Untimely Meditations* represented, despite the long and perilous journey which still remained to be completed, did not remain a dead letter or merely a 'word', it was because Nietzsche had signed the pact (with the devil) which committed him to himself with his tears and with his blood, with fervour, with an intense suffering. This work – like all those that will follow – is not cut off from what Nietzsche lives and experiences, and this is what makes it a true 'commitment'. What dominates, though, and 'heralds' the writing of the final period, is a tone of great freedom;[19] 'a wind of *great* freedom' says *Ecce Homo*, to introduce a greater continuity with the 'lightning bolt' to which he nowadays likens his style: a wind which already sought to carry everything away, make everything explode. Even if he seemed at that stage to attribute this idea to Schopenhauer, in *Schopenhauer as Educator*, quoting Emerson,[20] Nietzsche was actually already thinking of philosophy as an explosive imperilling the whole world – a conception which he opposes to the innocuous one of academic tradition, where philosopher-civil servants like Kant ruminate away peaceably (without 'ruminating' in the sense which section 8 of the 'Preface' to the *Genealogy* exhorts) in the service of the State, fashion, and the moment, in no sense legislators by themselves.[21] If the arrival of a great thinker, like the birth of a tremendous centre of forces, is dangerous, said Nietzsche:

> it is of course clear why our academic thinkers are not dangerous; for their thoughts grow as peaceably out of tradition as any tree ever bore its apples: they cause no alarm, they remove nothing from its hinges; and of all their art and aims there could be said what Diogenes said when someone praised a philosopher in his presence: 'How can he be considered great, since he has been a philosopher for so long and has never yet *disturbed* anybody?' That, indeed, ought to be the epitaph of university philosophy: 'it disturbed no-

body'. But this, of course, is praise of an old woman rather than of the goddess of truth.

If something of the third *Untimely Meditation* ought to 'remain' and return eternally, it is indeed this new conception of the philosopher and the educator. Because from this point of view it provides an invaluable lesson, this 'so-called' youthful text is reaffirmed by Nietzsche, with just one change: a change of title. The name of Nietzsche is substituted for that of Schopenhauer, which is decreed a mere metaphor. A substitution of one name for the other which is necessary in order to avoid confusion between what belongs to Nietzsche and what belongs to his antipode – the one who ultimately, like Wagner,[22] is diametrically opposed to him from a typological point of view and who, because he walks on his hands, inverts and perverts all values. To save himself from the risk of contamination by the miasmas coming from another hemisphere, and to preserve all his typological purity, Nietzsche erases the name of Schopenhauer and puts him in his place, which is not that of an identificatory model or a double, but an antipode, as such to be banished to the antipodes.

And yet Nietzsche needed to start by 'misinterpreting' Schopenhauer and Wagner, by deluding himself about them enough to seize hold of their masks for his use. His antipodes were a required detour in order for him to accede in full clarity to 'his name' and to the conquest of his own hemisphere. In the same way, he needed to make a detour by way of philological science in order to become an honest and rigorous 'philologist' – a 'philologist' who no longer has anything to do with what, before Nietzsche, was called philology. He needed to be many things (*vieles*) and in many places (*vielerorts*), to go from one pole to the other, in order to achieve unity and 'himself'. He needed to start by living in a quite different hemisphere, quite different atmospheres, before conquering his own native soil, in his own hemisphere, in his own climate. Thus he had to sojourn a while among the tribe of the scholars, which allowed him, as the third *Untimely Meditation* proves, to mark off better his distance from scientific activity, which, instrumental in essence, can only play the role of an accessory for the philosopher and his explosive mission. Only the philosopher posits aims and legislates; he can, and indeed must, use all the means at his disposal, since (and this is a law of life) the weakest forces owe obedience to the strongest forces, which, bending them to their perspective and subjecting them to their service, nevertheless claim for themselves alone the success of the collectivity.

When Nietzsche declares: 'Wagner and Schopenhauer were already me',[23] he is just applying to his own case this general law: the instruments for carrying out a task – such as the 'sub-wills' or 'sub-souls' which constitute the body, a collectivity of multiple souls, and which are in the service of this collectivity – are destined to be forgotten in the interest of the ruling class, which alone identifies itself with the result obtained: it can satisfy itself only by means of this 'forgetting' of genesis, which constitutes the illusion of a 'self' and is yet merely an effect.[24]

Nietzsche, who was able to accede to mastery over 'himself' only by first making the most opposing forces work for him, could feel fully 'himself' only by detaching himself from all the people and things that had been of service to him. It is the *pathos of distance* in him which always enabled him to distinguish what was mission, true task, great seriousness, from what was merely means, accessory, distraction: in this case, at the time of the third *Untimely Meditation*, the nobility of his flair allowed him to distinguish what was for him a mere trade (*Handwerk*), his philological activity, from his true, and truly philosophical task. The passage on the psychology of the scholar,[25] which the *après-coup* terms an 'astringent [*herbes*] piece', signs this awareness of the difference between what is an end and what is merely a means, and the distancing of everything that is merely an 'accessory' – finally banished to the antipodes – after it has served in constructing what is essential, an 'own' single self, and in accomplishing its 'mission'.

However, in the *Druckmanuskript*, before corrections, Nietzsche does not give exactly the same version: he says that even though he clearly distinguished between the philosophical 'genius' and the scientific worker, he himself at this time was absolutely not a philosopher, and everything 'astringent' written against the scholar was directed, in fact, against himself:

> Do people want a sample of how I felt about myself at that time – degenerated practically into a scholar, one more bookworm [turning over and over][26] crawling [through] around the ancient metricians with meticulous precision and bad eyes, [busy] obsessed with a trade which not only used up three quarters of my energy but deprived me of the very time I needed simply to think of replacing [the] energy? I give [that abysmal] that astringent piece of psychology of the scholar which suddenly leaps out in your face in this work, as if [hurled forth by an unspeakable something] arising from an unspeakable experience. (KSA 14, 488ff.)[27]

The definitive version deletes this passage, for in fact, far from wanting to insist on his experience at that stage of the scholar's trade, with which he was 'obsessed', Nietzsche is keen, as throughout *Ecce Homo*, to emphasize the continuity between yesterday's and today's 'Nietzsche'.

His ability to describe scientific activity in such a pejorative way becomes, in the *après-coup*, the symptom of the following: the fact that Nietzsche, at his full noble distance, was already managing to draw away from what was for him simply an accessory, a source of income, a trade (*Handwerk*), and for which – opposing it to what philosophy requires – he felt a thoroughly Platonic contempt.[28] He only ever used this *Handwerk* in order to 'get his hand in', to master himself in his true interests, to grasp better the profound unity of a will which, from the beginning, distinguishes him from the tribe of the scholars, the multiplicity of whose instincts always remains in a multicoloured state, for want of a single centre of perspective which could hierarchise and unify them. In the 'young' Nietzsche nothing was ever isolated fragments[29] or a chemical type of mixture, even if in order to accede to an awareness of the unity of his own will, he necessarily had to go via alterity: whether by identifying himself with types which were not yet fixed, onto which he unwittingly projected his own richness and fertility, offering himself up as a tribute as if to the Minotaur; or by plying 'trades' at the antipodes of his philosophical task. Such were the 'detours' which his instinctive intelligence (*Klugheit*), well aware of what it was doing, necessarily imposed on him, at the risk of first having him taken, and take himself, for anything but what he was. For example Wagner and Schopenhauer; for example a scholar, banished *après coup* to his prop room (*magasin des accessoires*) by Nietzsche, who alone legislates and is truly a master.[30]

NOTES

Translated by Duncan Large. Translator's Note (hereafter 'TN'). The French version of this text appeared as a chapter (pp. 158–74) in the second volume of Sarah Kofman's two-volume study of *Ecce Homo*, *Explosion* (*Explosion I: De l' "Ecce Homo" de Nietzsche* (Paris: Galilée, 1992); *Explosion II: Les enfants de Nietzsche* (Paris: Galilée, 1993)). The French title (*'Accessoires'*) implies not only things of secondary importance, 'inessentials', but (theatrical) 'props' and, as will become apparent, stages in Nietzsche's 'accession to himself'.

The following published Nietzsche translations have been used: *The Anti-Christ*, in *Twilight of the Idols* and *The Anti-Christ*, trans. by R. J. Hollingdale (Harmondsworth: Penguin, 1968), pp. 113–87; *Ecce Homo*, trans. by R. J. Hollingdale (Harmondsworth: Penguin, 1979); *Nietzsche contra Wagner*, in *The Portable Nietzsche*, ed. and trans. by Walter Kaufmann (Harmondsworth: Penguin, 1976), pp. 661–83; *Selected Letters of Friedrich Nietzsche*, ed. and trans. by Christopher Middleton (Chicago and London: University of Chicago Press, 1969); *Untimely Meditations*, trans. by R. J. Hollingdale (Cambridge: Cambridge University Press, 1983). All other Nietzsche passages have been translated from the German.

The following abbreviations are used: GOA – *Nietzsche's Werke* (*'Grossoktavausgabe'*), 19 vols (Leipzig: Naumann; Kröner, 1901–13); KSA –

Friedrich Nietzsche: Sämtliche Werke ('*Kritische Studienausgabe*'), 15 vols, ed. by Giorgio Colli and Mazzino Montinari (Munich: dtv; Berlin and New York: de Gruyter, 1980).

1 TN: cf. the chapter ('*Attaques*', pp. 133–43) which Kofman devotes to this section earlier in *Explosion II*: 'This section is like a musical overture where the themes subsequently reprised are simply "struck up" ["*attaqués*"]' (p. 137).

2 Before corrections, the *Druckmanuskript* [TN: final handwritten version] added: 'despite the gratitude which certain intelligent admirers of both great men expressed to me precisely for this reason, too – including A. Bilharz, the most scientific of them' (KSA 14, 488). A. Bilharz (1836–1925), physician and philosopher, corresponded with Nietzsche in 1879.

3 Cf. *Richard Wagner in Bayreuth*, 7: 'one might assume the existence in him of an original histrionic talent which had to deny itself satisfaction by the most obvious and trivial route and which found its expedient and deliverance in drawing together all the arts into a great histrionic manifestation'.

4 TN: as the French term implies, Kofman stresses that Nietzsche's 'flair' lies in his having a good nose, 'like a police dog' (*Explosion I*, p. 168). Cf. *Ecce Homo*, 'Why I am a Destiny', 1: 'My genius is in my nostrils'.

5 TN: the perspective from 'after the event' (although the 'event' may not have been); retrospective (re)interpretation. The French translation of the psycho-analytic term 'Nachträglichkeit' ('deferred action', 'retroaction').

6 Cf. *The Case of Wagner*, 7.

7 Cf. *The Case of Wagner*, 8 and 11. Cf. also *Nietzsche contra Wagner*, 'Where I Offer Objections': 'Wagner [. . .] was essentially a man of the theatre and an actor, the most enthusiastic mimomaniac, perhaps, who ever existed, *even as a musician.*' 'Music as a means to clarify, strengthen, and lend inward dimension to the dramatic gesture and the actor's appeal to the senses – and the Wagnerian drama, a mere occasion for many interesting poses!'

8 Cf. *Explosion I*, 'Comment l'on devient ce que l'on est' ['How One Becomes What One Is', pp. 55–69].

9 Is Nietzsche imagining that, by doing this, Schopenhauer confirms the mistrust which Kant, in the *Critique of Judgement*, shows towards rhetorical methods?

10 Cf. Sarah Kofman, *Nietzsche and Metaphor*, ed. and trans. by Duncan Large (London: Athlone Press; Stanford, CA: Stanford University Press, 1993), 'The Rhetorical Paradigm', pp. 32–4. Cf. also Philippe Lacoue-Labarthe, 'The Detour', trans. by Gary M. Cole, in Philippe Lacoue-Labarthe, *The Subject of Philosophy*, ed. by Thomas Trezise (Minneapolis and London: Minnesota University Press, 1993), pp. 14–63.

11 Cf. the 'Introduction' to *Explosion I* ['Explosion I: Of Nietzsche's *Ecce Homo*', trans. by Duncan Large, *diacritics*, 24/4 (Winter 1994), 51–70], and, among other texts of Nietzsche's, *Beyond Good and Evil*, 190.

12 Cf. the letter to Rohde of 25 October 1872, in *Selected Letters of Friedrich Nietzsche*, p. 104.

13 Cf. *Explosion I*, 'Comment l'on devient ce que l'on est'.

14 Cf. *Ecce Homo*, 'Why I Am So Clever', 9 and *Explosion I*, 'Voies de traverse' ['Byways', pp. 367–75].

15 Cf. *On the Genealogy of Morals*, 'Preface', 3. [TN: for further discussion of Nietzsche's relation to the Jews, cf. Sarah Kofman, *Le mépris des Juifs:*

Nietzsche, les Juifs, l'antisémitisme (Paris: Galilée, 1994) (English trans. forthcoming from Macmillan Press, 1996).]

16 TN: cf. *Ecce Homo*, 'Why I Am So Clever', 1 ('moraline-free virtue') and *Explosion I*, p. 278.

17 TN: cf. *Explosion I*, p. 64, where Kofman quotes from Nietzsche's letter to Gersdorff of 7 April 1866: 'What to me [. . .] were the eternal "Thou shalt", "Thou shalt not"! How different the lightning, the wind, the hail, free powers, without ethics! How fortunate, how strong they are, pure will, without obscurings from the intellect!' (*Selected Letters of Friedrich Nietzsche*, p. 12).

18 ' "Neither by land nor by sea shalt thou find the road to the Hyperboreans": Pindar already knew that of us. Beyond the North, beyond the ice, beyond death – *our* life, *our* happiness. [. . .] Better to live among ice than among modern virtues and other south winds! [. . .] We became gloomy, we were called fatalists. *Our* fatality *was* the plenitude, the tension, the blocking-up of our forces. We thirsted for lightning and action, of all things we kept ourselves furthest from the happiness of the weaklings, from "resignation". . . . There was a thunderstorm in our air, the nature which we are grew dark – *for we had no road*' (*The Anti-Christ*, 1).

19 Cf. *Schopenhauer as Educator*, 8: 'freedom and again freedom: that wonderful and perilous element in which the Greek philosophers were able to grow up'.

20 Cf. the epigraph to *Explosion I*, and *Schopenhauer as Educator*, 8.

21 For all this, cf. Sarah Kofman, 'Le/les "concepts" de culture dans les *Intempestives* ou la double dissimulation' ['The "Concept(s)" of Culture in the *Untimely Meditations*, or the Double Dissimulation'], in *Nietzsche aujourd'hui?*, 2 vols (Paris: UGE, 1973), II ('Passion'), pp. 119–46; reprinted in Sarah Kofman, *Nietzsche et la scène philosophique* (Paris: UGE, 1979; Galilée, 1986), pp. 337–71.

22 Cf. the 'Preface' to *Nietzsche contra Wagner*: read one after the other, his writings on Wagner would leave no doubt, either about Richard Wagner or about himself: they were antipodes. In the chapter entitled 'We Antipodes', having shown that he had enriched Wagner and Schopenhauer with himself, that he had as it were offered himself up to them as a tribute, he shows how they both respond to the need of those impoverished of life, for whom avenging themselves on life itself represents the most voluptuous kind of intoxication: 'they negate life, they slander it, hence they are my antipodes.'

23 TN: cf. *Ecce Homo*, 'Why I Write Such Good Books', 'The Untimelies', 1: 'Schopenhauer and Wagner *or*, in *one* word, Nietzsche', and *Explosion II*, pp. 141–3.

24 Cf. *Beyond Good and Evil*, 62 and 19. [TN: for further discussion of the forgetting of genesis, cf. 'Genesis of the Concept and Genesis of Justice' in *Nietzsche and Metaphor*, pp. 42–9.]

25 Above all sections 3 and 6. Themes are set out here which will continually return in the rest of the works; the scholar is cited among the powers which patronize culture without knowing its goal – which, for Nietzsche in this period, is the production of genius. He is cold and dry. He has no love and knows nothing of the self-annoyance, dissatisfaction, or longing proper to the self. . . . Science ossifies its servants; the scholar is not a man but a rattling of bones. The scholar, who fingers all the most venerable things in the world, deserves in turn to be dissected, a task to which Nietzsche devotes himself in these pages of the third *Untimely Meditation*, as he strives to disentangle the

network of various instincts and impulses which characterises him. He grants him probity and a taste for simplicity – which are simply the reverse side of his inexperience in dissimulation and his lack of malice – and a clear-sightedness for things that are close up, the correlate of which is a great myopia for the distant and the general. He has a most restricted field of vision and has to bring an object right up to his eyes till they touch it. He fragments every thing and reconstitutes its unity only by induction. Thus, unlike the philosopher, whom he can only hate, he has absolutely no sense of the general. The scholar has a prosaic and vulgar nature which makes him incapable, if he is a historian, of understanding what is rare, great, uncommon. Furthermore his modesty reveals his lack of self-esteem: banished to a dark corner, scholars of this kind feel neither sacrificed nor humiliated; they seem to know that they are not flying, but creeping, creatures. This is why they crowd around a master and initiator, to whom they remain loyal. They continue along the road onto which they have been pushed, and seek the truth mechanically, in accordance with the habit they have adopted. Unlike the philosophers, they dread leisure for fear of getting bored. Their consolation lies in books: by listening to someone else think differently to themselves, they succeed in killing time. Industrious (*Besogneux*), they are also the men of need (*besoin*): hence they serve only a profitable truth. They respect their colleagues and fear their contempt, vying with each other to give their name to an invention. Scholars are such from vanity or for fun, and in general they lack the noble instinct for justice which would be enough to inflame their lives and their activity, ennobling it to the extent of making them forget the multicoloured mixture from which they spring. But most of the time the scholar is unfruitful by himself and feels resentment towards the fruitful man, the genius with whom he is always at odds: the former wants to kill nature and dissect it in order to understand it; the latter wants to augment it by adding to it a second nature which is new and living.

26 TN: material in square brackets in passages translated from Nietzsche's *Druckmanuskript* was deleted in the manuscript itself.

27 Cf. also *Human, All Too Human* I, 252 and, in *Ecce Homo*, the third section devoted to *Human, All Too Human*.

28 In his 1875 Basel lecture course 'Der Gottesdienst der Griechen' ['Greek Worship'], Nietzsche wrote: 'Thinking, in customs of worship, inventing and uniting, is essentially the activity of men of *leisure*, it is part of the χάλῶζ οχολάζειν, the guiding principle of the noblest Hellenism: on account of this principle the Greeks are the men of distinction' (GOA, XIX, 6).

29 Cf. also *On the Genealogy of Morals*, 'Preface', 2.

30 (Extra note for the English translation.) My thanks to Duncan Large for correcting a number of misprints and referencing mistakes which existed in the French edition.

REFERENCES

Primary

Works quoted from:
Friedrich Nietzsche, *The Antichrist*, in *Twilight of the Idols* and *The Antichrist*, trans. by R. J. Hollingdale, Harmondsworth: Penguin, 1968, pp. 113–87.

——, *Ecce Homo*, trans. by R. J. Hollingdale, Harmondsworth: Penguin, 1979.
——, *Friedrich Nietzsche: Sämtliche Werke* ('*Kritische Studienausgabe*'), 15 vols, ed. by Giorgio Colli and Mazzino Montinari, Munich: dtv; Berlin and New York: de Gruyter, 1980.
——, 'Der Gottesdienst der Griechen', in GOA, XIX, 1–124.
——, *Nietzsche contra Wagner*, in *The Portable Nietzsche*, ed. and trans. by Walter Kaufmann, Harmondsworth: Penguin, 1976, pp. 661–83.
——, *Nietzsche's Werke* ('*Grossoktavausgabe*'), 19 vols, Leipzig: Naumann; Kröner, 1901–13.
——, *Selected Letters of Friedrich Nietzsche*, ed. and trans. by Christopher Middleton, Chicago and London: University of Chicago Press, 1969.
——, *Untimely Meditations*, trans. by R. J. Hollingdale, Cambridge: Cambridge University Press, 1983.

Other works cited:
Friedrich Nietzsche, *Beyond Good and Evil*.
——, *The Case of Wagner*.
——, *Human, All Too Human*.
——, *On the Genealogy of Morals*.

Secondary

Immanuel Kant, *Critique of Judgement*.
Sarah Kofman, 'Le/les "concepts" de culture dans les *Intempestives* ou la double dissimulation', in *Nietzsche aujourd'hui?*, 2 vols, Paris: UGE, 1973, II ('Passion'), pp. 119–46; reprinted in Sarah Kofman, *Nietzsche et la scène philosophique*, Paris: UGE, 1979; Galilée, 1986, pp. 337–71.
——, *Explosion I: De l'Ecce Homo' de Nietzsche*, Paris: Galilée, 1992.
——, *Explosion II: Les enfants de Nietzsche*, Paris: Galilée, 1993.
——, *Nietzsche and Metaphor*, ed. and trans. by Duncan Large, London: Athlone Press; Stanford, CA: Stanford University Press, 1993.
——, *Le mépris des Juifs: Nietzsche, les Juifs, l'antisémitisme*, Paris: Galilée, 1994.
——, 'Explosion I: Of Nietzsche's *Ecce Homo*', trans. by Duncan Large, *diacritics*, 24/4 (Winter 1994), 51–70.
Philippe Lacoue-Labarthe, 'The Detour', trans. by Gary M. Cole, in Philippe Lacoue-Labarthe, *The Subject of Philosophy*, ed. by Thomas Trezise, Minneapolis and London: Minnesota University Press, 1993, pp. 14–63.

10
Shamanic Nietzsche

Nick Land

God said to Nietzsche:
That'll Tietzsche,
You irritating little Krietzsche.
Anonymous graffito

Will Christendom ever *reap the whirlwind* it has sown? That it should try
to pass without the vulnerability of interval from a tyranny to a joke is
certainly understandable, but that its enemies should do nothing to
obstruct its evasion of nemesis is more puzzling. How can there be such
indifference to the decline of our inquisitors? Is it that they succeeded so
exorbitantly in their project of domestication that we have been robbed
of every impulse to bite back? Having at last escaped from the torture-
palace of authoritarian love we shuffle about, numb and confused,
flinching from the twisted septic wound of our past (now clumsily
bandaged with the rags of secular culture). It is painfully evident that
post-christian humanity is a pack of broken dogs.

Georges Bataille is the preeminent textual impediment to Christianity's carefully plotted *quiet death*; the prolongation of its terminal
agonies into the twentieth century. Having definitively exhausted itself
after two ugly millennia of species vivisection, Christianity attempts to
skulk away from the scene, aided by the fog of supine tolerance which
dignifies itself as 'post-modernity'. It does not take a genius to see whose
interests are served by this passage from militant theism to postmodern
ambivalence.

A despot abandons any game that begins to turn out badly. This has
been the case with metaphysics. From Kant onwards exploratory philosophy ceased to generate the outcomes favourable to established

(theistic) power, and we were suddenly told: 'this game is over, let's call it a draw'. The authoritarian tradition of European reason tried to pull the plug on the great voyages *at exactly the point they first became interesting*, which is to say: atheistic, inhuman, experimental, and dangerous. Schopenhauer – refusing the agnostic stand-off of antinomy – was the first rallying zone for all those disgusted by the contrived peace entitled 'the end of metaphysics'. Bataille is his most recent successor. The forces of antichrist are emerging fanged and encouraged from their scorched rat-holes in the wake of monotheistic hegemony, without the slightest attachment to the paralytic tinkerings of deconstructive undecidability. 'An attitude which is neither military nor religious becomes insupportable in principle from the moment of death's arrival' (II 246). The war has scarcely begun.

It is hard to imagine anything more ludicrous than Descartes, or Kant, having erected their humble philosophical dwellings alongside the baroque architectural excesses of the church, standing in the shadows of flying buttresses and asking pompously: how do we know the truth? It surely cannot solely be due to Nietzsche that we see the absurdity of an 'epistemological' question being asked in such surroundings. When a philosopher has a priest for a neighbour, which is to say, a practitioner of the most elaborately constructed system of mendacity ever conceived upon earth, how can a commitment to 'truth' in a positive sense even be under consideration? Truth in such situations is a privilege of the deaf. There is no question of 'error', 'weakness in reasoning', or 'mistaken judgement' when addressing the authoritative discourses on truth in the western tradition, those cathedrals of theological concept building that ground our 'common sense'; no, here one can only speak of a deeply rooted and fanatical *discipline of lying*. In other words, one fraction of the radicality of the atheistic thinking escalated through Schopenhauer, Nietzsche, and Bataille is that it overthrows the high-bourgeois apologetic-epistemological problematic in modern philosophy by asking clearly for the first time: where do the lies stop?

The great educational value of the war against Christendom lies in the *absolute* truthlessness of the priest. Such purity is rare enough. The 'man of God' is entirely incapable of honesty, and only arises at the point where truth is defaced beyond all legibility. Lies are his entire metabolism, the air he breathes, his bread and his wine. He cannot comment upon the weather without a secret agenda of deceit. No word, gesture, or perception is slight enough to escape his extravagant reflex of falsification, and of the lies in circulation he will instinctively seize on the grossest, the most obscene and oppressive travesty. Any proposition passing the lips of a priest is *necessarily* totally false, excepting only insidiouses whose message is momentarily misunderstood. It is impossible to deny him without discovering some buried fragment or reality.

There is no truth that is not war against theology, and even the word 'truth' has been plastered by the spittle of priestcraft. It cannot be attachment to some alternative conviction that *cuts* here, but only relentless refusal of what has been told. The dangerous infidels bypass dialectics. It is the sceptic who assassinates the lie.

Whenever its name has been anything but a jest, philosophy has been haunted by a subterranean question: what if knowledge were a means to deepen unknowing? It is this thought alone that has differentiated it from the shallow things of the earth. Yet the glory and also the indignity of philosophy is to have sought the end of knowing, and no more.

Once blatant sophisms are exempted, the fact that scepticism has never been *enacted* is the sole argument of the dogmatists, and it is a powerful one, despite its empirical flavour. There can be little doubt that the philosophical advocates of disbelief have tended to exploit the very conventions they profess to despise as the shelter for an insincere madness. As was the case with Socrates, philosophy has sought to peel itself away from sophism by admitting to its ignorance, as if unknowing were a pathos to be confessed. Profound ecsanity ['Ecsane' – out of one's mind] alone is effective scepticism, in comparison to which sceptical philosophies fall prey to naïve theories of belief, as if belief could simply be discarded, or withheld. We know nothing of course, but we do not remotely know even this, and mere assertion in no way ameliorates our destitution. Belief is not a possession but a prison, and we continue to believe in achieved knowledge even after denying it with intellectual comprehensiveness. The refusal to accept a dungeon is no substitute for a hole in the wall. Only in a voyage to the unknown is there real escape from conviction.

The dangerous sceptics are those Kant fears, 'a species of nomads, despising all settled modes of life' (K 8) who come from a wilderness tract beyond knowledge. They are explorers, which is also to say: invasion routes of the unknown. It is by way of these inhumanists that the vast abrupt of shamanic zero – the ἐποχή of the ancients – infiltrates its contagious madness onto the earth.

Ἐποχή is a word attributed to Pyrrho by way of indirect reportage, but in its absence the philosopher's name would lose what slight sense invests it. Although it might be argued that we owe ἐποχή to Pyrrho, it is from ἐποχή that the name Pyrrho comes to us, as a cryptograph of the unknown. Even were it not for Pyrrho's silence – a silence far more *profound* that the literary abstinence of Socrates – ἐποχή would surely not be something of which we could straightforwardly know the truth, far less a method, or a subjective state.

Ἐποχή is a report of the abrupt, and an escape.

1. [. . .]
2. the world of 'phenomena' is the adapted world which we feel to be real. The 'reality' lies in the continual recurrence of identical, familiar, related things in their logicized character, in the belief that here we are able to reckon and calculate;
3. the antithesis of this phenomenal world is not 'the true world,' but the formless unformulable world of the chaos of sensations – *another kind* of phenomenal world, a kind 'unknowable' for us;
4. questions, what things 'in-themselves' may be like, apart from our sense receptivity and the activity of our understanding, must be rebutted with the question: how could we know that things exist? 'Thingness' was first created by us. The question is whether there could not be many other ways of creating such an apparent world. (WP 569)

How much industrialism lies buried in the notion of thought! As if one could ever *work things out*. One does not think one's way out, one gets out, and then sees (that it wasn't one . . .).

Bataille's Nietzsche is not a locus of secular reason but of shamanic religion; a writer who escapes philosophical conceptuality in the direction of ulterior zones, and dispenses with the *thing in itself* because it is an item of intelligible representation with no consequence as a vector of becoming (of travel). Shamanism defies the transcendence of death, opening the tracts of 'voyages of discovery never reported' (R 327). Against the grain of shallow phenomenalism that characterizes Nietzsche readings, Bataille pursues the fissure of abysmal scepticism, which passes out of the Kantian *Noumenon* (or intelligible object) through Kant and Schopenhauer's *thing in itself* (stripping away a layer of residual Platonism), and onwards in the direction of acategorial, epochal, or *base* matter that connects with Rimbaud's 'invisible splendours' (R 296): the immense deathscapes of a 'universe without images' (R 293). Matter cannot be allotted a category without being retrieved for ideality, and the Nietzschean problem with the *Ding an Sich* was not its supposed dogmatic materialism, but rather that it proposed 'an ideal form of matter' (I 179), as the transcendent (quarantined) site of integral truth, a 'real world'. There are no things-in-themselves because there are no things: 'thingness has only been invented by us owing to the requirements of logic' (WP #558) (which ultimately revert to those of grammar). The *Ding an Sich* is a concept tailored for a God (supreme being) desperately seeking to hide itself: a cultural glitch turned nasty, but on the run at last. 'Root of the idea of substance in language, not in beings outside us' (WP #562)!

> The antithesis of the apparent world and the true world is reduced to the antithesis 'world' and 'nothing'. (WP #567)

Materialism is not a doctrine but an expedition, an Alpine break-out from socially policed conviction. It 'is before anything else the obstinate negation of idealism, which is to say of the very basis of *all* philosophy' (I 220). Exploring acategorial matter navigates thought as chance and matter as turbulence 'beyond all regulation' (VI 97). It yields no propositions to judge, but only paths to explore.

This is Nietzsche as a fanged poet at war with the philosophers (with the new priests), a thinker who seeks *to make life more problematic*. Bataille locks onto a desire that resonates with the reality that confounds us, and not with a 'rationality' that would extricate us from the labyrinth. Nietzsche is the great exemplar of complicating thought, exploiting knowledge in the interest of interrogations (and this is not in order to clarify and focus, but to subtilize and dissociate them). Complicating thought strengthens the impetus of an active or energetic confusion – delirium – against the reactive forces whose obsessive tendency is to resolve or conclude. Rebelling against the fundamental drift of philosophical reasoning, it sides with thought against knowledge, against the tranquillizing prescriptions of the 'will to truth'.

If Nietzsche is locked in an extraordinarily furious struggle with philosophy it is because it is philosophy that has claimed, with the most cynical explicitness, to negate problems. Philosophy has always wanted to retire; Schopenhauer is simply its most honest examplar. The 'absolute' is humanity's laziest thought. Nor does it suffice to argue that thought can be complicated within itself, or – as the philosophers have said for some time – 'immanently', for we know where this path of thinking leads. An intellection in need of immanent critique is one that is already nudging against an ultimate solubility. 'The intellect finds its limits within itself' – it does not even need to move to consummate interrogation! It is thinking such as this, whose most eminent model is the Kant of the critical philosophy, that generated such distrust in Nietzsche for writers who work sitting down.

Wisdom (*sophia*) substitutes for travelling, hollowing it out into a Baudelairean caricature of the *Voyage* – redundantly reiterating a moral dogma – and to love it is to seek to be still. In obedience to narco-Platonic Eros, philosophy defers to the end of desire. Nietzsche reaches back beyond this Hellenic priest-philosophizing, and forward beyond its modern limit, reassembling *sophia* as escape:

> Indeed, we philosophers and 'free spirits' feel, when we hear the news that 'the old god is dead,' as if a new dawn shone on us; our heart overflows with gratitude, amazement, premonitions, expectations. At long last the horizon appears free to us again, even if it should not be bright; at long last our ships may venture out again, venture out to face any danger; all the daring of the lover of knowledge is permitted again; the sea, *our* sea, lies open again; perhaps there has never yet been such an 'open sea'. (GS #343)

The death of God is an opportunity, a chance. It makes sense to ask *what is meant* by the word 'noumenon', but 'chance' does not function in this way, since it is not a concept to be apprehended, but a direction in which to go. 'To the one who grasps what chance is, how insipid the idea of God appears, and suspicious, and wing-clipping' (VI 116)! Monotheism is the great gate-keeper, and where it ends the exploration of death begins. If there are places to which we are forbidden to go, it is because they can in truth be reached, or *because they can reach us*. In the end poetry is invasion and not expression, a trajectory of incineration; either strung-up in the cobwebs of Paradise, or strung-out into the shadow-torrents of hell. It is a route out of creation, which is to each their fate interpreted as enigma, as *lure*. 'Now a hard, an inexorable voyage commences – a quest into the greatest possible distance' (VI 29). 'I said good-bye to the world' (R 330). Even the most angelic curiousity – when multiplied to the power of eternity – must find its way to end in the abyss.

It can seem at times as if Bataille owes almost everything to Christianity; his understanding of the evil at the heart of erotic love, the hysterical affectivity of his writing, along with its excremental obsession, its epileptoid conception of delight, its malignancy, the perpetual stench of the gutter. Yes, this is all very Christian; well attuned to a doctrine gestated in the sewers of the empire. Yet from out of the aberrant intensity and disorder of Bataille's writings an *impossible* proposition is perpetually reiterated: that far from being the acme of religion – let alone its telic blossoming – God is the principle of its suppression. The unity of *theos* is the tombstone of sacred zero, the crumbling granitic foundation of secular destitution. This is so exorbitantly true that the existence of God would be an even greater disaster for him than for us. How infinitely trivial the crucifixion of Jesus appears beside the degrading torture of being God, after all, existence is so indistinguishable from defilement that one turns pale at the very thought of an eternal being's *smell*. Perhaps this is why God 'is profoundly atheistic' (V 121), leading Bataille to remark that '[w]hilst I am God, I deny him to the depths of negation' (V 152) ('nihilism . . . might be a *divine way of thinking*' (WP #15) Nietzsche anticipates). God can only redeem the universe from its servility by burning his creation into ash and annihilating himself. Such is the 'God of blinding sun, . . . this God of death that I sought' (IV 203). Bataille invokes the dark undertow of a self-butchering divinity: 'God of despair, give me . . . your heart . . . which no longer tolerates that you exist' (V 59). (If God is an explorer, then there is no God.)

Bataille's texts are 'a hecatomb of words without gods or reason to be' (V 220), led back down through the crypts of the West by a furious impulse to dissociate theism and religion, and thus to return the sacred to its shamanic impiety, except that nothing can ever simply return, and Hell will never be an innocent underworld again. The depths have become infernal, really so, quite irrespective of the fairy tales we are still told. '[F]lames surround us / the abyss opens beneath our feet' (III 95) reports Bataille from the brink of the impossible, 'an abyss that does not end in the satiate contemplation of an absence' (V 199) because its lip is the charred ruin of even the most sublimed subjectivity. 'I have nothing to do in this world' he writes '[i]f not to burn' (IV 17). 'I suffer from not burning . . . approaching so close to death that I respire it like the breath of a lover' (V 246). It is not only due to the inquistion that all the great voyagers have for a long time been *singed*. For well over a century all who have wanted to see have seen: no profound exploration can be launched from the ruins of monotheism unless it draws its resources from damnation.

The death of God is a religious event – a transgression, experiment in damnation, and stroke of antitheistic warfare – but this is not to say it is pre-eminently a crime. Hell has no interest in our debauched moral currency. To confuse reactive dabblings in sin with expeditions in damnation is Christian superficiality; the Dantean error of imagining that one could earn oneself an excursion in Hell, as if the infernal too was a matter of justice. Our crimes are mere stumblings on the path to ruin, just as every projected *Hell on Earth* is a strict exemplar of idolatry. Transgression is not criminal action, but tragic fate; the intersection of an economically programmed apocalypse with the religious antihistory of poetry. It is the inevitable occurrence of impossibility, which is not the same as death, but neither is it essentially different.

This ambivalence responds to that of death 'itself', which is not ontological but labyrinthine: a relapse of composition that is absolute to discontinuity, yet is nothing at the level of immanence. The very individuality that would condition the possibility of a proprietary death could only be achieved if death were impossible. One dies because discontinuity is never realized, but this means that there is never 'one' who dies. Instead there is an unthinkable communication with zero, immanence, or the sacred. 'There is no feeling that throws one into exuberance with greater force than that of nothingness. But exuberance is not at all annihilation; it is the surpassing of the shattered attitude, it is transgression' (X 72).

> The question of the mere 'truth' of Christianity – whether in regard of its origin, not to speak of Christian astronomy and natural science – is a matter of secondary importance as long as the question of the value of Christian morality is not considered. (WP #251)

What if eternal recurrence were not a belief? ('The most extreme form of nihilism would be the view that *every* belief . . . is necessarily false because there simply is no *true world*' (WP #15).) Bataille suggests:

> The return *immotivates* the instant, freeing life from an end and in this ruining it straight away. The return is . . . the desert of one for whom each instant henceforth finds itself immotivated. (VI 23)

Christianity – the exemplary moral 'religion' – 'substituted slow suicide' (WP #247) and representation (belief) for shamanic contact with zero-interruption, but with the (re-)emergence of nihilisitic recurrence, caution, prudence, every kind of 'concern for time to come' (VI 50, 167, etc.) is restored to the senselessness of cosmic 'noise'. With recurrence comes a '*future*, [which is] not the prolongation of myself across time, but the expiry of a being going further, passing attained limits' (VI 29). A religious crisis can no longer be deferred.

In the final phase of Nietzsche's intellectual life the eternal recurrence is grasped as a weapon, a 'hammer,' the transmission element between diagnosis and intervention. Where Christendom recuperates decline to preservation, deflecting it from its intensive plummet to zero, eternal recurrence re-opens its abyssal prospect, precipicing affect onto death. This is the predominant sense of 'selection' in Nietzsche's texts; a vertiginous extrication of zero from the series of preservative values, cutting through 'the ambiguous and cowardly compromise of a religion such as Christianity: more precisely, such as the church: which, instead of encouraging death and self-destruction, protects everything ill-consti-tuted and sick and makes it propagate itself' (WP #247).

The notes assembled into section 55 of *The Will to Power* develop this morbid thread. Either 'existence as it is, without meaning or aim, yet recurring inevitably without any finale of nothingness' (a box), or 'the nothing (the "meaningless"), eternally' (WP #55). The nihilism of re-currence is ambivalent between its (Christian) historical sense as the constrictive deceleration of zero and its cosmic (non-local) virtuality as a gateway onto death. Christendom is to be attacked because it was its 'morality that protected life against despair and the leap into nothing' (WP #55).

> Morality guarded the underprivileged against nihilism. . . . Suppos-ing that the faith in this morality would perish, then the underprivi-leged would no longer have their comfort – and they would perish. (WP #55)

The religious history of mankind is based upon a technics of ill-health: dehydration, starvation, mutilation, deprivation of sleep, a general 'self-destruction of the underprivileged: self-vivisection, poisoning, intoxica-tion' (WP #55). A journey was underway which Christian preservative moralism – generalized species cowardice – privatized, representa-tionalized, crushed under the transcendent phallus, froze, obstructed, and *drove elsewhere*. Christianity is a device for trapping the sick, but recurrence melts through the cages:

> What does 'underprivileged' mean? Above all, physiologically – no longer politically. The unhealthiest kind . . . (in all classes) furnishes the soil for this nihilism: they will experience the belief in the eternal recurrence as a curse, struck by which one no longer shrinks from any action; not to be extinguished but to extinguish everything. (WP #55)

To relate sickness to death as cause to effect is itself a sign of health. Their morbid interconnection is quite different. Sickness is not followed by death within the series of ordered representation. It opens the gates.

Genealogy does not reduce sickness to a historical topic, since sickness – the inability to suspend a stimulus – eludes mere unfolding in pro-gressive time, tending towards the disappearance of time in epochal interruption. The reflex-spasm at (and by) which reactivity gropes is the atemporal continuum beneath the crust of health. Death is 'that which has no history' (GM II #13), and Nietzsche's method is syphilis. 'Only religion assures a consumption that destroys the proper substance of those that it animates' (VII 316).

Philosophy is a ghoul that haunts only ruins, and the broken croaks of our hymns to sickness have scarcely begun. Borne by currents of deep exhaustion that flow silent and inexorable beneath the surface perturbations of twitch and chatter, damned, shivering, claw-like fingers hewn from torture and sunk into wreckage drawn with unbearable slowness down into the maw of flame and snuffed blackness twisted skewerish into fever-hollowed eyes. Eternal recurrence is our extermination, and we cling to it as infants to their mother's breasts.

'*Poetry leads from the known to the unknown*' (V 157) writes Bataille, in words that resonate with Rimbaud. Poetry is fluent silence, the only venture of writing to touch upon the sacred (= 0), because 'the unknown . . . is not distinguished from nothingness by anything that discourse can announce' (V 133). To write the edge of the impossible is a transgression against discursive order, and an incitement to the unspeakable: 'poetry is immoral' (V 212).

Rimbaud writes from the other side of Zarathustrean descent/death (*Untergang*), anticipating the labyrinthine spaces of a *Nietzsche for the sick*, and of what escapes from/due to the cultural convulsion Nietzsche reinforces. 'The poet makes himself a *visionary* by a long, immense and rational *deregulation* of *all the senses*' (R 10), and this deregulation is a source of '[i]neffable torture' (R 11), 'the sufferings are enormous' (R 6) Rimbaud insists. No organism is adapted to 'arrive at the unknown' (R 6), which makes deregulation as necessary as it makes pain inevitable. Our nerves squeal when they are re-strung upon the phylogenetically unanticipated, 'experiences strike too deeply; memory becomes a festering wound' (EH 230): a descent into the inferno. *Nuit de l'enfer*, where the entrails of nature dissolve meanderous into lava, 'this is hell, eternal pain' (R 313), and Rimbaud burns, 'as is necessary' (R 313).

Yes, the poet must be a visionary. The East knows a true lucidity, but to be an inheritor of the West is to hack through jungles of indiscipline, devoured by vile ants and words unstrung from sense, until the dripping foliage of delirium opens out onto a space of comprehensive ruin. This has never been understood, nor can it be. The foulness of our fate only deepens with the centuries, as the tracts of insanity sprawl. From bodies gnawed by tropical fevers we swim out through collapse to inexistence in forever, destined for Undo.

True poetry is *hideous*, because it is base communication, in contrast with pseudo-communicative discourse, which presupposes the isolation of the terms it unites. Communication – in the transgressive non-sense Bataille lends it – is both an utter risk and an unfathomable degradation, associated with *repellent* affect. The ego emerges in the flight from communicative immanence, from deep or unholy community, initiating a history that leads to the bitter truth of the desertification of the isolated being. From the anxiety of base contact, which it can only experience as dissolution, the ego stumbles into the *ennui* of autonomy, the antechamber to a harsh despair, whose horror is accentuated by the fact that it arises at the point where escape has exhausted itself, where the ego has quarantined itself to the limit of its being against extraneous misfortune. *Ennui* is not any sort of response to the compromising of the ego from without, it is not an impurity or a contamination (the negation of such things are for it a condition of existence), but rather, it is the very truth of achieved being; the core affect of personal individuality. *Ennui* cannot be mastered, surpassed, resolved, *aufgehoben*, because it is nothing but the distillate of such operations, indeed, of action as such. *Ennui* is insinuated into the very fabric of project, as 'the necessity of leaving oneself' (V 137). If the soil of Bataille's writing is volcanic it is not only due to the sporadic convulsions of a devastating incandescence, but also because its fertility is anticipated by a monstrous sterilization. Beneath and before the luxuriant jungles of delirium is the endless crushing ash-plain of despair.

'I believe that I am in hell, therefore I am there' (R 313). Blake might have written such words, although their sense would then have been quite different. Drooled from Rimbaud's pen they point less to a potency of imagination than to a geological crisis of justification, approaching a perfect epistemological irresponsibility. It is not for us to defend the rights of truth, truth is decreed by the masters. What matters is to adapt, nursing the meagre resources of our reactivity, of our base cunning. 'Belief' – the cloak of confession – is too precious a resource to be squandered on the zealotry of idealism. What value is there to be extracted from a committed belief, from a last-ditch belief? Such things are for the strong (or for dupes), for the allies and slaves of light, for all those who do not rely on the subterranean passages beneath belief to avoid the panoptic apparatuses. Adaptability can only be lamed by commitments. We have seen enough true Christians: rabbits transfixed by headlights. When draped about the inferiors beliefs are not loyalties, but rather sun-blocks against inquisition. We creatures of shadow are hidden from their enlightenment. We believe exactly what they want.

The inferior race 'await God with greed' (R 304), scavanging at Christ 'like wolves at an animal they have not killed' (R 302). Creation, testamental genealogy, the passion of Christ . . . none of it is their story, nor is any other, for they are too indolent to have a story of their own, only theft and lies are 'proper' to them: 'pillage' (R 302). Rimbaud's inheritance, 'above all', consists of 'mendacity and sloth' (R 301). 'I have never been a Christian; I am of the race which sung under torture' (R 307–8) he remarks. It is precisely obliviousness to Christianity, to fidelity or duty, to privileged narratives, that eases the inferior race into singing the praises of the Nazarene. The white man has guns, *therefore* the truth. 'The whites disembark. The cannon! It is necessary to submit to baptism, dress oneself, work' (R 309).

In contrast to the pompous declarations of the orthodoxies, which come from on high (like a stroke of the whip), an infernal message is subterranean, a whisper from the nether-regions of discourse, since 'hell is certainly below' (R 315). Just as the underworld is not a hidden world – a real or true (*Wahre Welt*) – but is that hidden by all worlds, so is the crypt-mutter from hell something other than an inverted scene, concept, or belief. In their infernal lineaments words are passages, leading into and through lost mazes, and not edifications. Acquisition is impossible in hell. There is nothing *en bas* except wandering amongst emergences, and what is available has always come strangely, without belonging. Infernal *low-life* has no understanding for property. Even the thoughts of the inferior ones are camouflage and dissimulation, their beliefs mere chameleon dapplings of the skin.

Poetry does not strut logically amongst convictions, it seeps through crevices; a magmic flux resuscitated amongst vermin. If it was not that the Great Ideas had basements, fissures, and vacuoles, poetry would never infest them. Faiths rise and fall, but the rats persist.

Rimbaud's *saison en enfer* pulsates through a discourse without integrity. Teaching nothing, it infects. Like matter cooked-through with pestilential 'contagions of energy' (V 111), it collapses into a swarm of plague-vectors. Substance is only its host. '[W]ords, books, monuments, symbols, and laughters are nothing but the paths of this contagion, its passages' (V 111).

> I never could conclude anything . . .
> Zero does that.
>
> *Towards New Seas*
>
> That way is my *will*; I trust
> In my mind and in my grip.
> Without plan, into the vast
> Open sea I head my ship.
>
> All is shining, new and newer,
> Upon space and time sleeps noon;

Only *your* eye – monstrously,
Stares at me, infinity
(GS 371)

REFERENCES

Raw Roman numerals refer to volumes of Bataille's *Œuvres Complétes*, published by Gallimard, Paris. Hash marks refer to section (rather than page) numbers.

EH: Nietzsche, *Ecce Homo*, see below.
GM: Nietzsche, *On the Genealogy of Morals*, published together with *Ecce Homo*, New York 1969.
GS: Nietzsche, *The Gay Science*, New York 1974.
WP: Nietzsche, *The Will to Power*, New York 1968.

K: Kant, *The Critique of Pure Reason*, London 1990.

R: Rimbaud, *Collected Poems*, Harmondsworth 1986.

11
Traces of Discordance:
Heidegger–Nietzsche

Will McNeill

"Nietzsche is the *one* that he is . . ."[1]

1 Nietzsche's Name

There is little that can be said with confidence about Heidegger's *Nietzsche*. Certainly, it would be imprudent to take issue with Derrida when he remarks that "the thesis of Heidegger's mighty tome is much less simple than people generally tend to say."[2] Assuming of course that it has a thesis, a single thesis that could be authoritatively identified and demonstrated. To this we might add that the collection of apparently disparate lectures and essays comprising the two volumes that were published under the single title *Nietzsche* is just as much about Heidegger as it is about Nietzsche. And it is just as much about the tradition of philosophizing as it is about either of these two figures. Or perhaps it is not really "about" any of these. When we read these texts closely, they themselves seem to speak of something else. That "something else," presumably, will be traceable via what the texts call *die Sache des Denkens*, the matter or issue of thinking. Perhaps, then, it would, at the outset, be prudent to suspend our deeply rooted prejudice that what is at issue in these texts is the judgment of one thinker on another. All those readings – too many to name – that are quick to accuse Heidegger of a stubborn blindness toward Nietzsche and his "radicality," of "doing violence" or "injustice" to him, doing him a disservice, as it were, seem to rest on the presumption (however strenuously denied) that it is Nietzsche "himself," his "message" or his "philosophy" – *his*, precisely –

that is the issue. Which is hardly to do a great service to the *Sache* Nietzsche, or for that matter to Nietzsche "himself." And to note this is no more to defend "Heidegger" than it is in general to have decided already what lies in wait behind the name of a thinker. We would do well to remind ourselves of the opening words of the 'Foreword" (*Vorwort*, the word before the word, as it were) announcing the publication of Heidegger's *Nietzsche* volumes, volumes which, in the original German edition, simply bore the title *heidegger nietzsche*:

> "Nietzsche" – the name of the thinker stands as title for *the issue* [*die Sache*] of his thinking.

And what is this issue? Heidegger continues:

> The issue, the conflict [*Streitfall*], is in itself confrontation [*Auseinandersetzung*]. To let our thinking enter upon the issue, to prepare thinking for this issue – such is the content of the present publication.[3]

Yet what are we to understand by confrontation, *Aus-einander-setzung*?[4] A confrontation between Heidegger and Nietzsche? Undoubtedly. If only we knew what these names meant. If only we knew who they were, or are, these two: Heidegger and Nietzsche. Who they are: each of them, that is, and then perhaps we could ask concerning both of them, together, concerning the confrontation itself "between" them. Who each of them is: this will no doubt always be a source of conflict and confrontation; people will always argue over who "Nietzsche" really is, over what "Heidegger" or his "philosophy" really represents. This is a source of conflict, to be sure. Yet perhaps something else is at issue in Heidegger's *Aus-einander-setzung* with Nietzsche – something other than a confrontation between two "positions," two positions already set, set in place for the confrontation. Perhaps the issue lies elsewhere.

> "Nietzsche" – the name of the thinker stands as title for *the issue* of his thinking.

> But this issue, the matter of conflict, is "*in itself*" *Aus-einander-setzung*. This issue: the issue, that is, of "*his*", Nietzsche's thinking. *This* one, this *one*, "Nietzsche," would thus already be two, *if* the *Aus-einander-setzung* indeed involves two, two at least. The name "Nietzsche" would thus name both singularity and being taken apart. More precisely, it would – if Heidegger's claim is correct – name a singularity that itself *is* being taken apart.

What would it mean to read Nietzsche? To read Nietzsche "himself"? To read one who himself writes, "I am one thing, my writings are another"?[5] To read the one who says "*non legor, non legar*"?[6] Can one read "Nietzsche"? Can one read this name? Above all, can one read its singularity? And is the singularity named in this name a singularity that *belongs* to someone, to an author or reader? Or will it not, rather, always already have withdrawn from every λόγος, every name and every text, leaving but a trace – yet a trace that is never of "itself." Like the book *Thus Spoke Zarathustra*, perhaps, a book "for everyone and no one." A book to be read by everyone who can read and that is yet for no one: for no *one*, because it was written by this "no one" *for* this very "no one." "– And so I narrate my life to myself. . . ."[7]

This one, "Nietzsche," may already be such disintegration, may already be this singular *Aus-einander-setzung*, which, "in the end" (which is to say: from the outset, from the origin), when it tries to name itself, can only name itself "all the names of history." And yet, still, all these names are "me," this one, Nietzsche. This one, whose own Foreword says: "Above all, do not confuse me!" "*Verwechselt mich vor allem nicht!*"[8] Do not involve me in that kind of exchange or *Wechsel* in which this singularity, "me," becomes like every other. The title "Nietzsche," the name of the thinker, is not the title deed to some property. It is, we might say, a title for the *Aus-einander-setzung*: title – deed, λόγος – being, name – life.

In the present chapter, I shall restrict myself to examining Heidegger's first lecture course on Nietzsche. Heidegger's reading of Nietzsche will not – at least not in the first instance – attempt to read Nietzsche "himself." His reading will concern, rather, the way in which Nietzsche's writing (and specifically the later writings, approaching the period of *Ecce Homo*), the λόγος of his texts, attempts to tell of being itself. Heidegger's reading will attempt to lead us into the issue that he calls *Aus-einander-setzung*, the issue "Nietzsche." It will attempt to read the trace of being in Nietzsche's texts. More precisely, it will attempt to read what Heidegger will refer to in the first lecture course as a "trace of discordance" in Nietzsche's telling of being. Yet this trace, perhaps, is also and inevitably the trace of somebody: of some body so singular it is no one. . . .

2 Nietzsche and Us

In the first of his three major lecture courses on "Nietzsche," the 1936/37 course entitled "The Will to Power as Art," Heidegger gives us some clues as to how to understand the *Aus-einander-setzung*. The course

begins with some reflections on what is entailed in *Auseinandersetzung* –
in this context written as one word, without hyphenation. Speaking of
the *Auseinandersetzung* with Nietzsche, Heidegger indicates that it is to
be conceived as engaging "Western thought hitherto." Such will be the
case if, "in Nietzsche's thinking, the prior tradition of Western thought
is gathered and completed in a decisive respect."⁹ Yet such an
Auseinandersetzung with Nietzsche's thinking – with the issue of his
thinking as a "decisive" (*entscheidende*) gathering and completion of
Western thought – has yet to begin. The reason, Heidegger tells us, is
that "Nietzsche's thought and language [*Sagen*] are still too contemporary [*gegenwärtig*] for us. He and we have not yet been sufficiently set
apart historically [*Er und wir sind geschichtlich noch nicht hinreichend
auseinandergesetzt*]; we lack the distance necessary for a sound appreciation of this thinker's strength."¹⁰ Yet if he, Nietzsche, *is* the tradition,
gathered and completed in a decisive respect, then what is at stake in the
Auseinandersetzung is an opening up, a decision or *Entscheidung* – the
opening up of a scission – with respect to the tradition itself. But what
identity remains of "the tradition itself" in such an *Auseinandersetzung*?
The "we" – he and "we" are not yet sufficiently taken apart
(*auseinandergesetzt*) – this "we" would refer also and precisely to "the
tradition": the tradition as itself not yet sufficiently *auseinandergesetzt*;
"we" who lack the distance, "we" are still too close, still too immersed in
"the tradition," *we are still too much the tradition* for us to be able to see
the *Auseinandersetzung* in, and of, the tradition: the *Auseinandersetzung*
that awaits "us," the *Auseinandersetzung* that "he," Nietzsche, already
was – the *Auseinandersetzung*, in short, of identity itself, whether of
"him," of "the tradition," or of "us."

Yet if "we" – the tradition – and "he" – the *Auseinandersetzung* of that
tradition – are "not yet sufficiently taken apart historically," then what is
this future, this "not yet" that awaits us? Is it merely a matter of waiting
a few years, or a few hundred years, by which time we would come
to understand and appreciate Nietzsche's thinking? In which case
Heidegger's *Auseinandersetzung* would be rather superfluous. He, too,
could have waited. Or has not this future, this *Auseinandersetzung*, already happened? Is it not the opening up or irruption of another history,
not "beyond" or "outside of," but, if anything, *within* "our" tradition –
assuming for a moment that this tradition could contain such a rupture,
such a crisis or critique, assuming that what we call "the tradition" could
have anything like the form of a container or vessel. Hasn't this future,
this *Auseinandersetzung* already happened? Is it not "he," Nietzsche: he
who waits to be read, to be recollected, he who is a destiny, he who
knows his future? . . .

I know my fate. One day my name will be associated with the recollection of something tremendous – of a crisis such as there has never been on earth, of the most profound collision of conscience, of a decision evoked *counter* to everything that had hitherto been believed, demanded, hallowed.[11]

The *Auseinandersetzung* Heidegger – Nietzsche, "Heidegger's" *Auseinandersetzung* with and reading of "Nietzsche," the name, would then be a recollection and intensification of a crisis that has already happened, yet which "we," we who have yet to read "Nietzsche," do not yet sufficiently heed.[12] It would, in other words, be a recollection and intensification (perhaps indeed a celebration[13]) of a singular *Auseinandersetzung* – one that dare not be confused.

3 Truth and Discordance

In the first *Nietzsche* course, the *Auseinandersetzung* concerns the relation between art and truth. Both art and truth represent, for Nietzsche, particular configurations of the will to power, which for its part is understood as "the innermost essence of being."[14] Being itself is another word for "life."[15] Whereas art is the will to the sensuous as appearance (*Schein*), truth, ever since Plato's interpretation of being, has meant the will to the suprasensuous, the ideas. Heidegger frames the implicit conflict between art and truth in terms of a fragment from one of Nietzsche's notebooks:

From the earliest point I came to take seriously the relation of *art* to *truth*: and even now I stand in a sacred horror before this discordance. My first book was dedicated to it; *The Birth of Tragedy* believes in art on the background of another belief: that it *is not possible to live with the truth*: that the "will to truth" is already a symptom of degeneration.[16]

The conflict between art and truth is referred to by Nietzsche as a *Zwiespalt*: a discordance, specifically, one that gives rise to "a sacred horror" (*ein heiliges Entsetzen*). Heidegger does not comment further on the horrifying nature of this discordance at this point. The statement indeed sounds "monstrous" (*ungeheuerlich*), but loses its strangeness if we read it "in the correct way," whereby the "will to truth" is to be understood as referring to truth in the Platonic-Christian interpretation of the suprasensuous world. For Plato, the suprasensuous world is the true world, the realm of true being. For Nietzsche, by contrast, "the sensuous stands higher and more properly *is* than the suprasensuous."[17] Whereas the philosophical, metaphysical will to truth is a turning away from the sensuous, thus from the vitality of life, art is an affirmation of the sensuous and hence "*worth more*" than truth.[18]

Heidegger initially says little more regarding this fragment on the relation between art and truth. Yet it is this very fragment that becomes central to his interpretation some eighty pages later, following a long excursus on Nietzsche's physiology of art. In the section translated as "The Raging Discordance between Truth and Art," Heidegger again recalls Nietzsche's characterization of the relation between art and truth as one of discordance. Paraphrasing Nietzsche, Heidegger describes the relation as "*ein Entsetzen erregender Zwiespalt*," a discordance that arouses horror.[19] In order to understand how the relation between art and truth can be one of discordance, Heidegger tells us, we first need to examine more closely Nietzsche's conception of truth, specifically in relation to Plato and Platonism.

Heidegger frames his discussion of Nietzsche's conception of truth in terms of the claim that Nietzsche, despite his inversion or overturning (*Umkehrung*) of Platonism, fails to think "the essence of truth." Nietzsche's understanding of the word "truth" occurs via a path that turns away from truth's essence.[20] This is in effect a reiteration of the earlier claim in terms of which Heidegger stages his overall reading of Nietzsche, namely the claim that Nietzsche indeed poses the *guiding* question of philosophy (What are beings?), but fails to ask the *grounding* question (What is being itself?).[21] The first question asks concerning the truth of beings, the second concerning the truth of being. How we are we to understand this claim?

Truth means, for Nietzsche, that which is true. In the history of Platonism (which Heidegger, initially at least, distinguishes from Plato's thought[22]), what is true is that which we know to be true; knowledge comprises our access to truth, to that which truly is, to beings in their truth. And truth in this sense, as what is true about something, is to be found in the *idea* corresponding to that thing, i.e., in the suprasensuous. To know what this sensuous object we call a "table" is means to know what it *truly* is, and this entails knowing the idea that corresponds to, or agrees with, this object. Knowing what this (sensuous) thing here truly is, knowing that it is a table, means seeing the (suprasensuous) idea that fits it, the idea that corresponds to *any* object having this sensuous appearance: the idea of a table in general. Knowing, as such "seeing," is a pure contemplation ($\theta\epsilon\omega\varrho\acute{\iota}\alpha$) that brings the suprasensuous idea before us.

For the history of Platonism, the truth of what things are is located not in sensuous appearances themselves, but in the suprasensuous realm. The suprasensuous ideas first tell us what beings themselves truly are. For Nietzsche, however, this represents a devaluation of the sensuous. Nietzsche early on characterizes his philosophy as "inverted Platonism" (*umgedrehter Platonismus*[23]), which, Heidegger suggests, implies that the hierarchy whereby the suprasensuous provides the measure of the sensuous is to be inverted, so that the sensuous would, for Nietzsche, become the measure of what truly is. This position would seem to correspond to that of positivism, though Heidegger insists that such an identification would be premature.[24] Nietzsche's thought is not to be equated with positivism. Above all, Nietzsche's inversion of Platonism, and the need for such an inversion, must be understood in the light of Nietzsche's "fundamental experience," namely his "growing insight into the fundamental fact [*Grundtatsache*] of our history"[25]: the experience of nihilism. By nihilism, Heidegger comments, Nietzsche means "the historical fact [*Tatsache*], i.e., the event [*Ereignis*], that the highest values become devalued, all goals are annihilated and all estimations of value turn counter to one another [*sich gegeneinander kehren*]".[26] With the advent of nihilism, the meaning of values themselves becomes arbitrary; all measure is lost.

In the light of this experience of nihilism, Heidegger notes, Nietzsche's inversion of Platonism takes on another meaning. It is not merely the mechanical substitution of a positivistic perspective in place of a theoretical, epistemological one. Rather, the inversion entails, first, disrupting the priority of the suprasensuous as an ideal that posits the measure for the meaning of beings, for what beings are meant to be; and, second, as a countermove to such philosophy of the ideal, it entails "seeking out and establishing that which is, [it entails] the question: what are beings themselves?"[27] That is, the essential question becomes: *how are we to understand the sensuous itself?* If the suprasensuous, as that which tells us what the sensuous truly is as such, comes to be disrupted or shattered (*erschüttert*), then *we no longer know what anything (truly) is.* It is nothing less than our very perspective upon beings – and thus all stability, meaning and ground – that is shattered when the ideas, as that which provide permanence, ground and meaning to existence, come to nothing. Two things need to be noted regarding Heidegger's interpretation at this point: First, the kind of question that remains following the experience of nihilism: the question "what are beings?, what is the sensuous itself?" What is important for Heidegger is that this question, as a question, remains a question *concerning beings*, concerning that which somehow still "is" or can "be," *and not a question concerning the very meaning of the "is," i.e., of being itself as such.* Furthermore, because in the

question "what is . . . ?" we implicitly understand: "what is, *in truth*,
. . . ?"; because, in short, being and truth are understood as belonging
together,[28] this question remains a question concerning *truth*, and specifically one concerning the *truth of beings* – that is, it remains within what
Heidegger calls the "guiding question" or *Leitfrage* of metaphysics. Second, however – and this goes hand in hand with the first point – what
also remains implicit and unquestioned in the way this question is posed
is that it concerns a question of *knowledge*, since our access to truth has,
since Plato, been understood as the path of knowledge. When we ask:
what are sensuous beings, in truth?, we are implicitly asking: *how do we
know* what the sensuous is? Thus Heidegger argues that "In this inversion of Platonism, invoked and guided by the will to overcome nihilism,
what remains is the conviction, shared with Platonism and maintained as
self-evident, that truth, i.e., that which truly is, must be secured by way
of knowledge."

What remains, following the disruption of the suprasensuous realm,
what remains as that which is, is simply the sensuous. It, the sensuous,
is left as that which truly is. Yet what remains is also, or rather in the first
instance, a question: What do the "is" and the "truly" now mean? Thus,
Heidegger emphasizes, what remains following such disruption can only
be the sensuous. "But what the essence of the latter [the sensuous]
consists in is not yet thereby given; its determination is given as a task."[29]
Nevertheless, the *realm* within which that which truly is may be determined, and thus "the essence of truth" (*das Wesen der Wahrheit*), is
presupposed as given, namely knowledge.

If the inversion of Platonism leaves the sensuous remaining as that
which truly is, however, then the realm of the true is *also* the realm of art.
Art is understood by Nietzsche as the supreme affirmation of the sensuous and thus as a countermovement to nihilism. In the inversion of
Platonism, both *art* and *truth* come to designate our relation to the
sensuous. Heidegger sums up the predicament as follows:

> Against Platonism, the question to be asked is: What is that which
> truly is? Answer: that which is true is the sensuous.
>
> Against nihilism, the creative life, i.e., preeminently art, must be set
> to work. But art creates out of the sensuous.[30]

Art and truth thus enter into relation to one another in terms of a
single guiding perspective, that of "rescuing and configuring the sensuous." This relation is not merely a comparative or extrinsic one consist-
ing of two possibilities, existing side by side, of relating to the sensuous,

but, as Heidegger puts it, an intrinsic coming together in the realm of "a new historical existence."[31] Yet this coming together is an uneasy one. If we consider the relation between art and truth in Platonism, then we can readily see that this relation is a hierarchical one, in which truth stands higher than the sensuous and knowledge is thus higher than art in terms of our access to what truly is. Here, the relation of truth to art appears to be one of "exclusion, opposition, and disseverance [*Entzweiung*], thus one of discordance [*des Zwiespaltes*]."[32] Hence, where Platonism is inverted, such that both art and truth come to be conceived as an affirmation of the sensuous, we might expect the relation to become one of "univocity and concordance" (*Einstimmigkeit und Eintracht*). And yet – Heidegger argues – for Nietzsche it remains one of discordance. For Nietzsche speaks of this horrifying discordance not prior to his inversion of Platonism, but in 1888, i.e., during the period following this inversion, when he considers the inversion already "decided," when the true world has become the realm of the sensuous. What remains is a horrifying discordance. Yet why does a discordance remain following this inversion? What kind of discordance is it, and what can it tell us about Nietzsche's inversion, conceived as an overcoming of nihilism?

Before examining this issue, Heidegger provides a detailed interpretation of the relation between art (as mimesis) and truth (as idea) in Plato's *Republic*.[33] This turn to Plato is necessary because, as Heidegger puts it, it is already "questionable" whether there is indeed a discordance between art and truth in Plato's work.[34] On the one hand, the excursus on Plato is an attempt to safeguard Plato's works from any oversimplified or totalizing interpretation that would reduce it to "Platonism"; on the other hand, it is an attempt to situate the origin and "trace" (*die Spur*) of discordance that emerges in Nietzsche's inversion of "Platonism."[35] Heidegger's reading of Book X of the *Republic* shows that in this particular context, art, whose essence is μίμησις, is situated at a distance from truth. Whereas truth is to be found in our contemplation of the εἶδος as ἰδέα, art as μίμησις is regarded as producing or bringing forth a mere εἴδωλον or likeness, a lesser version of the idea. μίμησις is a kind of producing, a bringing forth (*Hervorbringen, Herstellen*), in Greek, a ποίησις. It is not, therefore, to be understood as a process of reproduction; rather, μίμησις as "imitation" means a subordinate kind of production or bringing forth. It is subordinate precisely because it is unable to bring forth the εἶδος in its fullest presence, as ἰδέα. This interpretation of the relation between art and truth is, Heidegger emphasizes, based upon an implicit understanding of being as plenitude of presence. It is in the εἶδος as the most constant outward appearance (*Aussehen*) of something that that thing is most present, least dissimulated, thus most fully *is*. "*The interpretation of being as* εἶδος, *presencing in outward appearance,*" states Heidegger, "*presupposes the interpretation of truth as* ἀλήθεια, *non-dissimulation [Unverstelltheit]*."³⁶

Plato's understanding of truth and art in the *Republic*, implicitly articulated in terms of the different ways and degrees to which beings can be present, thereby arrives at a hierarchical ordering in which art is subordinate to truth. Art lies "far removed" from truth. It would seem that we have discovered a "discordance" between art and truth that is inherent in Platonism. And yet, somewhat surprisingly, Heidegger now argues that such remoteness or distance (*Abstand*) is *not* discordance. What lies behind this claim, and why does Heidegger make such a claim at this point?

If the inversion of Platonism is to be understood as an overcoming of nihilism, an overcoming through which the sensuous is affirmed and valued more than suprasensuous truth, then, as noted, we might expect that the discordance that seems to be inherent in Platonism would become a concordance. For Nietzsche, the affirmation of the sensuous may be expressed in the insight that "art is *worth more* than truth."³⁷ Platonism, by contrast, asserts that truth is worth more than art. Yet the straightforward reversal of the Platonic hierarchy, Heidegger notes, by no means entails that the discordance between art and truth – assuming that there is such a discordance in Platonism – must disappear. On the contrary, it merely implies that such discordance would come to the fore "in the reverse form." Presumably, therefore, this reverse form would be the discordance of which Nietzsche speaks, the discordance implied in the statement that art is worth more than truth. *Yet does this statement express the discordance?* Or does it rather *conceal* the discordance? Heidegger now suggests that the latter is the case. And this is why he also claims that the relation between art and truth in Platonism (if we identify "Platonism" broadly speaking with the interpretation given of Plato's *Republic*), the hierarchical relation, is one involving "remoteness" (*Abstand*), but not discordance. Discordance does not mean hierarchical ordering. If there *is* discordance in Plato's work regarding the relation between art and truth (and Heidegger will argue that there is), it is not to be read simply in terms of an already installed hierarchy. Likewise, if there *is* discordance in Nietzsche's work following the *overcoming* of Platonism – which overcoming, Heidegger will proceed to show, entails more than a straightforward reversal – it may not simply be read in terms of the reversal or inversion of a hierarchy. Evidently, there is a discordance for Nietzsche, for the *Sache* Nietzsche: the work itself speaks of it. But evidently also, "Evidently," says Heidegger – though in fact this is not so immediately evident – "Evidently, the discordance is concealed [*verbirgt sich*] in this statement [that art is worth more than truth]."³⁸ It is *the trace of this concealment*, of the concealment of such discordance, that Heidegger's first *Nietzsche* course will attempt to read. The reading presented here, in this course, will thereby prove to be a much more generous reading of both Nietzsche and Plato than a reading that would simply confine either of these figures within an already installed metaphysical hierarchy.

Yet what, then, does discordance mean, what is Heidegger attempting to understand as *Zwiespalt*, if it is not to be understood in terms of a hierarchy? Heidegger:

What does discordance mean? Discordance is the opening of a gap between two [things] that are dissevered. Of course, a mere gap does not yet constitute a discordance. We do speak of a "split" in relation to the gap that separates two soaring cliffs; yet the cliffs are not in discordance, and never could be; to be so would require that they, of themselves, relate to one another. Only two things that are related to one another can be opposed to one another. But such opposition is not yet discordance. For it is surely the case that their being opposed to one another presupposes a being drawn toward and related to one another, which is to say, their converging upon and agreeing with one another in one respect. Genuine political opposition – not mere dispute – can arise only where the selfsame political order is willed; only here can ways and goals and basic principles diverge. In every opposition, agreement prevails in one respect, whereas in other respects there is variance. Yet whatever diverges in the same respect in which it agrees slips into discordance. Here the opposition springs from the divergence of what once converged, indeed in such a way that precisely by being apart they enter into the supreme way of belonging together. But from that we also conclude that disseverance is something different from opposition, that it does not need to be discordance, but may be a concordance. Concordance too requires the twofold character implied in disseverance.

Thus "discordance" is ambiguous. It may mean, first, a disseverance which at bottom can be a concordance; second, a disseverance which must be a discordance (being torn asunder).³⁹

Heidegger here implies that there is both a broad and a narrow sense of *Zwiespalt*. *Zwiespalt*, discordance, in the broad sense means disseverance, *Entzweiung*. Disseverance, *Entzweiung*, can for its part be understood either as concordance, harmony (*Einklang*), or else as a

discordance in the narrow sense of *Zerrissenheit*, being torn apart or
asunder.[40] Now this ambiguity or ambivalence (*Zweideutigkeit*, double
meaning: again, the term resonates with duality or twofoldness, *Zweiheit*)
of the word *Zwiespalt* is in fact pivotal (the very pivot, one might say) for
Heidegger's attempt to read a trace of concealment in "Nietzsche."
Thus, he "deliberately" allows the word this ambiguity:

> For now, we shall deliberately allow the word "discordance"
> ["*Zwiespalt*"] to remain in this ambiguity [*Zweideutigkeit*]. For if a
> discordance prevails in Nietzsche's inverted Platonism, and if this is
> possible only if there is discordance already in Platonism; and if the
> discordance is for Nietzsche a horrifying one; then for Plato it must
> be the reverse, that is, it must be a disseverance that is nevertheless
> a concordance [*Einklang*]. In any case, two things that are supposed
> to be able to enter into discordance must be counterbalanced, be of
> the same immediate origin, of the same necessity and rank. An
> "above" and "below" can stand in a relation of distance or opposi-
> tion, but never in discordance, because they lack any equivalent
> standard of measure. The "above" and "below" are in each case
> different in what they themselves are, and do not agree in any
> essential respect.[41]

It is not just the word *Zwiespalt* that carries the ambiguity of
Heidegger's reading here, however. The little word "in" also – and
more importantly – sustains the work of ambiguity. *If* for Nietzsche a
discordance (in some sense) prevails "in" inverted Platonism . . . but
Heidegger has just suggested that this is *not* the case, not, that is, if by
"in" we mean "within," or more precisely "in terms of the polarities of,"
for Heidegger has just argued that discordance cannot exist in terms of
a hierarchical ordering, even if it is inverted (since hierarchy remains
following the inversion, the hierarchy of a "*worth more*"); and *if* this is
possible only insofar as there is already discordance "in" Platonism –
but, again, we have just seen Heidegger argue that this is not the case,
that there is no discordance, but only remoteness; and if for Nietzsche
the discordance is a horrifying one – but is the horror of discordance "in"
inverted Platonism as an inverted hierarchical order?; *then* – then the
conclusion would seem just as dubious or unstable, namely that for
Plato, the discordance must be the reverse of horrifying, a disseverance
that is concordance. *Unless* the word "in" precisely carries the ambiguity
referred to, the ambiguity that would allow it to be read *either* as meaning: in terms of the already installed polarities of Platonism (the true *as
opposed to* the sensuous, the apparent); *or* as meaning: latent or implicit

within the very emergence and installing of such polarities yet precisely not coming to the fore, that is, *concealed* by these very polarities in *their* appearing, in their very installation. And *unless, also,* Heidegger here deliberately writes "Plato" as irreducible to "Platonism." In that case, discordance would conceal itself just as much in "Platonism" as in "inverted Platonism," and reading "Plato" would be just as delicate an undertaking as reading "Nietzsche." In each case, "evidently," we might say, a discordance would appear to conceal itself. *That is, it would conceal itself in the very λόγος of each of these two, "Plato" and "Nietzsche."* Assuming, of course, that they too are two.

4 Discordance and the Sensuous

Where, then, is discordance to be found "in" Plato's work? Where do we find discordance that is not hierarchy, remoteness, or opposition? In pursuing these questions, however, it will not *simply* be a matter of a concordant or harmonious discordance in Plato that would be the opposite or inverse of the horrifying discordance attested to in Nietzsche. This predicament is indeed suggested by Heidegger's own apparent qualification, with which he begins the next sentence: "In any case . . ." ("*Jedenfalls . . .*"). Such qualification is needed because inversion is simply not the issue. Moreover, not only have we yet to find discordance in Plato; we have yet to locate it "in" Nietzsche. If discordance is not to be located in Platonism, that is, in "the tradition" of metaphysics, then it is Platonism or the tradition itself that stands between "Plato" and "Nietzsche," Platonism itself that conceals discordance and its possible forms.

Yet is there discordance between art and truth in Plato? This is the question Heidegger now interjects. He notes that Plato does speak in the *Republic*, albeit somewhat obscurely, of "a certain ancient disseverance between philosophy and poetry" (παλαιὰ μέν τις διαφορὰ ψιλοσοφίᾳ τε καὶ ποιητικῇ), i.e., between knowledge (truth) and art.[42] The word "disseverance" (*Entzweiung*) here translates the Greek διαφορά. In this context too, διαφορά or disseverance does not simply mean "distinction" (*Unterschied*); yet if, according to Heidegger, disseverance or διαφορά is discordance in the broad sense, then given the framework and terms of the *Republic*, we nevertheless find no discussion of such discordance. The διαφορά referred to must be *more ancient* than the mere distance of art from truth as instituted in the *Republic*. Thus, in his search for a trace of discordance between art and truth, Heidegger now turns to Plato's

Phaedrus, a dialogue concerned with the beautiful, but also, as Heidegger notes, with themes such as the soul, love, τέχνη, truth, λόγος, and μανία – madness (*Wahnsinn*), rapture (*Rausch*), being carried away or transported (*Wegsein*). Finally, it is also and always concerned with being and the ideas. The relation of human beings to other beings and to being itself forms the overall context of the dialogue.

How does discordance between art and knowledge, beauty and truth, come to the fore in Heidegger's account of the *Phaedrus*? Human beings are implicitly understood as those beings that can relate to and comport themselves toward other beings. Yet in order to do so, they must have caught sight of the being of those beings. For Plato, being is nothing sensuous, and can thus be "seen" only through θεωρία, through a vision of the suprasensuous. It is this vision of being, Heidegger notes, that first lets us see what diversity and equality are, what is meant by sameness and oppositionality, law and order. That is, for Plato it is the precondition for understanding all difference and identity, all divergence and relationality, all discord and agreement, and all ordering (hierarchical or otherwise). Thus the *Phaedrus* states that the human soul could never assume this form of life unless it had caught sight of τὰ ὄντα, "beings in their being," as Heidegger translates.[43] In order for the human being to be "this particular human being, living and bodying forth," in order for a particular human being to be as particular, as different, and to be able to relate to other particular beings as such, he or she must already have caught sight of and understood being, being different, being identical, and so forth.

Yet the human vision of being can never be a catching sight of being in itself as such, in its own "unclouded brilliance." Rather being itself can be seen only when encountering this or that particular being; for humans exist among beings in the realm of the sensuous and their vision is, moreover, "captivated in the body."[44] Thus, most humans scarcely see being at all, they merely steal a glance at it or see it out of the corner of their eye (*schielen*); they are content to feed off the views things offer them, the way that particular beings appear to them in *doxa*, in the prevalent view and opinion of things. In humans being turned toward beings and their views of beings, what occurs is a "concealment of being," λανθάνει. This concealment of being is not due to some human failing; it is a *self-concealing* of being. Its consequence, however, is that λήθη befalls most human beings: they tend to "forget" being in their preoccupation with beings as they appear to be.[45] Yet how, once the human response to the self-concealment of being has fallen into such forgottenness of being, can humans come to remember being, how can they come to see being "in" and through those beings they encounter in the realm of appearance, in the sensuous? Heidegger's answer: through ἔρως.

> As soon as human beings, in their vision of being, let themselves be bound by being, they are transported out beyond themselves, so that they are stretched, as it were, between themselves and being and are outside themselves. Such being raised out beyond oneself and being drawn toward being itself is ἔρως. Only to the extent that being, in its relation to human beings, is able to unfold "erotic" power are human beings capable of thinking of being itself and of overcoming oblivion of being.[46]

The human relation and attraction to being, the way humans are attracted and drawn (*angezogen*) to being, is the "erotic" power of ἔρως. But how does this power manifest itself and unfold in the realm of the sensuous? Plato's answer in the *Phaedrus* is that it unfolds by way of the beautiful, τὸ κάλον. The beautiful is that which we encounter *in* beings, in the sensuous, yet which transports us toward being, toward that which is usually "most remote" from the initial appearance of things. The beautiful is that which transports us into a vision of being itself. It is that which is most "erotic," that which superlatively transports us, *das Entrückendste*, as Heidegger translates Plato's τὸ ἐρασμιώτατον: "However [in the essential order within which being is illuminated], to beauty alone has this fate been allotted: namely to be that which is most radiant, yet also that which most transports us."[47]

What does this tell us about the relation between beauty and truth in the *Phaedrus*? To answer this, Heidegger turns back to the statement that identifies the vision of being as belonging to the nature or essence (φύσις) of the soul that has assumed the human form of life. We noted above that Heidegger translates τὰ ὄντα at 249E as "beings in their being." This translation is now justified by reference to 249B. For Plato does not simply say that the precondition for assuming the human form is having seen τὰ ὄντα, if by that we understand "beings as such" (as Heidegger now renders it); rather he states that "the soul would never have assumed this form, had it not already caught sight of the unconcealment of beings, i.e., beings in their unconcealment."[48] Heidegger here renders the Greek ἀλήθειαν (usually translated as "truth") as "unconcealment."

This vision of being is an opening up of that which, from the perspective of beings and the sensuous, is concealed (namely being), bringing it into unconcealment as the true being of beings, letting us see what and how beings truly are. The beautiful thereby accomplishes an opening up of beings *in* their truth, in their true being, their unconcealment. This unveiling of beings in their truth is thus also an opening up of being, of truth. The opening up of the *truth* of beings thus occurs *by way of the beautiful*. In other words, Heidegger concludes, the relation between truth and beauty is not one of remoteness or distance entailing hierarchical ordering, as in the *Republic*, but a relation of belonging together with respect to the same:

> Truth and beauty are, in their essence, related to the Same, to being; they belong together in the One decisive respect of making being manifest and keeping it open.[49]

Heidegger's translation of ἀλήθεια as "unconcealment," *Unverborgenheit*, here allows us to think an ambiguity inherent in Plato and in the Platonic conception of being, an ambiguity which the accepted translation of ἀλήθεια by "truth" can only cover up. His reading of the *Phaedrus* thereby provides, first, a perspective from which to problematize the remoteness and distance that come to be installed between art and truth in the *Republic*. Second, it gives us a perspective from which to think through the *Zwiespalt* that emerges in Nietzsche's overcoming of Platonism. Third, however, it perhaps points us toward another site of discordance intrinsic to the *Auseinandersetzung*: Heidegger – Nietzsche.

With regard to the first point, it is clear that the translation of ἀλήθεια by truth precisely *obscures* our understanding how there could be a harmony or concord between the sensuous appearance of beings as the beautiful and the *being* of such beings. It thereby introduces a *concealment* into the possibility of our understanding disseverance and discordance as a belonging-together of that which diverges.[50] For if ἀλήθεια is rendered as truth, as true being, then this immediately suggests to us the understanding of being argued in the *Republic*, namely being as the *non-* and *supra* sensuous idea, severed from the sensuous. We are thus already *within* a remoteness and a hierarchical ordering of being, and thereby also already excluded from seeing that perspective from which such polarization could open up; excluded, that is, from the essential dimension of discordance. If, on the other hand, ἀλήθεια is understood as the unconcealment of beings, as beings *in* their unconcealment (being), then beings and being cannot yet be understood in terms of difference, i.e., we are not yet dealing with two distinct realms or "worlds," and negativity has not yet been installed within being in general (within the beingness of beings).

Yet how, then, does negativity come to install itself within the being of beings? The experience of the beautiful in the sensuous opens us precisely to the experience that things *are* not what they seem or *appear* to be. A "not," a negativity announces itself as belonging to the prevailing and being of beings. This "not" belongs to the being or prevailing of beings, to ψύσις, as the coming into appearance and shining forth of that which appears. It belongs to being itself as the Same, the One, the common "essence" prevailing as beauty *and* being, ἀλήθεια, "truth." When Heidegger writes: "Truth and beauty are in their essence [*Wesen*] related to the Same, to being . . . ," we must emphasize *in their essence*, and "truth" (*Wahrheit*) is to be read as the ambiguity of ἀλήθεια. For "truth" itself is a translation of being, of presence, unconcealment, ἀλήθεια. On the one hand, "truth" in this statement refers to the not yet metaphysically determined being of beings, to unconcealment experienced *in* (but not yet *as*) the beingness of beings and in the "erotic" view of a negativity, thus of a discordance, in the appearing of beings themselves. It is drawn into (*bezogen auf*) the singular prevailing, *Wesen*, of being itself. On the other hand, the very use of the word *truth* to name *unconcealment* here – as Heidegger translated ἀλήθεια just a moment earlier – already evidences the imminent divergence and disseverance of being from the appearing of beings. It announces, in effect, the imminent installation of negativity *within*, and indeed *as* the very beingness of beings. Thus Heidegger writes:

> Yet in that in which they [namely truth and beauty] belong together, they must diverge from one another [*auseinandergehen*] for human beings, they must become dissevered [*sich entzweien*]; for, because for Plato being is the nonsensuous, the openedness of being too, namely truth, can only be nonsensuous illumination. Because being opens itself only in a vision of being, and such vision must always be torn [*herausgerissen*] from its oblivion of being and thus requires the initial shining of appearance, the opening up of being must occur where, judged from the perspective of truth, the μὴ ὄν (εἴδωλον), that which is not, prevails. This, however, is the site of beauty.[51]

From that moment on, things will not – will no longer be what they seem to be. Yet that moment arrives, not with the experience of being itself as the nonsensuous, but only with the reductive determination of beings and the beautiful to "nonbeings," μὴ ὄν, that is, only when beings are judged or evaluated (*geschätzt*) "from the perspective of truth," for this is the moment at which ἀλήθεια is isolated from beings in advance, the moment at which hierarchy and negativity are installed within being, the moment in which nothing comes to be. The *precondition* for this moment, however, is the implicit understanding of being itself as presence, namely as the presence *of beings*: what, in the first instance, things *are, is* not – and only then, only secondarily, is *not* – what they (at present) appear to be. Being, in its full intensity and plenitude, is then the negation of sensuous being, of being understood as the appearance of the sensuous, as beings in their unconcealment.

It is thus that we arrive at the understanding of being evinced in the *Republic*. Heidegger's "aletheic" reading of this moment both looks back to an implicit understanding of being as unconcealment and forward to the emergent understanding of being as eidetic truth. Indeed, Heidegger continues with a reference to the remoteness that he earlier identified in Plato's *Republic*: "If, in particular, we consider that art, insofar as it brings forth the beautiful, resides in the sensuous, and is therefore far removed [*im weiten Abstand*] from truth, then it becomes clear how truth and beauty, in their belonging together in One must nevertheless be two [*zwei*], must become dissevered [*sich entzweien*]." Heidegger, of course, has argued that remoteness is not disseverance; thus, the disseverance mentioned here must refer to one that is precisely *concealed* in the removal of truth that occurs in the *Republic*, and yet in retrospect is also the precondition for such removal to occur. Thus, Heidegger immediately locates this discordance not in the *Republic*, but in the "felicitous" (*beglückende*) disseverence he reads in the *Phaedrus*: "Yet this disseverance, discordance in the broad sense, is for Plato not one that arouses horror, but a felicitous one. The beautiful raises us beyond the sensuous and carries us back into the true. Harmony [*Einklang*] prevails in such disseverance, because the beautiful, as radiant and sensuous, has in advance installed its essence in the truth of being as the suprasensuous." "Truth" as the "suprasensuous" must here imply that which lies out beyond the sensuous and yet is accessible precisely in the harmonious and "erotic" transport of the beautiful. The "essence" or essential prevailing of the sensuous lies *in* this very transport, and not yet in some realm determined as other.

5 Twisting Free

Yet how does the ambiguity in Heidegger's translation of ἀλήθεια help us to think through the discordance experienced by Nietzsche in his attempted overcoming of Platonism? As Heidegger emphasizes, there is no discordance or *Zwiespalt* in Platonism, if by "Platonism" we mean the hierarchical understanding of being in Plato's *Republic*. But this implies that no discordance will emerge either in a straightforward inversion

(*Umdrehung*) of Platonism in which the sensuous becomes the true and the suprasensuous idea is merely the apparent. Heidegger argues, however – citing a passage from *Twilight of the Idols* in testimony[52] – that Nietzsche himself went beyond a mere symmetrical inversion of Platonism, an inversion in which the polarities of the true and the apparent would be exchanged yet precisely maintained as polarities. This "twisting free" (*Herausdrehung*) from Platonism, whereby the polarities, and thus the oppositionality between them, are themselves abolished, occurred, according to Heidegger, only late in Nietzsche's life, "shortly before the curtailment of his thoughtful work."

It is because twisting free, and not straightforward inversion, becomes the issue for Nietzsche during the period when he speaks of the horrifying discordance between art and truth that Heidegger attempts to read this discordance not in terms of art and truth as indicative of the polarities of Platonism (inverted or otherwise), but with a view to the task of the overcoming of Platonism as a twisting free from such polarities. Reading "Nietzsche" in respect of this task therefore also entails reading "Platonism" in all its ambiguity, with a view to what it conceals.

Heidegger's reading has just located a disseverance between truth and beauty in Plato's *Phaedrus*, a disseverance which appears to be a harmonious, concordant one, one which thus falls on one side of the ambiguity conveyed in the word *Zwiespalt*, allowing this disseverance to be termed a discordance "in the broad sense," as Heidegger puts it, a "felicitous" discordance. Yet Heidegger now complicates the scenario, in suggesting that this *appearance* of harmony is itself a concealing:

> If we look more precisely, there is also a discordance in the strict sense to be found here. But it is the essence of Platonism to avoid this discordance by positing being in such a way that it is capable of such avoidance, without this avoidance becoming visible as such. Yet when Platonism is inverted everything that characterizes it must also become inverted, and whatever allowed itself to be concealed and veiled and could be claimed as felicitous must, conversely, emerge and arouse horror.[53]

These remarks bring back into play the ambiguity (*Zweideutigkeit*) of *Zwiespalt* as *Entzweiung*. What appears or seems to be a harmonious discordance in fact conceals, avoids, and veils "discordance in the strict sense," i.e., discordance that would be *Zerrissenheit*, arousing horror. And the moment of this veiling is the advent of "Platonism." Heidegger's recourse to the word "Platonism" here suggests that such concealment must already be at play in the *Phaedrus*. And this in turn implies that the account of beauty in the *Phaedrus* is already complicit with emergent Platonism, that the *Phaedrus* cannot be regarded as the voice of "Plato himself," of "Plato's work," his own, "proper" work, as distinct from its appropriation by Platonism. It follows that, while Heidegger, apparently siding with Nietzsche, subsequently affirms that "Plato's work is not yet Platonism,"[54] that Nietzsche "consciously sets Plato apart [*absetzt*] from all Platonism, protecting him from it,"[55] Heidegger's reading in fact problematizes any ascription of the work to Plato "himself," any attempt to identify Plato "set apart from" Platonism. It would, in short, problematize our understanding in terms of an authorial name whatever "setting apart" occurs in the work that bears the proper name. Where Nietzsche's gesture appears as one of "protection," Heidegger's is rather one of exposure. But exposure to what, exactly?

If it is impossible to locate precisely, that is, to *isolate* the discordance that lies, somehow concealed, "in" Platonism, impossible to isolate it "in" any proper moment, whether historical, textual, or authorial; if, in short, such a moment could be situated only where it "occurs" (in the sense of the "history" or "occurrence" of being itself), that is, in the nexus of being and λόγος, then it will surely prove no less impossible to isolate the moment of discordance "in" Nietzsche's inversion of and twisting free from Platonism. Nonetheless, for Heidegger's reading the task remains "to locate the place and context where, within Nietzsche's conception of art and truth, the disseverance of these two must spring forth [*entspringen*]."[56] Our reflections on Heidegger's reading of truth and beauty in the *Phaedrus* suggest a certain negativity at the very root of disseverance and discordance. Yet this negativity, and hence discordance, belongs to being itself, to being itself as irreducible to any metaphysical determination thereof. Thus, Heidegger affirms that "Both beauty and truth are related to being, namely by way of an unveiling [*Enthüllung*] of the being of beings. . . . If, for Nietzsche, beauty and truth enter into discordance, then they must first belong together in One. That One can only be being and our relation to being."[57] Specifically, the nature of the discordance for Nietzsche will depend upon the way in which negativity is thought with respect to being.

Heidegger approaches this problem from the perspective of the sixth and final stage in the history of Platonism, as documented by Nietzsche in "*How the 'true world' finally became a fable. The History of an Error,*" from *Twilight of the Idols*. In the preceding five stages, Nietzsche recounts the development of Platonism from out of Plato's work, up to the abolition of the 'true world' as a useless and superfluous idea. With the abolition of the true world, what remains is the sensuous, knowledge of which is supposed to be gained via positivism. Yet positivism itself still contains, indeed as its very foundation, an implicit appeal to truth. What the sensuous (truly) *is* is to be discovered by way of (scientific) knowledge. The being of beings is understood in advance as *true being*, and access to truth is – just as in Platonism – to be determined via knowledge. Platonism, in other words, has not yet been overcome; on the contrary, it remains all the more deeply entrenched and concealed. Positivism merely represents the inversion of Platonism, in which the polarities of truth versus appearance are maintained, and indeed maintained as determinative. What is still called for is an "*Auseinandersetzung*" with positivism in its very foundations.[58] What is called for is a twisting free from Platonism.[59]

Nietzshe describes as follows the aporia in the sixth stage of this history:

> 6. We abolished the true world: what world remained? the apparent one, perhaps. . . . But no! *along with the true world we also abolished the apparent one!*

Nietzsche writes this stage of the history of Platonism in the past tense, as though in retrospect, as though from a great distance, as though he, Nietzsche, were no longer part of that history. The fact that Nietzsche adds a sixth stage here, notes Heidegger, shows clearly that he had to go "beyond the mere abolition of the suprasensuous."[60] The realization documented in this sixth stage and its implications coincides with the "moment" (*Augenblick*) of Zarathustra's arrival. And because the relation to the "true world," the suprasensuous, is at each stage invested in a particular kind of human being, the twisting free of Platonism entails a "transformation of human beings," a "decision" (*Entscheidung*), as Heidegger puts it, concerning the essence of humanity;[61] a decision concerning whether the "last man" remains as "the necessary consequence of undefeated nihilism," or whether the "last man" can be overcome with the arrival of the "overman." The "overman" refers to that kind of human being who passes over and beyond humanity hitherto.

What remains when both the "true," suprasensuous world and the "apparent," sensuous world are abolished? Abolition here cannot mean sheer annihilation or dissolution into nothingness, notes Heidegger, for Nietzsche seeks precisely to overcome nihilism in all its forms. The designations "true" and "apparent" merely represent an *interpretation* of beings as a whole in accordance with Platonism. It is this interpretation that is to be overcome and abolished, not the sensuous or nonsensuous *per se*. Thus Heidegger writes:

What is needed is neither abolition of the sensuous nor abolition of the nonsensuous. On the contrary, it is a matter of eliminating the misinterpretation and deprecation of the sensuous, as well as the hyperbolic elevation of the suprasensuous. It is a matter of clearing the path for a new interpretation of the sensuous in terms of a new order and ranking of the sensuous and nonsensuous.[62]

The sensuous and its intrinsic negativity still remain following the abolition of "true" and "apparent," following the first moment in twisting free from Platonism. But what remains also, and above all, is the question: *What is the sensuous?* How is it to be delimited? Where does the sensuous end and the nonsensuous begin? What relation now prevails between sensuous and nonsensuous? What remains, as Heidegger puts it, is the need for *a new interpretation of sensuousness.*

Heidegger considers the emergent new interpretation of sensuousness, i.e., of what the sensuous is, from the perspective of being and of Nietzsche's understanding of being as will to power. Following the abolition of the true and apparent worlds, the sensuous remains as that which is, as the sole reality. Reality, being, life as will to power is conceived as a perspectival shining forth, a coming into appearance within the multiple and changing perspectives belonging to the bodying forth of organic life. Whatever appears in such coming into appearance, however, appears to be whatever it is within a momentary perspective in the flux of appearing. But such momentary appearances are also *mere* appearance, in the sense that they appear to be stable, to be, to be that which is, and thus do not accord with reality as a coming to appear (*Erscheinen*). Here too, then, we find appearance in the sense of mere appearance, semblance. The being of whatever appears *to be* is mere appearance, *Schein*. For Nietzsche, such mere appearance or "error" belongs to the essence of life as pespectival. Thus, he writes of truth, being, that which appears to be true, as "*that kind of error* without which a particular kind of living entity could not live."[63]

Heidegger's reading now focuses on this ambiguous[64] sense of the word *appearance, Schein,* for Nietzsche. He argues that there is an *ambiguity* to this "fateful" word *Schein,* an ambiguity that Nietzsche knows of, yet fails to master. On the one hand, Nietzsche, in a fragment that Heidegger dates from 1886 at the latest, claims to understand appearance as "the actual and sole reality of things":

Hence I do not posit "appearance" ["*Schein*"] in opposition to "reality," but on the contrary take appearance to be reality, which resists being transformed into an imaginative "world of truth." A particular name for this reality would be "will to power."[65]

On the other hand, when such appearance becomes fixed within a perspectival horizon and comes to be regarded as that which *is*, it is to be understood as mere appearance, *Schein* in the sense of semblance. This ambiguity of the word *appearance* corresponds to what remains following the inversion of Platonism: the true world, the world of being, of permanence, is no longer to be found in the suprasensuous, but in the sensuous itself. In this realm, "being" is a congealing of becoming, of the coming into appearance of the sensuous. Such "being" (truth according to the Platonist conception) is now (for Nietzsche) *mere* appearance, illusion, error, as opposed to "true" appearance: the becoming of the sensuous, its coming to appear and its disappearing in the flux of becoming. Yet is this merely an *inversion* of Platonism, or is it already a *twisting free*? It would remain an inversion, or entangled in the process of inversion, if the relation between illusion or "mere" appearance (being) and "true" appearance (becoming) remained one of *hierarchical* ordering and remoteness. In that case we would indeed be dealing with an *opposition*. Yet Heidegger's reading implies rather that a movement of *twisting free* is already occurring here, for there is no longer a remoteness, but instead a *necessary belonging* of truth as mere appearance to becoming: "If truth is taken as appearance, i.e., mere appearance, as error, then this means: truth is that fixated appearance [*Schein*] or semblance [*Anschein*] that necessarily belongs to perspectival appearing [*Scheinen*]."[66] Here, then – precisely in this ambiguity of the *logos* – we have the basis for a *discordance* between truth as fixated appearance and that appearing or shining forth that is affirmed in art as the creative transformation of the sensuous into the beautiful. Thus Heidegger writes:

> We can now also see to what extent the relation between art and truth must become a discordance for Nietzsche and for his philosophy as inverted Platonism. Discordance is present only where the elements that become dissevered must diverge from one another [*auseinandergehen*] in terms of and from out of the unity of their belonging together. The unity of their belonging together is given via the *one* reality of perspectival appearing [*Scheinen*]. To such appearing there belong [mere] appearance [*Anschein*] and radiant appearing [*Aufscheinen*] as transfiguration. In order for what is real (living) to *be* real, it must on the one hand secure itself within a particular horizon and thus remain in the [mere] appearance of

truth. Yet in order for what is real to *remain* real, it must on the other hand simultaneously transfigure itself by going beyond itself, surpassing itself in the radiant appearing of that which is created in art, i.e., by going counter to truth. In their belonging equally primordially to the essence of reality, art and truth diverge from one another and go counter to one another.[67]

This discordance between art and truth is thus one that emerges *in Nietzsche's twisting free* from Platonism, not in a mere inversion. Art and truth belong together in the unity of being or reality understood as the perspectival appearing and shining forth of the sensuous. And it is in this same respect that they also turn against and counter to one another, become dissevered. Heidegger's reading has thereby *located* that discordance of which Nietzsche speaks between art and truth, interpreting it *not* in terms of a mere inversion of Platonism, but in the process of a *twisting free*. The discordance thus located is precisely that which was earlier said to *conceal itself* in Nietzsche's assertion that *art is worth more than truth*. Clearly, the discordance conceals itself in this assertion because the words "worth more" seem precisely to imply hierarchy, ordering in terms of rank, evaluation.

And yet – why is this discordance a "horrifying" one for Nietzsche? Why is it not harmonious? Is the discordance that is experienced as a belonging together in the very moment of twisting free from Platonism perhaps still held or magnetized by a certain tension bound up with hierarchical and evaluative thinking? At this point Heidegger indicates a further ambiguity of the word *Schein* for Nietzsche:

Yet because for Nietzsche appearance [*Schein*], even as perspectival, still retains the character of the nonactual, of illusion and deception, Nietzsche is forced to say:

"The will to *appearance* [*Schein*], to illusion, to deception, to becoming and change is deeper, more 'metaphysical' [i.e., more in keeping with the essence of being] than the will to *truth*, to actuality, to being." (XIV, 369)[68]

In this citation, appearance as becoming – which in the inversion and twisting free from Platonism is supposed to be the "true" reality, that which truly is, that which is truly in keeping with the "essence of being," as Heidegger puts it – is equated with illusion, i.e., with *mere* appearance. Yet this implies that coming-into-appearance, which is now supposed to *be* reality, continues to be understood as in conflict with being, i.e., with being in the Platonic sense of permanence. What is supposed to be

"truth," being, reality *after* the twisting free from Platonism continues to
be interpreted in terms of being and truth in the Platonic sense, i.e., in
an interpretation that is still entangled in or engaged with the stage of
mere inversion. This very entanglement would thus be what prevents the
discordance from being a harmonious one. Heidegger writes:

> Art and truth are equally necessary for reality. As equally necessary
> they stand in a disseverance. Their relationship, however, first be-
> comes horrifying when we consider that creating, i.e., the meta-
> physical activity of art, acquires yet another necessity at that
> moment in which the fact of the most monumental event, the death
> of the God of morality, comes to be recognized. For Nietzsche,
> existence can now be endured only in creating. Bringing reality into
> the power of its law and of its supreme possibilities now alone
> guarantees being. Yet creating, as art, is will to appearance [*Schein*];
> it stands in a disseverance to truth.[69]

With the death of the God of morality, i.e., the collapse of any positing
of a suprasensuous goal and meaning, the unfolding of nihilism in which
the "true world" comes to nothing, there is no longer any meaning or
directionality to existence. Existence can now find meaning only in the
creative activity of art, in which the sensuous is affirmed in being transformed and transfigured into its highest possibilities, the supreme intensity and radiance of becoming as shining forth. Such transfiguration
precisely affirms the sensuous as what it ultimately *is*, lets becoming itself
appear in its ultimate being. Yet if art as this will to *appearance* is the will
to appearance *in what it, appearance, is*, and if such being is understood
in terms of the Platonic conception of being as permanence, then what
results is indeed a horrifying discordance between appearance as coming-into-appearance, as becoming, and the *being* of such appearance, the
fact that such becoming also *is*. Thus, Heidegger writes, Nietzsche in his
thinking of being as will to power attempts to think together – in a way
that is no longer oppositional, but discordant – the ancient opposition
between being and becoming.[70]

These considerations in fact bear on Heidegger's claim that Nietzsche
remains within the *guiding* question of metaphysics and does not attain
the grounding question; that he remains, in other words, within the
question of what beings are, and does not ask concerning the essence of
being itself as truth. If we consider Nietzsche's statement that "truth is
an error," we can see that it is in fact entangled in two different conceptions of the *essence* of truth. According to Heidegger's favorable reading
of this assertion, "truth" means "the true," that which is true, this or that

particular truth. Yet how is truth itself understood here? "Truth" as the true is meant in the Platonic sense of the true as the permanent. Yet clearly such "truth" is not an error in the Platonic sense. In what sense, then, can it be said to be an error? In what sense is it not something true? It is not true insofar as it is not in keeping with that which now (in twisting free from Platonism) truly is, namely becoming. The essence of truth itself is now implicitly understood as *concordance with that which is, with becoming.*

Heidegger does not explicitly examine this "extreme" transformation of the essence of truth into ὁμοίωσις as concordance or *Einstimmigkeit* until the third *Nietzsche* course, "The Will to Power as Knowledge" (1939).[71] It remains to be pointed out, however, that Nietzsche's implicit entanglement with this transformed, yet ultimately Platonic conception of truth that also allows a principle of *evaluation* and evaluative thinking to remain, even if such evaluation is now in service of "life itself," and no longer in prospect of a Platonist "beyond." Art can be said to be *"worth more"* that truth in the sense that it is more *in keeping with* what now is, the sensuous as becoming. Yet for Heidegger such thinking fails to pose the grounding question of what being itself is, the question of the "truth" of being as the question of the being or essence of truth, because its implicit understanding of the being of what is remains an understanding of being *as truth*, precisely. That which now is, the sensuous in its coming-into appearance, is still understood by Nietzsche as that which *truly* is; being as expressed in the "is" continues to be understood implicitly as truth, and such being as truth remains entangled in a Platonic conception of ἀλήθεια, a conception in which ἀλήθεια is drawn into a λόγος of ὁμοίωσις. What in Nietzsche's attempted twisting free from Platonism verges on Heidegger's understanding of being as φύσις, coming-into-appearance, ἀλήθεια, continues to be translated as that which *truly* is, and is not yet thought as unconcealment. That is, it is not yet thought in terms of concealment itself, of a concealment that could never be homologous with any saying of being as the issue and issuing of a determinate discordance.

What, if anything, remains to be said concerning the discordance experienced by Nietzsche in his twisting free? Is it conceivable, perhaps, that such discordance could become so horrifying that one could no longer distinguish between being and becoming? Especially if one were not simply standing "before" (*vor*) this discordance, but, in already experiencing it as horrifying, oneself became aroused by it, drawn into it, befallen by it: if what one once stood "before" were one's own future and destiny. And especially considering that this discordance is a discordance within *being itself* and what it means to be. "During the time when the inversion of Platonism became for Nietzsche a twisting free from it," writes Heidegger, "madness befell him [*überfiel ihn der Wahnsinn*]." And *this* inversion – namely the inversion that became a twisting free – was, Heidegger adds, Nietzsche's "last step."[72] The German *Wahnsinn* suggests, literally, being "without sense or meaning," out of one's senses, in this case, perhaps, in a realm in which one would no longer know what meaning is, nor what being means, yet be *possessed* precisely by such desire to know: to know the truth of what is, of what and who I am.[73] To be *aroused* by such horrifying discordance, to be *befallen* by madness: these terms that Heidegger uses to interpret what occurs in discordance and in Nietzsche's twisting free from Platonism suggest that here we are not simply dealing with "theories" of being that could subsequently be applied to the sensuous (for that would be precisely to remain within the oppositional λόγος of Platonism). The terms imply, rather, that *it is the body itself that is seized, aroused and befallen by the λόγοι or voices in this* Aus-einander-setzung, *the body as living and bodying forth (leiben) in and into sensuous appearance.*[74] The body "itself," we should write, perhaps, in the case of "Nietzsche," in the case of some body aroused and possessed by a horrifying discordance, by a discordance that, as Heidegger adds parenthetically, means "being torn apart," *Zerrissenheit*.

Heidegger closes his Foreword to *heidegger nietzsche* with the words:

Whence the *Aus-einander-setzung* with Nietzsche's issue comes, whither it goes, may show itself to the reader when he himself sets off along the path that the following texts have taken.[75]

NOTES

1 *Nietzsche ist der Eine, der er ist . . .* (NI, p. 79; tr., p. 66).
2 *Spurs*, bilingual edition, trans. B. Harlow (University of Chicago Press: Chicago, 1979), pp. 72–3ff (translation modified).
3 NI, p. 9. All references are to the two-volume Neske edition (Pfullingen, 1961), cited as NI and NII respectively. In English, these are available in Harper Collins paperback edition, translated and edited by David Farrell Krell (New York, 1991). Where appropriate, I have modified the existing translation to suit the readings proposed in this present essay. Krell's Analysis of the first *Nietzsche* course (pp. 230–57 in the English edition) provides an excellent introduction to the *Auseinandersetzung* discussed here.
4 I shall leave this word untranslated in what follows, for the multiple register of its meaning, which I shall discuss in a moment, is important for approaching Heidegger's text.
5 *Das eine bin ich, das andre sind meine Schriften* (*Ecce Homo*, "Why I Write Such Good Books").
6 "I am not real, I will not be read" (ibid.).

7 – *Und so erzähle ich mir mein Leben. Ecce Homo,* Preface to "Why I Am So Wise."
8 *Ecce Homo,* Foreword, (1).
9 NI, p. 13, tr., p. 4.
10 Ibid.
11 *Ecce Homo,* "Why I Am a Destiny," 1, translated by W. Kaufmann (Random House: New York, 1969). Translation modified. In German, "*Warum ich ein Schicksal bin*":

> Ich kenne mein Los. Es wird sich einmal an meinen Namen die Erinnerung an etwas Ungeheures anknüpfen – an eine Krisis, wie es keine auf Erden gab, an die tiefste Gewissens-Kollision, an eine Entscheidung, heraufbeschworen *gegen* alles, was bis dahin geglaubt, gefordert, geheiligt worden war.

12 Cf. here some remarks made in a first draft of Heidegger's 1937/38 course *Grundfragen der Philosophie,* remarks concerning Nietzsche's "madness" (*Wahnsinn*) and the necessity of *our* being "deranged" (*verrückt*) from our present position back into a relation to being itself. The reference to Nietzsche's *Wahnsinn,* Heidegger states, is all too often used as an excuse for keeping his "most decisive meditation," the thought of eternal return, at a distance, literally: for keeping it away from one's body (*vom Leibe halten*). For something astonishing has been happening since Western history has had some intimation of its own end, via its most profound meditations. The astonishing thing is that those who undertook such meditation, those who "thus already bore something quite other [*das ganz Andere*] within their knowing" – Schiller, Hölderlin, Kierkegaard, van Gogh, and Nietzsche – were prematurely torn from the wakefulness of existence, each in their own way. Did they merely "break down" (*zerbrechen*"), asks Heidegger, "or was a new song sung to them"? These *names,* he continues "are like enigmatic signs [*Zeichen*], inscribed in the most concealed ground of our history" (GA Bd. 45, p. 216). Heidegger's first *Nietzsche* course, as we shall see, will attempt to bring the name, the *Auseinandersetzung* "Nietzsche," back into proximity with the body and the "concealed ground" upon which history is inscribed.
13 Heidegger concludes this first section of "The Will to Power as Art" by characterizing the course as a preparation for a "feast" and "celebration" of thinking. See NI, pp. 14–15; tr., pp. 5–6.
14 *The Will to Power,* No. 693. Henceforth cited as: WM, 693.
15 WM, 582. Cited at NI, pp. 82–3.
16 XIV, 368. Cited at NI, pp. 88–9. References to the Nietzsche *Nachlaß* are to the *Großoktav* edition, as cited by Heidegger.
17 NI, p. 89.
18 WM, 853; NI, p. 89.
19 As the note in the English translation points out, the section title chosen by Heidegger is a condensation of this phrase. The German *die erregende Zwiespalt,* rendered as "the raging discordance," is difficult to translate into English, because the adjective *erregende* – from the verb *erregen*: to arouse, provoke, stimulate, excite (also in the sexual sense) – is to be understood in the transitive sense, i.e., referring to a discordance that *arouses* or *excites* something. See the translator's note on p. 142 in the English edition.

20 NI, p. 174; tr., p. 148.
21 Ibid., pp. 80–1.
22 This initial distinction, however, will subsequently be complicated via Heidegger's reading.
23 Ibid., p. 180; tr., pp. 153–4.
24 See NI, pp. 177ff, tr., pp. 151ff, for Heidegger's summary of positivism.
25 Ibid., p. 182; tr., p. 156.
26 Ibid., p. 183; tr., pp. 156–7.
27 Ibid., pp. 187–8; tr., p. 160.
28 Concerning the intrinsic belonging together of being and truth, see the section entitled "The Fundamental Question and the Guiding Question of Philosophy" (ibid., pp. 79–81; tr., pp. 67–8). For an earlier overview of this issue, see especially the 1927 course *Die Grundprobleme der Phänomenologie* (GA Bd. 24, Frankfurt: Klostermann, 1975), Part One, Chapter Four. (Tr. A. Hofstadter, *The Basic Problems of Phenomenology* (Bloomington: Indiana University Press, 1982).
29 NI, p. 188; tr., p. 160.
30 Ibid., tr., p. 161.
31 Ibid., p. 189; tr., p. 161.
32 Ibid., tr., p. 162.
33 I shall not pursue the details of Heidegger's very careful and nuanced reading of the question of truth in the *Republic* in the present context, since my interest here concerns the emergent conception of *Zwiespalt* or discordance as a kind of *Auseinandersetzung*.
34 Ibid., p. 190; tr., p. 162.
35 Ibid., p. 191; tr., pp. 163–4. Heidegger will also refer to the task of reading Nietzsche as that of reading a trace in his 1939 course (his third course on Nietzsche), "The Will to Power as Knowledge." Heidegger there writes: "What solely concerns us is the *trace* [Spur] that [Nietzsche's] thought-path toward the will to power has made into the history of being – which means into the still untravelled regions of future decisions" (NI, p. 475; tr., Vol. III, p. 4).
36 Ibid., p. 212; tr., p. 182.
37 WM, 853. Cf. NI, pp. 89ff; tr., pp. 74ff.
38 NI, p. 218; tr., 188.
39 Ibid., p. 219; tr., p. 189. I cite the German text in full because of the difficulty of translating this passage into English:

Was heißt Zwiespalt? Der Zwiespalt ist das Auseinanderklaffen von Zweien, die entzweit sind. Das bloße Klaffen macht freilich noch nicht den Zwiespalt. Zwar sprechen wir in Bezug auf das Klaffende zwischen zwei ragenden Felsen von einem Felsspalt; doch die Felsen sind nicht im Zwiespalt und können es nie sein; denn dazu gehört, daß sie, und zwar von sich aus, sich aufeinander beziehen. Nur was sich aufeinander bezieht, kann gegeneinander sein. Aber auch die Gegensätzlichkeit ist noch nicht Zwiespalt. Das Gegeneinander setzt freilich das Aufeinanderbezogensein, d.h. das Übereinkommen in einer Hinsicht voraus. Ein echter politischer Gegensatz – nicht bloße Händel – ist nur da, wo die politische Ordnung des Selben gewollt wird; hier erst können Wege und Ziele und Grundsätze auseinandergehen. Im Gegensatz herrscht jeweils in der einen Hinsicht Übereinkunft, in einer anderen Verschiedenheit. Was nun aber in derselben Hinsicht, in der es übereinkommt, zugleich auch auseinandergeht, gerät in den Zwiespalt. Hier ist das Gegeneinander aus dem Auseinandertreten des Zusammengetretenen entsprungen, so zwar, daß es als Auseinander gerade in die höchste Zusammengehörigkeit tritt. Daraus ersehen wir aber zugleich, daß Entzweiung etwas anderes ist als Gegensatz, daß aber auch die Entzweiung nicht notwendig Zwiespalt sein muß, sondern Einklang sein kann. Auch der Einklang verlangt die Zweiheit der Entzweiung. "Zwiespalt" ist daher zweideutig: 1. Entzweiung, die aber im Grunde Einklang sein kann. 2. Entzweiung, die Zwiespalt werden muß (Zerrissenheit).

40 Krell's translation renders *Zerrissenheit* as "abscission." The word is frequently used by Hegel, and often translated as "diremption." Heidegger has in fact already cited its use by Hegel in a section from the Preface to the *Phenomenology of Spirit* in which Spirit is said to find itself in "absolute *Zerrissenheit*" in the face of the power of the negative, the presence of death. See NI, pp. 73–4 (tr., pp. 61–2). Here Miller's translation renders *Zerrissenheit* as "dismemberment," while Bailey has "being torn asunder." I have preferred this more literal translation for the purposes of the present essay. (My thanks to Stephen Houlgate for some of these references.)

41 Ibid., pp. 219–20; tr., pp. 189–90.

42 *Republic*, 607B, cited at NI, p. 220; tr., p. 190.

43 *Phaedrus*, 249E. πασα μὲν ἀνθρώπου ψυχὴ ψύσει τεθέαται τὰ ὄντα, ἢ οὐκ ἄν ηλθεν εἰς τόδε τὸ ζῷον Heidegger renders this as "every human soul, emerging of itself, has already caught sight of beings in their being, otherwise it would never have entered into this form of life" (NI, p.223; tr., p. 192).

44 "*in den Leib gebannt . . .*" (NI, p. 224; tr., p. 193). This appears to be a reference to the *Phaedrus* 250C, where the soul is said to be "imprisoned" (δεδεσμευμένοι) in the body. Krell's translation of *in den Leib gebannt* has "exiled in the body. . . ." The German *bannen*, however (which also appears on NI, p. 229), also suggests being bound in the sense of "spellbound," "entranced"; the word is used by Heidegger in precisely this sense in his analyses of boredom, as our being "entranced" by time, in his 1929/ 30 lecture course *Dic Grundbegriffe der Metaphysik. Welt – Endlichkeit – Einsamkeit* (GA Bd. 29/30, Klostermann: Frankfurt, 1983). I have rendered *gebannt* as "captivated" to suggest this double sense.

45 The term "befalls" (*befallen*) implies that such λήθη occurs as an attunement or *Stimmung*; it is a way in which the human being in their bodying forth is *affected*, thus one way in which disclosure occurs ("positively") through disposition (*Befindlichkeit*). Presumably, such λήθη occurs for the most part (though not exclusively) through an attunement of *indifference* (*Indifferenz* or *Gleichgültigkeit*), which Heidegger analyses most incisively in the 1929/30 course (see previous note) in terms of *boredom*, but which also plays a role in *Being and Time* as the "average everydayness" of Dasein from which the analytic of Dasein takes its departure (see especially SZ, § 9).

46 NI, p. 226; tr., p. 194. Note that Heidegger's use of the term *entrückt*, "transported," here invites an attempt to read the question of ἔρως back into *Being and Time*, where the same term is used to characterize the temporal transport of ecstasis. On questions of ἔρως and *Auseinandersetzung* in

Heidegger, see especially Derrida's essay "Heidegger's Ear: Philopolemology (*Geschlecht* IV)," in: *Reading Heidegger: Commemorations*, ed. John Sallis (Indiana University Press: Bloomington, Indiana, 1993), pp. 161–218.

47 NI, p. 227; tr., p. 196.

48 οὐ γὰρ ἦγε μήποτε ἰδοῦσα τὴν ἀλήθειαν εἰς τόδε ἥξει τὸ σχῆμα (NI, p. 229; tr., p. 198).

49 NI, p. 230; tr., p. 198.

50 What is at issue here is ultimately the question of how difference and negativity come to be installed within being in such a way as to conceal the *essence* or essential prevailing (*Wesen*) of negativity, that is, to conceal concealment itself, thereby (i.e., as a "consequence") giving rise to human oblivion of being. It is, in short, the story of *how nothing comes to be*, of the advent of nihilism in terms of the history of being (*Seinsgeschichte*).

51 NI, p. 230; tr., p. 198.

52 See the analysis of "How the 'True World' Finally Became a Fable" (NI, p. 233ff, tr., p. 202ff).

53 Ibid., pp. 230–1; tr., pp. 198–9.

54 Ibid., p. 236; tr., p. 204.

55 Ibid., p. 237; tr., p. 205.

56 Ibid., p. 231; tr., p. 200.

57 Ibid.

58 Ibid., p. 240; tr., p. 207.

59 On the issue of this "twisting free" as encountered by Heidegger, see John Sallis, "Twisting Free: Being to an Extent Sensible" (*Research in Phenomenology*, Volume XVII, 1987, pp. 1–22). Cf. also chapter 13 of his book *Delimitations* (Indiana University Press: Bloomington, Indiana, 1986).

60 NI, p. 240; tr., p. 208.

61 Heidegger's second *Nietzsche* course, "The Eternal Recurrence of the Same" (1937), will attempt to understand this decision as the moment or *Augenblick* in which the eternal return of the same is thought. And this is also the moment and time of *Auseinandersetzung*. Thus Heidegger will write that the moment itself *is* "that decision in which history hitherto is confronted [*zur Auseinandersetzung gestellt*] and at the same time overcome as the history of nihilism" (NI, p. 445; tr., p. 182).

62 Ibid., p. 242; tr., p. 209.

63 WM, 493; cited at NI, p. 247; tr., pp. 214–15.

64 *vieldeutig.* having a multiplicity of meanings.

65 NI, p. 248; tr., p. 215.

66 Ibid., p. 248; tr., p. 215.

67 Ibid., p. 250; tr., p. 217.

68 Ibid., pp. 250–1; tr., p. 217. Heidegger also cites WM 853, I, at this point.

69 Ibid., p. 251; tr., pp. 217–18.

70 Ibid., p. 251; tr., p. 218.

71 See NI, pp. 473–658; tr., Vol. III, pp. 1–158. Cf. especially the sections "Truth and the distinction between the 'true and apparent worlds'," and "The most extreme transformation of truth as metaphysically conceived" (NI, p. 616ff, tr., pp. 123ff).

72 Ibid., p. 233; tr., p. 202.

73 Cf. Heidegger's interpretation of the word *Wahnsinn* in a much later text and a very different context: the 1953 essay *Die Sprache im Gedicht* (*Unterwegs zur Sprache*, Neske, 1979, pp. 35–82) which attempts to find the "location" or

"locus" [*Ortschaft*] of Trakl's poetry. The *Wahnsinn* of which Trakl speaks, and which Heidegger discusses at the beginning of Part II of the essay, is not that of Nietzsche. Yet it is still to be thought in the context of duality and twofoldness [*Zwiefalt*], of an "unsayable" harmony [*Einklang*] and gathering in the "ambiguous ambiguity" [*zweideutigen Zweideutigkeit*], polysemy, and multiplicity of meaning in the *logos* of Trakl's poetry. Heidegger there suggests that *Wahnsinn* does not mean "mental illness," but the site of "departedness" from which a "more gentle" twofoldness of the sexes can be glimpsed. For commentary on these issues, see in particular Derrida's essays on *Geschlecht*, and David Krell's *Daimon Life* (Indiana University Press: Bloomington, Indiana, 1992).

74 Thus Heidegger, much earlier in the course, when discussing "The Will as Affect, Passion, and Feeling," writes:

> Anger, for instance, is an affect. In contrast, by "hate" we mean something quite different. Hate is not simply another affect; it is not an affect at all, but a passion. Yet we call both of them feelings. We speak of a feeling of hatred or of an angry feeling. We cannot plan or decide to be angry. Anger befalls us, seizes us [*überfällt uns, fällt uns an*], "affects" us. Such seizure is sudden and turbulent. Our being is stirred in the manner of being aroused [*unser Wesen regt sich in der Weise der Erregung*]; such seizure excites us [*regt uns auf*], i.e., lifts us beyond ourselves, yet in such a way that in being seized and aroused in this way we are no longer masters of ourselves. We say that someone "acted on impulse [*im Affekt*]." Ordinary discourse is very keensighted when it says of someone who is excited and acts excitedly that he is not really "together" [*beieinander*]. When we are seized by excitement, our being properly "together" vanishes and becomes transformed into a being "untogether" [*ein Auseinander*]. We say that someone is "beside himself [*außer sich*] with joy." (NI, pp. 56–7; tr., pp. 45–6)

In his later essay "*Der Weg zur Sprache*" (1959), Heidegger will identify *Regen*, excitation or rousing, with the showing and telling [*Sage*] of language in its "propriating" [*Eignen*]. (See also its use in the 1936 *Schelling* and 1942/43 *Parmenides* courses.)

75 NI, p. 10; tr., p. xl.

12
Nietzsche and Critical Theory

William Outhwaite

Nietzsche's pervasive yet ambiguous influence on twentieth-century thought is nowhere more striking than in neomarxist critical theory. Whereas György Lukács, one of the main sources of critical theory, moved from an early adulation of Nietzsche to an intemperate attack on his contribution to the 'destruction of reason' in Germany, the key theorists of what came to be called the Frankfurt School – Theodor Adorno, Max Horkheimer, Herbert Marcuse and Walter Benjamin, and more recently Jürgen Habermas – took from the beginning a more nuanced and sympathetic approach to his work.

The so-called Nietzsche revival and what the sociologist Ferdinand Tönnies called 'the Nietzsche cult' was particularly strong in early twentieth-century Budapest; the young Lukács identified himself whole-heartedly with the man whom, along with Ibsen, he saw as the greatest prophet of the age.[1] Lukács' early books, *Soul and Form* (1910/1974) and *Modern Drama* (1911), are heavily influenced by Nietzsche. Although a personal tragedy in 1911 seems to have pushed Lukács into abandoning Nietzsche in favour of Kierkegaard, and in 1918 he became a communist, it was not until the 1930s, under political pressure in Moscow, that he joined in the anti-Nietzschean chorus of which his *The Destruction of Reason* (1954) later formed an important element.

More important than this later volte-face, however, is a certain affinity between Nietzsche and Marx which makes Lukács' turn to Marx at the end of the First World War seem less remarkable. François Fejtö, in a fictionalized dialogue of 1936, gives his Lukács character the following lines:

Both Nietzsche and Marx were sarcastic, sharp, and very French. They loved Heine and learned a lot from him. The language of

Nietzsche recalls the young Marx's language. From Nietzsche to Marx is a short step, rather than a leap. In my school years, Nietzsche opened my eyes, made me suspicious of phrases, encouraged me to face the world.[2]

Almost as important as Lukács (and his friend and admirer Ernst Bloch) among the immediate precursors of critical theory were the non-Marxist sociologists Georg Simmel and Max Weber. Lukács, whose early writing on culture is hard to distinguish from Simmel's, never had the academic connection with him which at one time he had sought. He was however a regular guest at Max Weber's house in Heidelberg, and his concept of reification (*Verdinglichung*) owes as much to Weber's 'rationalisation' as to Marx's 'commodity fetishism'. Nietzsche's influence on Weber, which was partly mediated by Tönnies' and Simmel's books on Nietzsche and the cult surrounding his work, has become an increasingly prominent theme of recent scholarship as this has become preoccupied with the concept of modernity. For Weber, Marx and Nietzsche were the twin poles of modern intellectual life: 'the seriousness[3] of a contemporary scholar can be measured by how he stands in relation to Marx and Nietzsche'.

The history of the Frankfurt Institute for Social Research and of what came to be called the Frankfurt School has been very fully discussed, most recently in Rolf Wiggershaus' massive study.[4] I shall focus here on Max Horkheimer, the Director of the Institute from 1931 until his retirement, Theodor W. Adorno, who was associated with the Institute through the 1930s and became Horkheimer's closest intellectual collaborator during their years in exile in the USA, Herbert Marcuse, another close associate, and Walter Benjamin.

One of the defining characteristics of these neomarxist thinkers is their openness to a wide range of intellectual influences: not just the obvious figures of Kant, Hegel and Marx, but also Freud, Schopenhauer, Kierkegaard, Heidegger and Nietzsche. As Peter Pütz noted in his classic article on 'Nietzsche and Critical Theory',[5] they tend to invoke him not as the introductory premise of their own writings (a role which in any case hardly suits him) but towards the end, as they draw to a point a line of argument in which often, as Adorno said in another context, only the exaggerations are true.

It was Nietzsche the man, the lonely oppositionist,[6] the critic of culture who was most congenial to the critical theorists; his trenchant aphorisms, directed at what he saw as a culture in decline, formed a model for their own. Max Horkheimer wrote, in a biting review of Karl

Jaspers' book on Nietzsche,[7] that he mercilessly 'analyzed the objective spirit of his time, the psychic state of the bourgeoisie (p. 408). . . . The independence which is brought to expression in his philosophy, the freedom from enslaving ideological powers is the root of his thought' (p. 414). As Adorno put it in a letter to Benjamin, criticising the latter's attempt to fit his study of nineteenth-century Paris into Marxist categories,

> God knows, there is only one truth, and if your intelligence lays hold of this one truth in categories which on the basis of your idea of materialism may seem apocryphal to you, you will capture more of this one truth than if you use intellectual tools whose movements your hand resists at every turn. After all, there is more about this truth in Nietzsche's *Genealogy of Morals* than in Bukharin's *ABC of Communism*.[8]

Benjamin, whose tragic suicide on his flight from Nazism occurred less than two years later, was perhaps closest to Nietzsche in his vigour of expression and his willingness to push his thought to its limits. He never found 'the time . . . to consider what meaning Nietzsche's writings might yield if put to the critical test (*im Ernstfall*)',[9] but his images, such as the famous angel of history (*Illuminations*) or of the present as 'a bull whose blood must fill the pit if the spirits of the departed are to appear at its edge'[10] could have come from Nietzsche himself. Benjamin goes so far as to endorse a version of nihilism which not only kicks over the traces but, in Brecht's phrase, effaces them. As Irving Wohlfarth puts it,

> Whenever Benjamin celebrates the effacement of traces, there is something at once messianic, Brechtian *and* Nietzschean in the air. 'On this sofa the aunt cannot but be murdered.' It is in the name of a 'new, positive barbarism', and with a barbaric Nietzschean laugh, that Benjamin welcomes the various efforts of a certain avant-garde to clear away the clutter of bourgeois culture.[11]

If anything, as Wohlfarth notes, Benjamin is even more destructive and and negative than Nietzsche, bent merely on a devaluation rather than a transvaluation (*Umwertung*) of values. More positively, however, though in a way which takes him very far from Nietzsche/Zarathustra, Benjamin advances a version of messianism which is cast in terms of moral obligation as well as opportunities for emancipation. 'Like every generation, that preceded us, we have been endowed with a *weak* Messianic power, a power to which the past has a claim.'[12] On one reading at least, this

implies an obligation to commemorate and atone for the sufferings of
previous generations.[13]

Two further, related themes in Benjamin's work lead us from the
critique of culture to the critique of knowledge which both Nietzsche and
Benjamin gestured towards but never fully articulated. Both are illustrated in the passage just quoted: the repetition of (in this case)
messianic power, and the form to be taken by our knowledge of the past.
The former refers of course to Nietzsche's doctrine of eternal recurrence,
the latter to his critique of historicism (in the sense of detached contemplation of the past). Benjamin was fascinated by the fact that

> the idea of eternal recurrence intrudes into the work of Baudelaire,
> Blanqui and Nietzsche at approximately the same moment. . . . In
> Baudelaire, the accent is on the new which is won with heroic effort
> from the 'ever-already-the-same'; in Nietzsche, it is the 'ever-
> already-the-same' which the person faces with heroic composure.
> Blanqui is much closer to Nietzsche than to Benjamin, but with him
> resignation prevails. In Nietzsche this experience projects itself
> cosmologically in the thesis: there will be nothing new anymore.[14]

As Winfried Menninghaus notes, in his sensitive discussion of this
theme, Benjamin alludes to eternal recurrence in a variety of different
ways, but 'they all partake equally of the fundamental dialectic of
Benjamin's thought on myth: the eternal recurrence of the same characterizes the historical compulsory relation *to be broken* apart, but equally
the temporal form of the "happiness" of the *exploded* mythical fate':

> Eternal recurrence is an attempt to link two antinomic principles of
> happiness with each other: namely that of eternity and that of the yet
> once again. The idea of eternal recurrence conjures up out of
> the misery of time the speculative idea (or phantasmagoria) of
> happiness.[15]

This theme combines with a second one: Benjamin's account of our
knowledge of history. Benjamin cites, in his sixteenth thesis 'On the
Concept of History', Nietzsche's famous remarks in the preface to 'On
the Advantage and Disadvantage of History for Life'[16]: 'Certainly we
need history. But our need for history is quite different from that of the
spoiled idler in the garden of knowledge.' Benjamin comments:

> A historical materialist cannot do without the notion of a present
> which is not a transition, but in which time stands still and has come

to a stop. For this notion defines the present in which he himself is writing history. Historicism gives the eternal image of the past; historical materialism supplies a unique experience with the past.[17]

And in Konvolut (file) N3,4 of the Arcades project on Paris, Benjamin recalls a conversation with Ernst Bloch:

in which I set forth how this project – whose method may only be compared to the splitting of the atom – releases the enormous energy of history that lies bonded in the 'Once upon a time' of classical historical narrative. The history that showed things 'as they really were' was the strongest narcotic of the century.[18]

Benjamin never articulated a theory of knowledge and truth which would match Nietzsche's equally fragmentary conception discussed below; but his notion of a practical imperative built into historical reflection is one which recurs in more systematic formulations of critical theory – notably in the work of Max Horkheimer to which I now turn.

In turning from Benjamin to Adorno, Horkheimer and Marcuse, we move from someone who might at a pinch be called a 'Nietzsche of the left' to thinkers who merely display a substantial respect for him, yet whose work has equally substantial Nietzschean resonances. To begin with the more obvious aspects, it is clear that their critiques of 'affirmative culture' or of the 'culture industry' have much in common with Nietzsche's – including, of course, a certain elitism.[19] Nietzsche is portrayed, like the other 'dark writers of the bourgeoisie' (to use one of Horkheimer's favourite categories), as showing up the truth of bourgeois society. As Horkheimer put it in 'The End of Reason',[20] 'Nietzsche proclaimed the death of morality; modern psychology has devoted itself to explaining it' (p. 36). Nietzsche was right, too, in his critique of scientism: 'It is not the victory of *science* that is the distinguishing mark of our nineteenth century, but the victory of the scientific *method* over science.'[21] Even Nietzsche's sceptical account of truth receives Horkheimer's qualified assent, in the service of a dialectical conception which would, it is implied, remove its purely negative and partial quality:

Nietzsche said that a great truth 'wants to be criticized, not worshipped'.[22] This is valid for truth in general. He might have added that criticism includes not only the negative and skeptical impulse but also the inner independence not to let the truth fall but to remain firm in its application, even if it may sometime pass away.[23]

This is of course an early essay, and Horkheimer's later position, under the influence of Adorno and of the general *misère*, becomes a good deal more gloomy. It is in fact in their later works that Adorno and Horkheimer come closest to Nietzsche; most obviously in their diagnosis of human history in *Dialectic of Enlightenment*. This bizarre but brilliant book has come to play a role as a kind of talisman in social and cultural theory in the last third of the twentieth century comparable to that of Nietzsche's writings in the late nineteenth century. Horkheimer and Adorno borrow explicitly from Nietzsche their basic motif: that of a deeply problematic process of enlightenment which links classical Greece and eighteenth-century Europe[24] and in which theoretical reason, science and a drive for mastery of the natural and the social world sweep aside old myths but end up falling into a new one. It is hardly too much to describe *Dialectic of Enlightenment* as a left Nietzschean book, and the following passage from *The Birth of Tragedy* would not look out of place in it: the Alexandrian or 'theoretical' spirit

> combats Dionysian wisdom and art, it seeks to dissolve myth, it substitutes for a metaphysical comfort an earthly consonance, in fact a *deus ex machina* of its own, the god of machines and crucibles, that is, the power of the spirits of nature recognized and employed in the service of a higher egoism; it believes that it can correct the world by knowledge, guide life by science, and actually confine the individual within a limited sphere of soluble problems.[25]

These neomarxists, or perhaps post-marxists, draw on Nietzsche to generalize a process which Marx (and to a considerable extent Max Weber too) had linked mainly to the emergence of capitalism. In so doing, Horkheimer and Adorno use Nietzsche in a way which is not wholly unlike Marx's use of Hegel, as someone who: (1) expressed the fundamental contradictions with which they are concerned; (2) remains in the end part of the problem rather than a solution; yet (3) offers elements of a method, or at least a form of analysis, for a more adequate response. In Reinhart Maurer's striking phrase, critical theory is 'a neomarxism crisscrossed by Nietzschean perspectives'.[26]

One important element in this is their own relationship to the philosophical tradition. Once again, the parallels between Nietzsche and Marx emerge in the notion of an end to philosophy or metaphysics. To put it in slogans, Marx wanted to realize philosophy; Nietzsche wanted to 'philosophize with a hammer', one last time, and Adorno famously remarked that 'Philosophy, which once seemed obsolete, lives on because the moment to realize it was missed'.[27]

What exactly is the dialectic of enlightenment as Horkheimer and Adorno present it? Perhaps the best way to sum it up is by way of Horkheimer's well-known claim in 1939, later disavowed, that 'he who does not wish to speak of capitalism should also be silent about fascism'.[28] *Dialectic of Enlightenment* in a sense makes the same claim for enlightenment as Horkheimer had earlier made for capitalism. It retains an emphasis on the capitalist organisation of labour as a crucial aspect of the implementation of enlightened reason, but the model is generalized. Homeric Greece was not a *capitalist* society, but the Odysseus legend already expresses 'the entanglement of myth, domination and labor',[29] and Francis Bacon in the early seventeenth century discerned the link between scientific knowledge and power. As Horkheimer and Adorno put it, 'What men want to learn from nature is how to use it in order wholly to dominate it and other men. . . . The only kind of thinking that is sufficiently hard to shatter myths is ultimately self-destructive' (p. 4). And it is Nietzsche who shatters the myth of the Enlightenment itself; it combines the critique of domination, 'to make princes and statesmen unmistakably aware that everything they do is sheer falsehood' (p. 44), with the extension of manipulation and domination in the name of progress. More radically still, Nietzsche's famous observation that reason cannot provide a knock-down argument against murder forms the basis of a chapter of the book which vertiginously combines Kant, Nietzsche and Sade's Juliette:

the *chronique scandaleuse* of Justine and Juliette is the Homeric epic with its last mythological covering removed: the history of thought as an organ of domination (p. 117). . . . Inasmuch as the merciless doctrines [of Sade and Nietzsche] proclaim the identity of domination and reason, they are more merciful than those of the moralistic lackeys of the bourgeoisie. (p. 119)

Or as Adorno put it:

Nietzsche belongs to that tradition of bourgeois writers who since the Renaissance have revolted against the untruth of society and cynically played its reality as an 'ideal' against its ideal, and by the critical power of the confrontation have helped that other truth [i.e. its ideal;] which they mock most fiercely as the untruth.[30]

This form of enlightenment can be genuinely emancipatory, as Horkheimer had argued in his *Dämmerung* in the early 1930s:

Nietzsche's goals are not those of the proletariat. But it can realise
that the morality which advises it to be complaisant is, according to
this philosopher of the dominant class, mere deception. He himself
impresses on the masses that it is only fear which prevents them
from destroying this apparatus. If they really understand this,
Nietzsche can even contribute to the transformation of the slave
revolt in morality into proletarian praxis.[31]

This same liberatory shock is what the critical theorists derive from
Nietzsche's critique of philosophical reason – including of course dialectic. Marcuse speaks in *One Dimensional Man* of the 'liberating atmos-
phere' of Nietzsche's thought, 'the realisation that neither aesthetic sense
nor philosophical concepts are immune to the intrusion of history'.[32]
This theme, an unshakeable sense of the conditioning of one's own
standpoint, is, as Alfred Schmidt notes in his afterword to Horkheimer's
Critical Theory, what defines the project of critical theory.[33] It is also what
makes Nietzsche a dialectical thinker, despite his explicit rejection of
dialectics. 'There are no contradictions (*Gegensätze*)', Nietzsche roundly
asserts; we falsely extrapolate logical contradictions onto things. But his
critique of oppositions is itself based on the idea that what we really
encounter are gradations and transitions. As Adorno noted, in a critical
comment on the way Soviet dialectical materialism had turned Hegel's
movement of the concept into a frozen article of faith,

> In contrast to this, there is still more of the motivating experience of
> dialectic in what Nietzsche expressed, long after Hegel, in the
> sentence that 'Nothing occurs in reality which strictly corresponds
> to logic.'[34]

Adorno's own main work, *Negative Dialectic*, is a brilliant development of
this negative conception in which, *contra* Hegel, 'the whole is the *un-
true*'.[35] In *Minima Moralia* (1951), Adorno's most Nietzschean book in
both form and content, he questions his own method of immanent
critique in a way which suggests that escape from the 'system of delusion'
(*Verblendungszusammenhang*) could only be a sudden and unpredictable
event.

Where critical theory diverges significantly from Nietzsche, however,
is when he drives his dialectical critique of knowledge into a complete
perspectivism:

> There is *only* a perspectival seeing, a perspectival perception; and *the
> more* affects we allow to be articulated about a thing, *the more* eyes,

different eyes, we know how to involve in the same thing, the fuller becomes the 'concept' of the thing, our 'objectivity'.[36]

This passage, which beautifully anticipates the concept of 'relationism' in Karl Mannheim's sociology of knowledge in the 1920s, is similarly open to a critique from the standpoint of critical theory.[37] Lacking any means in principle to mediate between or transcend these competing perspectives – something which would require a more totalising concept of *society*, Nietzsche remains an exponent of the approach whose barrenness he demonstrates. If Adorno's hope against hope[38] for an ultimate reconciliation is something he cannot justify in the face of Nietzsche's scepticism, he had at least provided, in his book on Husserl, an implicit critique of Nietzsche's presupposition that nature is wholly open to subjective construction: the domination of nature which Nietzsche makes the ultimate ground of his entire theory of knowledge would not be possible without a 'moment of fixity' in the objects themselves.[39] This amounts, once again, to the idea that the cognitive activities of human beings must be located in a broader naturalistic conception of human practice and the social totality which we must presuppose, though we cannot grasp it or 'drastically verify' it.[40] And here, too, Nietzsche points the way, with his critique of the fateful separation of the drive for knowledge from the 'whole world of practical interests'. For Nietzsche this entails sceptical consequences, though ones which we have to live with if we wish, *contra* Schopenhauer, to go on living. Adorno implicitly, and Habermas more explicitly, attempt to rescue Nietzsche's insight without giving up on truth.

In turning to the 'second generation' of critical theory in the work of its leading exponent, Jürgen Habermas, we encounter a much more restrained and ascetic conception of critical theory, closer in many ways to the original programme of the Institute for Social Research than to Adorno's and Horkheimer's wartime and postwar writings. Habermas is concerned, as the Institute was in the 1930s, with an interdisciplinary synthesis of philosophy and the individual social sciences. Nietzsche plays a significant, though largely negative role at two main points in Habermas' programme: first, in his brilliant critique of positivism at the end of the 1960s, and secondly in his more recent critique of 'post-structuralism'.

In his editorial postscript to an edition of Nietzsche's epistemological writings published in the same year as *Knowledge and Human Interests*, Habermas suggests that one can salvage the idea of transcendental 'subjective conditions of the possible objectivity of knowledge' without construing them, in the Kantian manner refuted by Nietzsche, 'as the a priori valid inventory of a timeless subject determined only by the unity of its synthetic performances'.[41] Nietzsche's 'epistemological completion of nihilism'[42] relies on a form of philosophical reflection – a 'reconstruction', as Habermas would later put it – of the cognitive and practical activity of the human species, which he uses only in a sceptical critique of the possibility of reflection'.

In *Knowledge and Human Interests*,[43] Habermas reconstructs the history of nineteenth-century philosophy and social theory so as to bring out an underlying reflexive model which uncovers the cognitive or knowledge-guiding interests corresponding to the different branches of thought. The natural or, as Habermas puts it, 'empirical-analytic' sciences are guided by an interest in the prediction and control of objectified processes by means of law-like knowledge (p. 308); this interest governs the construction and testing of theories and indeed the meaning of valid theoretical propositions. The 'historical-hermeneutic' sciences are governed by a 'practical' interest in mutual understanding (p. 309ff). 'Critical' social sciences, such as psychoanalysis and the critique of ideology 'go beyond' the production of systematic empirical knowledge 'to determine when theoretical statements grasp invariant regularities of social action as such and when they express ideologically frozen relations of dependence that can in principle be transformed' (p. 310). 'Critically oriented sciences' share with philosophy an emancipatory cognitive interest' (p. 310).

These passages are taken from Habermas' inaugural lecture of 1965, which is printed as an appendix to *Knowledge and Human Interests*; the book itself traces the history of reflection on the natural (from Comte and Mach to Peirce) and the cultural sciences (Dilthey), so as to bring out their dependence on a third concept of emancipatory knowledge found in the philosophical tradition from Kant to Marx and in the metatheory of psychoanalysis, where this is understood as concerned with the removal of causal obstacles to understanding.

All this might seem like an elaboration of Nietzsche's lapidary assertion that 'our needs interpret the world'; Max Scheler's typology of forms of knowledge, which seems to have been Habermas' immediate inspiration, itself owes a good deal to Nietzsche. For Habermas, however, Nietzsche 'naturalizes' and 'psychologizes' the guiding role of interests, making knowledge into one aspect among others of human self-preservation animated by a will to power. Habermas, by contrast, insists that the interest in self-preservation 'cannot be defined independently of the cultural conditions represented by work, language, and power' (p. 288).[44] 'As long as the interest of self-preservation is misunderstood in terms of naturalism, it is difficult to see how it could take the

form of a knowledge-constitutive interest without remaining external to
the function of knowledge' (p. 289). In other words, Nietzsche

> saw the connection of knowledge and interest, but psychologized it,
> thus making it the basis of a metacritical dissolution of knowledge as
> such. Nietzsche carried to its end the self-abolition of epistemology
> inaugurated by Hegel and continued by Marx, arriving at the denial
> of self-reflection (p. 290). . . . Nietzsche is so rooted in basic
> positivistic beliefs that he cannot systematically take cognizance of
> the cognitive function of self-reflection from which he lives as a
> philosophical writer. (p. 299)

This empiricist and reductionist conception of the conditions of knowledge, involving a denial of philosophical reflection, sets the scene for the
modern positivist conception in which methodology replaces the theory
of knowledge. The context of discovery, (the genesis of knowledge), is
sharply separated from questions of validity, (the context of justification). On this basis, Habermas concludes, 'modern positivism then
erected a pure methodology, purged, however, of the really interesting
problems' (p. 300).

Habermas' subsequent work on social and moral evolution and communicative action passes over Nietzsche's critique of morality, but he
returns to Nietzsche and his influence in his vigorous critique of post-
structuralism in *The Philosophical Discourse of Modernity*.[45] Habermas
begins with the very Nietzschean theme that 'the discourse of modernity,
which we are still conducting down to our own day', is marked by the
consciousness that philosophy is at an end, whether this is seen as a
productive challenge or only as a provocation (pp. 51ff). As other
disciplines become more professionalized, philosophy becomes less so.
Independent scholars such as Marx, Kierkegaard and Nietzsche play a
larger part than academic philosophers, and so do people like Darwin
and Freud developing independent branches of science. This makes the
common features of this discourse all the more striking: Enlightenment
reason is seen as an illusory phenomenon with a narrow, and ultimately
authoritarian, subjective conception of rationality (pp. 55ff). In this
sense, Habermas argues, 'we remain contemporaries of the Young
Hegelians' (p. 53). Subsequent thinkers lie in three broad lines of
development:

> Left Hegelian critique, turned toward the practical and aroused for
> revolution, aimed at mobilizing the historically accumulated poten-
> tial of reason (awaiting release) against its mutilation, against the

William Outhwaite

one-sided rationalization of the bourgeois world. The Right
Hegelians followed Hegel in the conviction that the substance of
state and religion would compensate for the restlessness of bourgeois society, as soon as the subjectivity of the revolutionary
cosciousness that incited restlessness yielded to objective insight
into the rationality of the status quo. . . . Finally, Nietzsche wanted
to unmask the dramaturgy of the entire state-piece in which both –
revolutionary hope and the reaction to it – enter on the
scene. . . . Reason is nothing else than power, than the will to power,
which it so radiantly conceals. (p. 56)

Whereas both left and right Hegelians basically accepted the superiority
of modernity to traditional ways of life, Nietzsche both generalizes (to
earlier historical periods) and undermines the rationality which had been
imputed to modernity. 'Nietzsche owes his concept of modernity, developed in terms of his theory of power, to an unmasking critique of reason
that sets itself outside the horizon of reason' (p. 96). Habermas sees an
ambivalence in Nietzsche, again no doubt arising from the Hegelian end-
of-philosophy problematic, which becomes a second major branching-
point in modern philosophy.

Nietzsche's critique of modernity has been continued along [two]
paths. The sceptical scholar who wants to unmask the perversion of
the will to power, the revolt of reactionary forces, and the emergence of a subject-centred reason by using anthrophological, psychological, and historical methods has successors in Bataille, Lacan,
and Foucault; the initiate-critic of metaphysics who pretends to a
unique kind of knowledge and pursues the rise of the philosophy of
the subject back to its pre-Socratic beginnings has successors in
Heidegger and Derrida. (p. 97)

In an earlier essay on 'the entwinement of myth and modernity', reprinted in *The Philosophical Discourse of Modernity*, Habermas refers to
'Horkheimer and Adorno's ambiguous attempt at a dialectic of enlightenment that would satisfy Nietzsche's radical critique of reason' (p.
105). Habermas stresses the 'thoroughly philosophical' intention of *Dialectic of Enlightenment*:

Reason itself destroys the humanity it first made possible – this far-
reaching thesis . . . is grounded in the first excursus [on Odysseus –
RWO] by the fact that from the very start the process of enlightenment is the result of a drive to self-preservation that mutilates

reason, because it lays claim to it only in the form of a purposive-rational mastery of nature and instinct – precisely as instrumental reason. (pp. 110ff)

The rest of *Dialectic of Enlightenment* aims to justify the claim that 'reason remains subordinated to the dictates of purposive rationality right into its most recent products – modern science, universalistic ideas of justice and morality, autonomous art' (p. 111). This 'astoundingly' (p. 112) oversimplified account of modernity, Habermas argues once again, 'does not do justice to the rational content of cultural modernity that was captured in bourgeois ideals (and thus also instrumentalized along with them)' (p. 113). The critique of ideology 'outstrips itself' (p. 127) in a Nietzschean manner that makes one 'insensitive to the traces and the existing forms of communicative rationality' (p. 129). Habermas' model is a more Hegelian one in which communicative rationality emerges with modernity, even if in a suppressed and distorted form.

Habermas' critical engagement with Nietzsche continues through his substantial discussion of the work of Michel Foucault. In Foucault's thought, 'the radical critique of reason' takes 'the form of a historiography of the human sciences' (p. 247), 'a kind of antiscience' (p. 242) which anatomizes their will to power both at the empirical level, in medicine, psychopathology, criminology, penology etc., and at the metatheoretical level of the constitution of their basic conceptual orientations. This however creates a fundamental problem in Foucault's thought – the same paradox of self-reference which we have encountered elsewhere in Habermas' critique of Nietzschean motifs in contemporary philosophy. The attempt to step out of modernity in a genealogical historiography grounded on the theory of power ends up as precisely the presentistic, relativistic, cryptonormative illusory science that it does not want to be (pp. 275ff).

Once again, the problem is that 'the internal aspects of meaning, of truth-validity, and of evaluating do not go without remainder into the externally grasped aspects of practices of power' (p. 276). First, Foucault cannot undercut the hermeneutic predicament in his search for a real history of underlying practices which goes below or behind the self-understandings of actors. These practices have no meaning except in relation to earlier and later ones and, from our point of view, to the present. To ignore this problematic is to fall victim to it: 'The unmasking of the objectivistic illusions of any will to knowledge leads to agreement with a historiography that is narcissistically oriented toward the stand-point of the historian and instrumentalizes the contemplation of the past for the needs of the present' (p. 278).

Secondly, genealogical historiography succumbs to a 'relativistic self-denial' (p. 281): 'if the truth claims that Foucault himself raises for his genealogy of knowledge were in fact illusory and amounted to no more than the effects that this theory is capable of releasing within the circle of its adherents, then the entire critical undertaking of a critical unmasking of the human sciences would lose its point' (p. 279). Foucault flirts with a Lukács-type argument that genealogy recovers subjugated or disqualified knowledge-forms, but he cannot give these the kind of 'cognitive privilege' that was afforded to the proletariat in Lukács' philosophy of history (p. 281).

Third, Foucault's apparently value-free or supra-normative position which 'resists the demand to take sides' masks a very clear critical standpoint, that of 'a dissident who offers resistance to modern thought and humanistically disguised disciplinary power' (p. 282). But Foucault cannot ground resistance and critique without moving onto the terrain of normative argument. The attempt to eliminate 'the categories of meaning, validity and value . . . not only on the metatheoretical, but on the empirical level as well' leaves Foucault 'with an object domain from which the theory of power has erased all traces of communicative actions entangled in lifeworld contexts' (p. 286). Foucault attempts 'to preserve the transcendental moment proper to generative performances in the basic concept of power while driving from it any trace of subjectivity' (p. 295). This leads him, as it had led Nietzsche, into the subjectivist paradoxes noted above.

In Habermas' view, neither Adorno, Foucault nor Derrida can adequately locate their own positions, either in terms of the conventional classification of the sciences – which they resist but by which they are nonetheless governed in their academic reception – or in the content of their thought. 'That the self-referential critique of reason is located everywhere and nowhere, so to speak, in discourses without a place, renders it almost immune to competing interpretations' (p. 337). These 'variations of a critique of reason with a reckless disregard for its own foundations' are also all driven by a critique of modernity, 'a special sensitivity for complex injuries and subtle violations', but having sacrificed such concepts as 'self-consciousness, self-determination and self-realization' (p. 338) they cannot sustain their normative critique with what remains. Finally, their critique of modernity is itself overblown and undifferentiated, paying too little attention to its enormous advantages for 'the mass of the population'.

I have tried to show here that critical theory is in large part defined by its relationship to Nietzsche – a relationship partly direct and partly mediated by Max Weber and others. This is clear in the case of Benjamin, Horkheimer and Adorno, despite the differences between them.[46] Even Habermas, who has much less sympathy for Nietzsche's style of thinking, gives him a crucial role as what Max Weber called a 'switchman' altering the points and sending philosophy and social theory down new tracks – towards scientistic positivism in *Knowledge and Human Interests* and to various forms of nihilism in *The Philosophical Discourse of Modernity*.

The difference between Habermas and the earlier generation of critical theorists in their reception of Nietzsche's work reflects important internal differences in intellectual orientation as well as style. Most importantly, as Jay Bernstein has brilliantly suggested, it points to a fundamental duality in critical theory as a whole. The defining motif of all critical theory, Bernstein argues, is the dialectic of enlightenment, the advance of instrumental reason devaluing other aspects of rationality. At the root of critical theory, then, is 'a Weberian reinscription of the Marxist analysis of capitalism' which

provides critical theory with its dual perspective: from traditional Marxism critical theory inherits its concern for the problem of justice, while from Weber's appropriation of Nietzsche critical theory inherits its concern for the problem of nihilism and the question of meaning.[47] . . . From our present vantage point, it is not difficult to identify the nature of the debate between first and second generation critical theory. Fundamentally, they differ with respect to the weight and focus they offer to the justice and meaning questions: Habermas believes that Adorno slights the question of justice in his engagement with the nihilism question, hence giving undue significance to the role of art in his theory and, by implication, espousing a position which could only be satisfied through a re-enchantment of the social and natural worlds. From an Adornoesque perspective, Habermas' focus on the justice problem entails surrender over the question of nihilism.

In other words, it is the Nietzschean problematic of nihilism and loss of meaning which pushes (or, in Bernstein's harsher judgement, needs to push) Habermas back towards a more Hegelian concern with the overall shape of ethical life (*Sittlichkeit*) in conditions of advanced modernity. This is not the place to examine these issues, which are central to current debates in critical theory.[48] But Nietzsche's unique combination of anti-moralising moralism and sardonic laughter haunts these debates, like so many others in our own fin de siècle.

218 *William Outhwaite*

NOTES

I am grateful to Drew Milne and participants in the English Graduate Colloquium at Sussex for their comments on this paper, to Keith Ansell-Pearson, Gareth Bish and Laura Marcus for reading and commenting on a draft, and to Caroline Welsh for help in deciphering a quotation from Horkheimer.

1 Quoted by Arpad Kadarkay, *György Lukács. Life, Thought, and Politics* (Oxford: Blackwell, 1991), p. 56. Lukács' identification extended to the cultivation of a Nietzsche moustache.
2 Kadarkay, *György Lukács*, p. 307.
3 He uses Nietzsche's term *Redlichkeit*; see E. Baumgarten (ed.), *Max Weber. Werk und Person* (Tübingen: Mohr, 1964), pp. 554–5. For an excellent discussion of the Nietzschean 'challenge' to Weber, and of recent accounts of this influence, see Martin Albrow, *Max Weber's Construction of Social Theory* (London: Macmillan, 1990), chapter 3, pp. 46–61.
4 Peter Putz, 'Nietzsche and Critical Theory', *The Frankfurt School* (Cambridge: Polity, 1992; first published 1986).
5 *Telos* 50, 1981–2, pp. 103–14; first published in *Nietzsche-Studien* 3, 1974, pp. 175–91.
6 Pütz, 'Nietzsche', p. 5.
7 'Bemerkungen zu Jaspers' "Nietzsche"', *Zeitschrift für Sozialforschung*, 6, 1937, pp. 407–14.
8 E. Bloch et al., *Aesthetics and Politics*, London: New Left Books, 1977, p. 131. See also Adorno's sharp defence of Nietzsche against Lukács in 'Reconciliation under Duress' (pp. 126–33) and his remark in *Negative Dialectics* (p. 381) that 'Thought honours itself by defending what is damned as nihilism'.
9 In a letter of 1932 to Gershom Scholem (Benjamin, *Briefe*, ed. Gershom Scholem and Theodor W. Adorno, 2 vols, Franfkfurt: Suhrkamp, 1966, p. 554), cited in Irving Wohlfarth, 'Resentment Begins at Home: Nietzsche, Benjamin and the University', in Gary Smith (ed), *On Walter Benjamin: Critical Essays and Recollections* (Cambridge, MA: MIT Press, 1988), p. 227. Cf. Scholem, *Walter Benjamin. The Story of a Friendship* (London: Faber, 1982; first published in 1975).
10 Walter Benjamin, *Gesammelte Schriften* III (Frankfurt: Suhrkamp, 1972), p. 259.
11 Irving Wohlfarth, 'Resentment Begins at Home: Nietzsche, Benjamin, and the University', in Gary Smith (ed.), *On Walter Benjamin. Critical Essays and Recollections* (Cambridge, MA: MIT Press, 1991), p. 244. (Cf. Wohlfarth, 'No-man's-land. On Walter Benjamin's "Destructive Character"', in A. Benjamin and P. Osborne (eds), *Walter Benjamin's Philosophy* (London: Routledge, 1994).
12 Walter Benjamin, 'Theses on the Philosophy of History', *Illuminations* (New York: Schocken, 1968), p. 254.
13 For an illuminating discussion of this theme, see in particular Axel Honneth, 'A Communicative Disclosure of the Past: On the Relation Between Anthropology and Philosophy of History in Walter Benjamin', *New Formations* 20, 1993, pp. 83–94, esp. pp. 91ff.
14 Benjamin, *Gesammelte Schriften* I, p. 673; quoted in Winfried Wenninghaus, 'Walter Benjamin's Theory of Myth', in Smith, *On Walter Benjamin*, p. 320.

Scholem writes (p. 60): 'According to him [Benjamin], Nietzsche was the only person who had seen historical experience in the nineteenth century, a time when people "experienced" only nature. Even Burckhardt skirted the historical ethic; his ethic was not the ethic of history but that of historiography, of humanism.'

15 Benjamin, *Gesammelte Schriften*, I, pp. 682ff, quoted by Menninghaus, p. 321.
16 Tr. Peter Preuss (Indianapolis: Hackett, 1980; 1894), p. 7.
17 Benjamin, *Illuminations*, p. 262.
18 The reference is of course to the nineteenth-century historian Otto Ranke's maxim that one should write history '*wie es eigentlich gewesen ist*'. Elsewhere, as Irving Wohlfarth notes, Benjamin refers to historicism as a 'lumber room' (Irving Wohlfarth, 'Resentment Begins at Home: Nietzsche, Benjamin and the University', pp. 236, 242); his critique of historicism is of course also, and this is the main theme of Wohlfarth's article, a critique of the academic world.
19 This comes out embarassingly, for example, in Adorno's diatribes against jazz and popular classics.
20 Max Horkheimer, 'The End of Reason', *Zeitschrift für Sozialforschung* IX, 1941, pp. 366–88.
21 Nietzsche, *Werke*, vol. III, ed. Schlechta (Munich: Hanser, 1966), p. 814; cited in A. Arato and E. Gebhardt (eds), *The Essential Frankfurt School Reader* (Oxford: Blackwell, 1978), p. 374.
22 Max Horkheimer, *Gesammelte Werke*, Musarion edition, XI: 15.
23 'On the Problem of Truth' (1935), tr. in Arato and Gebhart, *The Essential Frankfurt*, p. 439; cf. p. 424. For a sympathetic and suggestive reading of Nietzsche's theory of truth, see Gillian Rose, *Dialectic of Nihilsm* (Oxford: Blackwell, 1984), p. 110.
24 'The late German Romantic interpreters of classical antiquity, following on Nietzsche's early writings, stressed the bourgeois Enlightenment aspect in Homer', Max Horkheimer and Theodor W. Adorno, *Dialectic of Enlightenment* (London: Verso, 1973), p. 44.
25 Section 17; Vintage tr., p. 109.
26 Reinhart Maurer, 'Nietzsche und die Kritische Theorie', *Nietzsche-Studien* 10–11, 1981–2, p. 35.
27 Theodor W. Adorno, *Negative Dialectics* (London: Routledge, 1973), p. 3. Cf. Adorno, 'Wozu noch Philosophie?', *Eingriffe* (Frankfurt: Suhrkamp, 1963), pp. 11–28; Jürgen Habermas, 'Wozu noch Philosophie?' (Frankfurt: Suhrkamp, 1971), pp. 11–36, tr. as 'Does Philosophy Still Have a Purpose?', *Philosophical-Political Profiles* (London: Heinemann, 1983), pp. 1–19. I shall return to this theme in connection with dialectic.
28 Max Horkheimer, 'Die Juden und Europa', *Zeitschrift für Sozialforschung*, 8, 1–2, 1939, p. 115.
29 Max Horkheimer and Theodor W. Adorno, *Dialectic of Enlightenment* (London: Verso, 1973), p. 32.
30 Translation from Gillian Rose, *The Melancholy Science: An Introduction to the Work of Theodor W. Adorno* (London: Macmillan, 1978), p. 21.
31 Max Horkheimer, *Notizen 1950 bis 1969 und Dämmerung* (Frankfurt: Fischer, 1974), p. 248: 'Nietzsche and the Proletariat'.
32 Cf. Herbert Marcuse, 'On the Affirmative Character of Culture' (1937), *Negations*, pp. 88–133.

220 *William Outhwaite*

33 Cf. Alfred Schmidt. 'Zur Frage der Dialektik in Nietzsches Erkenntnistheorie', in *Zeugnisse. Theodor W. Adorno zum 60 Geburtstag* (Frankfurt: Europäische Verlagsanstalt, 1963).
34 Theodor W. Adorno, *Drei Studien zu Hegel* (Frankfurt: Suhrkamp, 1963, p. 92; cf. Pütz, p. 110). This theme returns in the more recent critical literature. On the one hand, Pierre Missac locates Nietzsche in an antidialectical 'call to order handed down from Nietzsche to Merleau-Ponty, passing by way of Popper' ('From Rupture to Shipwreck', in Smith (ed.), p. 212. On the other, Fredric Jameson is 'inclined to understand such paradoxical and self-implicating concepts as Sartrean authenticity . . . but also Wittgenstein's "therapeutic positivism" . . . , Nietzsche's genealogies; indeed the very Freudian analytical situation itself; as relatively specialized and distorted versions of what we have here described as dialectical self consciousness' (Fredric Jameson, *Marxism and Form* (Princeton NJ: Princeton University Press, 1971), p. 373).
35 Theodor W. Adorno, *Minima Moralia. Fragments from a Damaged Life* (London: Verso, 1974, p. 50). As Gillian Rose notes, 'Adorno's thought cannot be understood unless it is realized that any "Hegelian" terminology is reintroduced on the basis of a Nietzschean inversion' (*The Melancholy Science*, p. 22). A specific but important theme which Adorno derives explicitly from Nietzsche is his critique of nominal definitions. On this, see Theodor W. Adorno, 'Society', in *Aspects of Sociology* (London: Heinemann, 1973); Theodor W. Adorno, *Philosophische Terminologie*, 2 vols (Frankfurt: Suhrkamp, 1974), and William Outhwaite, *Concept Formation in Social Science* (London: Routledge, 1983).
36 Theodor W. Adorno, *The Philosophy of Nietzsche*, New York, 1927, quoted by Pütz, pp. 113–14.
37 On the critique of the sociology of knowledge, see Adorno, *Negative Dialectics*, p. 195; also, 'The Consciousness of the Sociology of Knowledge', in Adorno, *Prisms*, and in A. Arato and E. Gebhardt (eds), *The Essential Frankfurt School Reader*, pp. 452–565; also M. Jay, 'The Frankfurt School's Critique of Karl Mannheim and the Sociology of Knowledge', *Telos*, 20, 1974. Reprinted in Jay, *Permanent Exiles. Essays on the Intellectual Migration from Germany to America* (New York: Columbia University Press, 1985), pp. 62–78.
38 Cf. Rose, *The Melancholy Science*, p. 25.
39 Theodor W. Adorno, *Zur Metakritik der Erkenntnistheorie. Studien über Husserl und die phänomenologischen Antinomien* (Stuttgart: W. Kohlhammer, 1956), p. 28.
40 Theodor W. Adorno, 'Society', *Salmagundi* 10–11, 1969–70, p. 145.
41 Jürgen Habermas, *Friedrich Nietzsche. Erkenntnistheoretische Schriften* (Frankfurt: Suhrkamp, 1968), pp. 256ff.
42 On the concept of nihilism, see Adorno, *Negative Dialectics* 367–72, tr. 376–81, and Rose, *Dialectic of Nihilism*. As noted above, Rose defends Nietzsche against more radically nihilistic interpretations of his thought; see e.g. p. 110 and n. 2.
43 Jürgen Habermas, *Knowledge and Human Interests* (London: Heinemann, 1971 (1968)). Page references are given in the text.
44 On the origins of this trichotomy, see Jüren Habermas, 'Work and Interaction' in *Theory and Practice* (Cambridge: Polity, 1976).

45 Jürgen Habermas, *The Philosophical Discourse of Modernity* (Cambridge: Polity, 1988 (1985)). See also the essays on this book in Maurizio Passerin d'Entrèves and Seyla Benhabib (eds), *Habermas and the Unfinished Project of Modernity* (Cambridge: Polity, 1995).

46 As Gillian Rose has noted (*The Melancholy Science*, p. 5), the more obviously Nietzschean themes of instrumental reason and domination play a larger part in Horkheimer's thinking than in that of Adorno, who places more emphasis on the category of reification. Yet Nietzsche remains the 'fiery brook' (as Marx said of his own line to Hegel through Feuerbach) through which Adorno's Hegelianism passes.

47 'Adorno contrasts an identitarian logic with a logic of nonidentity; Marcuse seeks to recharge the utopian dimension of reason, re-fusing *eros* and *logos*, through the redemptive function of memory; while Habermas seeks to install the centrality of a communicative reason against the ravages of the subject-centred monologicality of instrumental rationality.'

48 The Kant/Hegel polarisation has been brought out most fully in discussions of Habermas' communicative ethics; see in particular S. Benhabib and F. Dallmayr (eds), *The Communicative Ethics Controversy* (Cambridge, Mass: MIT Press, 1990). Jay Bernstein's *The Politics of Transfiguration* (London: Routledge, forthcoming) is a superb critique of Habermas from a Hegelian-Adornian perspective.

13
Zarathustra/*Zarathustra* as Educator

Richard Schacht

To educate educators! But the first ones must educate themselves! And for these I write.[1]

This work stands altogether apart. Leaving aside the poets:
perhaps nothing has ever been done from an equal excess of
strength. My concept of the "Dionysian" here becomes a
supreme deed; measured against that, all the rest of human
activity seems poor and relative. . . . There is no moment in
this revelation of truth that has been anticipated or guessed by
even *one* of the greatest. There is no wisdom, no investigation
of the soul, no art of speech before Zarathustra.

EH III; Z: 6[2]

Whatever possessed Nietzsche to write *Thus Spoke Zarathustra* – and to
think so highly of it that one can hardly bear to read his ravings about it
in *Ecce Homo*? It was utterly unlike anything he had published previously,
preceded in print first by *The Birth of Tragedy* (henceforth "BT"),
then the four "untimely meditations," and then the various aphoristic
volumes of his "free spirit" series. He never again wrote anything like it.
  Zarathustra's various parts may have been written in bursts; but
Nietzsche published nothing else during the three years of their composition. Those three years were years of crisis for him in every respect; and
his personal and intellectual investment in a work written under such
conditions may have had something to do with his later feelings about it.
The fact that *Zarathustra* was as close as Nietzsche even came to com-
posing something that would rival Wagner's *Ring* may also be of some
relevance. Indeed, his claims for it (in *Ecce Homo*) suggest that he
regarded it not only as having bested Wagner's best shot, but also

those of Goethe, Shakespeare and Dante as well (not to mention "the greatest" among philosophers – presumably including his "educator" Schopenhauer).

But Nietzsche did not stop with that. He regarded *Zarathustra* as a work of world-historical significance, to which only the founding works of the world's great religions and cultures might properly be compared – and which it now superseded. This may be preposterous; and some at least of what Nietzsche says along these lines may be dismissed as symptomatic of his incipient madness. Yet I believe that he was trying to do something both unusual and important in this strange work, which renders his extravagant estimation of it at least comprehensible if not justifiable. Indeed, his unbridled enthusiasm for it to the end of his productive life is itself instructive in this respect; for it shows that he must have been – and remained – of the same opinion himself. But what is it that he was trying to do, and seems to have thought he had done?

What, in short, are we to make of *Thus Spoke Zarathustra*? And what, for that matter, are we to make of Zarathustra? Zarathustra is not merely Nietzsche's mouthpiece or stage-name; nor does this figure stand to Nietzsche as Hamlet to Shakespeare, Ahab to Melville or even Faust to Goethe. What are we to make of what might be called "Zarathustra's Progress," and of the relation of the Zarathustra of Part Four to the Zarathustra of the first three Parts – or, indeed, of the relation of the Zarathustra of the Prologue and First Part to the Zarathustra of the Second and Third? And what of the relation of Part Four of *Zarathustra* to the previous parts of the work? This question has received no little attention in the recent literature.[3] An adequate answer to it, however, requires an understanding of the entire enterprise I call "Zarathustra/ *Zarathustra*," which I believe has yet to be properly appreciated.

There are many related questions on which I hope to shed some light in this essay as well. What, for example, is to be made of Zarathustra's "speeches," and of his "teaching" of the "eternal recurrence"? And the notions of "*Übermensch*" and "higher" humanity, and the strange collection of "higher men" we encounter in Part Four? How are we to understand the relation between the Nietzsche of this work and the Nietzsche(s) of his previous and subsequent writings? And what is to be made of his suggestion in *Ecce Homo* that with this work "the Yes-saying part of my task had been solved"? (EH III; BGE: 1).

It seems to me that a key to answers to these questions is to be found in the third of Nietzsche's *Untimely Meditations*, written nearly a decade earlier: *Schopenhauer as Educator* (henceforth "SE"). In brief: I suggest that in and by means of Zarathustra and *Zarathustra*, Nietzsche sought to provide posterity with something capable of performing the kind of "educating" function he had discussed in that essay, and considered Schopenhauer to have performed for him. This is a special kind of education, requiring a special kind of educator – and Nietzsche was then and subsequently convinced that the experience of encountering such an educator is quite essential, if one is to find one's way to a new Yes to life that does not depend upon buying into the various forms of illusion he began (in BT) by thinking were the only means of avoiding Schopenhauerian pessimism and the calamity of dead-end nihilism.

I

In *On the Aesthetic Education of Man*,[4] written as a series of letters a half-century before Nietzsche's birth, Friedrich Schiller saw "aesthetic education" as the key to the attainment of a richer and more complete humanity than had been attained even by the Greeks – who, however, were seen as showing the way. Through such an education, according to Schiller, the "sensuous" impulses of our natural natures may be transformed, the cultivation of the "formal" impulses of our rational nature is made possible, and then the opposition between them can be overcome as a new impulse comes to the fore – a "play" impulse, joining elements of both of these other impulses as our higher (artistic/authentic) nature emerges, with a sensibility attuned to beauty and abilities employed creatively.

In this picture, as well as in the critique of the impoverished humanity produced by the operation of the modern world, much that we find in Nietzsche from BT to *Zarathustra* and beyond is anticipated. With Schiller in mind, the Apollinian–Dionysian distinction becomes a variation and deepening of a familiar theme. The employment of the idea of "play" in connection with the culminating state of spiritual development identified in Zarathustra's very first speech "On the Three Metamorphoses" (when one expects to find something like artistic creativity) becomes readily understandable. The ideas of an enhancement of life and an attainable higher humanity, contrasting with the quality of life that leaves so much to be desired in the modern world and throughout so much of history, become easily recognizable. And even the seemingly odd central thesis of BT, that "it is only as an *aesthetic phenomenon* that existence and the world are eternally *justified*" (BT 5 and 24), loses its strangeness.

What is even more to the point for present purposes is Schiller's explicit use of the notion of "education" (*Erziehung*) as the key to the enhancement of life, and his equally explicit indication that the kind of education meant has above all to do with the twofold cultivation of an aesthetic sensibility and artistic-creative powers. Nietzsche does more than merely echo Schiller; he deepens and extends these ideas in ways placing him well beyond Schiller and his early-romantic naivete. But in seeking to understand what Nietzsche is trying to do in *Zarathustra*, one does well to recall his Schillerian inheritance. Nietzsche's project too may be characterized as a version of Schiller's idea of the need for a further aesthetic education of humanity that might bring about a higher form of humanity – and *Zarathustra*, I suggest, was his greatest contribution to this campaign.

Nietzsche's first great case study of this kind of education and call for a new aesthetic education of humanity was *The Birth of Tragedy*. He may not have thought of it in precisely these terms at the time; but the central theme of the entire first half of the book is that, thanks to their artists, the Greeks received an extraordinary aesthetic education that was the key to both their kind and quality of culture and their ability to relish life as greatly as they did – despite their acute awareness of "the terror and horror of existence" (BT 3), and in the absence of anything like Christian-otherworldly consolation.

More specifically, Nietzsche regarded the Greeks' artists as their educators in the most important sense, cultivating their sensibility and transforming both their sense of themselves and their sense of their world in such a way that they were unsurpassed in their life-affirmation.[5] The Greeks' tragedians had educated their sensibility and self-consciousness, and had shown them a way of coming to terms with the harsh realities of life without succumbing to nausea and despair. They were the educators through whose efforts the wondrously affirmative and creative tragic culture of the Greeks achieved extraordinary heights. In BT Nietzsche looked to Wagner to serve as such an educator to modern European humanity. Wagner was to be their latter-day European counterpart, through whom a new tragic culture – no less affirmative and creative than that of the Greeks – was to be attained.

It was not long, of course, before Nietzsche's enthusiasm for Wagner-as-educator began to wane; and he soon (by the time of SE, two years later) settled upon Schopenhauer as being better suited to that role, at least in his own case. In SE Wagner still looms large in as the unnamed epitome of the "genius" through whom the flourishing of culture that is the locus of higher humanity can occur (if enough of the rest of us will play our supporting roles). But now the true educator – the one through encounter with whom we are transformed and impelled in the direction of at once "becoming those we are" and contributing to the enhancement of life – is depicted more as a stimulus than as a leader to be followed or a paradigm to be imitated. Such an educator may be a kind of *exemplar*; but this type of educator is anything but an instructor, from whom information is received or rules and procedures are learned. The most important things to be learned have to do more with admirable traits to be emulated and standards to be aspired to than with specific ideas and values to be accepted. So in SE Nietzsche celebrates Schopenhauer as his educator without even discussing any of Schopenhauer's views.[6]

Even in SE, however, Nietzsche did not suppose that Schopenhauer could or should be *everyone's* educator, and was already worrying about where the educator(s) needed – to do for others what Schopenhauer had done for him – would come from:

> Where are we, scholars and unscholarly, high placed and low, to find the moral exemplars and models among our contemporaries, the visible epitome of morality for our time? . . . Never have moral educators been more needed, and never has it seemed less likely they would be found. (SE 2, pp. 132–3)[7]

Nietzsche's intended audience here is all those "young souls" with the need, the courage and the ability to heed the call to "Become yourself" – understood not self-indulgently, but rather in the sense that "your true nature is not concealed deep within you but immeasurably high above you, or at least above that which you usually take yourself to be" (SE 1, p. 129). For their sake he raises a question and poses a challenge that he subsequently took up himself in a variety of ways:

> Who is there, then, amid these changes of our era, to guard and champion humanity, the inviolable sacred treasure gradually accumulated by the most various races? Who will set up the *image of man* when all men feel in themselves only the self-seeking snake and the currish fear and have declined to the level of the animals or even of automata? (SE 4, p. 150)

Nietzsche's prototype of the "free spirit" in SE is the "Schopenhauerian" type of humanity he goes on to sketch, in distinction not only from the all-too-human type of social-animal humanity he considers to be the human rule, but also from two alternative "images" or paradigms of a more genuine humanity he calls by the names of their most prominent representatives: Rousseau and Goethe. "Rousseauean man" for him represents naturalized humanity, renewed and revitalized through emancipation from the shackles of society and restoration to its basic instincts. "Goethean man" is the image of contemplative humanity, cultivated and sophisticated but detached from active involvement in life. "Schopenhauerian man" combines elements of both and also (for Nietzsche) supersedes both as the image of a "truly active" creative humanity, at once vital and spiritualized, and so most fully and truly human.

The significance of these images for Nietzsche in SE is that they have the power to liberate, stimulate and inspire – in short, to *educate*. Because of the diverse sorts of human development involved and the shortcomings associated with the first two of them, however, he takes them to differ not only in kind but also in value. Only the one he calls "Schopenhauerian" expresses and evokes the promise of an alternative form of humanity healthy and vital enough to be enduringly viable in this world, and sufficiently creative and spiritualized to justify itself – and human life and the world along with it. Cultural life is its domain; and so it is to the celebration and service of culture that Nietzsche looks in his response to the challenge he sets for himself when he writes:

> The hardest task still remains: to say how a new circle of duties may be devised from this ideal and how one can proceed towards so extravagant a goal through practical activity – in short, to demonstrate that this ideal *educates*. . . . Is it possible to bring that incredibly lofty goal so close that it educates us while it draws us aloft? (SE 5, p. 156)

Nietzsche's answer, of course, is in the affirmative; and it is of no little relevance to observe his elaboration upon it: "We have to be lifted up – and who are they who lift us? They are those true *men, those who are no longer animal, the philosophers, artists and saints*" (SE 5, p. 159). This is a veritable prescription projecting ahead to that "higher educator" we encounter in the pages of *Thus Spoke Zarathustra*, about whom there is something of each of this trinity of exceptions to the human rule. But *Zarathustra* was still years away, in conception as well as well as execution. Meanwhile Nietzsche could only observe that "The difficulty. . . lies for mankind in relearning and envisaging a new goal" (SE 6, p. 175). He was convinced that "the goal of culture is to promote the production of true human beings and nothing else" (SE 6, p. 164); but at this point he was clearer about the end than he was about what might be done to advance its achievement.

II

Nietzsche's concern with the inadequacies of what passed for education (and education of the highest quality at that) in his own time is reflected in his severe critiques, most notably in SE and his earlier series of lectures "On the Future of Our Educational Institutions." These critiques have as one of their recurring themes the contention that existing higher and lower forms of education alike were detrimental to intellectual as well as personal and human development, stultifying the minds and spirits of those submitting to them through over-specialization and regimentation.

This concern did not fade away in the years that followed. On the contrary, Nietzsche's aphoristic volumes from *Human, All Too Human* to the first edition of *The Gay Science* may be regarded as an initial if tentative series of efforts on his part to fill this need himself. Thus he wrote of these works, on the back of the original edition of *The Gay Science*, that their "common goal is to erect a new image and ideal of the free spirit."[8] Here Nietzsche, the heir of Voltaire and the Enlightenment, sought by way of this "new image and ideal" to provide a beacon of enlightenment and inspiration. This "free spirit" series constituted a kind of experimental effort to contribute to and promote a different type of education.

This series is educational in several respects. Through the hundreds of aphoristic reflections of which these books consist, Nietzsche was educating himself as well as his readers, working his way toward the kind of philosopher, thinker and free spirit he himself was becoming, while providing others with assistance in moving in the same direction themselves. And it is no system of doctrines that is set out here for the instruction of the reader, nor even a set of arguments advanced with the aim of compelling the reader's agreement. Rather, a variety of intellectual abilities and dispositions are being cultivated, with a view to fostering the emergence of the sort of human being realizing Nietzsche's conception of the "free spirit."

This involves a transformation of the way in which one understands oneself and relates to life and the world, along lines that Nietzsche clearly regarded as desirable. An indication of his underlying motivation is provided in the famous penultimate section of the original four-part edition of *The Gay Science* in which the idea of the eternal recurrence of every moment and episode of one's life is set forth with the question: "how well disposed would you have to become to yourself and to life to *crave nothing more fervently* than this ultimate confirmation and seal?"

(GS 341). An education capable of bringing that about, without sacrificing the intellect, would be an education indeed!

Having reached this point, however, Nietzsche seems to have concluded that something more was needed than the kind of thing he had
been doing in his "free spirit" series. One of the limitations of this series
is that this extraordinary experiment in consciousness-raising was far
stronger critically than it was constructively. The "free spirit" did not
itself fill the bill, or suffice for this purpose. In the fourth and (at that
time) final "book" of *The Gay Science*, however, and just prior to its
concluding invocation of Zarathustra, a number of themes are sounded
that point in the direction of this larger task.

These themes might be thought of as so many variations on a larger
theme, of the artistic transformation of our lives in ways endowing them
with value sufficient to warrant their affirmation. Learning to "'give
style' to one's character" (GS 299); learning to "live not only boldly but
even gaily, and laugh gaily, too" by learning to savor such forms of "war
and victory" as life affords – the pursuit of knowledge among them (GS
324); learning to love – for "love, too, has to be learned" (GS 334);
wanting and learning "to become those we are, human beings . . . who
give themselves laws, who create themselves" (GS 335); learning to
glimpse and move toward "the 'humaneness' of the future" (GS 337);
and learning to become capable of dealing with "the greatest weight,"
existence conceived as subject to "eternal recurrence" (GS 341) – these
are some of the variations on this theme with which this prelude to
Zarathustra resounds. It was left to *Zarathustra*, however, to take up the
challenge of this aesthetic education.

III

Nietzsche had begun in the early 1870s by thinking, or hoping, that
someone – the Greeks, Wagner, Schopenhauer – could be found to serve
as exemplars, mentors and educators for those like himself for whom
neither reason nor revelation would suffice. Ten years later he had
become disillusioned with all of those he formerly had revered. He had
come to be convinced that not only traditional modes of philosophical
and religious thought but also the available alternatives, both ancient and
modern (including the natural sciences and historical scholarship), all
fall radically short of educating our aspirations and valuations in a
manner conducive of human flourishing in a post-modern world in
which all gods have died. Indeed, he had come to see them not only as

all-too-human and inadequate but as positively detrimental to that flourishing, having effects that bode ill rather than well for the future, and requiring something serving as both an antidote and an alternative. The kind of galvanizing educator that was needed was nowhere to be found; and while his efforts to promote a "new image and ideal of the free spirit" might be necessary steps in the right direction, they were far from sufficient.

What more could Nietzsche do? He could write *Thus Spoke Zarathustra*. I suggest that Zarathustra and *Zarathustra* were conceived to meet this need, "for all and none" – for none, if none were ready for the encounter, but for all who might (come to) be up to it. A work capable of making such a difference on such a scale would indeed be a great gift to humanity, particularly if nothing remotely comparable were anywhere else to be found. In this light, Nietzsche's subsequent extravagant estimation of the work becomes at least comprehensible. It was no mere work of literature, scholarship or philosophy, but rather a unique educational device capable of making a real and great difference in human life.

In *Zarathustra* Nietzsche undertook to meet head on the challenge of Schopenhauer – not the "Schopenhauer" of SE, but the Schopenhauer whose radical pessimism led him to champion the negation of life, and whom Nietzsche took to foreshadow the advent of nihilism. How can one affirm life – and not merely endure it but relish it – if Schopenhauer was fundamentally right about the conditions of existence in this world (and the absence of any other, or any redeeming God beyond it), and if one refuses to sacrifice honesty and truthfulness?

Zarathustra is predicated upon the conviction that radical disillusionment, uncompromising truthfulness *and* unqualified life-affirmation are all humanly possible together, even under these circumstances. But it also proceeds from the recognition that this human possibility is not easily realized, and in fact requires the attainment of a new sensibility through an educational development that has free-spirited enlightenment as but its point of departure. To come to be capable of confronting what Nietzsche in *Ecce Homo* refers to as "the fundamental conception of this work, the idea of eternal recurrence, this highest formula of affirmation that is at all attainable" (EH III; Z: 1) with exhilaration rather than horror and despair, even the Zarathustra of the first parts of the work must undergo a major transformation. And Nietzsche shows us his education in a way that is designed to help effect ours as well, in the same direction and to the same ultimate effect.

But who – or what – is the educator here? Neither Zarathustra nor even Nietzsche himself at the outset, for both themselves had much to learn. The real educator, I suggest, is neither of them, but rather the work itself. What Nietzsche wrought in this work is the means of a remarkable possible educational experience and transformation that may reach into and affect the fundamental character of our humanity – a kind of spiritual *Bildungsroman,* akin perhaps both to Goethe's *Faust* and to Hegel's *Phenomenology,* but more radical than either of them. It is to *Zarathustra* rather than simply to Zarathustra that Nietzsche would above all have us respond. Zarathustra too has to be educated; and it is his education, as well as what he says and various other things about him, that is meant to serve ours.

IV

The term "education" must not be taken too narrowly here. As in the phrase and title *Schopenhauer as Educator,* it involves something quite different from mere instruction, or the imparting of information. Nietzsche's term for "educator" in SE is *Erzieher,* rather than *Lehrer;* and *Erziehung* for him means something closer to *Bildung* than to *Lehren* or to "learning" as these notions are ordinarily understood. The Nietzschean educator is closer to the Socratic "midwife," and perhaps closer still to something like a *catalyst* of change and transformation. The basic concern of his desired kind of education is not simply to increase our knowledge of the world as it merely is, or even of ourselves as we already are. Those kinds of knowledge – of which Nietzsche had acquired and conveyed a great deal in his "free spirit" series – are at most only points of departure. What matters more to him is to raise our sights and awaken us to possibilities we will have to reach out and exert ourselves to realize.

The object of such education is to "draw us out," as the terms *"erziehen"* and "educate" both fundamentally mean. Nietzsche would draw us out, beyond what we and the world already are, toward what we have it in us to become, and what we might make of ourselves and our world. And for him in *Zarathustra* as in SE, that calls for creativity rather than mere receptivity. Its general arena, beyond the empty abstractions and false dichotomies of the mental and the physical, the subjective and the objective, and the individual and the social, is the sphere of cultural life – Zarathustra's wilderness proclivities notwithstanding.

Zarathustra is not only the presentation of an educator who attempts to educate by free-spirited and wholesomely naturalistic enlightenment and counsel, doing a good deal of vivid debunking and reinterpreting and revaluing along the way – even though that *is* some of what we find,

particularly in the First Part. It also is the presentation of the educator's
education, and further the vehicle and record of its author's education –
and beyond that, the occasion and means of our own possible education;
and it is at these levels that the work does its real work, and serves to
perform its larger and deeper educative function.

Zarathustra thus is not only Nietzsche's answer to the *New Testament*,
but also his version of *Pilgrim's Progress*; and it is the whole multi-level
phenomenon by which we are to be educated in the sense of "*erziehen*,"
being drawn out and up, toward becoming those we are. Zarathustra's
speeches and reflections are part of it; but his transformations matter
more, and the transfiguration of the picture of humanity to which all that
transpires in the work contributes matters most of all. We are not taught
what to think, or how to live – but we are shown the prospect of a
possible humanity and the way toward a manner of life that Nietzsche
believes can sustain us beyond all disillusionment.

In such a work, the purpose of which is to educate our aspirations,
valuations and sensibility rather than to give us information and instruction, Nietzsche considers it fair game to make use of ideas that serve to
reorient our thinking regardless of their mere "truth-value" (or lack
thereof). The notion of the *Übermensch* is one, and the image of the
Eternal Recurrence is another. Indeed, the very figure of Zarathustra
"himself" is a third. They are neither the literal truth nor illusions, nor
are they even "noble lies," but rather something like the salient forms of
imagery figuring centrally in myths. Their "truth" or justification is a
matter of their value as means of enabling us to come to understand
something important about life and the world that they do not literally describe or designate. Nietzsche does not tell us things about
Zarathustra, and have Zarathustra proclaim and "teach" things about
the *Übermensch* and the Eternal Recurrence, in order to have us "learn"
them. Rather, he does so in the course of (and as part of) his effort to
prompt us to the sort of response that may foster and further the
enhancement of our lives.

As it is pursed in *Zarathustra*, Nietzsche's educational endeavor at
once reflects and transcends the kinds of educating that had previously
figured importantly in his thinking – in BT, in SE, and in the "free spirit"
series. But it continues to undergo development in the course of the four
parts of the work, in each of which something crucial is added, without
which the kind of humanity attained would be seriously lacking. The
successive transformations of sensibility that are explored supersede
rather than negate previously attained forms; but the subsequent transformations are important. The sensibility of Part One is still basically
that of the Nietzschean "free spirit"; and it is still some distance from

that which is barely envisioned in the penultimate section of *The Gay Science*, in which the idea of the "eternal recurrence" is invoked to assess one's disposition to oneself and to life (GS 341). In a large sense, the task of *Zarathustra* may be said to consist in the educational project of cultivating a sensibility capable of passing this "Recurrence Test" – and so of affirming life under what Nietzsche considers to be the most daunting of possible descriptions.

It is important to observe that, while Nietzsche retains the rubric of "tragedy" in connection with this new sensibility (Zarathustra is introduced in GS 342 under the heading "*Incipit Tragoedia*"[9]), he departs markedly and very significantly from the standpoint of BT in rejecting recourse to *illusion* as the key to life-affirmation. He makes much of this point in subsequent remarks about the figure of Zarathustra. Life-affirmation may require *more* than "truthfulness"; but the kind of life-affirmation Nietzsche associates with Zarathustra also requires nothing less. For nothing short of uncompromising truthfulness is immune to the threat of disillusionment in the aftermath of the severest critical scrutiny. Nietzsche does insist upon the importance of learning to appreciate and esteem surfaces, appearances, creations and even fictions as a part of the new sensibility he envisions; but in this sensibility such appreciation and esteeming are conjoined with truthfulness and honesty rather than indulged at their expense. So, in *Ecce Homo*, Nietzsche makes much of the point that "Zarathustra is more truthful than any other thinker" and "posits truthfulness as the highest virtue" (EH IV: 3).

But that is not the whole story, as Nietzsche makes clear in going on to state "what Zarathustra wants" in the following striking passage, which was nearly (and might well have been) his last word:

> this type of man that he conceives, conceives reality *as it is*, being strong enough to do so; this type is not estranged or removed from reality but is reality itself and exemplifies all that is terrible and questionable in it – *only in that way can man attain greatness*. (EH IV: 5).

Truthfulness may be the "highest virtue"; but what Nietzsche here calls "greatness" is the highest goal. And much of *Zarathustra* has to do with the cultivation of a new sensibility appropriate to this revalued valuation of human life and possibility.[10]

Zarathustra is full of talk of "teaching;" but it would be a great misunderstanding to identify its educating function entirely or even primarily with the imparting of the contents of Zarathustra's many speeches. That is only one of the levels or forms of education here; and while it is not to be overlooked, it is perhaps the least interesting. In these speeches, with a few major exceptions, we encounter a good deal of material that one would expect from the author of the "free spirit" series, making many analytical, interpretive and critical points that are quite relevant to fleshing out Nietzsche's naturalistic account of human life and revaluation of many traits and practices.

This is all well and good; but for the most part it does not add significantly to what one finds in that earlier series. The greatest exception is the idea that supposedly is Zarathustra's central teaching, but which he never proclaims in the mode of his early speeches: the idea of the Eternal Recurrence. Others are the ideas of "remaining faithful to the earth," and of the "*Übermensch*" as "the meaning of the earth." These notions function more as "guiding ideas" than as markers of cognitive claims, setting the context for the many reinterpretive and revaluative speeches and remarks Zarathustra makes.

The basic educational function performed by these many speeches elaborating upon the ideas of "faithfulness to the earth" and of the *Übermensch* as the "meaning of the earth" does not reduce to the specific points advanced in the various speeches. Rather, I would suggest, it consists in their use to give one a feeling for a genuine alternative to what Nietzsche elsewhere calls the "Christian-moral" scheme of the interpretation and evaluation that we have come to take largely for granted – and that he believes is bound to collapse in the aftermath of "the death of God." What might it mean to achieve a reorientation of the way in which we think about ourselves that would make this life in this world the locus of meaning and value, and that would link them to considerations of differential quality of life and possible enhancements of life?

The educational task of the First Part of *Zarathustra* may thus be said to be that of confronting the "death of God" and rising to the challenge Nietzsche had sketched in *The Gay Science* a year earlier: "God is dead. . . . And we – we still have to vanquish his shadow too" (GS 108). "When will we complete our de-deification of nature? When may we begin to '*naturalize*' humanity in terms of a pure, newly discovered, newly redeemed nature?" (GS 109).[11] This is a kind of crisis Nietzsche had already been addressing in his "free spirit" series; but here he gives life to his belief in the possibility of an alternative to the "nihilistic rebound" from the death of God.

But the outlook attained and expressed in the First Part is only the beginning; and its insufficiency is brought home in the Second Part, which dwells on the pervasiveness of the all-too-human, and moves toward a crisis that the resources of aesthetic-naturalistic enlightenment are not adequate to meet. Zarathustra and his wisdom have to "ripen" further before he can either comprehend it or meet it. The crisis reaches a climax in the Third Part, in which that "ripening" proceeds far enough that Zarathustra has the resources to be capable of coming through it with a more profound wisdom rooted in an aesthetically transfigured "ecstatic naturalism" (to borrow a phrase Paul Tillich used to use[12]).

That climax is followed by another, however, or rather by a kind of anti-climax. The educator's education, and ours, is far from complete at the end of the Third Part. A great gulf has opened up between the soaring height to which it rises at its end and the solid (or at any rate mundane) ground of daily life and human reality. A "Monday morning Dionysianism" may not be a human (or even a conceptual) possibility; but in the Fourth Part we find that there is a way of bringing it all down to earth that is not entirely a descent from the sublime into the ridiculous. The all-too-human remains, and indeed is very much in evidence in the bizarre array of specimens of "higher humanity" Zarathustra collects; but by the end one can begin to understand what it actually can mean to go on – without illusions and false hopes, yet undeterred by the circumstances that might inspire pity and do warrant talk of tragedy, and sustained by a life-sized reaffirmation of life as the very ambiguous thing it is.

V

The lesson Nietzsche had learned from the Greeks, and the lesson of *The Birth of Tragedy*, has to do with the role the arts – and tragic art in particular – can play in effecting a transformation of our consciousness in such a way that not only our experience but our lives and the very aspect of existence are transformed, in a manner enabling us to affirm life and the world despite all. He may have given up on Wagner in this respect; but he did not abandon the very idea of what in BT he had called the "justification" of "existence and the world" as an "aesthetic phenomenon." *Zarathustra* was to do what Wagner had counterfeited, and so succeed where he had failed – in achieving a rebirth of tragedy ("*Incipit tragoedie*"), as a sensibility attuned to our finitude and yet infused with a fundamentally Dionysian affirmative spirit.

The educational task of *Zarathustra* is to assist those capable of doing so to attain this sensibility, and the associated forms of aspiration and valuation. Hence the "greatest weight" and Recurrence Test; for this is the education called for by Nietzsche's question, "how well disposed would you have to become to yourself and to life to crave nothing more fervently than this ultimate eternal confirmation and seal?" (GS 341). Hence also Nietzsche's characterization in *Ecce Homo* of "what Zarathustra wants" (EH IV: 5, cited above).

This kind of education may be conceived as Nietzsche's version of what in an earlier time had been called the cultivation of an "aesthetic sensibility"; and the need for it had already been intimated in BT in his contention that "it is only as an aesthetic phenomenon" that life and the world can ultimately be "justified" and so esteemed and affirmed. It further may be regarded as an attempt to understand and work out the implications of his conviction that we must learn to sustain and nourish ourselves by means of the kind of thing to which Nietzsche alludes in the section of *The Gay Science* on "Our ultimate gratitude to art," in which he has in mind "art as the *good* will to appearance," and writes:

> As an aesthetic phenomenon existence is still *bearable* for us, and art furnishes us with eyes and hands and above all the good conscience to be *able* to turn ourselves into such a phenomenon. (GS 107)

Nietzsche recognizes we may well need an education of the right sort to come to appreciate and find this not only a sufficient but also an invigorating diet. If we are to come to be able to relish life on the only terms it offers without the veils of illusion the Nietzsche of BT had deemed indispensable, we must learn not only to accept but also to love and cherish it under some possible interpretation or attainable configuration.

It is the educational task of *Zarathustra* to enable us to do so. To this end, like the tragic literature and culture whose earlier birth and demise Nietzsche had contemplated in BT, it must provide us with a way of facing and coming to terms with what he then had called "the terror and horror of existence" (BT 3) under the worst and bleakest of descriptions without being devastated by the encounter – and with a way of emerging from this encounter in a non-naive but nonetheless exhilarated and affirmative manner. Indeed, it is of the utmost importance for Nietzsche in *Zarathustra* (and beyond) that one get beyond all naivete and disillusionment, and leave behind not only despair, nausea, vengefulness, resentment and pity (including feeling sorry for oneself as well as others), but also all optimistic illusions, idealistic fantasies and the foolish belief in the sufficiency of fine sentiments and lofty principles.

This project by no means reduces to the inculcation of the secular-humanist maxims and principles one so often finds coming out of Zarathustra's mouth, especially in the first two parts of the work. Nietzsche may subscribe to the latter as far as they go; but one of the most important points of the work, brought out by Zarathustra's own transformation and abandonment of that mode of discourse, is that the "free spirit" mentality they express is far from sufficient as a way of thinking by which one might live. I see no reason to think Nietzsche does not mean us to take seriously the counsel Zarathustra offers in the first parts of the work. Quite clearly, however, he does at least mean to suggest that such rhetoric needs supplementing, not only by means of additional principles but also by way of a fundamentally modified outlook; and that without the needed supplement this free-spirited enlightenment is incapable of carrying the day and sufficing to get one through the "dark night of the soul" by which Zarathustra himself is subsequently – if only temporarily – overwhelmed.

The enlightened humanistic outlook expressed in Zarathustra's early speeches and on a number of occasions thereafter is all very well and good as far as it goes; and it would be a most welcome thing if it could be much more widely attained. But Nietzsche did not stop there, and has Zarathustra venture further; for the attainment of this outlook is only a step in the right direction, and must be followed by others Nietzsche uses Zarathustra and *Zarathustra* to enable us to see – and to try to prompt us to take. These steps lead from the sunny Apollinian heights Zarathustra loves and evokes at the outset (in the First Part) through the dreary all-too-human swamps into which he descends (in the Second) – and into the dark Dionysian depths underlying all of human existence, which give way to the strange and problematic brightness that is the other face of Dionysian reality (in the Third); and at length (in the Fourth Part) back into a human world in which we can recognize ourselves again – but with a difference. This last part of the journey and educational process is absolutely essential, in my view; and for me this endows the Fourth (and final) Part of the work with a significance that is seldom appreciated.

It is particularly important, in this connection, to recognize that Nietzsche employs both the figure of Zarathustra and such notions as the *Übermensch* and Eternal Recurrence as devices in the context of his educational project of transforming our sensibility, rather than literalistically. In the language of BT, the image of the *Übermensch* represents his version of the Apollinian moment in this process, while the notion of the Eternal Recurrence represents the Dionysian – and neither, by itself, is enough. The *Übermensch* may be regarded as an image introduced and employed to provide the (re-)education of our aspirations and our thinking about the enhancement of life with a kind of compass, enabling us to gain a sense of direction even if not a clear description of our goal (which would be impossible). Its upshot for our lives is the notion of attained and attainable "higher humanity." (The relation of these two images may usefully be conceived as somewhat analogous to the relation between the Greeks' Olympian deities and their heroes.) The notion of the Eternal Recurrence, on the other hand, is the idea Nietzsche appropriates and employs in a central way in connection with a larger and more fundamental (re-)education of our sensibility, as the touchstone of the transformation of our basic disposition toward ourselves and our lives and world. Translated into its upshot, it becomes Nietzsche's conception of the affirmation of life, with *amor fati* as its insignia.

If there is any such counterpart figure to the third (tragic) moment in BT in which these other two moments come together and are *aufgehoben*, I would suggest that it can only be the figure of Zarathustra himself. And by this I do not mean simply the Zarathustra we encounter in the First Part, but rather the Zarathustra who begins as a well-meaning en-lightened humanist (almost as naive as Oedipus Rex), but winds up as the Zarathustra of the end of Part Four (far wiser and more human, as was Oedipus at Colonous, although in considerably better shape in other respects – at least for the moment). The upshot for us and our lives, in this case, is the newly and more truly human "future humanity" Nietzsche had recently envisioned and described (GS 337), possessed of what he went on (a year after completing the Fourth Part of *Zarathustra*) to call the "great health" (GS 381).[13] Here one would be neither preoccupied with the dream of he *Übermensch* nor obsessed with the vision of the Eternal Recurrence, but rather concerned to get on with one's life and work (in the spirit of Zarathustra's parting lines at the end of the Fourth Part), as the only meaningful way of "becoming who one is."

At this point mythic imagery gives way to actual human life as it must and can be lived – but now finding or working out one's own way ("This is my way; where is yours?"), in a spirit of transformed aspiration and sensibility. Neither the "meaning of the earth" associated with the image of the *Übermensch* nor the "affirmation" and *amor fati* associated with the Eternal Recurrence remain the talk of the town, or become the elements of a new creed and catechism; for their work is done when they have supplemented the "free spirit" and seen the latter-day pilgrims through their educational progress and childhood's end.

The *Übermensch*, Eternal Recurrence and Zarathustra himself thus all have their places *within* the educational process Nietzsche crafts for us, rather than at its end, as its results. They are among the materials of a ladder that is to be dispensed with once it has been climbed. If we become fixated upon them, we have made mere means of this education into its end; for their role is not to capture and hold our attention, but rather to aid us in reaching the developmental point at which we can go on without them – as Zarathustra himself suggests often enough.

Nietzsche earlier (in the time of BT, and even in the *Untimely Meditation* on history) had been much concerned with the role of myth in making life possible, worth living and capable of flourishing; and he had been persuaded that, for better or worse, is efficacy in this respect depended upon *illusion*. As was earlier observed, however, he subsequently had second thoughts on this matter. While he continued to make much of the ubiquity and indispensability of fictions, lies and errors in human life, I believe than he came to understand that he had been guilty of a number of oversimplifications here, and that in particular it is a mistake to suppose that everything in the entire domain of human thought must be either "true" (in some impossible absolute sense) or "false." This is a false dichotomy; and what is important about the contents of myth and art alike is something else altogether – namely, their power to shape our dispositions and ways of thinking, feeling and esteeming.

Nietzsche subsequently (after BT and the "meditations") moved away from the celebration of myth, and during his "free spirit" years flirted with the idea that we may have to learn either to get along without it or to resign ourselves to the inescapability and necessity of all-too-human forms of untruth. He retained or soon regained the conviction that no healthy and vital culture and humanity can be attained and sustained without something of the sort. But he would seem to have come to the realization that the "something of the sort" need not be either myths of the kind by which we long have lived or the newer myths of scientism, nationalism and Wagnerianism. Something like *Zarathustra* might do the job, in a way that does not exact too high a price, does not entail the sacrifice of honesty and intellectual integrity – and does not self-destruct at its own hands when the truthfulness it promotes is brought to bear upon itself.

To do the kind of job that myth has done, compelling images and representations of alternative interpretations are still required. Something on the order of the fare Nietzsche serves up in *Zarathustra* is needed, if our thinking is not to remain confined to the dead end of mere critique. It is a myth-substitute for the modern world, intended for a humanity (or at least for its vanguard) in transition, ready to be weaned away from its dependency upon myths, and yet still not fully mature – either too cavalier or too desperate at the prospect of having to make do without them. It engenders a new enthusiasm, and then provides its own antidote (in the form of the Fourth Part) to ensure that the new enthusiasm does not congeal into a new dogmatism. For Niezsche understood that we must be able eventually to distance ourselves from the means of our education, even if we must initially be seduced and induced to engage with it and take it seriously enough to be affected by it. As in the case of myth, literal truth is not what it is all about; and a fundamentalist turn of mind with respect to the "teachings" of Zarathustra would have been no more welcome to Nietzsche among would-be disciples than among detractors.

The Fourth Part makes it clear, if the first three do not (and as Nietzsche may have feared after writing them that they did not), that these teachings are not intended to be embraced as gospel truth. Its irony, parodies, grotesqueries and humor are more than sufficient for this purpose. But the whole of the work shares in this double effect, as a kind of self-parodying quasi-myth that we are expected both to take seriously and to see for what it is. It is offered to us as no *mere* self-parody, however, as Nietzsche's hyperbolic hype with respect to it in *Ecce Homo* renders obvious. He realized that it would take something approaching a miracle to enable humanity to get from where it is to where it needs to go without meeting one or another of the sorry fates he envisions – and *Zarathustra*, he believed, *is that miracle*.

But it can do its work only if it is taken seriously. Getting anything of the kind taken seriously, however, especially by the very readers Nietzsche wanted most to reach (with their modern and perhaps nascently post-modern sophistication), might seem to be a virtual impossibility. But this is a part of the genius of the work he came up with: its self-parodic character is *neither* what it is all about *nor* a hopeless stumbling block to sophisticated readers. Rather, it is the very device that *enables* such readers *to take it seriously*. We bear witness to that ourselves.

By the time of *Zarathustra*, Nietzsche both felt the need for something more than the ever-increasing sophistication of the "free spirit" series, and knew better than to think that anything on the order of Wagner's new mythology – or any of the older ones around, including that to which Wagner had returned – could be embraced by anyone like himself. He therefore sought to come up with something that would incorporate the means of coming to discern and attain an appropriately transformed and promising sensibility, in a form that protects it was well as possible against dismissal for reasons of intellectual integrity. *Zarathustra* is the result. We can take it seriously precisely because it is made clear that *we are not expected to believe it*. What is to be taken seriously in and about it is not the cognitive content of the images and ideas by means of which our attention is attracted and our thinking is engaged (let alone the story line). Rather, it is the human possibilities that are reconfigured and opened up to us as the work unfolds, and as we respond.

VI

Zarathustra: a pedagogical reading

Prologue. Education is thematized from the outset; and the kind of education that is at issue is clearly distinguished from both indoctrination and mere instruction. Zarathustra sets out to impart his "wisdom" to others, having already been transformed himself; for in place of the ashes he carried into the mountains, he now bears fire that he would bring to humanity in the valleys below. Or rather: "I bring men a gift" (Z P: 2) – a gift for all or none, depending on their receptiveness. His gift is a new way of thinking that endows life with greater value than it has under prevailing modes of interpretation and evaluation. His formula for it, expressing his conviction of the importance of "remaining faithful to the earth" and making the most of life as an earthly affair, is that "the *Übermensch* is the meaning of the earth" (Z P: 3).

Zarathustra knows that all loving needs to be learned, and so attempts to educate his hearers in the matter of learning how to love that in ourselves which relates to the enhancement of life (Z P: 4). Dismissing what ordinarily passes for "education," and also disparaging the sorry excuse for humanity (the "last man") that aspires to nothing more than an insipid happiness, he advocates a different kind of education, the thrust of which is to inculcate and cultivate *aspiration* (Z P: 5). As things stand, he observes, "Human existence is uncanny and still without a meaning" (Z P: 7). Yet its transformation into something meaningful is humanly possible, he proclaims, if only we will heed him.

But Zarathustra's preaching to the multitude to this effect is to no avail. It is not in this way, and with such an audience, that any meaningful education can occur – except on the part of Zarathustra and the reader, who both may come away somewhat the wiser from the all-too-believable failure of this attempt (and any such attempt) to transform the way people are disposed to think by telling them things they are neither prepared nor interested to hear. Zarathustra now understands that real education cannot take place in that way, and that he needs companions rather than just an audience if he is to have any success as an educator. So he proposes "to lure many away from the herd," with the thought that "I shall show them the rainbow and all the steps to the overman" (Z P: 9). But his optimism is tempered: "That I might be wiser!" (Z P: 10). And with this the Prologue concludes. The first steps in the education of the educator (and reader) are taken, and the stage is set for those to follow – beginning with a goodly number of sermonettes, this time presumably addressed not to the multitude but to those among the multitude who might be responsive to the kind of rhetoric in which the First Part consists. It is only a beginning; but unless a beginning is made, nothing further can happen.

First Part. In the 22 speeches of the First Part we see what Zarathustra's initial wisdom amounts to – and also what sorts of things Nietzsche associates with the ideas of "remaining faithful to the earth" and the *Übermensch* as "the meaning of the earth." It is with these notions that Zarathustra starts out in the Prologue; and it is with their reaffirmation that the First Part ends, in a concluding reflection on "the gift-giving virtue" – power (Z I: 22). Much good naturalistic sense and worldly wisdom is to be found in these speeches, beginning on a high note with the famous discussion of "The Three Metamorphoses" of the spirit – metaphorically speaking, becoming first as a camel, then as a lion, then as a child (Z I: 1). This is revealing of the kind of thing Nietzsche has in mind in speaking of the enhancement of life and what is involved in the passage from animality toward higher humanity and *Übermenschlichkeit*; and it also provides a sketch of a model of the multi-stage educational process that is his point of departure.

It is significant, however, that this *is* only his point of departure rather than his summary statement on this topic, and that the First Part ends with Zarathustra's withdrawal from those to whom he has been preaching, bidding them to "lose me and find yourselves" (Z I: 22: 3). Their education has only begun, he realizes, even if they have comprehended and taken to heart the entire content of the intervening score of speeches. This content ranges from disparagement of the antiworldly, the otherworldly, and the ascetically minded and puritanical to celebration of the body, sublimation (as opposed to repression) of the passions, love, friendship, fighting the good fight, and creativity, with a mixture of barbed commentary on various all-too-human and insidious tendencies and developments and Nietzsche's own all-too-human musings on women, marriage, and children.

What are we to make of all of this? A part of the answer to this question surely is suggested by the fact that Nietzsche neither stopped with the First Part nor merely continued to churn out further parts just like it. Zarathustra's concluding rejection of discipleship with respect to all that has gone before (Z I: 22: 3) is also relevant and revealing. It is not mere instruction in the rules of right living that is imparted in these speeches, but rather a general outlook reflecting the fundamental reinterpretation and revaluation Nietzsche had been seeking (prior to *Zarathustra*) to carry out with respect to human life, and continued to promote and pursue subsequently. The soundness or unsoundness of any particular piece of advice or observation matters less than their collective drift, which is all well and good as far as it goes – but which, for Nietzsche (as the next parts show), does not go nearly far or deep enough.

Some of these speeches give vivid expression to ideas that are central to his thought. They serve to enhance both the comprehension and the appreciation of these ideas in any reader who is at all receptive to them: e.g., "On the Despisers of the Body" (Z I: 4), "On Enjoying and Suffering the Passions" (Z I: 5), "On the Thousand and One Goals" (Z I: 15), "On the Way of the Creator" (Z I: 17) and "On the Gift-Giving Virtue" (Z I: 22) in particular. But Nietzsche seeks to do more than get these ideas across; and mere agreement with them is not sufficient either. One needs to earn one's right to them; and by themselves they do not add up to a firmly rooted way of thinking that can dispense with all external support and withstand any doubt.

Second Part. Zarathustra's task in the Second Part is to begin to try to come to terms with various threats to this way of thinking and its affirmative character that are quite capable of subverting it. He is represented as having changed; for we are told that "his wisdom grew," and had become a "wild wisdom," at once "pregnant" and "foolish," with Dionysian overtones and undercurrents (Z II: 1).

Zarathustra's first major speech ("Upon the Blessed Isles") is one of the high points of the entire work, reaffirming the basic thrust of the First Part, and also extending it by both celebrating creation and emphasizing the inseparability of creation and destruction (Z II: 2). Much of what follows, however, is troubled, both by skirmishes and distractions and by deeper worries about the problematic relations between life, spirit and wisdom. There are many things that pass for education that do more harm than good; and they need to be dealt with and dispatched. Even if one manages to avoid becoming caught in their snares, however, it is still deeply worrisome whether there is any educational antidote to the doubts, anxiety and incipient despair that cast a deepening shadow over this Second Part, culminating in the crisis with which it ends. A hint of a solution is offered in the central section "On Self-Overcoming" (Z II: 12); but it is with profound dissatisfaction, distress, and foreboding that Zarathustra once again withdraws at the Second Part's conclusion. Nothing he has understood or conveyed up to this point is adequate to the challenges that dawn upon him in "On Redemption" (Z II: 20) and "On Human Prudence" (Z II: 21).

This, however, is itself an important educational advance. Coming to know what one does not know, to comprehend the nature and magnitude of the problem one faces, and to grasp the inadequacy of ways of thinking already at one's disposal in relation to it, may be no solution; but one will never find a solution if one does not understand the situation, and is not impelled to seek some way of doing something about it.

Third Part. In the course of the 16 sections of the shorter Third Part (with which *Zarathustra* originally concluded), a provisional solution is achieved, in the form of a profound transformation of the way in which life and the world and one's own existence are regarded, both interpretively and evaluatively. It begins with a renewed call (in "The Wanderer") to self-overcoming, the enhancement of life and the aspiration to human greatness (Z III: 1); and it ends with the Dionysian "Other Dancing Song" (Z III: 15) and "Seven Seals" hymn (Z III: 16), in which an ecstatic affirmation of life – embraced in Nietzsche's version of *sub specie aeternitatis* – is expressed. The idea of life as eternally recurring in the same (specific or general) way, unredeemed by anything beyond or after it or by any significant alteration of its basic character, ceases to be experienced as a devastating, unbearable and "most abysmal thought" that cannot be faced. Indeed, this idea comes to be not only celebrated but drawn upon to provide the outlook elaborated previously (in the First Part and earlier in the Second) with legs to stand on.

This outlook and the polemics accompanying its initial elaboration are recapitulated and reaffirmed in the early speeches of the Third Part, following Zarathustra's first intimation – in "On the Vision and the Riddle" (Z III: 2) – that it may be possible after all to come to terms affirmatively with the notion of Eternal Recurrence. These speeches culminate in two of the most notable perorations in the entire work: "On the Three Evils" (Z III: 10) and "On Old and New Tablets," with its paean to creativity as the key to the enhancement of life and its meaningfulness: 'he who creates . . . creates man's goal and gives the earth its meaning and its future" (Z III: 12: 2).

Accompanying this reaffirmation of these ideas is the elevation to prominence of what had been a relatively minor theme in the First Part. As it is developed here, with applications at all levels (up to that of the Eternal Recurrence itself), it becomes clear that it is crucial to the transformation that occurs in the Third Part. It also is of profound educational importance, and is one of the keys to the conception of the kind of education with which Nietzsche is concerned. This is the idea that the basic condition of the possibility of all affirmation is *learning to love*.

In "On Passing By" (Z III: 7) the point is made that "passing by" is the best thing to do where one cannot love; and then, as the Third Part unfolds, the idea of the importance of loving and learning to love is explored in a variety of contexts, from "learning to love oneself" (Z III: 11: 2) to learning to appreciate "the many good inventions on earth" and grasp that "for their sake, the earth is to be loved" (Z III: 12: 17), to loving "life" (Z III: 15) and even "eternity" (Z III: 16). The "three evils" rehabilitated and celebrated – sex, lust to rule, and selfishness – are three basic forms of loving that we must both learn to affirm and learn to cultivate beyond their simplest forms of expression.

Zarathustra's wisdom is powerless to sustain him by itself. What he can love, however, he can affirm, and find meaningful; for love bestows value and meaning. Here life expresses itself as the fundamentally Dionysian phenomenon Nietzsche takes it to be. And at the conclusion of the Third Part, he attempts to construct a means not only of conveying this point but of enabling us to ascend his version of the ladder of love to its ultimate height, from which even a world viewed under the aspect of Eternal Recurrence can be affirmed.

Fourth Part. One cannot live, however, at such a height. How can the spirit of such a Dionysian love be preserved in some way when one descends to the plane of life as we must live it? Nietzsche may not have intended initially to extend *Zarathustra* past its first three parts; but had he not done so, the educational project of the work would have been seriously incomplete. Like a great symphony or grand opera, the Third Part ends with a rapturous and glorious climax. But even if it succeeds in momentarily transporting us along with Zarathustra as we reach that point, what then?

Nietzsche knew as well as we do that even exceptions to the human rule will continue to have much of the all-too-human about them; and if depression is not to set in once again with this recognition, one's education will have to continue further, to provide one with ways of coming to terms with this circumstance without illusions. If one is well advised to turn away and pass by where one cannot love, where does this leave one who is acutely aware of the all-too-human with the dawning of the cold clear light of day, when the raptures evoked in the concluding songs of Part Three have subsided?

Here the motley collection of "higher men" Zarathustra assembles in the Fourth Part serve the purpose providing another kind of test, somewhat analogous to the Recurrence Test. If "higher humanity" were to amount to nothing more than the sort of thing this strange and ludicrous crew represents, could one still affirm it with open eyes, and adhere to the way of thinking that ties the "meaning of the earth" to the enhancement of life? In the end Zarathustra passes this test; and if the Fourth

Part accomplishes its educational task for us, we should be able to pass it as well.

In that event, one would not have to be in the throes of "Seven-Seal" rapture to be able to embrace the conception of "higher humanity" as the upshot of the idea of the *Übermensch* and the basis of a fundamental and comprehensive affirmative stance. One may have to learn to overcome the susceptibility to be overwhelmed by feelings of "pity" for "higher humanity," such as it is; and indeed this "temptation" may actually be heightened in the aftermath of the Third Part. Yet here we see that this is humanly possible, even if the only "higher" types around leave a great deal to be desired *and* are viewed utterly without illusions.

This requires yet a further "ripening" of Zarathustra's nature, and another chapter in the educational process with which Nietzsche is concerned. The section "On the Higher Man" (Z IV: 13), with its 20 sub-sections, makes it clear that Nietzsche still means the idea of "higher humanity" to be taken very seriously, despite the comical procession of "higher" types to which we have been introduced. But a part of what *enables* it to continue to be taken seriously is that Nietzsche is effectively countering any tendency one might have to take it seriously *in the wrong way*, using comedy and absurdity to overcome "the spirit of gravity" (Z IV: 17).

This is one expression of one of the central points of the Fourth Part – that one must learn not only to love but also to *laugh*, and to dance. It is with this theme that the last half-dozen sub-sections of the discourse "On the Higher Man" are concerned (Z IV: 13: 15–20). To be sure, they are followed immediately by the "old magician's" anguished "Song of Melancholy" (Z IV: 14); but this only serves to underscore the point. The magician has not yet managed to incorporate the very lesson Zarathustra has just taught. His real education is still incomplete.

But not all laughter is of the same kind, as Zarathustra observes: "And if they have learned to laugh from me, it is still not *my* laughter that they have learned" (Z IV: 17: 1). And the same applies with respect to affirmation, as the "Yea-Yuh" braying of the ass in the ensuing "ass-festival" shows. Indeed, it even applies with respect to the affirmation of the idea of Eternal Recurrence (Z IV: 19: 1). Zarathustra himself is still struggling with all of this right to the very end of the Fourth Part, falling back on the theme of the Third Part's end to fortify himself in "The Drunken Song" – albeit with greater self-consciousness this time, and with more explicit awareness of its implications for human life. It is only at the conclusion of the final section that he seems finally to arrive at the human maturity toward which his educational course has been tending. The conclusion clearly affirms that course, and shows that the Fourth

Part is by no means a *reductio ad absurdum* of the entire work. But it also resists any reduction of the educational project of Zarathustra/ *Zarathustra* to a formula; for like creativity, maturity admits neither of any complete description nor of any specific prescription.

VII

Where does this leave Zarathustra, and how are we to imagine him after he again leaves his cave, "glowing and strong as a morning sun that comes out of dark mountains," having finally "ripened" and arrived at his realization of what finally does and does not matter? (Z IV: 20). His education has been extraordinary: "The ladder on which he ascends and descends is tremendous," Nietzsche tells us three years later in *Ecce Homo* (EH III: 7: 6). Nietzsche's retrospective apotheosis of him there actually only serves to underscore his profound commitment to what Zarathustra and *Zarathustra* are all about.

Zarathustra may fall short of deserving Nietzsche's claims for it, and may have fallen short of his hope for it as well; and as a literary vehicle for his philosophical ideas it may leave a good deal to be desired, as anyone who has tried to use it to "teach Nietzsche" in a philosophy course can attest. Yet regarded as an educational device of the kind I have been describing, and assessed by any more modest standard of success than Nietzsche's own, it would seem to me to be a truly remarkable accomplishment. Most of humanity has been and is likely to remain untouched by it (for better or worse); and it has lent itself to uses and abuses both silly and sinister, as well as to others it is less awkward to acknowledge. Yet it does have the power to do – at least for some – the sort of thing Nietzsche attributed to his encounter with Schopenhauer; and it can have a great and profound educational effect upon the sensibilities of kindred spirits.

Zarathustra may deal in consciousness-raising and attitude-adjustment; but it is almost in a class by itself among efforts of this kind in the philosophical literature after Plato. Anecdotal evidence suggests that it not only is what first attracted many of us to Nietzsche, but also has figured importantly in the attraction of many others to philosophy who have long since left Nietzsche behind. And it has at least rocked the boats of countless students and others who have happened upon it.

This may be a far cry from saving humanity from the Scylla and Charybdis of fanaticism and nihilism, on whose rocks we may yet founder. But I do believe that the kind of education one can get from

Zarathustra can enable those who worry about such things to navigate through and beyond those straits at least as well as anything else around. For those who do not worry about such things, however, it is better dead than read. It is, after all, a book for all and none. (But what if they offered an education and nobody came?)

NOTES

1 Nietzsche, manuscript source uncertain. Cited elsewhere as "VII: 215."
2 I shall follow the common practice of identifying Nietzsche citations whenever possible by the acronyms of the English titles of the works or other volumes from which they are taken, in the translations indicated below. In the case of citations from *Ecce Homo*, the roman numerals identify the main parts of the work, and the internal acronyms identify the writings he is discussing in the third part, "Why I Write Such Good Books." In the case of citations from *Thus Spoke Zarathustra*, "P" refers to the Prologue to the First Part, roman numerals refer to the four main parts of the work, and the first arabic numerals refer either to the numbered sections of the Prologue or to the numbers of the speeches or sections of the four main parts of the work. (While not numbered in print, the speeches and sections can easily and usefully be given numbers.) Subsequent arabic numerals refer to numbered sub-sections within these speeches or sections.

BT = *The Birth of Tragedy*, in *The Birth of Tragedy and The Case of Wagner*, trans. Walter Kaufmann (New York: Vintage, 1967)
EH = *Ecce Homo*, in *On the Genealogy of Morals/Ecce Homo*, trans. Walter Kaufmann (New York: Vintage, 1967)
GS = *The Gay Science*, trans. Walter Kaufmann (New York: Vintage, 1974)
SE = *Schopenhauer as Educator*, in *Untimely Meditations*, trans. R. J. Hollingdale (Cambridge: Cambridge University Press, 1983)
Z = *Thus Spoke Zarathustra*, in *The Portable Nietzsche*, trans. Walter Kaufmann (New York: Viking, 1954)

3 See, for example, Harold Alderman, *Nietzsche's Gift* (Athens, Ohio: Ohio University Press, 1977); Bernd Magnus, *Nietzsche's Existential Imperative* (Bloomington, Indiana: Indiana University Press, 1978); Laurence Lampert, *Nietzsche's Teaching* (New Haven: Yale University Press, 1986); Kathleen Marie Higgins, *Nietzsche's ZARATHUSTRA* (Philadelphia: Temple University Press, 1987). Alan White, *With Nietzsche's Labyrinth* (New York: Routledge, 1990); Greg Whitlock, *Returning to Sils-Maria* (New York: Peter Lang, 1990).
4 Friedrich Schiller, *On the Aesthetic Education of Man*, trans. Reginald Snell (New York: Frederick Ungar, 1965).
5 See my *Nietzsche* (London: Routledge & Kegan Paul, 1983), chapter 8.
6 See my Introduction to *Schopenhauer as Educator* in *Unmodern Observations*, ed. William Arrowsmith (New Haven: Yale University Press, 1990), pp. 147–61.

7 Page numbers in quotations from SE refer to the page numbers in Hollingdale's translation. They are given, as well as Nietzsche's section numbers, because the sections are quite long.

8 See the Kaufmann translation of this work (New York: Vintage, 1974), p. 30.

9 "The tragedy begins." This is the heading Nietzsche gave to the final section of the last part of the original edition of *The Gay Science*, which consists in a version of the opening of the Prologue to the First Part of *Zarathustra*, published the next year but obviously already well underway.

10 See my *Nietzsche*, chapters 5 and 6, esp. pp. 326–40 and 380–94.

11 See my "Nietzsche's *Gay Science*, Or, How to Naturalize Cheerfully," in *Reading Nietzsche*, eds Robert C. Solomon and Kathleen M. Higgins (New York: Oxford University Press, 1988), pp. 68–86.

12 In lectures at Harvard University (in which, as an undergraduate, I first made Nietzsche's acquaintance).

13 It is well worth noting that Nietzsche returned to the project of *The Gay Science* after finishing the four parts of Zarathustra and writing *Beyond Good and Evil*, publishing an expanded second edition with a new Fifth Book and a new Preface in 1887, just prior to *On the Genealogy of Morals*. *Zarathustra* thus did not mark the end or abandonment of that project, but rather only an extended intermission in it – albeit a very important and perhaps necessary one for Nietzsche.

14
Putting Nietzsche to Work: The Case of Gilles Deleuze

Alan D. Schrift

> The time for me hasn't come yet; some are born posthumously.
>
> *Ecce Homo*

> A new species of philosophers is coming up: I venture to baptize them with a name that is not free of danger. As I unriddle them, insofar as they allow themselves to be unriddled – for it belongs to their nature to *want* to remain riddles at some point – these philosophers of the future may have a right – it might also be a wrong – to be called *experimenters* [*Versucher*]. The name itself is in the end a mere experiment [*Versuch*] and, if you will, a temptation [*Versuchung*].
>
> *Beyond Good and Evil*

In a 1972 conversation with Michel Foucault, Gilles Deleuze remarked that a "theory is exactly like a box of tools. . . . It must be useful. It must function. And not for itself."[1] Even a cursory examination of the theoretical productions within recent French philosophy reveals that the writings of Friedrich Nietzsche function as a central tool in their collective toolbox. This is particularly true in the case of Gilles Deleuze, whose career exhibits a continuing willingness to employ that tool named "Nietzsche." Deleuze's use of this tool, moreover, can be seen to take one of two forms. In the first, while ostensively offering an interpretation of Nietzsche, he uses this occasion of interpretation as a forum within which to challenge what he holds to be a (the?) dominant philosophical voice of the day. In the second, whether or not Nietzsche is named explicitly, Deleuze appropriates various Nietzschean motifs which he puts to work in the development of his own critical project. In the following few pages, I want to touch briefly upon the first form and make a few remarks about Deleuze's early text on Nietzsche; then I will devote the remainder of the paper to tracking some of the Nietzschean traces that run through Deleuze's later work.

Claiming One's Place: from Nietzsche to Hegel/Heidegger

We can begin to mark the importance of Nietzsche for Deleuze's philosophical project by comparing the interpretive strategy Deleuze adopts in his early text on Nietzsche with the strategy that guides the interpretation of Nietzsche offered a decade later by Jacques Derrida. While neither Deleuze nor Derrida are commonly characterized as "transparent" writers, they make little attempt to conceal their respective agendas in *Nietzsche and Philosophy* and *Spurs: Nietzsche's Styles*.[2] This is to say, while their immediate task is to offer a reading of Nietzsche, these early texts each *use* Nietzsche for reasons other than simply explicating his thought. Deleuze acknowledges explicitly the anti-Hegelian polemic[3] that motivates his reading of Nietzsche, and Derrida, for his part, is only slightly more circumspect in his use of Nietzsche to confront Heidegger and the Heideggerian hermeneutic. This surface similarity of choosing Nietzsche to challenge Hegel and Heidegger should not obscure an important difference, however, since Derrida's relationship with Heidegger is far more congenial than Deleuze's relationship to Hegel. As Derrida's subsequent writings have gone on to show, he approaches Heidegger as a fellow traveller, intent upon correcting certain Heideggerian excesses but ultimately committed to the Heideggerian project of overcoming the ontotheological-cum logocentric tradition. Deleuze, on the other hand, declares war on Hegel, and his subsequent works show equally his consistent identification of Hegel with the state apparatus against which his nomad war machine continues to struggle.

In his early works, Derrida makes frequent reference to Nietzsche in his own attempt to deconstruct the logocentric tendencies of metaphysical thinking. More specifically, Nietzsche often appears in the Derridean text as an alternative to the nostalgic longing for full presence that Derrida locates at the core of Western metaphysics.[4] In fact, "Nietzsche" often comes to function as a proper name for the possibility of thinking otherwise, a shorthand marker for the other of logocentrism.[5] In *Spurs: Nietzsche's Styles*, we see again the Derridean strategy of providing Nietzsche as an example of thinking otherwise, this time with respect to Heidegger's own nostalgic tendencies.[6] The discussion in *Spurs* is structured around three questions addressed to Nietzsche's writing, each unfolded as a critical foil with which Derrida will joust with Heidegger. These three questions are the question of the text, the question of the proper (*propre*), and the question of style. In raising the first question, Derrida focuses on Nietzsche's conception of woman and he uses this focus to raise the question of truth in Nietzsche's text. In so doing, the Heideggerian reading, among others, is implicitly chastised for its lack of attention to the position of woman, a lack which betokens an inadequate conception of the intricacies of the Nietzschean text while repeating the phallogocentric tradition's blindness to questions of gender and women. From here, Derrida proceeds to consider Nietzsche's place within the metaphysical tradition. He explicitly marks his departure from Heidegger's situating Nietzsche within that tradition as its last great representative when he transmutes the Heideggerian-metaphysical question of Being into the Nietzschean-axiological question of the proper. Last, we find the discussion of Nietzsche's forgotten umbrella. Here, Derrida most directly addresses the question of Nietzsche's styles as they pertain to Nietzsche's text, to the question of the text in general, and to the problematics of interpretation. Derrida's discussion of the heterogeneity of Nietzsche's styles, which issues a challenge to what he calls "hermeneutics," reiterates many of the points raised in his earlier critical discussion of the "Heideggerian hope" in the essay "*Différance*."[7] But here as elsewhere, the nature of the Derridean response to Heidegger is far from obvious, as Derrida's interpretation is not offered as either replacement for or refutation of Heidegger's interpretation. Instead, it provides a *supplément* to these earlier readings and, as with other Derridean questions of supplementarity, this *supplément* both depends upon and exceeds what it supplements. This is to say, Derrida's strategy in his discussion of Nietzsche's styles is double: while he wants to make it clear that the question of style exceeds the Heideggerian reading, he at the same time wants to make it no less clear that things are never simple with Heidegger and that the critique of Heidegger must always proceed obliquely, indirectly. In this sense, *Spurs* offers us another example of philosophical "undecidability," this time with respect to the adequacy of the Heideggerian reading of Nietzsche and, in particular, to the success of Heidegger's attempt to include Nietzsche within the history of Western metaphysics while extricating himself from that same history. As a text, *Spurs* thus stands as a signpost for Derrida's ambivalent relationship to Nietzsche/Heidegger, an ambivalence that marks a certain undecidability in his own thinking observable in many of his writings prior to 1980.

Ambivalence is not a term that comes to mind when reading Deleuze's *Nietzsche and Philosophy*. Published during the period when he was primarily engaged in fairly straightforward philosophical analyses of more or less canonical figures within the history of philosophy, *Nietzsche and Philosophy* is an excellent study that contributed as much as any single work to the renewed interest in Nietzsche's thought in France during the 1960s and 1970s.[8] In this text, Deleuze directs himself against what he regards as a misguided attempt to strike a compromise between the Hegelian dialectic and Nietzsche's genealogy; his desire to offer an interpretation of Nietzsche's philosophy is matched by a desire to show the impropriety of reading Nietzsche as a neo-Hegelian dialectician. Where Hegel's thinking is always guided by the movement toward some unifying synthesis, Nietzsche, in contrast, is seen to affirm multiplicity and rejoice in diversity.[9] In fact, Deleuze comes to view the entirety of Nietzsche's corpus as a polemical response to the Hegelian dialectic, one which opposes its own discovery – "the negativity of the positive" – to the famous Hegelian discovery of the "positivity of the negative."[10] Focusing on the qualitative difference in Nietzsche between active and reactive forces, Deleuze argues that the mastery of the *Übermensch* is derived from her or his ability *actively* to negate the slave's reactive forces, even though these reactive forces may exceed quantitatively the active forces. In other words, whereas the slave moves from the negative premise ("you are other and evil") to the positive judgment ("therefore I am good"), the master works from the positive differentiation of self ("I am good") to the negative corollary ("you are other and bad"). There is, according to Deleuze, a qualitative difference at the origin of force, and it is the genealogist's task to attend to this differential and genetic element of force which Nietzsche calls "will to power."[11] Thus, whereas in the Hegelian dialectic of master and slave, the reactive negation of the other has as its consequence the positive affirmation of self, Nietzsche reverses this situation: the master's active positing of self is accompanied by and results in a negation of the slave's reactive force.[12]

While much can be learnt reading *Nietzsche and Philosophy*, this text remains content to express Nietzsche's thought more or less within the discursive practices of traditional ontology. For this reason, it is not the most interesting place to locate what one might call the Nietzsche-effect within Deleuze's writings. In fact, we can allow Deleuze himself to speak, albeit obliquely, against his early work on Nietzsche. The history of philosophy, he writes, is "philosophy's own Oedipus," and although Deleuze confesses to being a member of "a generation, one of the last generations, who were more or less ruined by the history of philosophy," he was "pulled out of all of this" by Nietzsche.[13] In a remark that recalls

Foucault's account of the normalizing power of the disciplinary rules that govern institutionalized discourse,[14] Deleuze writes that the history of philosophy has always played the repressor's role as the agent of power in philosophy:

> [H]ow can you think without having read Plato, Descartes, Kant and Heidegger, and so-and-so's book about them? A formidable school of intimidation which manufactures specialists in though – but which also makes those who stay outside conform all the more to this specialism they despise. An image of thought called philosophy has been formed historically and it effectively stops people from thinking.[15]

Deleuze goes on to claim that he prefers philosophers who appear to be part of the history of philosophy but who escape from that "bureaucracy of pure reason" in one respect or altogether.[16] Deleuze's text on Nietzsche comes close to escaping the bounds of traditional philosophical discourse insofar as it develops Nietzsche's affirmation of difference as an alternative to the Hegelian paradigm for resolving opposition, the *Aufhebung*. It is in his later texts, however, where Deleuze moves from the interpretation *of* Nietzsche to an experimentation *with* Nietzsche, that we see him begin to operate outside of the "official language" of philosophy, outside of those organizing rules that govern what can and cannot be said within philosophy, and outside as well of the typical power plays that operate within philosophy insofar as these later texts acknowledge the political and libidinal dimensions inscribed in every philosophical gesture.

In Deleuze's later works, Nietzsche's texts exemplify the deterritorializing politics to which all texts should aspire by presenting themselves as tools to be used rather than privileged objects to be understood. Like Foucault but unlike Derrida, Deleuze is not particularly comfortable with the language games of textuality, and in his later works, he comes to reject the entire project of "interpretation," opting instead for a process of *experimentation* whose explicit intent is to promote or incite political change.[17] Since the "signifier" was invented, Deleuze writes in *Dialogues*, things have not yet sorted themselves out, as the obsession with interpreting sends readers off in all directions looking for hidden, secret meanings.[18] In contrast to the hermeneutic project of interpretation which aims to recover "sense" and the structuralist project which tracks the play of signifiers, Deleuze places his emphasis on codes, decoding, and recoding. The processes of codification, whether legal, contractual, or institutional, constitute for Deleuze the very being of politics, and Nietzsche's originality, Deleuze claims, lies in part in his having written a new kind of book, one that defies codification insofar as his aphorisms transmit forces rather than signify meanings.[19] In this regard, his response to a question posed to him following his presentation of the paper "Pensée nomade" at the Cerisy Colloquium on Nietzsche in 1972 is significant. When queried on the relation between his thought and "deconstruction," Deleuze responded:

> If I understand you, you say that there is some suspicion on my part of the Heideggerian point of view. I'm delighted. With regard to the method of deconstruction of texts, I see well what it is, I admire it greatly, but I don't see it having anything to do with my own. I never present myself as a commentator on texts. A text, for me, is only a little wheel in an extra-textual practice. It is not a question of commenting on the text by a method of deconstruction, or by a method of textual practice, or by any other method; it is a question of seeing what use a text is in the extra-textual practice that prolongs the text. You ask me if I believe in the nomad's response. Yes, I believe it.[20]

While not directed in response to Derridean deconstruction per se, this remark points out an important difference between Deleuze's and Derrida's positions with respect to Nietzsche – the difference between use and method.[21] Bearing this distinction in mind, one notes that Derrida methodically reiterates the proper name "Nietzsche" at significant points in his commentaries on several of the privileged texts and canonical thinkers in the history of philosophy. As suggested above, "Nietzsche" in fact comes to function as a metonymy for the possibility of thinking otherwise than logocentrically. This should not be taken to imply that the iteration of the name "Nietzsche" lacks political implications, either within or outside the academy. In fact, I would claim just the opposite, offering Derrida's other texts "on" Nietzsche – "Interpreting Signatures (Nietzsche/Heidegger)" and *Otobiographies: The Teaching of Nietzsche and the Politics of the Proper Name*[22] – as evidence of his attempt to address issues concerning academic/intellectual and world politics respectively. But acknowledging the political dimension of Derrida's writings should not obscure the fact that this dimension is textually contextualized, that is, it appears in the context of a methodological intervention into the practices of reading and interpretation. For Deleuze, on the other hand, the question is never one of method. Where Derrida offered as a motto the now infamous *"Il n'y a pas de hors-texte,"*[23] Deleuze seeks instead to exit the text: insofar as reading is a political act, the task is not to remain within the textual network but to execute lines of escape into extra-textual practice (not to interpret the world, Marx would say, but to change it!). In another context, Deleuze, this time speaking with Guattari, makes this same point in terms of their notion of assemblage (*agencement*). "A book," they write, "exists only through the outside and on the outside."[24] As an assemblage, a book exists in connection with other assemblages; it exists in terms of what it can be conjoined with, what it can be made to function with. In order to develop further the difference between use and method – and develop further the contrast between Deleuze's textual practices and Derridean deconstruction – we must now examine some of the assemblages Deleuze constructs with Nietzsche's texts, some of the connections he makes between Nietzsche's texts and extra-textual practices; in other words, some of his Nietzsche-experiments.

Willing, Power, Desire

Nietzsche announced, in the remark that would become the closing entry in the non-book published as *The Will to Power*, that the solution to the riddle of his Dionysian world was that "*This world is will to power – and nothing besides!* And you yourselves are also will to power – and nothing besides!"[25] In so doing, he issued a challenge to all future dualisms: it would no longer be possible for understanding to proceed according to a model that operated in terms of a simple binary logic. Opting instead for a polyvalent monism which distinguishes among both degrees and kinds of will to power, Nietzsche's announcement stands as a challenge to all subsequent dualistic attempts to divide and hierarchize the world neatly into dichotomous groups: good or evil, minds or bodies, truths or errors, us or them. The world is much more complicated than such dualistic thinking acknowledges, and Nietzsche's announcement that everything is will to power suggests that the radically contextual and contingent nature of all conceptual distinctions makes suspect any appeal to a rigidly hierarchized metanarrative of binary opposition. But while Nietzsche acknowledged that "the typical prejudice" and "fundamental faith" of all metaphysicians "is the faith in opposite values,"[26] he nevertheless continued to utilize such oppositional pairs as master morality and slave morality, Apollonian and Dionysian, life-enhancement and life-negation, and so on. And as a consequence, his texts present us with the recurring problem of how to understand his use of dualistic concepts in a non-oppositional way. To pose this problem as starkly as possible, alongside the monistic final note, quoted above, from Nietzsche's most (in) famous unpublished work, that "this world is will to power – and nothing besides," we need only set the final remark of his final (albeit posthumously) *published* work, which appears to pose the ultimate binary choice: "Have I been understood? – *Dionysus versus the Crucified.*"[27]

Nietzsche's semiotically condensed formula has its analog in what Deleuze and Guattari call their "magic formula . . . PLURALISM = MONISM."[28] Like Nietzsche, Deleuze and Guattari collapse the distinction between monism and pluralism, and they likewise follow Nietzsche in their willingness to utilize binary concepts *strategically*. This willingness to adopt a binary format marks one of the most obvious points at which Deleuze and Guattari differentiate themselves from Derrida and other recent French thinkers as well as from the Hegelian tradition. While the Hegelian *Aufhebung* resolves dualistic opposition in a higher synthesis, Derrida traces binary opposition to a more primordial transcendental "non-concept" (for example, "*archi-trace*" as condition for the possibility of the opposition between writing and speech or "*différance*" as what makes possible both the presentation or absence of the being-present).[29] In contrast, even a brief survey of some of their basic analytic categories – paranoia and schizophrenia, molar and molecular, arborescent and rhizomatic, state apparatus and nomad war machine, smooth and striated – shows Deleuze and Guattari to be content to work within the framework of a certain kind of binarism, one which seeks not to dissolve but to multiply dualistic concepts. While Nietzsche leaves unthematized the problem of utilizing dualistic concepts in non-oppositional ways, Deleuze and Guattari confront this issue directly in the introduction to *A Thousand Plateaus*, where they admit to using dualisms but only in order to challenge other dualisms. When binary concepts are employed, "mental correctives are necessary" to undo those dualisms that one does not "wish to construct but through which [one must] pass" as one moves beyond dualisms to the realization of a pluralist monism.[30] One can use dualistic concepts, indeed their use may be necessary; but one must take care both to avoid privileging and reifying these dualisms as absolute while remembering that these dualisms mark *differences* rather than oppositions and remembering as well that their use is always provisional.

Arriving at the perspective of a pluralist or polyvalent monism which can acknowledge differences without falling victim to conceiving these differences as marking inherently opposed subjects is one of the central points of contact between the projects of Nietzsche and Deleuze. When Nietzsche claimed that everything is will to power, he drew our attention away from substances, subjects, and things and focused that attention instead on the relations *between* these substantives. Such relations, according to Nietzsche, were relations of forces: forces of attraction and repulsion, domination and subordination, imposition and reception, and so on. If there is a metaphysic in Nietzsche, and I'm not at all sure that there is or that it is particularly helpful to view Nietzsche in these terms (as Heidegger did), then this metaphysic will be a dynamic, "process" metaphysic and not a substance-metaphysic, a metaphysic of becomings and not of beings. These processes, these becomings, will be processes of forces: becomings-stronger or becomings-weaker, enhancement or impoverishment. There is, for Nietzsche, no escaping these becomings other than death. The goal he advocates, therefore, is not to seek Being but to strive for the balance-sheet of one's life to include more becomings-stronger than -weaker, more overcomings than goings-under.

When we look to Deleuze's work, we can see him making double use of Nietzsche's will to power. Deleuze engages in a project that reformulates traditional binary disjunctions between given alternatives in terms of a pluralistic continuum in which choices are always local and relative rather than global and absolute. When, for example, he speaks with Guattari of a continuum of desiring production, the model they appeal to takes the form of Nietzsche's "monism" of the will to power understood as the differential of forces rather than in the Heideggerian sense of will to power as Nietzsche's foundational answer to the metaphysical question of the Being of beings.[31] This is to say, where Heidegger, himself the consummate metaphysician, understood will to power in terms of a logic of Being, an onto-logic, Deleuze situates will to power within a differential logic of affirmation and negation that facilitates the interpretation and evaluation of active and reactive forces. Will to power thus operates at the genealogical and not the ontological level, at the level of the qualitative and quantitative differences between forces and the different values bestowed upon those forces rather than at the level of Being and beings.[32] In going beyond good and evil, beyond truth and error to the claim that all is will to power, Nietzsche attempted to think relationality without substances, relations without relata, difference without exclusion. And in so doing, his thought serves as a model for Deleuze's desiring assemblages conceived in terms of a logic of events.

In addition to using Nietzsche's formal structure as a model, Deleuze seizes upon what we might call the "content" of Nietzsche's will to power and he offers expanded accounts of the two component poles: will and power. While French thought in general has been working for the past thirty years under the aegis of the three so-called "masters of suspicion," Nietzsche, Freud, and Marx, we can understand Deleuze privileging Nietzsche over Marx and Freud on precisely this point. Marx operates primarily with the register of power and Freud operates primarily within the register of desire. Yet each appears blind to the overlapping of these two registers, and when they do relate them, one is clearly subordinate to the other. Nietzsche's will to power, on the other hand, makes impossible any privileging of one over the other, and his thinking functions in terms of an inclusive conjunction of desire and power. That is to say, for Nietzsche, "will to power" is redundant insofar as will wills power and power manifests itself only through will. In privileging Nietzsche over Marx or Freud, Deleuze recognizes the complicity between the poles of will and power and, as a consequence, he can focus on one of the poles without diminishing the importance of the other pole or excluding it altogether from his analyses.[33]

In his own studies and especially in his work with Guattari, Deleuze has focused on the *willing* of power – desire. Like Foucault, he refrains from subjectifying desire while recognizing the intimate and multiple couplings of desire and power. In *Nietzsche and Philosophy*, Deleuze first linked the notion of desire with will to power, and the insight that desire is productive develops out of his reflection on will to power in terms of the productivity of both active and reactive forces. In *Anti-Oedipus*, he and Guattari introduced the desiring machine as a machinic, functionalist translation of Nietzschean will to power. A desiring machine is a functional assemblage of a desiring will and the object desired. Deleuze's goal, I think, is to place desire into a functionalist vocabulary, a machinic index, so as to avoid the personification/subjectivation of desire in a substantive will, ego, unconscious, or self. By avoiding the organicist connotations of a discrete subject characterized by a realm of interiority within which desire will be located, Deleuze can avoid the paradox Nietzsche sometimes faced when speaking of will to power without a subject doing the willing or implying that will to power was both the producing "agent" and the "object" produced. Insofar as the machinic language of assemblages connotes exteriority – connections with the outside are always already being made – to speak of desire as part of an assemblage, to refuse to reify or personify desire at the subject pole, recognizes that desire and the object desired arise together. Deleuze rejects the account of desire as lack – a view shared by Freud, Lacan, Sartre, and many others[34] – which assumes that desire arises in response to the perceived lack of the object desired or that desire is a state produced in the subject by the lack of the object. Instead, for Deleuze desire is a part of the infrastructure:[35] it is constitutive of the objects desired as well as the social field in which they appear.[36] Desire, again like Nietzsche's will to power, is productive. And as Nietzsche sought to keep will to power multiple so that it might appear in multiple forms, at once producer and product, a monism and a pluralism, so too Deleuze wants desire to be multiple, polyvocal.[37] Nietzsche encouraged the maximizing of strong, healthy will to power while acknowledging the necessity – indeed, the inevitability – of weak, decadent will to power. Deleuze advocates that desire be productive while recognizing that desire will sometimes be destructive and will sometimes have to be repressed, while at other times it will seek and produce its own repression. Analyzing this phenomenon of desire seeking its own repression is one of the goals of Deleuze and Guattari's schizoanalysis, and we should not fail to notice the structural similarity between desire desiring its own repression and Nietzsche's "discovery" in *On the Genealogy of Morals* that the will would rather will nothingness than not will.[38]

To speak very generally, we can say that as Deleuze appropriates Nietzsche, will to power is transformed into a desiring-machine: Nietzsche's biologism becomes Deleuze's machinism; Nietzsche's "everything is will to power" becomes Deleuze's "everything is desire"; Nietzsche's affirmation of healthy will to power becomes Deleuze's affirmation of desiring-production. Now, what is to be gained, one might ask, through this transformation? By way of answering this question, I will proffer two textual experiments. In the first, moving from Deleuze to Nietzsche, I will show how one could use a Deleuzian approach to offer a novel interpretation of one of Nietzsche's central themes: the *Übermensch*. In the second experiment, I will reverse the direction and show how attending to Nietzsche's genealogical critique of Christian morality highlights a number of features in Deleuze and Guattari's critique of psychoanalaysis.

Becoming-*Übermensch*

One of the themes frequenting Deleuze's later work is the process he calls "becoming." He distinguishes becoming from several other transformative processes with which it can be confused, most notably evolution. The central feature distinguishing becoming is the absence of fixed terms:

What is real is the becoming itself, the block of becoming, not the supposedly fixed terms through which that which becomes passes. . . . Becoming produces nothing other than itself. . . . [A] becoming lacks a subject distinct from itself. . . . Becoming is a verb with a consistency all its own; it does not reduce to, or lead back to, "appearing," "being," "equaling," or "producing."³⁹

What Deleuze finds lacking in all of these apparent synonyms for "becoming" is the focus on process itself. Whereas evolutionary language focuses our attention on the beginning and endpoint of a process in a way that obscures the passage between them, the language of compound becoming draws our attention to what happens *between* these ever-receding endpoints. Becomings take place *between* poles, they are the in-betweens that pass only and always along a middle without origin or destination.⁴⁰

The experimental value of these movements of becoming are displayed, for example, in Deleuze and Guattari's reading of Kafka, especially in terms of Kafka's use of metamorphosis as a counter to metaphor. Whereas metaphor recalls relations of resemblance and imitation, metamorphosis inscribes processes of becoming. They read "The Metamorphosis" not as an allegory of an individual who considers himself to be as insignificant as an insect, a reading that would interpret the insect as a metaphor or symbol of dehumanized humanity. It is, instead, the becoming-insect of Gregor that is the "subject" of the story: Gregor's becoming-insect deterritorializes the politics of the family, only to be re-territorialized by his family, as his refusal to give up the picture of his sister leads to the throwing of the apple which eventually results in Gregor's becoming-dead. Likewise, the becoming-machine of the officer in "The Penal Colony" or the becoming-human of the ape in "Report to an Academy" is at issue in Kafka's short stories. This attention to becoming allows Deleuze and Guattari, and their readers, to experiment with alternative notions of subjectivity as a process of multiplicity in which Kafka's characters are freed radically to transform themselves while becoming-other. This is to say, Kafka's characters are freed from the constraints imposed upon them by the more traditional psychoanalytic or existential interpretations, which overdetermine these subjects as fixed and fully formed, albeit Oedipally crippled or socially/inter-subjectively alienated. On Deleuze and Guattari's reading, on the other hand, anything is possible – the subject is a process of multiple becoming in which anything can be connected to anything else; humanity becomes insect becomes ape becomes killing machine becomes humanity, *da capo*.

An attention to becoming can also be put to use in terms of experimenting with Nietzsche's *Übermensch*, and many of the interpretive paradoxes concerning the *Übermensch* can be avoided if one refrains from interpreting *Übermensch* as Nietzsche's model of the ideal subject or perfect human being. Unfortunately, many of Nietzsche's most influential interpreters, including among others Heidegger and Kaufmann, have viewed the *Übermensch* in just this way. Caricaturist images from the left and right thus portray Nietzsche's *Übermensch* alternatively as a model of the Maslowian self-actualized individual or a fascist moral monster. We thus find, on the one hand, Arthur Danto writing:

> The *Übermensch*, accordingly, is not the blond giant dominating his lesser fellows. He is merely a joyous, guiltless, free human being, in possession of instinctual drives which do not overpower him. He is the master and not the slave of his drives, and so he is in a position to make something of himelf rather than being the product of instinctual discharge and external obstacle.[41]

And on the other hand, we have the example of J. P. Stern:

> [Nietzsche] seems unaware that he is giving us nothing to distinguish the fanaticism that goes with bad faith from his own belief in the unconditioned value of self-realization and self-becoming – that is, from his own belief in the Superman. We for our part are bound to look askance at this questionable doctrine. We can hardly forget that the solemn avowal of this reduplicated self – the pathos of personal authenticity – was the chief tenet of fascism and national socialism. No man came closer to the full realization of self-created "values" than A. Hitler.[42]

Nietzsche himself warned against interpreting the word *Übermensch* either as "a higher kind of man" or in a Darwinistic, evolutionary fashion.[43] It therefore seems mistaken to read Nietzsche as a philosopher of the Superman or as someone who seeks to exalt Man as that being who will serve as God's replacement in terms of some new anthropo-theology following the death of God. As Deleuze himself notes in the Appendix to his book on Foucault, it is not Nietzsche but Feuerbach who is the thinker of the death of God and who seeks to install Man in the space vacated by God's absence.[44] For Nietzsche, on the other hand, God's death is an old story, of interest only to the last Pope,[45] a story told in several ways, more often as comedy than tragedy.[46]

Rather than trying to understand what Nietzsche means by *Übermensch* in terms of some model of ideal humanity, a Deleuzian approach would experiment with how the *Übermensch* functions in the Nietzschean text. One notes immediately that we are told very little about what an *Übermensch* is like, and Nietzsche nowhere gives us as detailed a picture of the *Übermensch* as we have of the last man, the higher men, the free spirit, or the slave and master moralists. As Deleuze remarks, "we have to content ourselves with very tentative indications if we are not to descend to the level of cartoons."[47] Unfortunately, too often the discourse descends to this level as Nietzsche's commentators seek to provide an answer to the question "Who is Nietzsche's *Übermensch*?" If we look to how "*Übermensch*" functions in the Nietzschean text, however, we find it functioning not as the name of a particular being or type of being. "*Übermensch*" is, rather, the name given to a certain idealized conglomeration of forces, what Nietzsche calls, in *Ecce Homo*, "a type of supreme achievement."[48] Nietzsche does not provide, in *Thus Spoke Zarathustra* or anywhere else, a philosophical guidebook for *Übermensch*; he provides instead suggestions for steps to take in order to become-*Übermensch*. Following Deleuze, I would suggest we construe becoming-*Übermensch* with a hyphen as a compound verb marking a compound assemblage. In so doing, we draw attention to the active process of assembling rather than hypostatizing, re- or deifying the endpoint to be assembled. We can only speak of the becoming-*Übermensch* of human beings, of the process of accumulating strength and exerting mastery outside the limits of external authoritarian impositions. Nietzsche called this process of becoming-*Übermensch* "life-enhancement," and he indicated by this a process of self-overcoming and increasing of will to power rather than an ideal form of subjectivity. Nietzsche's failure – or more accurately, his refusal in *Thus Spoke Zarathustra* – to present an *Übermensch* in any form other than as a vision or a riddle thus leads to the conclusion that the answer to the question "Is S an *Übermensch*?" will always be "No" insofar as "*Übermensch*" does not designate an ontological state or way of being that a subject could instantiate.[49] By experimenting with the different possibilities of becoming-*Übermensch*, we can read *Thus Spoke Zarathustra* not as providing the blueprint for constructing a centered super-subject called "Overman," as was tragically the case in several readings of Nietzsche offered earlier this century. Instead, an experimental approach attends to Zarathustra's own experimentalism, noting as he does that one must find one's own way, "for *the* way – that does not exist."[50] This approach will emphasize not a way of Being but the affirmation of self-overcoming and transvaluation that makes possible the infinite processes of becoming that I am here suggesting we call becoming-*Übermensch*.

Anti-Oedipus, or the Genealogy of Psychoanalysis

As we turn now to the second experiment, I must admit that the details of Deleuze and Guattari's critique of psychoanalytic theory and practice and the relations between psychoanalysis and capitalism are far too complex to be addressed in a short chapter. What I would like here to suggest is that the outlines of their critique can be sketched in terms of the ways this critique follows an analytic pattern elaborated nearly a century earlier by Nietzsche in *On the Genealogy of Morals*.[51] While no one would question the author of the *Antichrist* having influenced the development of the argument by the authors of the *Anti-Oedipus*, I want to bring clearly into view several of the ways Deleuze and Guattari draw upon Nietzsche's genealogical account of church practices as they analyze the practices of psychoanalysis.

It will be helpful at this point to rehearse very quickly some of the central issues in Nietzsche's analysis of the origins of bad conscience and the alliance between the church and the state that appear in the *Genealogy*, a work Deleuze and Guattari cite as "*the* great book of modern ethnology."[52] In the first essay, Nietzsche chronicles "the birth of Christianity out of the spirit of *ressentiment*."[53] The inability to respond actively leads to the invention of a concept that will legitimate and justify this inability – the concept "subject." By the invention of the subject, the slave creates a substratum (ultimately the soul) which underlies and supports activity and is conceived as *free not to act*. The slave can now demand of strength that it should not express itself as strength, that it should not desire to overcome nor desire to be master. Slave morality thus draws the moral implication that the strong don't have to be evil; they could have chosen, like the weak, to be good, not to act. Like a lamb who regards itself as a bird of prey that *chooses* to refrain from action, the slavish type's invention of the subject/soul as a fiction separating force from what it can do allows it to interpret itself as good, to interpret its essential lack of strength as a voluntary, meritorious achievement; in other words, the invention of the subject allows the slaves to interpret their weakness as freedom.

The second essay traces the cruel history of disciplinary mnemotechnics involved in breeding the powers of memory that make possible guilt, bad conscience, punishment and responsibility – that is, morality – in human beings. Pain, Nietzsche notes, it the most powerful aid to mnemonics: if something is to remain in memory it must be burned in, it must hurt.[54] To explain the mechanics of this breeding, Nietzsche turns first to the origins of guilt and bad conscience. These origins lie in the economic relation of creditor and debtor. The moral concept "guilt," conceived as a debt that is essentially unredeemable, has its origin in the economic, legal notion of debt as essentially repayable. We see this in the origin of punishment, which as retribution emerges from the inability to repay the debt. *Schuld*, debt/guilt, is part of the strange logic of compensation which seeks to establish equivalences between creditors and debtors: because everything has its price and all things can be paid for, the debtors, having made a promise to repay, would offer a substitute payment of something they possessed: their body, their spouse, their freedom, even their life. Here we see the primitive intertwining of guilt and suffering: suffering will balance debts to the extent that the creditors get pleasure from making suffer. There is, for Nietzsche, a basic joy in the exercising of mastery, and by making suffer, the creditors thus participate in the pleasures of the masters. For Nietzsche, the degree to which cruelty constituted a pleasure for primitive people is evidenced by their turning this suffering into a festival play for themselves and the gods.

When he turns to modern cultures, Nietzsche observes a spiritualization and deification of cruelty. Whereas the primitives were cheerful, modern man is ashamed of his instincts for cruelty. Modern man has to invent free will to justify suffering: punishment now appears as deserved because one could have done otherwise, which is to say, punishment now appears no longer as the result of the human desire for pleasure and mastery but instead as the consequence of God's judgment. The "moral" function of punishment is thus to awaken the feeling of guilt, and it is supposed to function as an instrument to create bad conscience. To this account, Nietzsche offers his own account of the origin of bad conscience as a serious illness contracted when human beings entered into communities. Anticipating both the general Freudian model of tension-reduction and the specific account of the functioning of the superego that Freud offers in Chapter VII of *Civilization and its Discontents*, Nietzsche claims that upon entering into a community, the prohibition against discharging one's instincts externally led to these instincts being turned inward. This "internalization [*Verinnerlichung*] of man,"[55] Nietzsche argues, is the origin of "bad conscience," as the instinct for hostility, cruelty, joy in prosecuting and attacking, the desire for change and destruction are inhibited from being discharged and are instead turned against the possessor of these instincts. Bad conscience, that uncanniest of illnesses, Nietzsche thus concludes, is man's suffering of himself.

In an analytic move that clearly inspires Deleuze and Guattari's materialist psychiatry, Nietzsche links this psychological account of bad conscience to the origin of the state as he offers an account of the establishment of society from out of the "state of nature," a tale which echoes the one told by Hobbes much more than the myth told by Locke or Rousseau. Bad conscience does not originate gradually or voluntarily, but all at once. This change is initiated by an act of violence: the institution of the state. The state is a violent, tyrannical, oppressive machine, created by those unconscious, involuntary artists and beasts of prey – the conquerors and masters who impose form on nomadic, formless masses. Although the masters themselves lack bad conscience, it originates through their making latent in others the instinct for freedom. When repressed and incarcerated, this instinct for freedom – the will to power as autonomous imposition of form – can only be turned against itself. In other words, while masters and artists are able to vent their will to power on others, the weak can only vent their will to power on themselves and they can experience the joy in making suffer only by making themselves suffer.

While its origin resides in the institution of the primeval state, bad conscience plays a central role in the evolution of the state's modern form. Bad conscience, Nietzsche tells us, is an illness as pregnancy is an illness,[56] and he concludes the Second Essay by exposing this illness's progeny to be Christian morality and the church. As society evolved, the creditor/debtor relation took the form of a relation between the present generation and its ancestors: we pay back our ancestors by obeying their customs. Our debt to our ancestors increases to the extent that the power of the community increases. Ultimately, our ancestors are transfigured into gods and, in successive generations, this unpaid debt to our ancestors is inherited with interest. As the power of the community increases, as the community advances toward a universal empire, the divinity of the ancestors also increases. With Christianity, Nietzsche sees a "stroke of genius" in the eventual moralization of debt/guilt and duty, as the Christian God, "the maximum God attained so far," is accompanied by maximum indebtedness. Christianity's stroke of genius was to have God sacrifice himself for the guilt of humanity. By sacrificing himself for the debtor, the creditor both removed the debt and made the debt eternal and ultimately unredeemable. The origin of the Christian God is this mad will to guilt and punishment, this will to a punishment incapable of becoming equal to the guilt. This new guilt before God results in the complete deification of God as holy judge and hangman, at once man's infinite antithesis and the ultimate instrument of his self-torture.[57]

Nietzsche's *On the Genealogy of Morals* shows the ways in which the ascetic priests, in the form of the founders of Christianity and the ideologues of science, have constructed an interpretation of the modern world in which they are made to appear essential.[58] Deleuze and Guattari argue that the psychoanalyst is the "most recent figure of the priest"[59] and throughout *Anti-Oedipus* their analyses of the practices of psychoanalysis parallel the practices of Christianity as analyzed by Nietzsche. Like the early priests, psychoanalysts have re-interpreted the world in a way that makes themselves indispensable. The whole psychoanalytic edifice is constructed on the basis of the Oedipal drama, and the primary task of psychoanalysis is to successfully Oedipalize its public: "Oedipus is the disease," the psychoanalysts announce, "and we have the cure!" Nietzsche showed how much of Christianity's practice requires convincing its adherents of their guilt and sin in order to make tenable Christianity's own claim of redemptive power. Deleuze and Guattari take a similar approach, developing at length the ways in which the psychological liberation promised by psychoanalysis requires first that it imprison libidinal economy within the confines of the family. To Nietzsche's "internalization of man," they add man's Oedipalization: Oedipus repeats the split movement of Nietzschean bad conscience – projecting onto the other while turning back against oneself – as the unsatisfied desire to eliminate and replace the father is accompanied by guilt for having such desire. They view psychoanalytic interpretive practices as no less reductive than the interpretations of Nietzsche's ascetic priests. Just as Nietzsche's priests reduce all events to a moment within the logic of divine reward and punishment, Deleuze and Guattari's psychoanalysts reduce all desire to a form of familial fixation. Like Nietzsche's ascetic priests, psychoanalysts have created for themselves a mask of health that has the power to tyrannize the healthy by poisoning their conscience. Where Nietzsche notes the *irony* of the Christian God sacrificing himself for humanity *out of love*, Deleuze and Guattari ironically chronicle the various expressions of the psychoanalysts' concern for their Oedipally crippled patients. The ultimate outcomes of these ironic twists also parallel one another: where Christianity's self-sacrificing God makes infinite its adherents guilt and debt, psychoanalysis creates its own infinite debt in the form of inexhaustible transference and interminable analysis.[60]

What is, I think, the most interesting transformation of Nietzsche's analysis is the way Deleuze and Guattari adapt Nietzsche's link between the rise of Christianity and the rise of the state to their discussion of libidinal and political economy. They want to introduce desire into the social field at all levels and this prompts their critique of psychoanalysis. Freud could only view libidinal social investments as subliminal and, as a result, he interpreted all social relations as desexualized representations of unconscious desire. Likewise, when sexual relations do appear in the social field, they are interpreted by Freud as symbolic representations of the Oedipal family. Deleuze and Guattari want to liberate desire from its enslavement within the theater of representation, and they reject the reductive familialism which sees the family everywhere while it obscures all relations of wealth, class, gender, race – that is, all social relations outside the family. They criticize Freud for failing to acknowledge the sexual dimension of economic dependence, a failure exemplified in his consistent reduction of women of subordinate social standing ("maids," "peasant girls," and so on) to substitutes for incest with the mother or sister (for example, in the case of the "Rat Man" or the "Wolf Man").[61] For Deleuze and Guattari, on the other hand, every investment, libidinal or otherwise, is social.[62] "One can put it best by saying that social investments are themselves erotic and, inversely, that the most erotic of desires brings about a fully political and social investment, engages with an entire social field."[63] Insofar as social production is libidinal and libidinal production is social, they claim it is a mistake to desexualize the social field.

> The truth is that sexuality is everywhere: in the way that a bureau-crat fondles his records, a judge administers justice, a businessman causes money to circulate; in the way the bourgeoisie fucks the proletariat; and so on. And there is no need to resort to metaphors, any more than for the libido to go by way of metamorphoses. Hitler got the fascists sexually aroused. Flags, nations, armies, banks get a lot of people aroused.[64]

Revising both Marx and Freud, Deleuze and Guattari conclude that insofar as desire is constitutive of the social field, "social production is desiring-production *under determinate conditions*."[65]

In linking desire to production in this way, Deleuze and Guattari "replace the theatrical or familial model of the unconscious with a more political model: the factory instead of the theater."[66] The question of desire is, *pace* Freud, a question not of dramatic familial representation but of material production, which is to say, a political question, a question of experimentation, power and justice. This is the point at which they replace psychoanalysis with schizoanalysis or, as they put it, this makes clear the need to "schizoanalyze the psychoanalyst."[67] Psychoanalysis has failed to recognize that the successful Oedipalization of its public depends upon the phenomenon discussed earlier of desire desiring its own repression. For Deleuze and Guattari, the discovery of this phenomenon is associated first and foremost with Wilhelm Reich,[68] who refused to explain fascism in terms of the false consciousness of the masses. Instead, Reich formulated an explanation that takes the desires of the masses into account: they *wanted* fascism, and it is this perverse manifestation of desire that must be explained. For Reich, the explanation comes in terms of the pleasures of exercising authority that are vicariously experienced by the "little man's" identification with the "Führer."[69] Deleuze and Guattari's account of this desire, along with their fascination with the relation of the officer to the machine in Kafka's "Penal Colony" and their analyses of psychoanalysis, leads them to Nietzsche's *Genealogy of Morals*. Here, in Nietzsche's account of the will to nothingness as preferable to not willing and in bad conscience choosing to make itself suffer rather than relinquish the pleasure in making suffer, they locate their answer to Reich's question of the link between psychic repression and social repression in the libidinal economy of fascism. Where Reich saw desire activated through a passive identification of the masses with their fascist master (s), Nietzsche saw the ascetic desire to make itself suffer as perverse but fundamentally *active* and ultimately *positive* because through this perverse desire, "*the will itself was saved.*"[70]

On the basis of their experimentations with Reich and Nietzsche, Deleuze and Guattari draw the following conclusion: desire is productive, it must be productive, and it will be productive. If a social field does not allow for desire to be productive in non-repressive forms, then it will produce in whatever forms are available to it, even those that it recognizes to be socially or psychically repressive. Like Nietzsche's will to power, Deleuze and Guattari conclude that desire can only be analyzed locally, relative to the social field in which it operates. There can be no global, universal or totalizing judgment concerning desire. As Nietzsche's Third Essay of the *Genealogy of Morals* analyzed the concrete practices of the ascetic priests in terms of the enhancement and impoverishment of will to power, Deleuze and Guattari continued this critique, questioning political and psychoanalytic practices in terms of productive and repressive libidinal capacities, microproductivities and microfascisms. The question that must ultimately be placed to their work, a question first articulated by Nietzsche with regard to truth which Deleuze and Guattari themselves articulate in terms of the challenges posed by desire, is not "what does it mean?" or "is it true?" but "does it work?"[71] In the preceding pages, we have seen some of the ways that it does.

Conclusion

In *Dialogues*, Deleuze wrote that "my ideal, when I write about an author, would be to write nothing that could cause him sadness, or if he is dead, that might make him weep in his grave. . . . To bring back to an author a little of that joy, that force, that amorous and political life, that he knew how to give and invent."[72] In the case of his writings on Nietzsche, I think Deleuze has met this ideal. Nietzsche often noted the posthumous character of his work, predicting that in the next century, he would find his rightful heirs, the "philosophers of the future" to whom his works were addressed. There can be little doubt that Deleuze is one of those philosophers, and his work, along with the work of Derrida and Foucault, is largely responsible for the ascription of "Nietzscheanism" to recent French thought.[73] That Nietzsche would find his rightful heirs among the French, with whose culture and language he felt a special kinship, would neither have surprised nor displeased him.[74] A century earlier, Nietzsche remarked that he found the most recent Frenchmen "charming company," noting that it would be hard to find anywhere in past history "such inquisitive and at the same time such delicate psychologists as in contemporary Paris."[75] More significantly, perhaps, he included the French among his "most natural readers and listeners."[76] To be a reader of Nietzsche, we must recall, is not to receive his words as truths or to follow him as a disciple, two situations he openly tried to forestall. "We honour the great artists of the past," Nietzsche wrote in *Assorted Opinions and Maxims*, "less through that unfruitful awe which allows every word, every note, to lie where it has been put than we do through active endeavours to help them to come repeatedly to life again."[77] Rather than an aesthetics of reception, Nietzsche's works call for a performative hermeneutics. As someone who considered "to have been written in vain every word behind which there does not stand a challenge to action,"[78] Nietzsche's "rightful readers" will be those incited to action by his works, to the action of transvaluing values. Recent French philosophy has answered Nietzsche's call and responded to his challenge. The diversity of readings often collected together as "the French Nietzsche" has played a significant role in the renaissance of interest in Nietzsche that has flourished since the 1960s. And with

Gilles Deleuze's "active endeavours" at the forefront, Nietzsche's words have come repeatedly to life again in France and elsewhere, both as an object for philosophical reflection and as a tool brought to bear upon the most pressing philosophical, political, and cultural problems of the present.

NOTES

An earlier version of this paper was presentd in October, 1988 at Northwestern University at the annual meeting of the Society for Phenomenology and Existential Philosophy. A somewhat different version was also presented in March, 1991 at a panel on the "French Nietzsche" organized by the North American Nietzsche Society. This later paper, published as "Between Church and State: Nietzsche, Deleuze and the Genealogy of Psychoanalysis" in the Summer, 1992 issue of *International Studies in Philosophy*, benefited from John T. Wilcox's editorial suggestions and includes several paragraphs from the present paper.

1 "Intellectuals and Power: A Conversation between Michel Foucault and Gilles Deleuze," trans. Donald F. Bouchard and Sherry Simon in Michel Foucault, *Language, Counter-Memory, Practice*, edited by Donald F. Bouchard (Ithaca: Cornell University Press, 1977), p. 208.
2 Gilles Deleuze, *Nietzsche et la Philosophie* (Paris: PUF, 1962); English translation: *Nietzsche and Philosophy*, trans. Hugh Tomlinson (New York: Columbia University Press, 1983); Jacques Derrida, *Éperons: Les Styles de Nietzsche/ Spurs: Nietzsche's Styles*, trans. Barbara Harlow (Chicago: University of Chicago Press, 1978). Derrida's text is a revised version of his presentation "*La question du style*" at the colloquium on Nietzsche at Cerisy-la-Salle in July, 1972.
3 The anti-Hegelian character of *Nietzsche and Philosophy* is the focus of the second chapter of Michael Hardt's *Gilles Deleuze: An Apprenticeship in Philosophy* (Minneapolis: University of Minnesota Press, 1993), pp. 26–55.
4 See, for example, the contrast drawn between Nietzsche and Rousseau in *Of Grammatology*, and the related contrast between Levi-Strauss and Nietzsche in "Structure, Sign and Play in the Discourse of the Human Sciences," in *Writing and Difference*.
5 The most famous example here is, of course, the concluding paragraphs of "Structure, Sign, and Play in the Discourse of the Human Sciences" in *Writing and Difference*, trans. Alan Bass (Chicago: University of Chicago Press, 1978), where "Nietzsche" appears as the name of that other interpretation of interpretation, of structure, of sign, of play (pp. 292–3).
6 What follows draws upon chapter four of my *Nietzsche and the Question of Interpretation: Between Hermeneutics and Deconstruction* (New York: Routledge, 1990), where I offer a much more detailed reading of *Spurs*.
7 Jacques Derrida, "*Différance*," in *Margins of Philosophy*, trans. Alan Bass (Chicago: University of Chicago Press, 1982), p. 27.
8 One of the few critics to discuss this work in the context of French post-structuralism is Vincent P. Pecora, in "Deleuze's Nietzsche and Post-Structuralism," *Sub-Stance*, 48 (1986): 34–50. Although largely critical of

Deleuze's reading of Nietzsche, Pecora is, I think, correct in indicating the formative role played by Deleuze's replacement of " *'le travail de la dialectique'* by the play of *'différence'* " in the emergence of post-structuralism (p. 36). The importance of Nietzsche in Deleuze's thought and post-structuralist French philosophy is also one of the leading themes of Ronald Bogue's fine introductory text *Deleuze and Guattari* (London and New York: Routledge, 1989); see, in particular, his concluding comments, pp. 156–63.

9 See Deleuze, *Nietzsche and Philosophy*, p. 197.

10 See Deleuze, *Nietzsche and Philosophy*, p. 180.

11 See Deleuze, *Nietzsche and Philosophy*, p. 50.

12 This discussion of *Niezsche and Philosophy* is a slightly revised and abridged version of my discussion in *Nietzsche and the Question of Interpretation*, pp. 82–3.

13 Gilles Deleuze, "Lettre à un critique sévère" (Michel Cressole, 1972), re-printed in *Pourparlers* (Paris: Éditions de Minuit, 1990), pp. 14–15.

14 See Michel Foucault, "The Discourse on Language," trans. Rupert Swyer as an appendix to *The Archaeology of Knowledge* (New York: Harper & Row, Publishers, Inc., 1972), pp. 215–37.

15 Deleuze and Claire Parnet, *Dialogues*, trans. Hugh Tomlinson and Barbara Habberjam (New York: Columbia University Press, 1987), p. 13. See also Deleuze's remarks in the preface to *Différence et Répétition* (Paris: PUF, 1968), pp. 4–5, on the relation between philosophy and the history of philosophy, where he comments that the ideal writing of the history of philosophy will be both a repetition of and differentiation from its own history.

16 Deleuze and Parnet, *Dialogues*, pp. 14–15; see also *Pourparlers*, p. 14. The phrase "bureaucracy of pure reason" is suggested by Deleuze's concluding remarks in "Nomad Thought," trans. David B. Allison in *The New Nietzsche*, edited by David B. Allison (New York: Dell Publishing Co., Inc. 1979), p. 149.

17 See, for example, the following remark in Gilles Deleuze and Félix Guattari, "Rhizome," trans. Paul Patton, *I&C*, 8 (spring 1981): "In a book, there is nothing to understand, but much to make use of. Nothing to interpret or signify, but much to experiment with" (pp. 67–8). This version of "Rhizome" was published separately prior to the appearance of *A Thousand Plateaus*, and it differs slightly from the version that introduced the second volume of *Capitalism and Schizophrenia*.

18 See Deleuze and Parnet, *Dialogues*, pp. 46–8.

19 See Gilles Deleuze, "Pensée nomade", in *Nietzsche aujourd'hui I* (Paris: Union Générale d'Éditions, 1973), pp. 159–74; "Nomad Thought," 142–9.

20 Deleuze, *Nietzsche aujourd'hui I*, p. 186. While this remark accurately char-acterizes Deleuze's post-1968 texts, his skill as a "commentator" in his earlier texts on Hume, Nietzsche, Kant, Bergson, and Spinoza should not be undervalued.

21 My formulation of this distinction between Deleuze and Derrida has ben-efited from the insightful comments of Jeffrey Nealon on an earlier draft of this essay.

22 Jacques Derrida, "Interpreting Signatures (Nietzsche/Heidegger): Two Questions," trans. Diane Michelfelder and Richard E. Palmer included in the present volume, pp. 53–68; and *Otobiographies: The Teaching of Nietzsche*

and the Politics of the Proper Name, trans. Avital Ronell in *The Ear of the Other*, ed. Christie V. McDonald (New York: Schocken Books, 1985), pp. 1–38.

23 It must be acknowledged that Derrida himself has responded to the facile understanding of this motto as advocating a pan-textualism. In the Afterword appended to *Limited Inc* titled "Toward an Ethic of Discussion," Derrida remarks that the "so badly understood" slogan of deconstruction "*il n'y a pas de hors-texte*" means nothing other than "there is nothing outside context." (*Limited Inc*, trans. Samuel Weber [Evanston: Northwestern University Press, 1988], p. 136.)

24 Deleuze and Guattari, "Rhizome," p. 67.

25 Friedrich Nietzsche, *The Will to Power*, trans. Walter Kaufmann and R. J. Hollingdale (New York: Random House, Inc., 1967), Section 1067; this note appears as fragment 38 [12] in Band 11 of the Colli and Montinari *Kritische Studienausgabe* (Berlin: de Gruyter, 1980).

26 Friedrich Nietzsche, *Beyond Good and Evil*, trans. Walter Kaufmann (New York: Random House, Inc., 1966), Section 2.

27 Friedrich Nietzsche, *Ecce Homo*, trans. Walter Kaufmann (New York: Random House, Inc., 1967), "Why I Am a Destiny," Section 9.

28 Deleuze and Guattari, *A Thousand Plateaus*, trans. Brian Massumi (Minneapolis: University of Minnesota Press, 1987), p. 20.

29 The issue of the transcendental character of Derrida's thinking is a complicated one which I only wish to raise here in order to sharpen the contrast with Deleuze. To be sure, unlike many other transcendental thinkers, Derrida's transcendental "non-concepts" are not foundational. But it seems to me impossible to overlook the transcendental nature of his "explication" of, for example, "*différance*" in the interviews collected in *Positions* as well as in the essay "*Différance*." While I do not want to question the innovative and radical character of Derrida's interventions into the history of philosophy, I do want to note the familiar, indeed traditional transcendental character of remarks like the following concerning *différance* being (albeit "*sous rature*") "*ce qui rend possible la présentation de l'étant-présent, elle ne se présente jamais comme telle* [what makes possible the presentation of the being-present, it never presents itself as such]." (*Marges de la philosophie* [Paris: Éditions de Minuit, 1972], p. 6.)

30 Deleuze and Guattari, *A Thousand Plateaus*, pp. 20–1.

31 See Deleuze, *Nietzsche and Philosophy*, pp. 49–55.

32 Cf. Deleuze, *Nietzsche and Philosophy*, p. 220: "Heidegger gives an interpretation of Nietzschean philosophy closer to his own thought than to Nietzsche's. . . . Nietzsche is opposed to every conception of affirmation which would find its foundation in Being, and its determination in the being of man." I address and criticize Heidegger's interpretation of will to power in some detail in *Nietzsche and the Question of Interpretation*, pp. 53–73.

33 Elsewhere I address many of these same points in the context of Foucault's analytic of power and its connection with Nietzsche. See my "Reconfiguring the Subject: Foucault's Analytics of Power," to appear in *Reconstructing Foucault: Essays in the Wake of the 80s*, edited by Ricardo Miguel-Alfonso and Silvia Caporale-Bizzini.

34 This tradition goes back at least as far as Plato, who argues in the *Symposium* (200a–d) that one who desires something is necessarily in want of that thing. I discuss the Deleuzian critique of "desire as lack" in more detail elsewhere;

see my "Spinoza, Nietzsche, Deleuze: An other discourse of desire" in Hugh Silverman, ed., *Philosophy and the Discourse of Desire* (New York: Routledge, forthcoming).

35 See the discussion of this point in Gilles Deleuze and Félix Guattari, *Anti-Oedipus*, trans. Robert Hurley, Mark Seem and Helen R. Lane (Minneapolis: University of Minnesota Press, 1983), p. 348.

36 We might put this point another way and, using Benveniste's distinction, say that desire situates itself as both the subject of the utterance (*sujet d'énonciation*) and the subject of the statement (*sujet d'énoncé*).

37 Cf. Gilles Deleuze and Félix Guattari, *Kafka: Toward a Minor Literature*, trans. Dana Polan (Minneapolis: University of Minnesota Press, 1986), p. 57.

38 See Friedrich Nietzsche, *On the Genealogy of Morals*, trans. Walter Kaufmann (New York: Random House, Inc., 1967), Essay III, Sections 1 and 28.

39 Deleuze and Guattari, *A Thousand Plateaus*, pp. 238–9.

40 Cf. Deleuze and Guattari, *A Thousand Plateaus*, p. 293.

41 Arthur Danto, *Nietzsche as Philosopher* (New York: Columbia University Press, 1980), pp. 199–200.

42 J. P. Stern, *A Study of Nietzsche* (Cambridge: Cambridge University Press, 1979), p. 117. For an excellent review of the literature concerning the "ideal type" interpretation of the *Übermensch*, see Bernd Magnus, "Perfectibility and Attitude in Nietzsche's *Übermensch*," *Review of Metaphysics* 36 (March 1983): 633–59, and "Nietzsche's Philosophy in 1888; *The Will to Power* and the *Übermensch*," *Journal of the History of Philosophy*, 24, 1 (January 1986): 79–98.

43 See *Ecce Homo*, "Why I Write Such Good Books," Section 1: "The word '*Übermensch*,' as the designation of a type of supreme achievement, as opposed to 'modern' men, to 'good' men, to Christians and other nihilists – a word that in the mouth of a Zarathustra, the annihilator of morality, becomes a very pensive word – has been understood almost everywhere with the utmost innocence in the sense of those very values whose opposite Zarathustra was meant to represent – that is, as an 'idealistic' type of a higher kind of man, half 'saint,' half 'genius.' Other scholarly oxen have suspected me of Darwinism on that account. Even the "hero worship" of that unconscious and involuntary counterfeiter, Carlyle, which I have repudiated so maliciously has been read into it. Those to whom I said in confidence that they should sooner look even for a Cesare Borgia than for a Parsifal, did not believe their own ears."

44 Gilles Deleuze, "On the Death of Man and Superman" in *Foucault*, trans. Seán Hand (Minneapolis: University of Minnesota Press, 1988), p. 130.

45 See Friedrich Nietzsche, *Thus Spoke Zarathustra*, trans. Walter Kaufmann in Kaufmann, ed., *The Viking Portable Nietzsche* (New York: The Viking Press, 1967), "Retired."

46 See Deleuze and Guattari's comments on the death of God and the death of the Oedipal father in *Anti-Oedipus*, pp. 106ff.

47 Deleuze, *Foucault*, p. 130.

48 Nietzsche, *Ecce Homo*, "Why I Write Such Good Books," Section 1.

49 And by implication, this also provides an answer to the interpretive question "Is Zarathustra an *Übermensch*?"

50 Nietzsche, *Thus Spoke Zarathustra*, "On the Spirit of Gravity," Section 2.

51 That the argument in *Anti-Oedipus* follows the same lines as Nietzsche's

argument in the *Genealogy* should not obscure the fact that it also follows the
outlines of Marx's own historical materialist outline of the socio-economic
stages that precede capitalism.

52 Deleuze and Guattari, *Anti-Oedipus*, p. 190. Emphasis added.
53 Nietzsche, *Ecce Homo*, "Genealogy of Morals."
54 The connection between Nietzsche's discussion of painful mnemotechnics
and Kafka's "In the Penal Colony" should not pass unnoticed.
55 Nietzsche, *On the Genealogy of Morals*, Essay II, Section 16.
56 Nietzsche, *On the Genealogy of Morals*, Essay II, Section 19.
57 Cf. Nietzsche, *On the Genealogy of Morals*, Essay II, Section 22.
58 Cf. Friedrich Nietzsche, *The Antichrist*, Section 26.
59 Deleuze and Guattari, *Anti-Oedipus*, pp. 108–12, 269, 332–3. See also *A
Thousand Plateaus*, p. 154.
60 See Deleuze and Guattari, *Anti-Oedipus*, pp. 64–5.
61 See Deleuze and Guattari, *Anti-Oedipus*, pp. 352–4.
62 Deleuze and Guattari, *Anti-Oedipus*, p. 342.
63 Deleuze and Guattari, *Kafka*, p. 64.
64 Deleuze and Guattari, *Anti-Oedipus*, p. 293. (Translation altered slightly.)
65 Deleuze and Guattari, *Anti-Oedipus*, p. 343.
66 Gilles Deleuze, Interview in *L'Arc*, No. 49, Second Edition (1980), p. 99.
See also *Anti-Oedipus*, p. 55.
67 Deleuze and Guattari, *Anti-Oedipus*, p. 365.
68 See Wilhelm Reich, *The Mass Psychology of Fascism*, trans. Vincent R.
Carfagno (London: Souvenir Press, 1970).
69 Cf. Reich, *The Mass Psychology*, pp. 63ff.
70 Nietzsche, *On the Genealogy of Morals*, Essay III, Section 28.
71 See Deleuze and Guattari, *Anti-Oedipus*, p. 109.
72 Deleuze and Parnet, *Dialogues*, p. 119. Translation altered slightly.
73 See, for example, Vincent Descombes, *Modern French Philosophy*, trans. L.
Scott-Fox and J. M. Harding (Cambridge: Cambridge University Press,
1980), pp. 186–90; and Luc Ferry and Alain Renaut, *French Philosophy of the
Sixties: An Essay on Antihumanism*, trans. Mary Schnackenberg Cattani
(Amherst: University of Massachusetts Press, 1990) pp. 68–121. Disclosing
French philosophy's "Nietzscheanism" is also a persistent theme in Jürgen
Habermas's *The Philosophical Discourse of Modernity*, trans. Frederick Law-
rence (Cambridge, MA: MIT Press, 1987).
74 See, for example, *Beyond Good and Evil*, Sections 253–4, *Twilight of the Idols*,
"What the Germans Lack," Section 4. *The Wanderer and His Shadow*, Section 214.
75 Nietzsche, *Ecce Homo*, "Why I Am So Clever," Section 3.
76 Nietzsche, *Ecce Homo*, "The Case of Wagner," Section 3.
77 Friedrich Nietzsche, *Assorted Opinions and Maxims* in *Human, All-Too-
Human*, trans. R. J. Hollingdale (Cambridge: Cambridge University Press,
1986), Section 126.
78 Friedrich Nietzsche, *Schopenhauer as Educator* in *Untimely Meditations*, trans.
R. J. Hollingdale (Cambridge: Cambridge University Press, 1983), p. 184.
Translation modified slightly.

15
The 'Spider's Web' and the 'Tool': Nietzsche *vis-à-vis* Rorty on Metaphor

Alessandra Tanesini

Metaphorical talk is a tricky business. Some metaphors become literal truths, others do not. Some are helpful, others cause one's thinking to go astray. Nietzsche knew that only a light-footed thinker could play with metaphors without having his feet cut by their sharp barbed edges (TI, VI: 2).[1] Others, notably Rorty, who have confused the light-footed thinker with the weak thinker,[2] have not escaped unscathed.

In this philosophical labour I address some questions concerning metaphors in the works of Nietzsche and Rorty. What is characteristic of both philosophers is that they take metaphors to be central to language and cognition, rather than mere additional embellishments. However, they have very different views on how metaphors work and on the consequences that this has for human cognition, and for the history of intellectual change. The metaphors that Rorty and Nietzsche can be taken to use as metaphors for metaphors are, respectively, the 'tool' and the 'spider's web'. I believe that Rorty's metaphor of the 'tool' is, so to speak, a poor tool for understanding the role of metaphor. Nietzsche's spider webs, on the other hand, are delicate enough to sustain the complexity of the issue; however, at times, Nietzsche spins his web in ways that cause this reader to lose track of the overall architecture of the construction.

Rorty presents himself as somebody who has improved on Nietzsche's position. Thus, whilst Rorty takes Nietzsche to be one of his 'ironist' predecessors from whom much is to be learned, he also accuses him of still being entangled in the snares of metaphysical thought.[3] However, I do not think that Rorty appreciates the subtleties of Nietzsche's thought; I believe that he badly interprets and uses Nietzsche's ideas, and that, partly because of this, at some crucial points whilst Rorty remains hooked by his own metaphors, Nietzsche light-footedly walks away.

1 Knowledge and Metaphors

There are many at least superficial similarities between Nietzsche and Rorty on the importance of metaphors for human knowledge. Nietzsche, for example, intimates that we never know anything about things as they are in themselves, and that 'we possess nothing but metaphors for things' (OTL, I, p. 83). Such a claim suggests that, according to him, we should interpret accumulation of knowledge as an accumulation of metaphors.

This suggestion is appropriated by Rorty in *Contingency, irony and solidarity* where he states that one of his aims is to show that the recognitions of the contingencies of language and conscience lead to

a picture of intellectual and moral progress as a history of increasingly useful metaphors rather than of increasing understanding of how things really are. (1989: 9)

Rorty follows Nietzsche in claiming that intellectual change is not a matter of getting closer to things as they really are, but a matter of adopting different metaphors. There is, nevertheless, a difference between Rorty and Nietzsche; whereas Rorty talks of 'a history of increasingly useful metaphors', Nietzsche claims that knowledge does not arise as something useful for life, but as something at odds with it (GS, 111). It is only when 'eventually knowledge and the striving for the true found their place as a need' that 'the impulse for truth has proved to be also a life-preserving power' (GS, 110). Rorty thinks that utility determines which metaphors become knowledge, whereas Nietzsche holds that some metaphors, which might be harmful, are instances of knowledge. Similarly, Rorty holds that those metaphors which become knowledge are ' "successful" in the sense that we find them so compelling that we try to make them candidates for belief' (1991a: 124). Nietzsche, on the other hand, claims that what we find compelling might very well be a source of error, and that in any case indispensability and compulsion prove nothing about the epistemic status of a claim (WP, 483). Rorty employs the language of 'utility' and 'success' because he thinks of metaphors as tools which we judge in terms of their efficient or inefficient use. He also points out the limits of this analogy when he says that the job to be done with the tools of metaphors is not known before the tools are invented (1989: 12–13). However, he does not notice that a consequence of this point is that it is only retrospectively that we can look at those metaphors that have become knowledge and declare their usefulness because what they are useful for does not precede them but is, instead, their result.

Whilst Nietzsche exposes this consequence in his account of the origin of knowledge, Rorty does not seem to be aware of it. Thus, he continues to talk of metaphors as tools, hit upon accidentally by thinkers, which are preserved if they happen 'to work better for certain purposes than any previous tool' (1989: 19). All this talk of metaphors as tools which are better or worse for a purpose suggests that Rorty's thinking is caught up in a metonymy. According to Nietzsche, a metonymy is a confusion of cause and effect; one of the forms taken by this confusion is the identification of the effects of a 'thing' with its essential characteristics. For example, he says:

> A synthetic judgment describes a thing according to its consequences, i.e. *essence* and *consequences* become *identified*, i.e. a *metonymy*. (P, 152)

Rorty's use of the metaphor of 'the tool' as a metaphor for the role of metaphors leads to a metonymical identification of the consequences of metaphors with their essence. Nietzsche, instead, avoids this confusion when he explicitly states that the utility of knowledge is something created by knowledge itself.

Nietzsche thinks metaphors as the stuff, which we have to manufacture ourselves, that constitutes the delicate conceptual material by means of which we construct our knowledge (OTL, I, 85). These webs of our own making do not have to be useful, do not have to satisfy a pre-existent need. Rather, they might be the cause for the creation of the need for more conceptual spinning.

In the passage from *Contingency, irony, and solidarity* quoted above, Rorty also seems to contrast the activity of producing understanding with that of producing metaphors. Such a contrast would suggest that he subscribes to the distinction between cognitive and rhetorical uses of language, and that he claims that all innovative uses are rhetorical rather than cognitive. At first sight, Rorty seems to hold a view according to which new metaphors might be better tools for doing things, but do not produce new ways of understanding reality.

However, this appears to go against what he says elsewhere when he encourages us to follow Davidson in thinking of the literal-metaphorical distinction as the distinction between old language and new language rather than in terms of a distinction between words which latch onto the world and those which do not. (1989: 28)

According to Rorty, the difference between metaphorical and literal uses of language is not a matter of their relations to extralinguistic reality; rather, it is a matter of novelty as opposed to familiarity. If this is the only difference between the two uses of language, it would seem that metaphors as much as literal language provide ways of understanding reality.

Perhaps, Rorty should be interpreted as saying that what we do not have is 'an increasing understanding of how things *really* are'; that is, we do not have accurate pictures or representations of reality. Hence, Rorty does not contrast metaphorical with cognitive uses of language; rather, he claims that metaphorical expressions, whose contents are not meant to picture or represent reality, can produce understanding. Since an opposition to representationalist theories of language is characteristic of many of Rorty's writings, it is not surprising that it is also at work in this case.

This view, according to which we can have true descriptions that are not representations of reality, requires a new definition of 'description'. In what follows whenever I say that a linguistic expression is a description I mean that it is a truth-value candidate; that is, something which can be either true or false. Furthermore, a description is something one can argue for or against. This is a notion of 'description' which, I think, is adopted by Rorty[4] and is consistent with what Nietzsche says on the topic.

The context in which Rorty claims that the difference between metaphors and literal language is matter of familiarity is one where he emphasises that metaphorical redescriptions are inventions rather than discoveries (1989: 28). Nevertheless, he holds that these inventions can provide understanding since what is to be understood is not 'a truth which was out there (or in here) all the time' (1989: 27). It seems that when Rorty contrasts 'understanding how things really are' with 'useful metaphors', he is not just saying that metaphorical re-description provides understanding without providing representations of reality, he is also suggesting that metaphors have such a role because there is no reality which could be understood *only* by being represented.

Nietzsche in 'The Philosopher' makes the same point as Rorty, concerning the difference between metaphorical and literal uses of language. However, Nietzsche derives from this point a conclusion which contradicts what Rorty has to say about the issue.

The most accustomed metaphors, the usual ones, now pass for truths and as standards for measuring the rarer ones. The only intrinsic difference here is the difference between custom and novelty, frequency and rarity.

Knowing is nothing but working with the favourite metaphors, an imitation which is no longer felt to be an imitation. Naturally, therefore, it cannot penetrate the realm of truth. (P, 149)

Both Rorty and Nietzsche adopt a position that inverts the traditional understanding of the relation between literal and metaphorical discourse. Whilst traditionally metaphors and other tropes were seen as additional to literal language, they both view literal discourse as a product of the process of familiarization that metaphors undergo. Hence, Nietzsche claims that 'the concept . . . is . . . merely the *residue of metaphor*' (OTL 1, p. 85).

By emphasizing the metaphorical 'origin' of all discourse both Nietzsche and Rorty attempt to undermine the conviction that literal language is employed to provide accurate pictures of things as they are. Both argue in favour of an anti-representationalist conception of language on the basis of the premise that descriptions are to be understood as stale metaphors.

But, in the passage quoted above, Nietzsche appears to maintain that metaphors are always outside the realm of truth. This is in opposition with Rorty's claim that there is no truth out there which precedes our descriptions. It would be too simplistic, however, to locate their disagreement at this level. This is so because Nietzsche is also the philosopher, who in another piece from the same period, has claimed that:

What then is truth? A movable host of metaphors, metonymies, and anthropomorphisms: in short, a sum of human relations which have been poetically and rhetorically intensified. . . . Truths are illusions which we have forgotten are illusions; they are metaphors that have become worn out. (OTL, I, p. 84)

What is claimed in this passage about the relation between truths and metaphors seems to contradict what is said in the passage quoted above. In order to avoid attributing contradictory views to Nietzsche, one is led to interpret 'truth' in two different ways in the different passages.

Thus, one could take the realm of truth which is never captured by metaphors, to be that realm of things in themselves to which our language does not correspond. At the same time, one could take worn out metaphors to be truths in so far as they are regarded as such by every language user. Although this way of interpreting the situation might be quite intuitive, it commits the intepreter to subscribe to the view that ultimately Nietzsche's position on these issues is inconsistent. The interpreter will either (1) take Nietzsche to endorse the Platonist claim in the first passage or (2) take Nietzsche to argue against the existence or validity of certain notions, such as correspondence to things in themselves, only because we have no use for them or because they are not accessible to us. In either case the interpreter is forced to attribute to Nietzsche views that he explicitly rejects elsewhere.

I would like to offer a different interpretation of what is going on in these passages. I would like to encourage you to think that Nietzsche does not employ the notion of 'truth' in two different senses; rather, he talks about two different kinds of truths – that is, truths about different kinds of subject matter. Worn out metaphors, according to him, might become literal truths, and be sources of knowledge. However, the knowledge they provide is limited to causal accounts of reality. What stale metaphors cannot give is an explanation of reality. Consider, for example, Nietzsche's claim that:

> [I]t is 'description' that distinguishes us from older stages of knowledge and science. Our descriptions are better – we do not explain any more than our predecessors. . . . 'Cause' and 'effect' is what one says; but we have merely perfected the image of becoming without reaching beyond the image or behind it. In every case the series of 'causes' confronts us much more completely, and we infer: first, this and that has to precede in order that this or that may then follow – but this does not involve any *comprehension*. . . . [N]obody has 'explained' a push. But how could we possibly explain anything? We operate only with things that do not exist. . . . How should explanations be at all possible when we first turn everything into an *image*, our image! (GS, 112)

At first sight one can read Nietzsche in this passage as saying that metaphors do not provide genuine explanations and knowledge *because* they are always *our* images. Since metaphors, as we shall see, consist in transferences between different sets of images, they never allow us to go beyond such images. Metaphors can constitute relations between images, but they do not relate images to things as they are in themselves. Furthermore, these images are always our images; that is, images that make an essential reference to the kind of beings we are. Hence, one could say that Nietzsche denies explanatory power to metaphors because they do not allow us to go beyond the anthropomorphic realm of appearance.

To read the passage in this way, however, is to take Nietzsche to contradict himself on this issue, since he is famously critical of the notion of a 'true' world (TI, V: 5). Furthermore, it is well known that Nietzsche holds that all knowledge is perspectival; that is, that all knowledge involves essential reference to a viewpoint. Hence, even if metaphors are inevitably and firmly situated in the empirical anthropomorphic realm, Nietzsche could not claim that this is a source of epistemic disadvantage.

The desire to attribute a consistent position to Nietzsche, however, is not the decisive reason for interpreting these passages in a non-standard way. If the problem with metaphors were that they are only images and do not capture things in themselves, how could Nietzsche say that they provide descriptions, some of which are better than others? Instead, I suggest that Nietzsche considers worn out metaphors as candidates for true empirical descriptions of reality. These descriptions are empirical because they give a causal account of how phenomena occur, they are true because there is no 'true' world beyond the realm of the empirical world. These truths, however, do not explain anything. For example, they do not tell us *what* a push is, although they tell us *how* it occurs and which are its effects. Since metaphors cannot give knowledge of what phenomena are, they cannot explain why (rather than how) things happen the way they do. Hence, according to Nietzsche, worn out metaphors can be descriptions but cannot be explanations of what things are, and why they are so.

In order to understand why for Nietzsche a language with metaphorical origins cannot be used to give explanations of the kind mentioned above, it is necessary to become clear about what metaphors are. This is the task that I undertake in the next section. However, if I am right about this, we have here a deep contrast between Rorty and Nietzsche. Nietzsche, I hold, believes that there is a kind of understanding which cognition, originated by metaphorical processes, cannot produce.

On the other hand, Rorty claims that those metaphors that have become literal truths give us all the explanations we need. Rorty adopts this position because he agrees with Nietzsche that worn out metaphors can give us true causal accounts of phenomena, and, contrary to Nietzsche, he holds that causal accounts are the only legitimate accounts. Thus, he endorses what he calls a 'Wittgensteinian attitude' which naturalizes mind and language by making all questions about the relation of either to the rest of universe *causal* questions, as opposed to questions about adequacy of representation. (1989: 15)

What Rorty points out here is that it makes sense to ask for the causes of language and of mind. In other words, it makes sense 'to ask how we got . . . from speaking Neanderthal to speaking postmodern' (1989: 15), what does not make sense is to ask for the reasons why we speak postmodern, or why speaking postmodern works. Hence, Rorty holds that it is legitimate to ask how linguistic expressions work, but it is not legitimate to ask why they work or, which is the same, why they are useful. Rorty, then, believes that, when we are concerned with the relation between language and reality, it does not make sense to ask for reasons, it only makes sense to ask for causes.

Rorty takes only causal questions about the relation between language and reality to be legitimate because he claims that causation is the only kind of relation to hold between language and reality. According to him, there are only three candidates for the role of word–world relation: causation, representation, and making true. An anti-representationalist, such as Rorty, rejects both representation and making true (1991a: 120) which is the converse of the first (1991a: 153).

Rorty expands on these views when he claims:

> The antirepresentationalist is quite willing to grant that our language . . . has been shaped by the environment we live in. . . . On an antirepresentationalist view, it is one thing to say that . . . an ability to use the word 'atom' as physicists do, is useful for coping with the environment. It is another thing to attempt to *explain* this utility by reference to representationalist notions. (1991a: 5–6)

Rorty believes that linguistic utterances are caused by, and have causal effects on the environment. He thinks of language in this way because he takes language to be a tool which, given our pre-established needs and interests, is useful to cope with and shape the environment. Rorty also claims that any questions, asking to explain why a given bit of language is useful, are ruled out. More precisely, they are ruled out if they appeal to representationalist notions, but this is inevitable in Rorty's framework where besides causal relations the only other candidates for the role of world–word relation are representationalist relations.

Rorty holds that it makes no sense to ask why, say, a scientific theory is useful. He believes that asking this question is the same as asking which state of the world makes the theory successful. Hence, he takes the quest for reasons for the utility of a theory to be a request for an account of the way in which the world is in virtue of which the theory works. In other words, he holds that asking for reasons for the utility of a theory is the same as asking for reasons for the truth of the theory. The latter, however, is a legitimate request only within a representationalist framework.

Nietzsche, on the other hand, does not believe that causal questions are the only legitimate kind of question. He holds that some requests for explanations are legitimate; for example, in the passage quoted above he claims that our scientific theories give us causal accounts, but that explanation is needed. Such explanations would give an account of why the causal theory works. Hence, for Nietzsche, those questions that Rorty rules out are legitimate.

I do not think that Nietzsche always falls pray of the representationalist trap by taking questions for explanation to be legitimate. Admittedly, Nietzsche seems to think that it is legitimate to inquire into the nature of phenomena such as a push. When he makes these claims he appears to accept the validity of representationalist questions. But, to ask why a causal theory works is not necessarily to ask a question about the nature of reality.

Rorty interprets the request for the reasons why a theory is useful as equivalent to asking for what makes the theory true, because he thinks of language as an instrument which we use to pursue our interests and fulfil our needs. Despite Rorty's disclaimers, his model makes sense only if we think of these needs and interests as already established before a particular bit of language is used. Within this framework it makes sense to ask how we achieve our goal by using language; but, to ask why that is possible is to ask for what in the world makes it possible. Since this is a representationalist question Rorty rejects it. Hence, it is impossible for Rorty to question an account that, by his standards, works. It follows that he must take utility to be a sufficient condition for truth. That is, in his account it is conceptually impossible for a metaphor to work and, at the same time, be false. Hence, in his view there is no need for an explanation of the truth of a stale metaphor.

Nietzsche, however, can interpret the request for reasons why a theory works in a different way. Instead of taking it as asking for what in the world makes the theory true, he can take it as asking for what kinds of needs and interests must exist or be created for viewing what the theory does as useful. For example, Nietzsche claims that what is conducive to scientific thought could have the effect of a poison. The impulses to doubt, wait, suspend judgment are not in many situations conducive to survival. However, when these impulses become organized in certain ways and new interests and needs are created, it is possible to look upon the employment of such impulses as useful and successful (GS, 113).

To summarize, according to Rorty, it is a mistake to believe that it is sensible to ask for a reason why a certain bit of language allows us to cope with our environment. Similarly, he thinks that to ask for a reason why a metaphor is useful and compelling is to ask the wrong question. In some sense utility is, for Rorty, basic; it explains why some events occur, but it does not itself need to be explained.

Nietzsche does not subscribe to such a view; he holds that it makes sense to ask why a theory works. In some contexts he appears to interpret this question as a question concerning the nature of the phenomena described. In these cases, he says that the question is legitimate even if we cannot answer it since the whole of our knowledge is derived from metaphors of our own making. In other contexts he interprets the question as one concerning the needs that are created by our theorizing that makes us see what the theory does as something useful. I discuss in detail the reasons and consequences of this disagreement in the following section of the paper.

2 What is a Metaphor?

Both Rorty and Nietzsche discuss at great length the role of metaphors. However, whilst Rorty is concerned only with the role of metaphors in language, Nietzsche is interested in understanding a more general phenomenon which he takes linguistic metaphors to exemplify.

Rorty, as we shall see, takes metaphors to play a role in a purely causal network. Hence, he only distinguishes between compelling and uncompelling metaphors. Nietzsche, instead, claims that some compelling metaphors are necessary to the acquisition of knowledge, whilst others which are equally compelling lead one's thinking astray.

Nietzsche holds that we have a metaphor when we identify things which are not the same (OTL, 177). He also believes that this is an inescapable condition of all human knowledge (P, 150). This is so because the process of abstraction – that is, omission of details – is necessary to the formation of concepts, and concepts are necessary to knowledge (OTL, I, p. 83). However, abstraction as omission of details is, according to Nietzsche, one way of treating as the same things which are only similar. Although he believes that this shows that it is impossible for us to have pictures or representations of reality, Nietzsche does not claim that abstraction makes it impossible for us to have knowledge.

Nietzsche also holds that one might commit a mistake when one proceeds from metaphorical abstraction to a metonymical exchange of cause and effect. For example, it is only 'by arbitrarily discarding . . . individual differences' that we form the concept of 'leaf'. Furthermore, the formation of this concept might lead one to believe that in addition to all the individual leaves, there exists also 'the leaf', and that 'the leaf is the cause of the leaves' (OTL, I, p. 83). In this case, 'the leaf' which is the result of abstracting from individual leaves is taken to be their cause and essence.

Besides this view of metaphor as the identification of what is only similar, Nietzsche also holds that metaphors involve some kind of transference or jump from one sphere to another; thus, he says of some metaphorical processes that 'there is a complete overleaping of one sphere, right into the middle of an entirely new and different one' (OTL, I, p. 82).

This Nietzschean notion of a metaphor as a transference or jump between two different spheres is of some consensequence. Firstly, according to him the jump does not merely occur at the linguistic level but is involved in all our cognitive activities. Hence, he says about sense perception that:

> To begin with, a nerve stimulus is transferred into an image: first metaphor. The image, in turn, is imitated in a sound: second metaphor. (OTL, I, p. 82)

Thus, when Nietzsche talks about metaphor, he is referring to a kind of phenomenon that is only exemplified by metaphors as they traditionally occur in language, but which has a much broader scope since it is also involved in sense perception. This broad conception of the metaphorical process has, however, repercussions on the issue of language, since the relations between descriptions of different spheres depend on those between phenomena pertaining to these different spheres. Secondly, Nietzsche claims that what is characteristic of a metaphor is that, when it becomes habitual, it produces an appearance of a relation of causal necessity with compelling force. Furthermore, he also holds that this appearance creates the illusion that only the result of the metaphorical jump is justified by the starting point. For example:

> [e]ven the relationship of a nerve stimulus to the generated image is not a necessary one. But when the same image has been generated millions of times . . . it acquires at last the same meaning for men it

would have if it were the sole necessary image and if the relationship of the original nerve stimulus to the generated image were a strictly causal one. . . . But the hardening and congealing of a metaphor guarantees absolutely nothing concerning its necessity and exclusive justification. (OTL, I, p. 87)

According to the traditional empiricist account of sense perception which Nietzsche opposes here, a mental image is the causal result of a given nerve stimulus which in turn is the causal result of a process that starts with objects in the world. Furthermore, these causal connections are viewed as providing a justification for holding that the image is an image *of* the objects in the world. Nietzsche rejects this view; he holds that no relation of causal necessity is involved in this phenomenon, and that we have no grounding for a justification of the image as a representation. Rorty is also opposed to the view that there are world–word relations of justification; however, he does not reach this conclusion by denying that there are strictly causal world–word relations, but by denying that these relations can also constitute justifications (1991a: 120).

Furthermore, in the passage quoted above Nietzsche stresses that there is no necessary relation between a phenomenon pertaining to one sphere and another belonging to a different sphere. In this context, to claim with Nietzsche that there is only a metaphorical relation between nerve stimuli and images is to say that it is not possible to reduce talk about images to talk about nerve stimuli. In other words, whenever we have only a metaphorical relation between two phenomena, we have a non-reductivist relation between two spheres of discourse. Rorty also claims to be an non-reductivist; however, as I discuss later, his non-reductivism is different from Nietzsche's.

According to Nietzsche, metaphorical transferences create relations between two phenomena or two linguistic expressions which were previously unrelated, and which also belonged to two unbridged spheres. Hence, he claims that 'between two absolutely different spheres . . . there is no causality, no correctness, and no expression; there is, at most, an *aesthetic* relation'. By which relation he means 'a suggestive transference, a stammering *post factum* translation into a completely foreign tongue – for which there is required, in any case, a freely inventive intermediate sphere and mediating force' (OTL, I, p. 86).

According to Nietzsche there is a certain arbitrariness involved in the transference from one image to the other. Because of such an arbitrariness, and because no causality is involved, there is no antecedent justification that connects the two relata of the metaphor. But then, say, the nerve stimulus cannot be an explanation for the concept, since the nerve being stimulated is neither a cause nor a reason for having the concept. Hence, it is not possible to use one of the relata of the metaphorical process to give an explanation of the other. It is because of this that metaphorical processes, for Nietzsche, cannot tell us anything about the nature of phenomena.

However, when the transference becomes habitual it acquires an aspect of compulsion. It is because of this that the transference acquires post-factum the characters of a causal process. It is this habitual repetition of an arbitrary process that institutes a kind of constant conjunction between the relata of the metaphor. Following Hume, Nietzsche holds that there is no causation besides regularity or constant conjunction. Differing from Hume, Nietzsche holds that constant conjunctions are the result of the repetition of metaphorical processes. Hence, according to Nietzsche, causation is the residue of the habitual occurrence of perceptual metaphors.

One should not interpret Nietzsche's claim that causation is a product of metaphors as implying that there is no causation in the world. Nietzsche takes metaphors to have productive powers; metaphors are the stuff of which the architecture of human cognition is made. They, like a spider's web, are the materials used to construct the empirical world of phenomena which is the only world we are in contact with.

Since metaphorical processes are constitutive of causal processes, metaphors can be used to provide descriptions. This is so because metaphors create constant conjunctions between, for example, concepts and images. Furthermore, since these conjunctions are the result of habits acquired by a given organism, the organism can be said to have acquired a disposition to think a certain concept whenever it has a certain image. In these cases, to say that the concept describes or is about the image is to say that the thinker has a disposition to think the concept whenever the image occurs. It is, thus, possible to attribute to Nietzsche a dispositional theory concerning the content of mental and linguistic expressions like the one adopted by Wittgenstein in *The Blue and Brown Books*.

To summarize, according to Nietzsche, metaphors are arbitrary transference which can become habitual, and when they do so they create causal processes. Also, stale metaphors can function as descriptions without being pictures. Words, for example, can be about images without picturing them; instead, they are about them by being constantly conjoined with these images. A language, however, which is the result of metaphorical processes cannot be used to provide explanations – that is, reasons or justifications – because the metaphorical process is always ultimately arbitrary.

If my attribution of a dispositional theory of content to Nietzsche is correct, then Nietzsche is committed to the view that metaphors have no meaning, but they acquire meaning when they become stale. I think that it is not implausible to attribute this view to Nietzsche since he holds that every concept is a stale metaphor. The view that metaphors, whilst alive, have no meaning is shared by Rorty. However, as we shall see, the similarities between the two thinkers stop at this very superficial level.

Rorty combines the view that the distinction between the literal and the metaphorical is a 'distinction between familiar and unfamiliar uses of noises and marks' (1989: 17) with the claim that metaphors are

> ways of producing effects on your interlocutor . . . not ways of con-
> veying a message. (1989: 18)

Rorty, that is, holds that metaphors have the effect they have because of their force rather than because of their meaning. To use an Austinian turn of phrase, metaphors are ways of doing things which have an effect on other people. According to Rorty, a metaphor succeeds if it has as a causal effect a modification of current linguistic use.

Metaphors, as such, do not have a meaning and do not, according to Rorty, describe or redescribe anything. Instead, they are just 'a noise having a place in a causal network'; however, when these 'unfamiliar noises acquire familiarity and lose vitality' they acquire also 'a place in a pattern of justification of belief' (1991a: 171). Furthermore, what allows this double role of a noise is not a matter of the intrinsic properties of the noise itself; it is, rather, 'a matter of what is going on in the rest of the universe' (1991a: 171).

Rorty holds that in literal uses of language we utter sentences with meaning; hence, he takes meaning to be an effect of the familiarity of uses of marks and noises (1989: 18). He acknowledges this commitment when he states that meanings are 'patterns of habitual use' (1991b: 14). In other words, a noise is endowed with a meaning when its occurrence has become more or less predictable (1991a: 168). The predictability of a noise is what makes it 'usefully describable . . . as an expression of belief' (1991a: 171). Once the occasions of utterance of a noise have become predictable, Rorty claims, it is possible to describe the noise as having an inferential role – that is, as having a place in a pattern of justification of belief. Hence, according to Rorty, the meaning of a literal utterance is its inferential role which is, in part, its role as a reason for uttering other familiar noises. A noise can be described as functioning as a reason rather than merely as a cause when and only when it has a causal role in a network which has become manageable by means of a theory about how to handle linguistic behaviour which is shared by some speakers (1991a: 169–70).

One could interpret Rorty's position as being, despite his claims to the contrary, reductivist about meaning because he explains meaning in terms of regularity of causal connections. Rorty's reply to this charge would be that since he is talking of double describability of noises as reasons and as causes he is not reducing either to the other; rather, he identifies the two. However, even if Rorty can escape the charge of being a reductivist he cannot escape the charge of being an attributivist about normative properties like meaning and justification.

The attributivist conception of normativity is, according to Lance, the view that normative judgements are 'mere descriptions of patterns of endorsement'; one variant of this view consists in the claim that the correct judgements about how linguistic expressions ought to be used in a given linguistic community are those which follow from the current patterns of usage endorsed by that community (Lance 1992: 2). Rorty adopts this attributivist conception since he identifies issues of correctness of linguistic use with issues concerning the regularity of linguistic behaviour. I believe that the attributivist conception is mistaken since it implies that it is a conceptual impossibility that a community might be wrong about normative issues.

I have claimed above that Nietzsche also takes content to emerge out of our habits and practices. However, I do not think that one can also charge Nietzsche with being an attributivist about normativity. This is so because to say that causation and description are the products of habitual patterns of behaviour, is not to commit oneself to the further claim that reasons are causes. Nietzsche's claims that metaphors produce descriptions but do not produce explanations suggests that he does not identify causes with reasons. Furthermore, whilst Rorty sees 'justification' just as a matter of patterns of endorsement displayed by a given community, Nietzsche talks of the origin of knowledge as a development against the 'natural' patterns of endorsement. According to him 'the weakest form of knowledge' emerges with the denial of those 'articles of faith, which were continually inherited, until they became almost part of the basic endowement of the species' (GS, 110).

3 Metaphors and Causation

In this final section of the chapter I would like to show how Rorty's thinking about metaphors and their role for human cognition is caught up in a series of metonymical inversions. I believe that Rorty's use of the metaphor of the tool as a metaphor for metaphors leads him to adopt a realist attitude toward causation. Such an attitude forces Rorty into a contradictory position: on the one hand, Rorty wants to put metaphors at the centre of human cognition and to show their relevance to understanding and truth; on the other hand, Rorty's position on causation forces him to say that metaphors are merely causal effects of external and internal influences, and that they do not provide any sort of understanding.

Rorty holds that causal stories can be the result of metaphorical invention, and should not be taken as providing representations of reality (1989: 28). However, it is significant that in this context Rorty is talking about 'causal stories' rather than about 'causality'. What Rorty is keen to point out is that even causal descriptions do not function as representations of reality.

For Rorty, even if causal stories have a metaphoric origin, causality itself is a relation between events which is not produced by metaphors. Causation is, for Rorty, 'out there'. I attribute this view to Rorty partly because he is a non-reductive physicalist.[5] Also because, in a pictorial representation of his position Rorty represents causation as the only kind of relation that connects us with our environment (1991a: 122), and also bits of the environment with other such bits (1989: 5). Furthermore, as far as I know, Rorty has not ever discussed in his work some of the problems concerning causation.

Rorty's position is that language both in its meaningful and metaphorical uses presupposes causality. It is only in a world where there are causal frameworks that metaphors can be produced as novel causal patterns, which, once they become predictable, can be interpreted as meaningful utterances in the realm of reasons.

From what I have said so far, it should be clear that Nietzsche would disagree with Rorty concerning what metaphors are and how they work. The only point of agreement is that they both hold that live metaphors do not strictly speaking have a meaning, and that this is why the meanings of metaphors cannot be paraphrased by means of literal language.

From Nietzsche's perspective, Rorty confuses 'cause' and 'effect' concerning the relation between metaphors and causality. Whilst Nietzsche holds that the very notion of 'causality' is a product of metaphorical transference, Rorty takes metaphors to have a purely causal role in a framework of causes that precedes them. Furthermore, whilst Nietzsche views causality as a consequence of metaphors, Rorty takes causality to constitute the essence of metaphors. Hence, if Nietzsche is right, Rorty is caught up in a metonymical inversion of cause and effect, consequence and essence.

It is, once again, Rorty's preference for the metaphor of 'the tool' as a metaphorical description of the role of metaphors that leads Rorty to make what Nietzsche would take to be a metonymical inversion. This is so because the idea of the 'tool' presupposes the existence of a framework of causal relations within which the tool can have an effect. Furthermore, as I have already pointed out at the beginning of this chapter, the metaphor of the tool suggests that the purpose which the tool is meant to serve is already clear. As a result of using 'the tool' as a metaphor for metaphors, Rorty is led to believe that metaphors have purely causal effects and are to be accepted only on the basis of whether they work.

Since Rorty takes causality to constitute metaphors and holds that metaphors are to be evaluated only in terms of their utility, it becomes impossible for him to question the epistemic status of compelling metaphors. There is no conceptual space in his account for the claim that a metaphor is both compelling and yet a worse metaphor for cognitive purposes than those which preceded it. Thus, Rorty holds that:

> [t]o accept the claim that there is no standpoint outside the particular historically conditioned and temporary vocabulary we are presently using from which to judge this vocabulary is to give up on the idea that there can be reasons for using languages as well as reasons within languages for believing statement. (1989: 48)

Rorty, then, is committed to the view that intellectual change which takes place by means of the introduction of new metaphors is entirely determined by causal forces. It seems that Rorty believes that once one has abandoned the idea of steady progress toward more adequate pictures of reality, one is committed to the view that there cannot be reasons for change. However, this is a picture of intellectual change that does not involve any kind of understanding: we are caused to change our patterns of linguistic use by the external causal influences of the environment and the internal causal influences of our needs.

The problems which emerge within Rorty's thought show that if we want to oppose representationalist theories of language, and embrace the view that metaphors are at the centre of human cognition and intellectual change, it is necessary to abandon a view according to which language functions as a tool for the purpose of fulfilling pre-established needs. Instead, we need to follow Nietzsche's claim that language is something we produce for no unique purpose. Like spiders which spin their webs, we produce the conceptual material that makes up the world we know. It is only after our world has been produced that those purposes that a given linguistic usage might serve emerge as needs or drives.

NOTES

1 Citations from Nietzsche's work are given in the text by abbreviation of the title followed by section number. The only exceptions are references to 'On Truth and Lies in a Nonmoral Sense' which are given by page number. A list of the abbreviations is presented below.

GS   *The Gay Science*
OTL 'On Truth and Lies in a Nonmoral Sense'
P   'The Philosopher'
TI   *Twilight of the Idols*
WP   *The Will to Power*

2 In his Introduction to his second volume of collected essays Rorty claims: 'My essays should be read as examples of what a group of Italian philosophers have called 'weak thought' (1991b: 6).
3 Rorty takes Nietzsche to be an anti-metaphysician and as such as still involved in metaphysical problematics which Rorty wants to abandon altogether.
4 What he says in 1989: 18 provides supporting evidence.
5 Rorty endorses physicalism in his paper 'Non-Reductive Physicalism' in 1991a.

REFERENCES

Nietzsche, Friedrich (1968) *Twighlight of the Idols*, in *The Portable Nietzsche*, ed. and trans. by W. Kaufmann, Harmondsworth: Penguin.
—— (1968) *The Will to Power*, trans. by W. Kaufmann and R. J. Hollingdale, New York: Random House.
—— (1974) *The Gay Science*, trans. by W. Kaufmann, New York: Random House.
—— (1979) 'On Truth and Lies in a Nonmoral Sense' in *Philosophy and Truth: Selections from Nietzsche's Notebooks of the Early 1870's*, ed. and transl. by D. Breazeale, New Jersey: Humanities Press.
—— (1979) 'The Philosopher' in *Philosophy and Truth: Selections from Nietzsche's Notebooks of the Early 1870's*, ed. and trans. by D. Breazeale, New Jersey: Humanities Press.
Lance, Mark (1992) 'Where do we go from here?', unpublished manuscript.
Rorty, Richard (1989) *Contingency, irony, and solidarity*, Cambridge: Cambridge University Press.
—— (1991a) *Objectivity, Relativism, and Truth*, Cambridge: Cambridge University Press.
—— (1991b) *Essays on Heidegger and Others*, Cambridge: Cambridge University Press.

Select Bibliography

Allison, David B., ed., *The New Nietzsche: Contemporary Styles of Interpretation* (New York: Dell, 1979).

Ansell-Pearson, Keith, *Nietzsche contra Rousseau* (Cambridge: Cambridge University Press, 1991).

—— *An Introduction to Nietzsche as Political Thinker: The Perfect Nihilist* (Cambridge: Cambridge University Press, 1994).

——ed., *Nietzsche and Modern Thought* (London: Routledge, 1991).

Bataille, Georges, *On Nietzsche*, trans. Bruce Boon (London: Athlone Press, 1992).

Blondel, Eric, *Nietzsche: the Body and Culture: Philosophy as a Philological Genealogy*, trans. Seán Hand (London: Athlone, 1991).

Boundary 2. ' "Why Nietzsche Now?" A *Boundary 2* Symposium', in *Boundary 2*, Vols 9, No. 3, and 10, No. 1, 1981.

Bridgwater, Patrick, *Nietzsche in Anglosaxony* (Leicester: Leicester University Press, 1972).

Burgard, Peter, ed., *Nietzsche and the Feminine* (Charlottesville and London: University Press of Virginia, 1994).

Clark, Maudemarie, *Nietzsche on Truth and Philosophy* (Cambridge: Cambridge University Press, 1990).

Conway, Daniel, 'Solving the Problem of Socrates: Nietzsche's "Zarathustra" as Political Irony', in *Political Theory*, No. 16, May 1988, pp. 257–80.

Deleuze, Gilles, *Nietzsche and Philosophy*, trans. Hugh Tomlinson (London: The Athlone Press, 1983).

Derrida, Jacques, *Spurs: Nietzsche's Styles*, bilingual edition, trans. Barbara Harlow (Chicago and London: University of Chicago Press, 1979).

—— *The Ear of the Other*, ed. Christie McDonald, trans. Peggy Kamuf and Avital Ronell (Lincoln and London: University of Nebraska Press, 1988).

Foucault, Michel, 'Nietzsche, Genealogy, History', in *Language, Counter-Memory, Practice*, ed. D. F. Bouchard, trans. D. F. Bouchard and S. Simon (Oxford: Basil Blackwell, 1977), pp. 139–64.

Gillespie, Allen, and Strong, Tracy B., eds, *Nietzsche's New Seas: Explorations in Philosophy, Aesthetics, and Politics* (Chicago: University of Chicago Press, 1988).

Harrison, Thomas, ed., *Nietzsche in Italy* (Saratoga, California: Anma Libri, 1988).

Heidegger, Martin, 'Who is Nietzsche's Zarathustra?', trans. Bernd Magnus, in *Revue of Metaphysics*, Vol. 20, No. 3, 1967, pp. 411–31.

——*Nietzsche*, trans. David Farrell Krell, 2 Vols (London: Routledge & Kegan Paul, 1981).

Heller, Erich, *The Disinherited Mind* (Harmondsworth: Penguin, 1961).

Hollingdale, R. J., *Nietzsche: The Man and His Philosophy* (London: Ark Paperbacks, 1985).

Kaufmann, Walter, *Nietzsche Philosopher, Psychologist, Antichrist* (Princeton NJ: Princeton University Press, 1974).

——*From Shakespeare to Existentialism* (Princeton, NJ: Princeton University Press, 1980).

Kofman, Sarah, *Nietzsche and Metaphor*, trans. Duncan Large (London: Athlone, 1993).

Krell, David Farrell, and Wood, David, eds, *Exceedingly Nietzsche: Aspects of Contemporary Nietzsche Interpretation* (London: Routledge, 1988).

Lampert, Laurence, *Nietzsche and Modern Times: A Study of Bacon, Descartes, and Nietzsche* (New Haven and London: Yale University Press, 1993).

Lukács, György, *The Destruction of Reason*, trans. Peter Palmer (London: The Merlin Press, 1980).

de Man, Paul, *Allegories of Reading: Figural Language in Rousseau, Nietzsche, Rilke, and Proust* (New Haven and London: Yale University Press, 1979).

Magnus, Bernd, Stewart, Stanley, and Mileur, Jean-Pierre, *Nietzsche's Case: Philosophy and/as Literature* (New York: Routledge, 1992).

Minson, Jeffrey, *Genealogies of Morals: Nietzsche, Foucault, Donzelot and the Eccentricity of Ethics* (London: Macmillan, 1985).

Nehamas, Alexander, *Philosophy in the Tragic Age of the Greeks*, trans. Marieanne Cowan (Chicago: Regnery Gateway, 1962).

——*Nietzsche: Life as Literature* (Cambridge: Harvard University Press, 1985).

Nietzsche, Friedrich Wilhelm, *The Birth of Tragedy*, trans. Walter Kaufmann, in *Basic Writings of Nietzsche* (New York: Modern Library, 1968); trans. Shaun Whiteside (Harmondsworth: Penguin, 1993).

——*Untimely Meditations*, trans. R. J. Hollingdale (Cambridge: Cambridge University Press, 1983).

——*Human, All-Too-Human*, Vols I and II (which includes *Assorted Opinions and Maxims*, and *The Wanderer and His Shadow*), trans. R. J. Hollingdale (Cambridge: Cambridge University Press, 1986).

——*Daybreak: Thoughts on the Prejudices of Morality*, trans. R. J. Hollingdale (Cambridge: Cambridge University Press, 1982).

——*The Gay Science*, trans. Walter Kaufmann (New York: Vintage Books, 1974).

——*Thus Spoke Zarathustra*, trans. Walter Kaufmann, in *The Viking Portable Nietzsche* (London: Chatto & Windus, 1971/New York: Penguin, 1976); trans. R. J. Hollingdale (Harmondsworth: Penguin, 1983).

——*Beyond Good and Evil*, trans. Walter Kaufmann, in *Basic Writings of Nietzsche* (New York: Modern Library, 1968); trans. R. J. Hollingdale (Harmondsworth: Penguin, 1981).

——*On the Genealogy of Morals*, trans. Walter Kaufmann, in *Basic Writings of Nietzsche* (New York: Modern Library, 1968).

——*On the Genealogy of Morality and Other Writings*, ed. Keith Ansell-Pearson, trans. Carol Diethe (Cambridge: Cambridge University Press, 1994).

——*The Case of Wagner*, trans. Walter Kaufmann, in *Basic Writings of Nietzsche* (New York: Modern Library, 1968).

——*Twilight of the Idols*, trans. Walter Kaufmann, in *The Viking Portable Nietzsche* (London: Chatto & Windus, 1971/New York: Penguin, 1976); trans. R. J. Hollingdale (Harmondsworth: Penguin, 1982).

——*The Antichrist*, trans. Walter Kaufmann, in *The Viking Portable Nietzsche* (London: Chatto & Windus, 1971/New York: Penguin, 1976); trans. R. J. Hollingdale (Harmondsworth: Penguin, 1982).

——*Nietzsche contra Wagner*, trans. Walter Kaufmann, in *The Viking Portable Nietzsche* (London: Chatto & Windus, 1971/New York: Penguin, 1976).

——*Ecce Homo*, trans. Walter Kaufmann, in *Basic Writings of Nietzsche* (New York: Modern Library, 1968); trans. R. J. Hollingdale (Harmondsworth: Penguin, 1979).

——*The Will to Power*, trans. Walter Kaufmann and R. J. Hollingdale (New York: Vintage Books, 1968).

——*Dithyrambs of Dionysus/Dionysos-Dithyramben*, bilingual edition, trans. R. J. Hollingdale (London: Anvil Press, 1984).

——*Philosophy and Truth: Selections from Nietzsche's Notebooks of the early 1870s*, ed. and trans. Daniel Breazeale (New Jersey: Humanities Press, 1979).

——*Sämtliche Werke: Kritische Studienausgabe*, eds Giorgio Colli and Mazzino Montinari, 15 Vols (Berlin: Walter de Gruyter, 1980).

Parkes, Graham, ed., *Nietzsche and Asian Thought* (Chicago: University of Chicago Press, 1991).

Pasley, Malcolm, ed., *Nietzsche: Imagery and Thought* (London: Methuen, 1978).

Rajan, Tilottama, 'Language, Music and the Body: Nietzsche and Deconstruction', in *Intersections: Nineteenth Century Philosophy and Contemporary Theory*, eds Tilottama Rajan and David L. Clark (Albany: State University of New York Press, 1994).

Reichert, Herbert W., and Schlechta, Karl, *International Nietzsche Bibliography* (Chapel Hill: The University of North Carolina Press, 1968).

Schacht, Richard, *Nietzsche* (London: Routledge & Kegan Paul, 1983).

Schrift, Alan D., *Nietzsche and the Question of Interpretation* (London: Routledge, 1991).

Strong, Tracy B., *Friedrich Nietzsche and the Politics of Transfiguration* (Berkeley: University of California Press, 1975).

Thiele, Leslie, *Friedrich Nietzsche and the Politics of the Soul* (Princeton: Princeton University Press, 1990).

Vattimo, Gianni, *The End of Modernity: Nihilism and Hermeneutics in Postmodern Culture*, trans. Jon R. Snyder (Cambridge: Polity Press, 1988).

——*The Adventure of Difference: Philosophy after Nietzsche and Heidegger*, trans. Cyprian Blamire (Cambridge: Polity Press, 1993).

Index

298

Index